Workers' Rights and Labor Compliance in Global Supply Chains

T0304176

This book provides insight into the potential for the market to protect and improve labor standards and working conditions in global apparel supply chains. It examines the possibilities and limitations of market approaches to securing social compliance in global-manufacturing industries. It does so by tracing the historic origins of social labeling, both in trade-union and consumer constituencies, considering industry and consumer perspectives on the benefits and drawbacks of social labeling, comparing efforts to develop and implement labeling initiatives in various countries and locating social labeling within contemporary debates and controversies about the implications of globalization for workers worldwide. Scholars and students of globalization, development, corporate social responsibility, human geography, labor and industrial relations, business ethics, consumer behavior and fashion will find its contents of relevance. Corporate social responsibility (CSR) practitioners in the clothing and other industries will also find this useful in developing policy with respect to supply chain assurance.

"Can consumer power be used to leverage improved working conditions and respect for labor rights in apparel global supply chains through social labeling? And, if so, under what conditions is social labeling likely to produce the best results? Combining an insightful historical perspective with a rich comparative analysis, the contributors to this volume convincingly suggest that social labeling can be fruitful if it is based on a global-industry standard, with broad stakeholder engagement, and effective verification along the entire supply chain."

—Mark Anner, *Penn State University, USA*

Jennifer Bair is Associate Professor of Sociology at the University of Colorado at Boulder. Her publications include articles on globalization, development, gender, and labor in *Social Problems, World Development, Global Networks,* and *Signs.* She is the editor of *Frontiers of Commodity Chain Research* (Stanford University Press, 2009) and coeditor of *Free Trade and Uneven Development: The North American Apparel Industry After NAFTA* (Temple University Press, 2002).

Doug Miller is Emeritus Professor, University of Northumbria, UK. With an academic background in industrial relations and trade-union studies, Doug was seconded between 2000 and 2008 as multinationals research coordinator for the Brussels-based International Textile Garment and Leather

Workers' Federation. Between 2008 and 2012, he was Inditex/ITGLWF Professor of Ethical Fashion and latterly Worker Rights in Fashion at Northumbria University.

Marsha A. Dickson is Irma Ayers Professor of Human Services and Chairperson in the Department of Fashion and Apparel Studies at the University of Delaware, USA. She is lead author of the book *Social Responsibility in the Global Apparel Industry* and has published on such topics as socially responsible consumer and business behavior, and public reporting in the apparel industry in peer-reviewed journals such as *Business & Society, Journal of Business Ethics*, and *Journal of Corporate Citizenship*.

Routledge Studies in Business Ethics

Workers' Rights and Labor Compliance in Global Supply Chains

Is a Social Label the Answer?

**Edited by Jennifer Bair,
Marsha A. Dickson, and Doug Miller**

NEW YORK AND LONDON

First published 2014
by Routledge
711 Third Avenue, New York, NY 10017

Simultaneously published in the UK
by Routledge
2 Park Square, Milton Park, Abingdon, Oxfordshire OX14 4RN

First issued in paperback 2016

*Routledge is an imprint of the Taylor & Francis Group,
an informa business*

Library of Congress Cataloging-in-Publication Data

Workers' rights and labor compliance in global supply chains : is a social
   label the answer? / edited by Jennifer Bair, Marsha Dickson, and Doug Miller.
     pages cm — (Routledge studies in business ethics ; 7)
   Includes bibliographical references and index.
  1. Sweatshops. 2. Clothing trade—Moral and ethical aspects. 3. Union
labels—Social aspects. 4. Social responsibility of business. 5. Employee
rights. 6. International trade—Social aspects. I. Bair, Jennifer, 1973–
II. Dickson, Marsha Ann.
  HD2337.W67   2013
  174'.4—dc23
  2013008794

ISBN 13: 978-1-138-21273-2 (pbk)
ISBN 13: 978-0-415-84385-0 (hbk)

Typeset in Sabon
by Apex CoVantage, LLC

Contents

PART III
Consumer and Business Perspectives on Social Labeling

PART IV
Contemporary Debates and Controversies

List of Figures

List of Tables

Part I

Introduction and Historical Overview

1   To Label or Not to Label

Is that the Question?

Jennifer Bair, Marsha A. Dickson
and Doug Miller

Over the last two decades, a vibrant, interdisciplinary literature has de-
bated the implications of globalization for economic development[1]. In particular, scholars have investigated the consequences of trade liberalization
and the internationalization of production for workers in global north and
south alike. As the classic 'starter' industry for developing countries and
the world's most widely dispersed manufacturing sector, apparel production
has long been at the center of the debate regarding the relationship between
globalization and worker well-being. This volume reveals the intensity and
plurality of this debate by providing an in-depth examination of one particular strategy for improving the well-being of workers in global supply
chains. Specifically, the contributors to this collection weigh the possibilities
and limitations of a 'social label' for securing a more ethical form of apparel
production in the global economy.

Although the social label is currently enjoying a renaissance as a possible bulwark against a global 'race to the bottom,' the idea is far from
novel. Defined as an attempt to provide consumers, via a physical mark,
some assurance about the social conditions surrounding a product's
manufacture (Urminsky 1998), the social label originated in somewhat
dubious circumstances in the United States during the latter half of the
nineteenth century; both trade unions and the embryonic consumer movement viewed it as the principal means by which abusive labor conditions
could be regulated through the power of the market. As we shall see, the
social-label approach proved highly contentious from the outset, and now,
more than a century later, this strategy has resurfaced in the form of new
efforts to certify the social conditions under which particular products
are manufactured. From proposals for a 'Good for Development' label
(Ellis & Keane 2008) to demands for the introduction of a harmonized
system requiring mandatory origin labeling for all clothing, shoes, and
textile imports into the European Union,[2] to the launch of a full range
of Fair Trade Certified™ clothing items,[3] consumers are now faced with
a veritable 'label maze' of garments bearing social or 'eco' marks, such
as the Soil Association certified-organic label or the Forest Stewardship
Council label.[4]

The reemergence of the social label is attributable to a range of factors. Foremost among these has been the inability of the international institutions to establish a global system for regulating the social dimension of global trade and production networks. The failure of the World Trade Organization (WTO) to include a social clause in trade agreements, and opposition to the International Labour Organization's (ILO) efforts to introduce a unilateral system of social compliance, including a global social label,[5] paved the way for a plethora of private initiatives addressing labor conditions in far-flung supply chains for light manufactures such as apparel and footwear (Chakravarthi 1997). Since the mid-1990s, these initiatives have evolved into a multi-million-dollar social-compliance industry. Corporate codes of conduct and private compliance programs, including auditing systems designed to monitor supplier performance, were originally developed as a risk-management tool in the wake of numerous sweatshop scandals involving contractors producing for well-known U.S. and European brands and retailers (Bartley 2005; Esbenshade 2004).

In recent years, the social-compliance industry has diversified into new initiatives that are based on a market differentiation logic that distinguishes them from the standard auditing model that most mass brands and retailers use to monitor their suppliers' compliance with local labor laws and/or their own corporate codes of conduct. The goal of such programs is to develop a label that can provide an emerging group of ethically conscious consumers with credible assurances that labeled goods are produced in a manner consistent with certain social and/or ecological standards. Ideally, then, a social label would enable consumers to identify ethically produced products and services among all those offered in the market (Piepel 1999).

It is no accident that this upsurge of interest and activity around social compliance in the global apparel industry over the last decade and a half has been occurring alongside a far-reaching liberalization of the global-trading regime for textile and apparel products. In 1995, the Agreement on Textile and Clothing established a decade-long schedule for phasing out the Multi-Fibre Arrangement (MFA), a multilateral regime that had regulated trade in textile and apparel products since the 1960s. Under the auspices of the WTO, quotas on clothing were gradually eliminated over a 10-year period, with the final quantitative restrictions on textile and apparel imports lifted on January 1, 2005. The inauguration of quota-free trade was expected to create new pressures on apparel manufacturers, since suppliers in some developing countries that had benefited from the quota regime would now be forced to compete for import market share with lower-cost suppliers (Bair 2008).

The scenario that trade liberalization would provoke a 'race to the bottom' among suppliers brought the social dimension of apparel production even more strongly to the fore. Some analysts suggested that a positive record of labor compliance might provide exporting countries with a competitive advantage, assuming that a positive record could be made a criterion that potential clients (i.e., foreign retailers and brands) would consider, alongside price, quality, and lead time, when choosing where to place their subcontracting orders. Thus, the restructuring of the post-MFA apparel industry has heralded a new chapter in the history of social labeling, as national governments and trade associations have sought to rebrand their apparel sectors as part of a business-to-business competitiveness strategy. At the same time, there is increasing consensus that the extant model of social compliance via private audits has failed to significantly improve working conditions or deter labor-rights violations in global supply chains (Locke et al. 2007; Seidman 2007). And new, market-driven, consumer-oriented initiatives, such as the one that Fair Trade USA is developing (see Chapter 11) are furthermore crowding the social-compliance field.

This is the context in which a group of academics, activists and industry practitioners met to debate social labeling in the global apparel industry at the University of Northumbria, United Kingdom, in September 2010. The perspectives presented at the meeting were interdisciplinary, and the debates were sometimes contentious. The 15 chapters collected here, which include a mix of papers presented at the conference and several solicited afterward, represent the most comprehensive, critical, in-depth look at social labeling yet assembled. They provide a detailed understanding of the central role a wide range of actors—individual consumers, businesses, governments, trade unions, nongovernmental organizations, and others—play in creating a system of production and trade that advances the welfare of workers in developing countries. It sheds unprecedented light on the contradictions and challenges inherent in developing, and communicating to consumers, a system for guaranteeing the integrity of the working conditions and labor practices along geographically dispersed and organizationally complex global supply chains. In short, this collection enables a deeper understanding of the political, ethical, economic, and logistical issues we must confront if we are to meaningfully pursue a more just and equitable apparel industry.

The remainder of this introduction mirrors the organization of the volume, which is divided into four main sections. We discuss the main contours of each section and provide brief summaries of each chapter, thus providing the reader with some sense of the breadth and depth of this examination into the promises and perils of social labeling. Before proceeding, however, a more nuanced conceptualization of the term social labeling is in order. Most broadly, social labeling is the effort to provide consumers with information and/or assurances regarding the conditions under which a product (in this case, apparel) was manufactured. We would describe those social labels that appear directly on the product and target the end-consumer as *primary social labels*. Such marks usually take the form of a swing tag that is used to market an unsold garment and/or a label on the actual item (see Chapters 6, 11 and 14).[6]

Table 1.1 An Overview of Social Labeling Initiatives

Country	Label	Initiator	Primary	Secondary
USA	Union label(s)	Trade unions	X	
USA	Sweat-free Communities	Municipalities		X
USA	Alta Gracia	Multistakeholder Group (WRC)	X	
Sri Lanka	Garments without Guilt	Manufacturers/Exporters' Association		X
Morocco	Fibre Citoyenne	Manufacturers/Exporters' Association and Government		X
Cambodia	Better Factories	International Institution (ILO)		X
Australia	Ethical Clothing Australia	Industry/ Trade unions	X	
Global	Better Work	International Institutions (ILO and IFC)		X
Global	Fair Trade	Non-profit Organization	X	

Secondary social labels are business-to-business initiatives. These are generally mounted by national associations of manufacturers, sometimes with government support, to assure international buyers (e.g., retailers and brands) that the labor (or environmental) standards prevailing in that country's apparel industry are high (see Chapters 3 and 5). However, secondary social labeling may take other forms, as in the case of public-procurement programs that seek to ensure that the uniforms of city or municipal employees are 'sweat-free' (see Chapter 13). Whether primary or secondary, social labels share the same goal, which is convincing the buyer—be it an individual consumer, a retailer, a university sourcing licensed apparel, or a local government—that the goods it orders will be produced under certain minimum standards. Table 1.1 provides an overview of some of the social labels this volume discusses.

1 A HISTORICAL OVERVIEW OF THE SOCIAL LABEL

As noted above, experiments in social labeling are not new, even if the highly globalized nature of today's apparel industry introduces new challenges for those advocating such an approach. A recurrent theme between the supporters and detractors of the market-oriented approach to social labeling concerns the issue of worker versus consumer agency, and the degree to which consumer power can bridge the terrain between the market and the world of work. Ross, in Chapter 2 of this volume, provides a historical overview of the origins of the social label in the U.S. trade-union movement and questions the theory of consumer sovereignty that underlies it. In Ross's view, the social-labeling strategy, and the consumer-sovereignty paradigm on which it rests, transfers power and agency to some actors—namely, consumers and internal or third-party auditors and, centrally, to the brands and retailers themselves who contract or outsource production—over others, most obviously, regulatory officials, direct employers, and workers, their organizations and their allies.

Ross provides a historical overview of the United States' experiment in social labeling that dates from the turn of the twentieth century. On the one hand, his account reveals the tensions that existed between the 'union label' that was promoted by organized labor and the 'white label' that Florence Kelley's National Consumers' League developed. Yet this distinction between workers and consumers should not be overstated. After all, the power of the consumer was also keenly observed by the Knights of Labor, and in the formation of 'label leagues' and the appointment of 'label agents' responsible for 'label agitation' within trade unions, there was a genuine sense that this device could not only hold the worst excesses of capitalism in check, but could also deploy the purchasing power of trade unionists into a form of moral control over production (see Glickman 1997). In this sense, advocates of the labeling approach within the labor movement agreed with Kelley, to some extent, that the sole emphasis was 'no longer on production or exchange but upon consumption' . . . with the consumer 'the real maker of goods' (1897: 33–34).

However, this emergent 'ethical consumerism' was at the outset saddled with a failure to acknowledge the absence of any transmission mechanism between the market and the workplace. In short, while the buying public (including trade-union members) could generate pressure for change via their own purchasing preferences, they did not have the capacity to bring about change at the point of production, since this is the jurisdiction of employers, trade unions and labor administrations. Secondly, and crucially, the middle-class nature of the emerging ethical consumerist movement during the Progressive era obscured the class implications of market-oriented initiatives; supporters failed to see that that shoppers differed in their ability and willingness to exercise consumer power. As Frank has argued, 'Working class women were less likely than middle class women to 'buy union,' in part because they had to stretch their budgets and time to do so, and also because they had been alienated from their husband's union activities' (1994: 243, Boyle 1903.)

The social/union label as it emerged at the turn of the century thus had a twofold function: first, to provide industrial governance by controlling the manufacture of goods in union-organized workplaces where working conditions could be regulated by collective bargaining and, second, to mobilize the power of labor and the wider public in the market as consumers.[7] It must be recognized that, from the beginning, the union label constituted an (albeit voluntary) *enforcement* tool, as trade unions sought to defend workplace institutions and norms that had been negotiated with an employer. Writing about the union label in 1912, P.H. Shevlin enumerated a set of expected trade-union workplace norms, some of which are not dissimilar from the content of today's corporate and multistakeholder codes of conduct:

> (a) The assurance that the work is done under sanitary conditions. (b) The assurance of the payment of a reasonable . . . and steadily improving wage. (c) The assurance of reasonable hours . . . of labor. (d) The assurance that child labor, the menace as well as the disgrace of modern civilization, has not entered into the product. (e) The assurance that so long as the intense and deplorable and inequitable forms of competition, as evidenced in our present-day industrialism, shall make it necessary for woman to earn her bread in shop and factory, she shall continue to enjoy economic equality with her male co-employee. (f) The assurance that the conditions of the workers are safer as to life and limb than are the surroundings of non-label toilers. (g) The assurance that the product is not prison made. (h) The assurance that the products are superior in workmanship and quality to the unlabeled articles. (i) The assurance that the label is the concrete expression and hallowed scutcheon of conscientious men, organized for the purpose of securing these results and maintaining them when secured (Spedden 1910: 10).

A comparative history of the union-label movement still has to be written, but from what is known, there was clearly an uptake of the union label elsewhere in the English-speaking world. In New Zealand, labeling was introduced as a state-backed initiative (Choppé 1908), whereas in Australia, a constitutional challenge prevented a union label from being recognized as a bona fide trademark (Ricketson 2009). In the United Kingdom, despite much 'label agitation' among the felt-hat makers,[8] the trade-union movement showed a greater disposition toward the use of fair lists in communicating to consumers where collectively bargained working conditions prevailed.[9]

Furthermore, it was one thing for trade unions and consumer groups to adopt labels; it was another thing actually to enforce them. Up until the 1920s, one of the two main apparel-industry unions in the United States, the International Ladies Garment Workers Union (ILGWU), had succeeded in securing union-label agreements with only 12 companies (Levine 1924: 111–113, quoted in Kleehammer 2001), and the normative content of these agreements could vary; as one contemporary observer felt compelled to remark: 'It is essential to bear in mind that the label stands primarily, not for any particular set of conditions, but for those conditions which the unions of each trade have found it possible and desirable to establish' (Spedden 1910: 54). Moreover, there was no strong demand for labeled goods, among either trade unionists or non-unionists (Boyle 1903, Spedden 1910: 63). According to some critics, there were salient reasons for this lack of take up. In his study of the union label in Milwaukee, Boyle quotes a union official, who expressed the view that:

> [t]he label is a mistake; it is contrary to human nature. It puts unnecessary burdens on the union man (sic) who is expected to purchase the label goods. The label is costly to print, to advertise like patent medicine on street cars and bulletin boards, to defend in court against counterfeits. A uniform label would have been better than the sixty or seventy labels now in use, but it is too late for that. There would be too much work to do all over again. We hope nothing from the label. We appreciate the fact, too, that there are many frauds connected with granting and using the label (1903: 171).

While union membership slumped during the Great Depression, when market conditions militated against any label agitation, the environment changed in the 1930s under President Franklin D. Roosevelt. The New Deal saw the creation of a National Recovery Administration (NRA) as part of the 1933 National Industrial Recovery Act (NIRA). The head of the NRA called on every business establishment in the nation to accept a 'blanket code' that incorporated a minimum wage of between 20 and 45 cents per hour, a maximum workweek of 35 to 45 hours, and the abolition of child labor. These provisions were then incorporated into industry-specific codes of fair competition. Significantly, this NRA initiative, which also allowed industry heads to set minimum prices collectively, was launched with a Blue Eagle label. All companies that accepted the Code of Fair Competition were permitted to display the NRA symbol in their shop fronts and on their packaging to show compliance with the NIRA (Himmelberg 1993; Morris 2005).

The Blue Eagle initiative proved short-lived, however. On September 5, 1935, following the invalidation of the compulsory code system after the Supreme Court ruled the NIRA unconstitutional, the emblem was abolished and its future use as a symbol prohibited (Marcketti 2010). Yet despite the abolition of the NIRA codes, apparel-industry unions made significant progress during the 1930s because of other New Deal legislation, including the National Labor Relations (Wagner) Act in 1935 and the Fair Labor Standards Act of 1938. The major industry unions, the Amalgamated Clothing Workers Union of America (ACWU) and the ILGWU grew in membership. It was in this new regulatory environment and the increased union density it helped generate that the ACWU adopted a new union label[10] and the ILGWU incorporated key provisions of the now-invalidated NRA Code of

Fair Competition into new collective agreements that were bargained between the union and employers (Bair 2012).

However, by the 1950s and 1960s, 'runaway' shops that relocated apparel production from the heavily-organized New York City area to cheaper production locations, first in the northeast and later in the American south, began to undermine the union's strength (Wolensky et al. 2002). The industry was even more dramatically transformed by the rise of global outsourcing in the 1970s and 1980s, as some apparel companies abandoned domestic manufacturing to set up offshore production in low-wage countries, and still others shifted to a subcontracting model in which they imported garments from foreign suppliers.

Organized labor tried to contend with the threat of outsourcing by promoting the union label as part of a 'buy American' campaign. In 1974, the ILGWU decided to change the colors of its label to red, white and blue, adding the line 'Made in USA' (Bird and Robinson 1972). All the promotional materials prepared in conjunction with the union's labeling campaign in the 1970s used the slogan 'Buy American: The Job You Save May Be Your Own'[11]—a sentiment which, to this day, appears to underpin the efforts of what remains of the union labeling department at the country's largest trade-union federation, the AFL-CIO.[12]

To note the decline of the union label in the country where it was strongest—the United States—is not to argue that the problems social labels were intended to address have disappeared. On the contrary, as Ross demonstrates, they reemerged in the backyard of the United States and over the border in Central America, as production was displaced into labyrinthine subcontracting networks stretching all the way back to the domiciles of a new, largely migrant working class. The ranks of those employed in today's global garment industry extend across the global south, encompassing Latin America, Asia, Africa, and the Middle East, as well as parts of Central and Eastern Europe.

As the international outsourcing of garment production grew apace during the last decades of the twentieth century, spurred by trade liberalization and the adoption by developing country governments of export-oriented growth strategies (Stiglitz 2003), the soft underbelly of global capitalism became increasingly exposed, thanks in part to the growth of the internet as a tool for disseminating information about sub-poverty wages, punishing working conditions, and underage workers in the factories supplying major brands and retailers. Key stakeholders, such as the International Textile Garment and Leather Workers Federation[13] (the global union federation for workers in the sector) and newly emerging nongovernmental (NGO) networks (e.g., Clean Clothes Campaign, Maquila Solidarity Network, Asia Monitor Resource Centre), publicized these conditions and insisted that northern-based corporations be held accountable for labor abuses occurring anywhere in their supply chains. These anti-sweatshop campaigns emerged on both sides of the Atlantic in the late 1980s, with the Dutch retailer C&A and the

American athletic shoe brand Nike among the first companies to be targeted for substandard working conditions and labor practices in supplier factories (Bair and Palpacuer 2012). Another major concern of human-rights, labor and child-welfare activists was the use of child labor to produce carpets for export in developing countries. Several of the first social labels to appear in the 1990s, including Rugmark[14] and Kaleen, were created to certify that the carpets manufactured in places like India, Pakistan, and Nepal were not made by children.

In 1996, following several well-publicized anti-sweatshop campaigns involving major companies such as Gap and Wal-Mart, U.S. President Bill Clinton and Secretary of Labor Robert Reich convened the Apparel Industry Partnership (AIP), a multistakeholder initiative involving brands, labor unions and NGOs. Initially, some of AIP's supporters hoped that it would lead to the creation of a 'No Sweat' label by which participating companies could assure consumers that they were effectively monitoring workplace conditions in their supply chains.[15] While such a label did not materialize, the Apparel Industry Partnership did lead to the creation of a new organization to address labor issues in the industry: the Fair Labor Association (FLA). Now more than a decade old, the FLA is the largest U.S.-based, multistakeholder initiative dedicated to monitoring labor compliance in global supply chains. It releases annual public reports and detailed tracking charts that include the results of the audits conducted of member companies' supplier factories (Dickson and Eckman 2008; cf Anner 2012).

Around the same time that the AIP was getting underway in the United States, the ILO in Geneva courted the idea of a global social label that could be awarded to countries demonstrating comprehensive respect for fundamental labor rights, as verified via reliable inspections.[16] However, the proposal soon foundered as developing countries criticized the initiative as a protectionist measure. This criticism was aptly expressed by the Indian workers' delegation to the ILO governing body:

> On the whole, the ILO's stand on social labelling, product labelling and so on, may give rise to protectionism, and this is going to be a unilateral decision . . . We are opposed to the system of [a] 'global social label' to be awarded to 'countries which show comprehensive respect for fundamental rights and principles, and agree to submit to reliable and legally autonomous international inspections' . . . This system will in future subject the developing countries to fall under pressure from countries which control the WTO (Chakravarthi 1997).

Similarly, the idea of a Europe-wide social label was explored and ultimately dismissed by the European Union (E.U.). While originally acknowledging the important role that consumers play in the creation of incentives for responsible business practices and ethical production, E.U. officials recognized both the impossibility of reconciling many diverse national product standards and labeling schemes into a single initiative, and the prohibitive expense of the monitoring systems that would be necessary to verify compliance with a Europe-wide social label. The recent decision by the European Council of Ministers to block the introduction of mandatory country-of-origin labeling, which would have brought the E.U. into line with China, the United States and Japan, reflects resistance to the proposal from European retailers and brands.[17]

In short, the anti-sweatshop movement of the late 1980s and 1990s ultimately spawned today's social-compliance industry, which is composed of NGOs, consultants, certification agencies, and global auditing and accountancy firms keen to lend their expertise to a range of voluntary initiatives, foremost of which has been third-party social auditing on behalf of brands and retailers (Sluiter 2010). Thus, while the problem of sweatshops has received increased attention in recent decades, the social-compliance model that has been proposed as a solution privileges factory audits, not social labels. This situation may be changing, however. A growing body of evidence suggests that the current approach, for the most part, is failing to markedly improve labor conditions in global supply chains—a conclusion that has been dramatically, if tragically, underscored by a spate of deadly fires and factory collapses in Bangladesh and Pakistan (Miller 2012). It is in this context that the possibility of social labels to protect and promote garment workers' rights is once again being explored. The remaining three sections of this volume focus on key dimensions of this controversy regarding whether and how social labeling may advance the pursuit of ethical production in global supply chains.

2   SOCIAL LABELS AND LABOR COMPLIANCE INITIATIVES IN COMPARATIVE PERSPECTIVE

The chapters comprising Part II of this volume examine four national labeling initiatives in comparative context. Together, they demonstrate how the expiry of the Multi-Fibre Arrangement has led to a rebranding of national apparel sectors in an effort to counteract expected shocks from trade liberalization. Rather than targeting consumers, three of the four compliance initiatives described here function as national-level programs developed and implemented by governments and industry actors who want to demonstrate to clients and potential clients—namely, foreign brands and retailers deciding where to source their apparel products—that they are working to upgrade social standards in their apparel sectors. In Chapter 3, Goger describes a homegrown compliance initiative called *Garments without Guilt* that was developed by Sri Lankan companies supplying both U.S. and European companies. Although *Garments without Guilt* was created, in part, to respond to the challenges of the quota phaseout, Goger emphasizes that the program was also intended to address domestic concerns about the perceived immorality of apparel-industry employment, especially when associated with urban-based, export-processing zones. In this context, not only must Sri Lankan manufacturers assure foreign buyers of the labor standards in their factories, but also, employers must simultaneously confront local concerns that sewing-factory employment is inconsistent with Muslim ideals of normative gender behavior because it corrupts young women, particularly when factories are producing the racy undergarments and lingerie with which the Sri Lankan industry has become associated. Thus, *Garments without Guilt* emerged out of a particular confluence of global and local concerns, and as such, it highlights the multiple meanings of 'ethical production.' Furthermore, the kinds of projects that participating companies have launched challenge the boundaries of conventional labor-compliance initiatives, which typically confine the space of ethical production to the factory floor, even when, as in the case of Sri Lanka, many garment workers are young migrant women who reside in company-owned dormitories.

The authors of Chapter 4, Brown, Dhejia and Robertson, provide a detailed assessment of what may be the best-known initiative to promote improved labor compliance in the apparel-exporting sector of a developing country. They examine whether the *Better Factories Cambodia* project, which was developed and implemented under the auspices of the ILO in 2005, has improved the compliance of local garment manufacturers with core labor standards. *Better Factories Cambodia* is important and unique, both because of its scope (every apparel-exporting factory in the country is required to participate to receive an export license) and because it served as the template for the new *Better Work* initiative. *Better Work*, which was developed jointly by the ILO and the International Finance Corporation (the private sector arm of the World Bank), is currently being implemented in a number of countries, including Haiti, Nicaragua, Lesotho, and Vietnam.[18] Given the influence of the *Better Factories Cambodia* project as the model for *Better Work*, it is critical to understand the degree to which the original initiative improved labor compliance. Analyzing data from the comprehensive factory audits that were carried out in Cambodia, Brown et al. found that *Better Factories Cambodia* did have a positive impact on labor-law compliance, though they also found that factory-level performance was affected by the presence of reputation-sensitive buyers and the program's policy (at one point, suspended) of disclosing the names of noncompliant factories.

Chapter 5 by Rossi examines another local initiative developed by an industry association concerned about the potential implications of the quota phaseout. Seeking to avoid the loss of business to lower-wage competitors, Morocco's national textile and garment industry association set out to brand Morocco as a 'high road' apparel exporter. The result was the *Fibre Citoyenne* (FC) project, which was launched in 2003 as a sector-wide code of labor practice. Drawing on factory-level field research in four locations (Casablanca, Rabat, Fez and Tangier), Rossi shows that the FC initiative has led to significant, positive changes in certain areas of labor compliance, including health-and-safety standards, minimum-wage commitments, and social-security contributions. However, Rossi concludes that the FC label has had limited impact on other dimensions, including on the core labor rights of freedom of association, collective bargaining and nondiscrimination. In this respect, Rossi's findings are similar to those of Goger's in Sri Lanka, insofar as neither the Sri Lankan *Garments without Guilt* initiative nor the *Fibre Citoyenne* label has improved compliance with two of the most contested and vexed issues in the domain of social compliance— namely, freedom of association and collective bargaining.

Chapter 6 shifts focus from the global south to the global north. In her contribution, Brien examines a national accreditation and social-labeling initiative in Australia. The Australian context is an interesting one because import penetration of the apparel market is lower than in most other developed countries. Furthermore, not only are Australian consumers still able to purchase domestically manufactured garments, but in a perhaps even more striking contrast with most of its peers, the Australian apparel industry continues to rely heavily on homeworkers, many of whom are immigrant women. In recognition of these circumstances and the specific challenges to labor compliance that they create, the textile and apparel-industry union, together with the industry association, created the *No Sweat Shop* label in 2001. However, as Brien explains, the *No Sweat Shop* label met with limited success in terms of company uptake and consumer response, which led to a redesigning of the program and its logo. Brien examines the reasons for this rebranding of the *No Sweat Shop* label as *Ethical Clothing Australia* and assesses the reactions of key stakeholders to the shift. She finds that businesses were more receptive to an initiative that emphasized the positive aspect of social compliance (the affirmation of ethical production, as opposed to the rejection of sweatshops) and the opportunities that consumers have to support it.

Brien's study departs from the others in this section insofar as the national labeling initiative she examines is geared toward the final consumer, as opposed to the foreign buyers who are the targets of the Sri Lankan, Moroccan and Cambodian initiatives. In this sense, her discussion of *Ethical Clothing Australia*, which suggests that effective social labels must find ways to communicate with and influence consumers, provides an apt transition to the third section of the volume.

3   CONSUMER AND BUSINESS PERSPECTIVES ON SOCIAL LABELING

Public opinion polls carried out worldwide indicate that a large majority of consumers care about working conditions in the global apparel industry; advocates of social labeling who believe that consumers have a role to play in improving conditions for garment workers frequently cite such polls. However, a growing body of rigorous studies suggests that the potential market of consumers who would use a social label to guide their purchasing is much smaller than the widely cited polls indicate. For example, one study suggests that this ethical-consumer segment constitutes about 1 percent of the British market for fashion apparel (Mintel 2009). Thus, the question arises: even assuming that a reliable social-labeling program could be developed and implemented in the global apparel industry, would businesses use it in marketing their products and communicating about their brands? And, if so, can we answer affirmatively that consumers would use that information when deciding what to buy?

In Chapter 7, one of the leading scholars in this area evaluates the extant evidence regarding consumer behavior with regard to ethical purchasing decisions. Dickson examines the methods used in consumer behavior research to explain what inferences can legitimately be made about consumers' potential use of such information. While information is generally lacking for consumers to make their purchasing decisions on the basis of brands' or retailers' performance on social compliance, opinion polls almost certainly overestimate what consumers *would do* with that information were it available. She argues that well-conceived studies using experimentally designed conditions and 'nearly real' market settings suggest that, under present conditions, only a fraction of the consumers who claim support for sweat-free apparel production would make purchasing decisions based on information about labor conditions. Dickson calls on researchers to develop action-based research initiatives that work to transform actual consumer behavior in support of worker rights, rather than continue to parade out study after study reporting that consumers care about these issues.

The study by Robinson, Meyer and Kimeldorf discussed in Chapter 8 is a prime example of the kind of research Dickson endorses. These authors have selected a company, American Apparel, which is widely perceived as an ethical retailer because it maintains domestic manufacturing facilities that are characterized by relatively good wages and working conditions. By interviewing consumers shopping at an American Apparel outlet in Michigan, Robinson et al. are able to determine how consumers use information about production conditions. The authors' main argument is that the disjuncture between consumers' professed concerns about ethical production and their actual purchasing practices do not reveal a lack of sufficient motivation by shoppers so much as a failure of the market to provide the products that potential ethical consumers want to purchase. By focusing on market context as opposed to consumer commitment, the authors provide a fresh perspective regarding the degree to which a social label might mobilize consumers. They conclude that the current absence of a sufficiently robust market niche for ethical apparel primarily reflects the industry's failure to understand and respond to the way that shoppers make decisions about what clothing they buy.

The first two chapters in Part III raise an important question regarding the propensity of apparel businesses to relay information about their global supply chains to consumers, and the size of the market for such information: if a substantial market of consumers were interested in using social compliance as a purchase criterion, would brands and retailers be aggressively marketing their achievements in this area? In Chapter 9, Roberts takes up this issue in a novel study that examines the degree to which British retailers use websites to convey information to consumers about working conditions in their supply chains and their efforts to improve them. He finds that large retailers in the United Kingdom do not make this information available to consumers directly from those pages of their websites visitors would access to make online purchases. Rather than make the information available on these prime 'shopping pages,' retailers often require consumers to navigate their sites through several additional clicks to access labor-compliance information. The seemingly low priority that British retailers place on making this type of information accessible suggests that they think mainstream consumers are not actively seeking it, let alone prioritizing labor-compliance criteria when making their purchasing decisions. Alternatively, retailers that are specifically targeting 'ethical consumers' make this information more accessible, either by ensuring it appears on the 'shopping pages' of their website or by locating it just one click away.

what factors would motivate a brand or retailer to make readily available information about its labor standards and compliance record? In Chapter 10, Valero and Dickson portray the evolution of companies' responses to the demands of various stakeholders, who first insisted that companies implement programs identifying and addressing violations of labor standards and later that companies provide public information about those programs and their effectiveness. In their study, Valero and Dickson interviewed representatives of companies with varied levels of transparency about their labor-compliance programs. They found that companies recognize benefits to public reporting while also emphasizing the difficulty of determining what to report and to whom (i.e., shareholders, nongovernmental organizations, employees, or consumers). Their informants also expressed concern about the voluntary nature of public disclosure, since it allows some companies to fly 'under the radar' while those corporations that are accurately reporting both their successes and their challenges in the area of labor compliance are putting themselves squarely in the sights of vocal critics.

4   CONTEMPORARY DEBATES AND CONTROVERSIES

The fourth and final section of the volume sharpens the focus on contending approaches to the question of labor compliance. It does so by honing in on one of the central fault lines in the social-labeling debate—that is, whether the livelihoods and working conditions of garment workers should be dependent on a market-differentiation strategy, which, after all, relies on consumers' willingness and ability to buy goods that are made under conditions distinct from those characterizing conventional apparel products. In a sense, this debate focuses on the two contending perspectives which Ross introduced in Chapter 2 as the *benevolence* versus *social-justice* approaches to improving labor standards. The final five chapters of this collection provide an in-depth examination of current proposals to address labor issues in global supply chains and the degree to which they represent either the benevolence or the social-justice approach to confronting the challenges and opportunities that globalization creates for garment workers worldwide.

Given the historical development of social labeling in the United States, it is perhaps not surprising that Fair Trade USA (formerly Transfair) chose to launch a full range of 'Fair Trade' garments sourced from India, Liberia, Peru and Costa Rica, originally as part of a wider pilot initiative by Fair trade Labelling Organizations International, which was intended to explore the possibility of labeling different parts of the apparel value chain (Krueger 2011).[19] This is an ambitious task, and in Chapter 11, Franzese explores the rationale behind applying the fair-trade approach to garment manufacturing. She reviews the failure of the existing social-compliance model to empower workers adequately and explains how the fair-trade approach might address some of these weaknesses. Franzese contends that, in some factories, the fair-trade premium has the potential to quadruple the earnings of sewing workers, although the impact may be moderated by the proportion of production in a particular production facility that is Fair Trade Certified. Franzese thus acknowledges one of the main challenges that any social-labeling initiative must confront: most apparel factories produce for more than one buyer, so unless the multiple buyers sourcing from a factory agree to adopt the same standards (in this case, paying prices that reflect a fair-trade premium), the ability of any one client to make a significant difference in terms of wages and working conditions remains essentially compromised. Must factories therefore dedicate production to a single client for this model to work? Significantly, in the wake of criticisms of the fair-trade garment project by trade unions and NGOs—particularly in relation to living wage and trade-union rights—the FLO's plans have not developed significantly to extend the Fair Trade Certified label to other parts of the apparel supply chain.

The authors of Chapter 12 provide a different perspective on the possible efficacy of market-oriented labeling initiatives. Athreya and Campbell underscore the limitations of the kind of approach that the Fair Trade Certified apparel pilot represents. While some have argued that social labels and other voluntary compliance initiatives can support labor rights by providing space for workers to organize, the authors caution against assuming that this is the case. Based on research conducted under the auspices of the International Labor Rights Forum, they conclude that the 'soft law' approach represented by voluntary initiatives such as Fairtrade and Social Accountability

International's SA8000 regime fails to ensure workers' rights. They argue that social-compliance programs, which have repeatedly failed to secure redress of workers' grievances, do not serve as functional equivalents of effective industrial-relations systems. Instead, Athreya and Campbell endorse the development of mechanisms that could serve to 'harden' soft-law initiatives, such as requiring participating companies to accept binding responsibilities that can be enforced through mandatory neutral mediation or arbitration processes with legitimate worker representatives.

Although he is similarly concerned about the limited efficacy of social labels, Claeson nevertheless suggests in Chapter 13 that such initiatives can be effective if they harness the purchasing power of a sufficiently large and educated consumer—in this case, the government. The SweatFree Communities movement that has developed over the past decade in the United States encourages local elected governments to establish 'sweatfree' procurement criteria to ensure that goods purchased with public funds are manufactured under acceptable labor conditions. As 'super consumers,' governments depart from traditional consumers in several ways that are auspicious from the vantage point of supporting a meaningful social label: aside from the size of their purchases, governments have the resources to gather adequate information and investigate compliance with the procurement standards that they set, and perhaps most importantly, governments can use sanctions to compel compliance with these standards. If traditional, consumer-oriented labeling initiatives represent the benevolent approach to labor compliance, then SweatFree Communities present an alternative model that leverages public procurement in the pursuit of social justice.

In Chapter 14, Nova and Kline argue that, after a decade and a half of corporate codes of conduct and monitoring programs, subpoverty wages and abusive working conditions remain the norm in global apparel supply chains. The underlying cause of this unchanging status quo, they argue, can be found in the pricing and sourcing practices of brands and retailers in North America and Europe—a root cause that is left unaddressed by the extant auditing model. Nova and Kline explain that, in light of this largely ineffectual social-compliance industry, the Worker Rights Consortium (WRC) has opted for a different 'fair list' approach known as the Designated Suppliers Program (DSP). The DSP is designed to achieve decent wages and conditions of work in unionized factories producing university-licensed/collegiate apparel by ensuring that suppliers are rewarded, not punished, for respecting worker rights. The authors critically assess a voluntary initiative that is currently underway in the Dominican Republic, which incorporates some of the key principles of the DSP and involves a new apparel brand, *Alta Gracia*. The U.S.-based manufacturer that produces the *Alta Gracia* label in its owned and operated factory in the Dominican Republic is committed to respect for worker rights and to pursuing a marketing strategy that depends in large part on social labeling. The emerging lessons from this unique case in progress illustrate three challenges that are relevant to issues of social labeling in a global economy: differentiating businesses based on their ethical practices, paying for necessary upgrades for workers and ensuring consumer support for the companies that are providing labeled products.

Finally, in Chapter 15, Dirnbach makes the case for a worker-oriented, as opposed to consumer-oriented, social-labeling system. Dirnbach first outlines a set of criteria for designing and evaluating such a label, including adherence to ILO standards, empowerment through collective bargaining, and transparency in the production network. He then provides a road map for establishing such a system via the negotiation of Global SweatFree Apparel Production (GSAP) agreements between workers and their organizations, contractors and apparel brands that would share rights and responsibilities throughout the global supply chain. Returning to the benevolence versus justice debate, Dirnbach questions whether the rights of workers to fair working conditions should depend entirely on the whims of distant consumers, however much they are allied politically in a common social-label project. A GSAP, he argues, might be the springboard to an alternative strategy for the development of an international and state regulatory model that would strengthen the ILO, enact a global living wage and enable stronger labor-law enforcement at the national level.

We conclude the book with a brief afterword that considers the overarching question of whether, in light of the research presented, social labeling is the answer for improving the well-being of the millions of workers employed in global supply chains. Although we are skeptical that a social label is 'the' answer, we acknowledge the role for a market-based approach to improving working conditions and securing labor rights, and suggest a path forward that builds on the successes and shortcomings revealed in this volume.

NOTES

1. The authors are grateful to Jessica Bair for her excellent assistance in preparing the manuscript and completing the index.
2. http://www.just-style.com/analysis/made-in-labelling-law-divides-eu-member-states_id109302.aspx last accessed 15.2.2011
3. Information to Stakeholders on the Textiles Project, FLO.pdf issued 13.2.2011
4. Although the Forest Stewardship Council was developed primarily for certifying timber and wood products, the label can also be applied to footwear that contains rubber.
5. "The ILO, standard setting and globalization." Report of the Director-General, International Labour Conference, 85th Session, 1997. Geneva: International Labour Office.
6. However, a social label is not necessarily a physical mark; companies can also convey information to the consumer electronically via the internet (see Chapter 9).
7. The Knights of Labor, for example, recognized the power of the consumer boycott above the strike as a weapon (Spedden 1910: 18).
8. http://www.pittdixon.go-plus.net/denton/jolly-hatters.htm last accessed 8.2.2011
9. TUC Archive University of Warwick MSS. 292/8.4 Fair Lists and Labels 1895–1958. The Waterproof Garment Makers Trade Union was successful in

getting a number of Manchester-based employers to operate a label scheme. Similarly, the Amalgamated Shirt and Jacket Workers Society had a union-label scheme in the early 1900s, and the Scottish Operative Tailors and Tailoresses considered resolutions at Conferences in 1908 and 1911 to create a union label. Between 1919 and 1939, the National Union of Boot and Shoe Operatives ran a labeling program, but with little effect (Fox 1958).
10. http://steelzipper.com/ACWA.html last accessed 11.2.2011 The Blue Eagle logo of the NRA was incorporated into the ILGWU's union label, and during this period, the International Ladies' Garment Workers' Union became one of the largest labour unions in the United States, with a membership of 200,000 by 1934, eventually growing to 300,000 as the NIRA offered protection to workers in their efforts to unionize. http://steelzipper.com/ILGWU.html last accessed 11.2.2011
11. http://steelzipper.com/ILGWU.html last accessed 11.2.2011. This is a tenet that was repeated in the British National Union of Hosiery and Knitwear Workers mark 'Look at the Label—Save our Jobs' (Carter 1995).
12. As the department's website states, "The Union Label and Service Trades Department, AFL-CIO, was founded in 1909 to promote the products and services produced *in America* by union members—especially those products and services identified by a union label, shop card, store card and service button"; see http://www.unionlabel.org/?zone=/unionactive/view_page.cfm& page=About20Us; accessed 15/2/2011; emphasis added.
13. In 2012, the International Textile Garment and Leather Workers Federation merged with the International Metalworkers' Federation and the International Federation of Chemical, Energy, Mine and General Workers' Unions to form a new union called IndustriALL.
14. Rugmark is now referred to as Goodweave.
15. See "Herman says Sweatshop Label Undecided at Conclusion of U.S.-EU Labor Symposium." *BNA Occupational Safety and Health Daily*, February 24, 1998.
16. "The ILO, standard setting and globalization," Report of the Director-General. International Labour Conference, 85th Session, 1997. Geneva: International Labour Office.
17. Among the industry groups opposing the measure was the Business Social Compliance Initiative, an organization that was created in 2003 by the Foreign Trade Association, a trade association representing large European retailers (Fransen 2012; see also http://www.consilium.europa.eu/uedocs/ cms_data/docs/pressdata/EN/foraff/116480.pdf
18. It is important to note that Better Work departs from the Better Factories project in a number of ways—most importantly, as the program's critics note, with mandatory participation for garment exporters in some countries (Jordan and Haiti), but optional involvement for others. For the latter, there is no link between factory compliance and import market access.
19. Fair Trade USA has since become an independent organization and is no longer a national labeling organization under the Fairtrade Labelling Organizations International.

REFERENCES

Anner, M. 2012. 'Corporate Social Responsibility and Freedom of Association Rights: The Precarious Quest for Legitimacy and Control in Global Supply Chains.' *Politics and Society* 40(4):609–644.

Bair, J. 2008. 'Surveying the Post-MFA Landscape: What Prospects for the Global South Post-Quota?' *Competition and Change* 12(1):3–10.

Bair, J. 2012. 'The Limits to Embeddedness: Triangular Bargaining and the Institutional Foundations of Organizational Networks.' Working Paper No. 2012–10, Institute of Behavioural Science, University of Colorado, Boulder, CO.

Bair, J. and F. Palpacuer. 2012. 'From Varieties of Capitalism to Varieties of Activism: The Anti-Sweatshop Movement in Comparative Perspective.' *Social Problems* 59(4):522–543.

Bartley, T. 2005. 'Corporate Accountability and the Privatization of Labor Standards: Struggles over Codes of Conduct in the Apparel Industry.' *Research in Political Sociology* 14(2005):211–244.

Bird, M.M. and J. W. Robinson. 1972. 'The Effectiveness of the Union Label and Buy Union Campaigns.' *Industrial and Labor Relations Review* 25(4): 512–523.

Boyle, J.E. 1903. 'The Union Label.' *American Journal of Sociology* 9(2):163–172.

Carter, P. 1995. *Beware of Foul Made Hats: Felt Hatting and the Union Label.* Salford, United Kingdom: Bulletin of the Working Class Movement Library.

Chakravarthi, R. 1997. 'ILO Director-General Backs Away from Social Label Proposal.' Geneva, Switzerland: Third World Network. Retrieved February 15, 2011 (http://www.twnside.org.sg/title/soc-cn.htm).

Choppé, A. 1908. *Le Label.* Paris, France: Thèse Droit.

Dickson, M.A. and M. Eckman. 2008. 'Media Portrayal of Voluntary Public Reporting about Corporate Social Responsibility Performance: Does Coverage Encourage or Discourage Ethical Management?' *Journal of Business Ethics* 83(4):725–743.

Ellis, K. and J. Keane. 2008. 'A Review of Ethical Standards and Labels: Is There a Gap in the Market for a New Good for Development Label?' London, United Kingdom: Overseas Development Institute. Retrieved June 7, 2011 (http://www.odi.org.uk/resources/download/2538.pdf).

Esbenshade, J. 2004. *Monitoring Sweatshops: Workers, Consumers and the Global Apparel Industry.* Philadelphia, PA: Temple University Press.

Fox, A. 1958. *A History of the National Union of Boot and Shoe Operatives.* Oxford, United Kingdom: Blackwell.

Frank, D. 1994. *Purchasing Power: Consumer Organising, Gender, and the Seattle Labor Movement.* New York: Cambridge University Press.

Fransen, L. 2012. *Corporate Social Responsibility and Global Labor Standards: Firms and Activists in the Making of Private Regulation.* New York: Routledge.

Glickman, L.B. 1997. *A Living Wage: American Workers and the Making of Consumer Society.* Ithaca, NY: Cornell University Press.

Himmelberg, R. 1993. *The Origins of the National Recovery Administration.* New York: Fordham University Press.

International Labor Rights Forum. 2010. *Missed the Goal for Workers: The Reality of Soccer Ball Stitchers in Pakistan, India, China and Thailand.* Washington, D.C.: International Labor Rights Forum.

Kelley, W. E. J. 1897. 'The Union Label.' *The North American Review* 165(488):26–37.

Kleehammer, M. 2001. 'Gender, Class Consciousness, and Ethical Consumerism: Early Twentieth-Century Labelling Campaigns in the Women's Garment Industry.' *Ex Post Facto: The History Journal of San Francisco State University* 10(Spring):113–122.

Krueger R. 2011. 'Information to Stakeholders on the Textiles Project.' Bonn, Germany: Fairtrade Labelling International. Retrieved March 12, 2012 (http://fairtrade.net/fileadmin/user_upload/content/2009/news/releases_state ments/2011-03-21_FLO-Textile-Stakeholder-Letter.pdf).

Locke, R., A. Brause, and F. Qin. 2007. 'Does Monitoring Improve Labor Standards? Lessons from Nike.' *Industrial Relations and Labor Review* 61(1):3–32.

Louis, L. 1924. *The Women's Garment Workers: A History of the International Ladies' Garment Workers' Union.* New York: B.W. Huebsch Inc.

Marcketti, S.B. 2010. 'Codes of Fair Competition: The National Recovery Act, 1933–35, and the Women's Dress Manufacturing Industry.' *Clothing and Textiles Research Journal* 28(3):189–204.

Miller, D. 2012. *Last Night Shift in Savar: The Story of the Spectrum Sweater Factory Collapse.* Alnwick, United Kingdom: McNidder and Grace.

Mintel Group. 2009. 'Mintel Ethical Clothing 2009-Marketing Intelligence.' London, United Kingdom: Mintel Group.

Morris, C.J. 2005. *The Blue Eagle at Work.* Ithaca, NY: Cornell University Press.

Piepel, K. 1999. 'The Ethics Deficit in Corporate Trade: Social Labelling and Codes of Conduct.' Kildare, Ireland: Trócaire. Retrieved July 6, 2011 (http://www.trocaire.org/resources/tdr-article/ethics-deficit-corporate-trade-social-labelling-and-codes-conduct).

Ricketson, S. 2009. 'The Union Label Case: An Early Australian IP Story.' Pp. 15–36 in *Landmarks in Australian Intellectual Property Law*, A.T. Kenyon, M. Richardson, and S. Ricketson. Melbourne, Australia: Cambridge University Press.

Robinson, I. and B. Athreya. 2005. 'Constructing Markets for Conscientious Consumers: Adapting the Fair Trade Model to the Apparel Sector.' Paper Presented at the Conference on Constructing Markets for Conscientious Apparel Consumers, April 1–2, Ann Arbor, Michigan.

Seidman, G.W. 2007. *Beyond the Boycott: Labor Rights, Human Rights, and Transnational Activism.* New York: Russell Sage Foundation.

Shevlin, P.H. 1910. *The Union Label; Its History and Aims: Prize Essays.* Washington, D.C.: American Federation of Labor.

Sluiter, L. 2010. *Clean Clothes: A Global Movement to End Sweatshops.* London, United Kingdom: Pluto.

Spedden, E.R. 1910. *The Union Label.* Baltimore, Maryland: John Hopkins University Press.

Stiglitz, J.E. 2003. *The Roaring Nineties: A New History of the World's Most Prosperous Decade.* New York: Norton and Co.

Urminsky, M. 1998. *Self-Regulation in the Workplace: Codes of Conduct, Social Labelling and Socially Responsible Investment.* Geneva, Switzerland: International Labour Organization.

Wolensky, K.C., N.H. Wolensky, and R.P. Wolensky. 2002. *Fighting for the Union Label: The Women's Garment Industry and the ILGWU.* State College, PA: Pennsylvania State University Press.

2 Consumers and Producers
Agency, Power and Social Enfranchisement

Robert J. S. Ross[1]

Social labeling tells consumers some ethically relevant, positive dimension of a commodity's production or distribution. Such labels are generally oriented to individual or retail consumers. Karl Marx (1852) wrote that history repeats itself, 'the first time as tragedy, the second time as farce.' One cannot say with confidence how that same commentator would characterize the third or fourth iteration of the same idea or policy, and in any event, it remains for us, the living, to erect from the bones of history a scaffold for useful knowledge. The proposition that social labeling is a way to combat 'sweatshop' conditions—in other words, intense exploitation and abuse of clothing workers—has returned repeatedly for at least 110 years and on both sides of the Atlantic. This history, a review of some research on consumer behavior, and strategic analysis of the global garment industry will help us to decide whether we should laugh or cry at new labeling initiatives. As I begin, let me be clear about where I want to end: with fully enfranchised, well-paid, healthy, empowered men and women who work at the needle trades and are able to take their lives in their own hands.

Besides the appeal to social ethics, consumption is also sometimes presented as a kind of civic responsibility. In a world where the 'big decisions' are made or transmitted through markets, good citizenship morphs into ethical consumption. Actually, on occasions such as the 9/11 crisis and during periods such as the Great Recession of 2007 to the present, good citizenship seems to call for consumption itself, whether or not of ethically produced items (Strasser et al. 1998, Stolle & Hooghe 2005).

It is interesting that formally disenfranchised—or, more accurately, *unenfranchised*—women should have been the pioneers of social labeling. As state regulation grew, and women gained the vote, their early approaches to social labels waned. But now, as globalization and neoliberal ideology push back the margins of law, consumption *cum* citizenship appears again. Is it too soon in our story to suggest that we now are all disenfranchised—casting about for potent means to combat exploitation, even as nonvoting women were a century ago?

1   THE WHITE LABEL AND UNION LABELS: CONSUMERS AND PRODUCERS

In 1899, Florence Kelley began her office as general secretary of the National Consumers League (NCL). An organization of prosperous and elite women, it was a confederation of clubs and associations in larger metropolitan areas. Having campaigned on behalf of women and child laborers, and pioneered factory inspection for the state of Illinois, in 1899, Kelley went to New York City and led the newly-formed league in the creation of its White Label. The White Label was awarded to items of women's white-cotton underwear that met the following criteria:

1. the goods bearing the label were made in factories that obeyed State factory laws,
2. the goods were fully assembled in the factory (and not in a sweatshop),
3. no overtime was worked at the factory,
4. no child under the age of seventeen was employed by the factory (Wiedenhoft 2002: 62).

Although an intellectual peer of Friedrich Engels and, earlier in her life, a committed socialist,[2] Kelley framed her anti-sweatshop struggle in classical consumerist fashion:

> The Consumers' League . . . acts upon the proposition that the consumer ultimately determines all production, since any given article must cease to be produced if all consumers ceased to purchase it (Kelley 1899).

Kelley was not naïve, however. She wrote:

> The great mass of producers have long had recourse to the more simple device of advertising. This can lay no claim to any educational quality. It is distinctly not meant to educate or instruct, but to stimulate, persuade, incite, entice, and induce the indifferent to purchase. Much of the current advertisement, of which the patent-medicine advertisement may be taken as the type, is directly aimed at the ignorance of the purchaser (Kelley 1899: 294).

So, Kelley thought a knowledgeable consumer could overcome the obfuscations of advertising if given the right signals. Her strategy of publicizing a positive recommendation to middle-class consumers has gained our attention because today's anti-sweatshop movement in the developed countries is based upon the same class as Kelley's NCL, with similar—if not the same— perspectives on their own potential power. For example, Fair Trade USA says in its mission statement:

As Americans become increasingly concerned about the state of the world and look for opportunities to use their power in the marketplace to make a positive difference, we seek to provide an avenue for consumers to vote with their dollar. As we educate and inspire more and more consumers, we hope to be a force for change (Fair Trade USA 2010).

Yet Kelley faced much the same complication that we now face.

The idea of a positively preferred list of ethically compliant manufacturers was the somewhat gentler twin of the boycott list. The boycott was a widely used tactic of the labor movement at the end of the nineteenth century. Both the Knights of Labor and its successor as the dominant American labor organization, the American Federation of Labor (AFL), used 'Don't Patronize' lists quite frequently. They met with enough apparent success to cause business organizations to combat them with both public relations and legal campaigns. These culminated in 1908, in a Supreme Court decision (Loewe v. Lawlor 1908) outlawing boycotts. The labor movement turned to its own version of a preferred list: the union label (Wiedenhoft 2002: 47).

Samuel Gompers, the crusty head of the AFL, had himself been a cigar maker. The original 'White Label' of 1875 had designated California cigars that had been made by white men, union labor, and not by Chinese 'coolies.' The semi-coerced, low-wage labor of Chinese immigrants produced a racially defined backlash among California workers, resulting in exclusionary immigration legislation in 1882. Subsequent union labels of cigar makers included the pejorative 'coolie' but also certified freedom from 'prison' and 'filthy tenement house workmanship.'[3]

The theme of labor standards requiring the suppression of subcontracting and outwork/ home workshops—the original definition of a sweatshop, after all—was unambiguously adopted by Kelley's NCL: only underwear made in factories could get a White Label. But, Gompers and the AFL were not pleased that the White Label had no wage standard, nor a union or a strike-free standard.

By 1904, the NCL White Label had about 60 factories signed up. With little change after that, the NCL White Label peaked at 68 factories in 1916 (Weidenhoft 2002: 63). My calculations suggest that this represents about one percent of wageworkers in women's clothing, with an upper limit of just over four percent (4.4 percent) and a lower limit of about 0.4 percent of all apparel and textile product workers.[4]

While workers' appeals to their fellows may evoke solidarity, it is fairly straightforward, both theoretically and empirically, that those with room for relative discretion in their purchasing behavior—those with more-than-adequate incomes—would be the main targets and instigators of such plans. Rather than solidarity, social-label appeals to retail consumers today are more usually appeals to conscience. The classes and subcultures in which such appeals are made are, in the language of social-movement analysis, 'conscience constituencies,' as distinct from 'beneficiary constituencies' (McCarthy and Zald 1977).

After the court decision of 1908, the AFL had turned aggressively to its own positive preference strategy, the union label. And so, what had been an irritation, the NCL's independence from the union movement, would become an almost-scripted confrontation. In 1916, a Boston White Label factory was struck. This redoubled the AFL antagonism toward the White Label, claiming that the White Label was used as a 'cloak' for employer 'hostility' to unions. This incident and confrontation provoked a rethink by the NCL. By 1918, the NCL reported, 'Our position is obviously untenable as friends of labor' . . . 'if we persist in pushing our label as a rival to the label of the American Federation of Labor against the protests of union officials' (Weidenhoft 2002: 166).

The White Label was withdrawn—but it was not deeply grieved by NCL members. According to Wendy Wiedenhoft, they had run into some limits, including: the effectiveness of volunteer inspectors and the complexity of their tasks; the size of the industry; and the growing importance, during the era of Progressive movement reform, of state (as distinct from federal) legislative achievements. They turned their attention to legislative reform at state and then national levels.

The famous culmination of this turn to regulation occurred with the coming of the Roosevelt New Deal. The former NCL staff member Frances Perkins, now secretary of labor, shepherded into law the Fair Labor Standards Act of 1938 (FLSA), embodying all of the NCL objectives: the end of child labor; a minimum wage for all (both men and women); restriction (though weak, only creating premium pay not maximum hours) of overtime work; and a prohibition of industrial homework in the vulnerable needle trades.

The demise of the White Label in favor of a campaign for reform by legal regulation and in favor of union labels was to see each of these broad objectives—legal regulation of labor standards and growth in union protection for masses of workers—achieved within 20 years.

In 1938, *Life* magazine had prematurely declared sweatshops a thing of the past, but by 1940, with military production ramping up and Secretary Perkins having finally closed down industrial homework, the needle-trades workers were on their way to what we might think of as 'normal working class' livelihoods—and these were emerging, after WWII, as middle-income lives.

2   LOOK FOR THE UNION LABEL

The era of relative decency for U.S. garment workers was to last but 40 years. About midway through this period, in 1958, the International Ladies Garment Workers Union (ILGWU) initiated one of the most storied social-labeling campaigns in U.S. history—with its impossible-to-forget jingle— *Look for the Union Label*. Between 1959 and 1971, the ILG, as it was known before merging numerous times with other unions—spent about $880,000 annually on the advertising campaign for its label. That is the equivalent of $4.6 million in early 2011 dollars. Certainly more was spent after 1975 when the campaign moved to TV—but at the same time union density was sinking, from 77 percent in the mid-1970s to 25 percent in the mid-1980s and now to under 6 percent (Ulrich 1995, Ross 2004). More than one million jobs were lost in this period (see Figures 2.1 and 2.2).

Figure 2.1 Apparel Workers' Average Weekly Earnings, as a Percentage of Average Manufacturing Earnings, 1947–2009

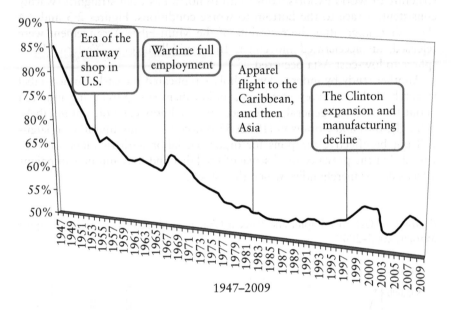

Figure 2.2 Employment of U.S. Apparel Production Workers, 1960–2010

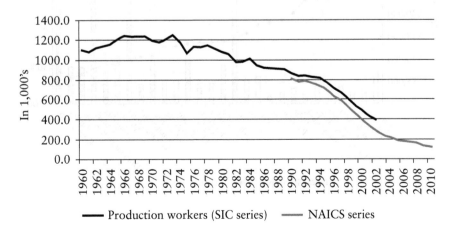

According to one scholar, the union commissioned only two studies of the effects of its union-label campaign, one in 1961 and another in 1975, before the campaign moved to television (Ulrich, op cit). Recognition of the union label declined from 68 percent to 44 percent; positive inclination to buy union also declined—from 23 percent to 17 percent. This was before the most recognizable union jingle ever produced hit the airwaves, but even then, union density, import penetration and jobs declined.

The clothing industry increasingly handled casual fashions and moved first to union-free Los Angeles and the Border States, and then to the Caribbean, and then to Asia (Laslett & Tyler 1989, Rosen 2002, Ross 2004). The structure of world exports from south to north has been straightforwardly consistent: a race to the bottom to worse conditions. Figures 2.3 and 2.4 show that, later, after the restraints of the Multi-Fibre Arrangement were released, an accelerated movement from middle-income Western Hemisphere to low-cost Asia occurred.

Another study by independent scholars replicated the earlier union-label research. A 1970 survey of Virginia union members' purchasing inquired about the subjects' general preferences for, or knowledge of, union labels. Tellingly, Bird and Robinson (1972: 520) note that: 'buy union' campaigns will not be effective weapons for organized labor until retailers are convinced that the presence or absence of the label and 'buy union' campaigns affect sales or merchandise which they stock.'

Figure 2.3   GDP per Capita and Percent Change in Share of U.S. Apparel Import Market, 2005–2008

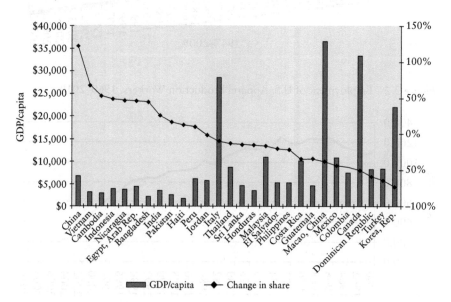

Figure 2.4 Shares of the U.S. Apparel Import Market, 2000–2009

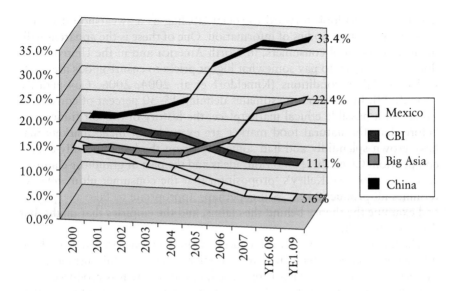

Though a small percent of union members did prefer and buy union products, the researchers concluded that:

> An important segment of the consuming public, union members, do not look for or recognize the union label and do not select brands which are union made over those which are not. Retailers, perhaps because they recognize this fact, make little effort to stock union-made products or to promote the fact that any of their merchandise is union made. Like the consuming public, industrial purchasers make little effort to purchase union-made products. Therefore, it is logical that manufacturers make little effort to promote their product as being union made (Bird and Robinson 1972: 523).

Among the speculations in which contemporary anti-sweatshop campaigners engage is that because there is so little union-made apparel on the shelves, retail shoppers might choose union-made apparel more often if it was available. But, we should note that when the ILG had 77 percent market penetration, it could not deter the tectonic shift of globalization, union evasion, and the loss of a culture of solidarity. The United States may be a polar case, but my speculation would be that the other broadly market-oriented societies of British heritage are similarly distinctive from those other OECD (Organization for Economic Cooperation and Development) political economies with lower levels of income inequality and higher levels of union influence. In the meantime, conscience appeals to ethical consumption may reach a broader public than union labels reach.

3   THE SEMI-SOVEREIGN RETAIL CONSUMER

It is tempting to look forward to social labeling as a sweatshop deterrent based on two other bodies of information. One of these is the apparent willingness of surveyed consumers, in North America and in the United Kingdom, for example, to pay somewhat higher prices to ensure goods are made under fair-labor conditions (Kimeldorf et al. 2004, 2006, Co-operative Bank 2009). In addition to estimates defining 15–30 percent of consumers as part of a possible ethical marketplace, the history of the fair trade, and, before that, the natural food market are examples of niche markets that have grown splendidly and had some impact on the less-than-fully-ethical competition. Given these ambitious ideas and the past of grandiose claims— remember Florence Kelley's 'proposition that the consumer ultimately determines all production . . .'—it is perhaps appropriate to take a step back and examine the theory behind the claims, and the empirics that might, but don't, support them.

The theory is straightforward: consumers in the retail market, as each individual purchase is aggregated, are sovereign—that is, in this instance, they can determine not only what is produced, but also how it is produced. This embodies, for purists such as Hayek, reason, a purposive individualism that regulation cannot embody, and rationality—a system result of broadly conceived freedom (Hayek 1984). 'The knowledge of the circumstances of which we must make use,' Hayek wrote, 'never exists in concentrated or integrated form but solely as the dispersed bits of incomplete and frequently contradictory knowledge which all separate individuals possess' (Hayek 1984: 212).

Thus, the consumer—the owner of that dispersed knowledge—a libertarian follower of Hayek proclaimed—is and ought to be 'king.' In a properly free market, 'the consumer is king, not the businessman,' announced Representative Ron Paul, and 'we should crown the consumers king and let them vote with their money on who should succeed and who should fail. . . . Consumer sovereignty simply means consumers decide who succeeds or fails in the market. Businesses that best satisfy consumer demand will be the most successful. Consumer sovereignty is the means by which the free market maximizes human happiness' (Paul 1999: H11683–H11684).

Clearly, Florence Kelley, the definitive translator of Engels and cofounder of the Intercollegiate Socialist Society (1905), was not in the same camp as Hayek—but they shared an error. Their error was the imagined power of the atomized individual retail consumer dictating conditions of production.

Consider the modern shopper. He or she wants peanut butter—not the kind that needs stirring—but is vaguely aware that certain kinds of oils are not so healthy. The consumer sovereign theory wants us to have all the information we can take to make informed decisions. So, the consumer reads the label of a popular brand; well, we have been alerted to the undesirability of 'fully hydrogenated vegetable oils,' but is 'under 2 percent' acceptable? And, what are mono- and diglycerides? Do you need college chemistry to be sovereign?

Now, let's move to the T-shirt shop to get a University of Michigan T-shirt for dear old dad, who graduated in 1963. In this make-believe world of intense ethical scrutiny, let us imagine we have an iPhone or Droidx and are internet connected. There is a Nike brand T-shirt with an attractive design. Michigan has a code of conduct that meets the criteria of the very competent Worker Rights Consortium (WRC)—a major creation of the student anti-sweatshop movement. Part of the accomplishment of that movement has been to force firms to disclose their contractor production sites. Nike disclosed to the WRC that it was sourcing from 256 factories in 21 countries as of its statement of 2009, accessed on August 5, 2010 (Worker Rights Consortium 2010). More broadly, Michigan logo gear is sourced from 567 separate contractors. Another one of them, Gear for Sports, sources from 16 factories in 11 countries. Not only is it impossible for a consumer to know if the T-shirt has been made under appropriate conditions, it is not in fact known by the WRC. The WRC, until its Designated Suppliers Program is fully operational, is a firehouse. It does not officially know about unsafe or exploitative conditions until a fire breaks out—that is, when and if workers or their advocates make a specific complaint. Then it sends a team in full gear—and has good success—until the plant closes and the brand contracts with another one in a less-regulated or more-repressive environment (Ross 2006).

There are reasons beyond cognitive complexity that make the individual retail consumer and her or his choices slender reeds upon which working conditions can depend. Among these are the combination of rational self-interest and the irrational loyalties and desires that join to produce consumption decisions. In the first instance, of course, most people want to pay the least for what they want. And, today, the combination of low prices and advertising and the humid swamp of contemporary cultural identity needs have led many to want a lot of clothes. In the United States in 2009, 1.8 pairs of jeans were purchased per capita; in 2008, Americans owned an estimated seven pairs of jeans each (Agarwal 2009, Cotton Inc. 2008). As recently as 2007, Americans bought eight pairs of shoes each (American Apparel and Footwear Association 2008). When consumers are willing to pay premium prices, they seem to be driven by brand images and loyalties. These are anything but rationally driven or decided affiliations—and therein lies one of the strategic keys to both social movement and corporate behavior today—the vulnerability of corporate or brand image.

4 NAMING AND SHAMING: EL MONTE AND KATHY GIFFORD AND THE AFTERMATH

In August 1995, the California Department of Labor Standards Enforcement (DLSE) and the (then) Immigration and Naturalization Service (INS) raided an apartment complex in El Monte, California—about 18 miles east of downtown Los Angeles. They had received a handwritten note in barely literate English telling them of a garment factory hidden in an apartment complex where people were being held against their will—in virtual slavery.

At the notorious El Monte apartments, the dawn raiders found 72 workers imprisoned—the longest for seven years, sewing clothes for the major brands and retail chains in California and nationally. A picture of the workers, moments after the raid, published by the *Los Angeles Times*, shows the women squatting on their haunches, on the sidewalk outside the apartment building, their postures suggesting their Asian or peasant background even as their faces conveyed a terrified helplessness that belongs somewhere else[5]—not here, not in the world's oldest democracy, not where government of the people had vanquished slavery 130 years earlier.

The El Monte slave-labor case projected the sweatshop issue into prominence in California and the West Coast (but not so much in the East), and gave Secretary of Labor Robert Reich and his head of the Wage and Hour Division, Maria Echeveste, dramatic justification to advance their anti-sweatshop campaign at the Department of Labor (DoL).

The El Monte case provided a window of public attention, and Reich and the Clinton administration used a never-before-employed section of the FLSA to leverage the 'manufacturers' to demand labor-law compliance from their contractors. The leverage was the authority, in the FLSA, to prevent interstate shipment of goods produced under conditions that violate the act ('hot cargo'). Reich and Echeveste began to require firms caught using contractors who broke the law to agree to inspect their contractors and certify that their contractors had obeyed the law. And so was born the late 1995 'trendsetters list'—the press immediately dubbed it the 'good guys' list—composed of firms who had signed agreements to monitor their contractors for labor-law compliance—'compliance monitoring.'

Compliance monitoring did reduce FLSA violations. In Southern California, in 1996, Esbenshade found: 'The percentage of garment firms found in compliance with FLSA minimum wage requirements increased nearly 20 percentage points (from 39 percent to 57 percent). Firms found complying with FLSA overtime requirements increased 23 percentage points (from 22 percent to 45 percent).' So, after 'signing up' firms, their contractors violated the minimum-wage law 43 of 100 times and failed to pay overtime in 55 of 100 cases (Esbenshade 2004). Using Esbenshade's data, I have estimated that compliance monitoring's 'success' in Southern California included wage theft of about $95 million annually in the mid-1990s (Ross 2005).

Jill Esbenshade's research and reflection on the brief experiment in compliance monitoring is relevant to the broader matter that is involved in social labeling. This is the substitution of private monitors for either worker collective agreement or legal standards with law enforcement. Gay Seidman (2008) later called these various private monitoring schemes 'voluntary, stateless regulatory schemes.' Esbenshade noted the sociological difference between labor-law enforcement and corporate-code compliance monitoring:

[W]orkers have no influence over the practices of monitoring . . . Enforcement, which relies on the power of local governments, and organizing, which depends on the power of workers, are floundering while
corporate campaigns and monitoring, which rely on publicity and con-
sumer/investor power, are on the upsurge. . . . Globalization has un-
dermined the ability of local governments to enforce their own laws.
Workers' power has been . . . decreased [while] . . . the power of investors
and consumers has been greatly increased (Esbenshade 2004: 55).

Monitoring has at least two broad types; one is internally sponsored,
even if conducted by a contractor, and this is the typical case in today's very
large corporate social responsibility (CSR) industry. Alternatively, there are
a variety of independent monitoring schemes and monitoring groups—both
profit and nonprofit, multistakeholder sponsored and independent. Garret
Brown estimated the CSR industry at $40 billion annually (Brown 2009).
Critics of CSR as a response to global exploitation charge that it is a largely
public relations–oriented strategy developed in response to what remains to
campaigners a weapon both potent and unreliable: 'naming and shaming.'
Some background will help.

While the garment workers' union, UNITE, was working intensely to
find a strategy to combat the spread of sweatshop conditions it had beaten
down by 1940, its outrage was not broadly noticed. Sweatshop conditions
in North America were still, as 1995 ended, a concern of the [shrinking]
unions, a few journalists, even fewer academics and a tiny handful of prophetic souls in the so-called NGO (nongovernmental) community. One of
those prophetic individuals was Charlie Kernaghan, the man who will be
known forever as the guy who made Kathie Lee cry.

5   THE FALL AND RISE OF KATHIE LEE GIFFORD:
A CASE OF NAMING AND SHAMING

Early in 1996, Charles Kernaghan traveled to El Salvador and Honduras, investigating abuses of workers' rights for his small organization, the National
Labor Committee. Near a factory called Global Fashions, he met with a number of women and girls who worked there. He had previously been told of
all-night, forced shifts, extremely low pay, 65-hour weeks, brutal discipline
and child labor. On this day, fearful that a company spy was in their midst,
the women did not speak very much, but one handed Kernaghan a label of
the type that they were sewing into the blouses they were making. It said
'Kathie Lee.' Kernaghan, not a daytime television watcher, did not realize the
potential of what he had in hand until he returned to the United States.

Kathie Lee Gifford was the cohost, with Regis Philbin, of a mid-morning
interview and chat show called *Live with Regis and Kathie Lee*. A former
model, Kathie Lee presented a pretty and wholesome appearance, and, quite

relevant to this story, presented herself as particularly concerned about children. Her own family was a frequent referent in her discussion on screen, and they appeared in advertisements she made endorsing products.

Kathie Lee endorsed a line of clothing sold in Wal-Mart stores—the largest chain in the United States and now the world. Ms. Gifford claimed, and this was on her labels, that some of the profit from her endorsement was devoted to children's charities. In this sense, Kathie had 'standing' concerning children's issues, but also vulnerability (Meyer and Gamson 1995).

On April 29, Kernaghan spoke to an informal 'hearing' composed of the Democratic members of the House Committee on Labor, meeting as the Democratic Policy Committee on Child Labor. The members heard testimony from a young Canadian activist involved with child labor issues (Craig Kielburger), and from Kernaghan. According to Kernaghan, the ample television coverage of the event was largely focused on the young man from Canada. Kernaghan returned home with no inkling of the tumult to come. The next day's *New York Times* carried a story about $1 million in back pay awarded to workers in California, including those Thai immigrants who had been held as semislaves in El Monte, and who were discovered in August 1995. The April 30 paper included no story about Kernaghan's charges about Kathie Lee's line of clothing, nor did the May 1 paper. By contrast, the *Los Angeles Times* did carry a business section story about the charges on April 30 (Salem 1996).

On May 1, Kathie Lee Gifford responded to Kernaghan's charges on her television show. According to the *New York Times* (May 2), Ms. Gifford 'held back tears,' denying that her clothes were made in sweatshop conditions. *People* magazine described her as quaking with teary rage as she denied the story. 'You can say I'm not talented . . . but when you say that I don't care about children. . . . How dare you?' (Howe et al. 1996: 60). '. . . [M]ister, you better answer your phone because my lawyer is calling you today' (Bearak 1996). Kernaghan reports this quite jovially, convinced it was the making of his ability to gain media attention for his views about the issue: Kathie Lee made *him* and *his issue* an object of attention (C. Kernaghan, interview with author, October 4, 1996).

Kernaghan arranged for one of the Global Fashions workers, Wendy Diaz, age 15, to come to the United States. On May 22, Ms. Gifford and her husband, Frank, a famous former football star and broadcaster himself, went on an ABC prime-time interview show. Ms. Gifford said she wanted to finance inspections of places where her line of clothing was made (Bearak 1996). As they waited airtime of the taped show, Frank and Kathie Lee learned that the Department of Labor had launched an investigation of Seo Fashions on West 38th in the heart of New York's garment district. Eventually, Seo was found to have cheated 25 men and women of two to four weeks' pay in the production of 50,000 Kathie Lee blouses (Howe et al. 1996), and the place had a list of grossly unsanitary conditions that filled out the sweatshop description.[6]

A few days later, on May 29, Kernaghan introduced Wendy Diaz, the Honduran employee of Global Fashions, to the Washington press corps. On May 30, Kathie Lee Gifford appeared with New York Governor George Pataki as he announced plans for New York State legislation that would outlaw sale of sweatshop-produced clothing. That day, Labor Secretary Reich met with Mr. and Ms. Gifford to discuss the sweatshop problem. On June 1, the *Los Angeles Times* reported that Ms. Gifford would help Secretary Reich organize a public forum for the fashion industry, to deal with the sweatshop issue.

In the meantime, Kernaghan was arranging a meeting between Ms. Gifford and Wendy Diaz: at issue were place, auspices and attendees. Finally agreed was June 5, at the residence of the Archbishop John Cardinal O'Connor of New York—St. Patrick's Cathedral in New York. Present were Kernaghan; Esperanza Reyes of the Committee for the Defense of Human Rights in Honduras; Rev. David Dyson of the People of Faith Coalition; Jay Mazur, president of the Union of Needletrades, Industrial and Textile Employees (UNITE); and Kathie Lee and Wendy. Kernaghan describes this as a moment of high emotion. Wendy Diaz, he says, was strong and articulate beyond the expectation of her years.

Afterward, Kathie Lee would advocate independent (third-party) monitoring of working conditions at contractor sites, and also express a desire to continue to send work to Global Fashions. One can see in this result Kernaghan striving to protect the Global Fashions workers from losing their jobs (through withdrawal of Wal-Mart contracts) because of speaking out. The model of third-party monitoring was adopted at this meeting for domestic work sites as well (C. Kernaghan, interview with author, October 4, 1996; Bearak 1996). Naming and shaming had produced a change.

On July 2, Ms. Gifford appeared at Gov. Pataki's press conference as he signed a New York anti-sweatshop bill, barring the sale of clothing made under conditions violating labor law. On July 16, Reich hosted a Fashion Industry Forum at which Ms. Gifford appeared, as well as 300 other leading spokespersons of the fashion and entertainment industry. The day before that event, Ms. Gifford went to Capitol Hill to urge passage of further child-labor protections. Also in Washington, Ms. Gifford met on August 2 with President Bill Clinton, Vice-President Al Gore, Secretary of Labor Reich and Senate Minority Leader Tom Harkin to discuss child-labor issues.

On August 23, the *Los Angeles Times* and the *New York Times* reported once again on Department of Labor raids on sweatshops found producing Kathie Lee clothing, and in September, there were reports of raids on firms making supermodel Kathy Ireland's line, sold at K-Mart stores.

By early Fall 1996, stories about Ms. Gifford's troubles continued to appear in newspapers and magazines, but a discerning observer would have noted that while she had become a spokesperson for moderate reform, others, for example, Michael Jordan, had eschewed responsibility for the conditions of production of clothing which bore their names. 'I don't know the complete situation,' Jordan told the Associated Press. 'Why should I? I'm trying to do my job. Hopefully, Nike will do the right thing' (Strom 1996).

Kathie Lee Gifford had moved into another realm: whatever one thought of her talent, and indeed, even if one had this or that quibble with the solutions she advocated, nevertheless, Kathie Lee Gifford had become a responsible moral agent. However much Ms. Gifford may have grown personally, it is the impact of her celebrity on the visibility of the sweatshop issue that explains the repeated return of movement activists to the 'celebrity' well. This episode was among the more dramatic examples of the 'naming and shaming' strategy of anti-sweatshop campaigning. What the Gifford case typifies—and what anti-sweatshop audiences appear to want—are entries in the victim Olympics: dramatically vulnerable and stereotypically innocent victims, like children or young mothers.

6   COMPASSION VS. JUSTICE; BENEVOLENCE VS. AGENCY

The Gifford affair doubled newspaper coverage of the sweatshop issue and tripled what remained the much smaller TV coverage of it (Ross 2004). It was a high point of naming and shaming. Shortly thereafter, the Clinton administration formed the Apparel Industry Partnership, which eventually became the Fair Labor Association (FLA). From the point of view of the social-labeling enterprise, the FLA story is strategically important. At the outset, it is clear that President Clinton and his secretary of labor, Robert Reich, wanted the result to be a social label. The president said this about the firms he had talked to before the initial meeting:

> They have agreed to do two things. First, they will take additional steps to ensure that the products they make and sell are manufactured under decent and humane working conditions. Second, they will develop options to inform consumers that the products they buy are not produced under those exploitative conditions. . . .
>
> I do hope they'll develop measures that might include labels, clear signs in stores, or other means of getting the information directly involved to consumers so that consumers at the point of sale have an opportunity themselves to be responsible citizens in their purchases (Clinton 1996).

A contentious ten months later, President Clinton once again expressed the goal for what became the FLA:

> It will also form an independent association to help implement the agreement and to develop an effective way to share this information

with consumers, such as labels on clothing, seals of approval in advertising, or signs in stores to guarantee that no sweatshop labor was used on a given product line (Clinton 1997).

The hoped for signals to consumers never happened. Agreement with unions could not be struck on wage criteria or freedom of association. Too many brands refused to commit to the moderate code of conduct proposed. But, the very complexity of the supply chain was also a factor. If a brand sources from hundreds of factories and only some of these are code compliant, the problem of labeling can become, depending on attitude and approach, overwhelmingly complicated,[7] or an invitation for subtle deceit as consumers are misled into thinking all of a chain's supply comes from equally ethical sources. Some think this is illustrated by the way Starbucks mixes fair-trade with conventionally sourced coffee in supermarket shelves.

7 THE PERFECT STORM ON THE HORIZON?

In 1991, a Halloween northeast hurricane joined a strong cold front to create 10-story high waves in the North Atlantic and $208 million damages in New England. Twelve lives were lost, including six on the fishing boat Andrea Gail. The confluence of cold fronts, subtropical air and a dying hurricane was rare, and thus, the phrase 'perfect storm' came into our language when Sebastian Junger (1997) told the tale.

From the outset of the American experience with the White Label, the nightmare scenario for workers and their allies has been the perfect storm: a widely acknowledged label that reassures and disarms conscience-based consumer allies, but one that cloaks or inadequately addresses abuse and exploitation of workers. Now the issue of producer agency and consumer sovereignty is brewing another potential perfect storm.

Florence Kelley and the National Consumers League eventually faced this issue and acceded primacy to the attempts at union label acceptance. Numerous NGOs, including the (now the International Labor Rights Forum, ILRF) and the National Committee on Labor and Human Rights (NCL), and labor-union participants anticipated this problem might arise with the nascent Fair Labor Association and withdrew in 1998. Led in part by the United Students Against Sweatshops, but also by the thoughtful collaboration of NGO leaders such as Scott Nova of the Worker Rights Consortium, Bama Athreya (ILRF), Bjorn Claeson (Sweatfree Communities), with academics such as Ian Robinson, the recent emphasis among anti-sweatshop campaigners has been the necessity for worker empowerment, sometimes called worker voice (e.g., Sweatfree Communities n.d.; Robinson and Athreya 2005).

The recent NGO emphasis on worker voice is a recognition of the problem of agency: who is the actor, and who the witness to action; who leads, who follows in the struggle for worker decency? The earlier tradition—I should note that my own view of it is positive, that it was noble—was one in which women of conscience worked on behalf of vulnerable workers—women and children—who were more or less voiceless on their own or as collectivities. On the other hand, the period in which workers in the garment industry, and indeed, workers throughout the developed world, gained more nearly decent standards of living were ones in which their own collective institutions were able to win gains directly in relation to employers and indirectly through public policy.

One way to view the comparison is in terms of framing devices: the compassion frame versus the justice frame, shopper benevolence and agency versus worker self-actualization and agency. The emphasis of the typically motivated individual ethical shopper is more like the earlier period of sympathy with a victim. Numerous studies have shown that both in opinion and in some cases behavior, a small, but not minute, fraction of shoppers wants goods fairly made (Hiscox & Smyth 2008, Dickson 2001, Shaw et al. 2007). Yet, the worker voice, and in particular, the union implication of this is rarely articulated by either the vendor or the buyer. The difficulty in finding information about brands and the meaning of different label schemes requires, like the consumer labeling of food, an enterprise in self-education, which is apt to be either rare or easily misled.

There is apt to be some considerable variation in the degree to which 'typical' ethical consumers in different political cultures understand the relevance of worker collective voice to the question of sweatshop abuse. Americans are almost certainly the most bereft of such comprehension. This means that for the fraction of the clothing market that does want an ethical signal, a perfect storm is brewing. A perfect storm for ethical labeling would be one in which a widely known and widely trusted brand or label certifies a garment made under standards that are inadequate—a widely believed false promise.

Let us imagine a producer that fulfills a labor standards obligation for worker voice by instigating what in the United States we call a company union—a plant-based worker association dominated by management. Let us further imagine a wage level at that factory that exceeds the national minimum wage—the proposed fair-trade labor standard criterion—by five percent. This minimum wage is widely acknowledged by official sources to be far below—at best half—what a family—even one sharing a toilet and bath with 20 other families—needs (United States Department of State 2009). Such a factory and brand 'may allow fair trade certification of products made by workers who are paid poverty wages and perhaps denied meaningful freedom of association' and might now earn a 'fair-trade apparel' label (International Labor Rights Forum 2009, Merk 2009)—a perfect storm of illusory ethical labeling.[8]

8   THE WAY FORWARD: THREE PILLARS OF DECENCY

Reflecting on the twentieth century—in particular on matters concerning garment workers—suggests three requirements for workers to achieve material decency and social enfranchisement. By material decency, I mean wages and benefits that bring working people within the broad ambit of normative consumption in their society. By social inclusion or enfranchisement, I mean those measures of policy that allow working people to participate broadly in the life of their society and culture: for example, universal free public education and access to post-secondary education, social insurances that form protection from the vicissitudes of the business cycle, social pensions, and health insurance.

In the first place, these requirements, these three supports for worker inclusion, what I have called elsewhere the 'three pillars of decency,' include the effective formation of workers' organizations for defense of their interests, primarily in the form of labor unions, but also in civil society (e.g., locality-based community organizations). Secondarily, the ability of workers and their organizations to form effective (even if de facto) alliances with reform, socialist or social democratic, or other egalitarian forces—usually middle class, and sometimes in their role as consumers—heightens worker strength in the industrial sphere and enables the achievement of the third support for worker decency. The last element of the supports for worker inclusion is effective public policy that provides elements of social wage, guarantees of associational rights and other elements of full participation in the life of the political culture—for instance, public education.

Monitoring, however independent, that produces a certification for a label recognized by an individual retail consumer cannot substitute for workers' own efforts at collective action. Such action moves the active agent from workers to certifiers; in turn, to their funders and sponsors—brands or retailer corporations. Unless motivated by particular 'naming and shaming' campaigns—the problems of supply-chain complexity, consumer education, the timeliness of remediation—all these overwhelm the endeavor.

The relevant question is how consumer decisions can aid in worker empowerment. Some elements of the recent history of consumer-oriented conscience constituency action are somewhat more instructive than others are. In the first instance, just as in the problem of air-pollution control, concentrated point sources are higher value targets then millions of dispersed household purchasers. This is why leverage over university-logo material and publicly contracted uniform purchases[9] makes some strategic sense: the consumers are aggregated into collective consumers, and their voice is more strategically focused and expertise is more efficiently marshaled. Even here, however, the volatility of the apparel supply chain, ease of entry and exit, and the upstream externalization of risk by the chain-governing brands (Gereffi et al. 2001) makes the maintenance of standards difficult at best and the protection of worker voice one hardly yet achieved.

And so one arrives where Florence Kelley did in 1918: adopting a consumer advisory to favor union labels—or, in the case of the collective consumer, to prefer union-made goods. Then, as allies to labor, struggle for legislation that protects both substantive labor standards (e.g., minimum wages and the prohibition of child labor) and labor rights (to organize and bargain). In turn, in a world of global capital and intensive interdependence, the clear implication of such a view is the reconstruction of the rules of international trade—one where workers are as protected as investors are. That's another story.

NOTES

1. April Lambert, Clark University 2010, provided vital research assistance for this chapter. The Mosakowski Institute for Public Enterprise at Clark University provided support to Ms. Lambert and the author, for which we are grateful.
2. Kelley was the translator of the still-authoritative American edition of Friedrich Engels's *The Condition of the Working Class in England in 1844*. J. W. Lovell Co. 1887.
3. See "The Union Label" website of the AFL-CIO for an image of this label at http://www.unionlabel.org/?zone=/unionactive/view_page.cfm&page=The20Union-20Label, accessed on February 3, 2011.
4. The *Statistical Abstract of the United States*. 1916. Department of Commerce. U.S. GPO, Washington, D.C., 185–186. http://www2.census.gov/prod2/statcomp/documents/1916-04.pdf. Using 1914 data, if underwear was made in factories the size of corset factories (120 wage workers on average), but the total employee base is corsets plus women's clothing, the result is 4.4%; if underwear was made in factories having more like the average for women's clothing (30 wage workers), the White Label fraction is 1%; the average between the two would 1.2%. If all "apparel and textile products" employment is used as the denominator, the 68 factories at the average establishment size for the whole industry (30 wageworkers) represents 0.4% of production workers. For this latter calculation, see *Historical Statistics of the United States*, Millennial Edition On Line, edited by Susan B. Carter, Scott Sigmund Gartner, Michael R. Haines, Alan L. Olmstead, Richard Sutch, and Gavin Wright, © Cambridge University Press 2006. 4–588 Series Dd13–231: http://hsus.cambridge.org/HSUSWeb/toc/showPart.do?id=D
5. The picture, by Rick Meyer for the *LA Times*, may be viewed at the Smithsonian Institution website: http://americanhistory.si.edu/sweatshops/intro/1t5.htm
6. Sweatshop: a place with multiple labor-law violations, particularly in reference to the Fair Labor Standards Act. See Ross, 2004.
7. See Ross, *Slaves. . .*, *op cit* for more on FLA history.
8. As this chapter goes to press, major splits in the global Fair Trade movement have occurred over, among other things, "hired labor standards." The European wing appears more "labor friendly" on the question of worker voice than the American one.
9. See Sweatfree Communities and Sweatfree Purchasing Consortium at http://www.sweatfree.org/about_us

REFERENCES

Agarwal, S. 2009. 'What is the Per Capita Consumption of Jeans in USA?' Retrieved August 5, 2010 (http://www.denimsandjeans.com/latest-denim-reports/denim-data-figures/what-is-the-per-capita-consumption-of-jeans-in-usa/).

American Apparel and Footwear Association. 2008. 'Shoe Stats 2008.' Arlington, VA: American Apparel and Footwear Association. Retrieved August 5, 2010 (http://www.apparelandfootwear.org/UserFiles/File/Statistics/ShoeStats2008_0808.pdf).

Bearak, B. 1996. 'Kathie Lee and the Sweatshop Crusade.' *Los Angeles Times*, p. 1.

Bird, M., and J. Robinson. 1972. 'The Effectiveness of the Union Label and Buy Union Campaigns.' *Industrial and Labor Relations Review* 25(4):512–523.

Brown, G. 2009. 'Genuine Worker Participation: An Indispensable Key to Effective Global OHS.' *New Solutions* 19(3):315–333.

Clinton, W. J. 1996. 'Remarks Announcing Measures to Improve Working Conditions in the Apparel Industry and an Exchange with Reporters.' Washington, D.C.: U.S. Government Printing Office. Retrieved September 28, 2011 (http://frwebgate2.access.gpo.gov/cgi-bin/TEXTgate.cgi?WAISdocID=gaVKOB/0/1/0&WAISaction=retrieve).

Clinton, W. J. 1997. 'Remarks on the Apparel Industry Partnership.' Washington, D.C.: U.S. Government Printing Office. Retrieved September 28, 2011 (http://frwebgate3.access.gpo.gov/cgi-bin/TEXTgate.cgi?WAISdocID=nPGMVN/0/1/0&WAISaction=retrieve).

Co-operative Bank. 2009. 'Ten Years of Ethical Consumerism: 1999–2008.' Manchester, United Kingdom: Co-operative Bank. Retrieved September 28, 2011 (http://www.goodwithmoney.co.uk/assets/Ethical-Consumerism-Report-2009.pdf).

Cotton, Inc. 2008. 'Denim Jeans: The U.S. Wardrobe Staple.' New York: Cotton, Inc. Retrieved August 5, 2010 (http://www.cottoninc.com/SupplyChainInsights/Denim-Jeans-US-Wardrobe-Staple/Denim-Jeans-US-Wardrobe-Staple.pdf).

Dickson, M. 2001. 'Utility of No Sweat Labels for Apparel: Consumers: Profiling Label Users and Predicting Their Purchases.' *Journal of Consumer Affairs* 35(1):196–119.

Engels, F. 1887. *The Condition of the Working Class in England in 1844*. Translated by F. Kelley. New York: J. W. Lovell Co.

Esbenshade, J. 2004. *Monitoring Sweatshops: Workers, Consumers and the Global Apparel Industry*. Philadelphia, PA: Temple University Press.

Fair Trade USA. 2010. 'Vision Statement.' Oakland, CA: Fair Trade USA. Retrieved February 8, 2011 (http://transfairusa.org/about-fair-trade-usa/mission).

Gereffi, G., J. Humphrey, R. Kaplinsky, and T. J. Sturgeon. 2001. 'Introduction: Globalization, Value Chains and Development.' *IDS Bulletin* 32(3):1–8.

Hayek, F. A.V. 1984. *The Essence of Hayek*. Nishiyama, C and K. Leube (eds). Stanford, CA: Hoover Institution Press.

Hiscox, M. J. and F. B. Smyth. 2008. 'Is There Consumer Demand for Improved Labor Standards?' Department of Government, Harvard University, Cambridge, MA. Unpublished manuscript.

Howe, R., R. Aria, L. McNeil, A. Otey, J. S. Podesta, and L. Wright. 1996. 'Labor Pains.' *People* 45(23): 58–67.

International Labor Rights Forum. 2009. 'Letter to Transfair USA Regarding Fair Trade Garments Pilot Project.' Washington, D.C.: International Labor Rights Forum. Retrieved September 28, 2011 (http://www.laborrights.org/creating-a-sweatfree-world/ethical-consumerism/resources/12254).

Junger, S. 1997. *The Perfect Storm: A True Story of Men against the Sea*. New York: Norton.

Kelley, F. 1899. 'Aims and Principles of the Consumers' League.' *American Journal of Sociology* 5(3):289–304.

Kimeldorf, H., R. Meyer, M. Prasad, and I. Robinson. 2004. 'Consumers of the World Unite: A Market-Based Response to Sweatshops.' *Labor Studies Journal* 29(3):57–79.

Kimeldorf, H., R. Meyer, M. Prasad, and I. Robinson. 2006. 'Consumers with a Conscience: Will They Pay More?' *Labor Studies Journal* 5(1):24–29.

Laslett, T. and M. Tyler. 1989. *ILGWU in Los Angeles 1907–1988*. Inglewood, CA: Ten Star.

Loewe v. Lawlor, 208 U.S. 274 (1908). Retrieved February 8, 2011 (http://www.law.cornell.edu/supct/html/historics/USSC_CR_0208_0274_ZS.html).

Marx, K. 1852. 'The Eighteenth Brumaire of Louis Bonaparte.' Retrieved September 28, 2011 (http://www.marxists.org/archive/marx/works/1852/18th-brumaire/ch01.htm).

McCarthy, J. D and M. Zald. 1977. 'Resource Mobilization and Social Movements: A Partial Theory.' *American Journal of Sociology* 82(6):1212–1241.

Merk, J. 2009. 'Stitching a Decent Wage across Borders: The Asia Floor Wage Proposal.' Washington, D.C.: Jobs with Justice. Retrieved September 28, 2011 (http://www.jwj.org/campaigns/global/tools/asia_floor_wage.pdf).

Meyer, D. and Gamson, J. 1995. 'The Challenge of Cultural Elites: Celebrities and Social Movements.' *Sociological Inquiry* 65(2):181–206.

Paul, R. 1999. 'Good Time for Congress to Reassess Antitrust Laws.' Washington, D.C.: The Library of Congress. Retrieved September 13, 2012 (http://thomas.loc.gov/cgi-bin/query/D?r106:7:./temp/~r1063WbG98).

Robinson, I., and B. Athreya. 2005. 'Constructing Markets for Conscientious Apparel Consumers: Adapting the Fair Trade Model to the Apparel Sector.' Paper presented at the Conference on Constructing Markets for Conscientious Apparel Consumers, April 1–2, Ann Arbor, MI.

Rosen, E. I. 2002. *Making Sweatshops: The Globalization of the U.S. Apparel Industry*. Ewing, NJ: University of California Press.

Ross, R. J. S. 2004. *Slaves to Fashion*. Ann Arbor, MI: University of Michigan Press.

Ross, R. J. S. 2005. 'Review of Monitoring Sweatshops: Workers, Consumers and the Global Apparel Industry.' *Social Forces* 83(4):1791–2.

Ross, R. J. S. 2006. 'Tale of Two Factories: Successful Resistance to Sweatshops and the Limits of Firefighting.' *Journal of Labor Studies* 30(4):1–21.

Salem, D. 1996. 'Human Rights Group Targets Disney, Kathie Lee Apparel Lines.' *Los Angeles Times*, April 30, p. 1.

Seidman, G. 2008. 'Transnational Labour Campaigns: Can the Logic of the Market be Turned against Itself?' *Development and Change* 39(6):991–1003.

Shaw, D., L. Hassan, G. Hogg, E. Shiu, and E. Wilson. 2007. 'Intending to be Ethical: An Examination of Consumer Choice in Sweatshop Avoidance.' *Advances in Consumer Research* 34(33). Retrieved from September 28, 2011 (http://www.acrwebsite.org/volumes/v34/500240_101176_v2.pdf).

Stolle, D. and M. Hooghe. 2005. 'Politics in the Supermarket: Political Consumerism as a Form of Political Participation.' *International Political Science Review* 26(3):245–269.

Strasser, S., M. Judt, and C. McGovern, eds. 1998. *Getting and Spending: European and American Consumer Societies in the 20th Century*. Cambridge, United Kingdom: Cambridge University Press.

Strom, Stephanie. 1996. 'A Sweetheart Becomes Suspect; Looking behind Those Kathie Lee Labels.' *The New York Times*, June 27, p. D1.

SweatFree Communities. n.d. 'Why Do We Promote Clothing Made by Democratic Unions and Worker-Owned Coops?' Northampton, MA: SweatFree Communities. Retrieved August 8, 2010 (http://www.sweatfree.org/shopping_suppliercriteria_popup).

Ulrich, P. 1995. 'Look for the Label: The International Ladies' Garment Workers' Union Label Campaign 1959–1975.' *Clothing and Textiles Research Journal* 13(1): 49–56.

United States Department of State. 2009. 'Human Rights Reports 2009—India.' Washington, D.C.: U.S. Government Printing Office. Retrieved September 28, 2011 (http://www.state.gov/g/drl/rls/hrrpt/2009/sca/136087.htm).

United States Department of the Treasury. 1916. 'Statistical Abstract of the United States.' Washington, D.C.: U.S. Government Printing Office. Retrieved April 29, 2013; (http://www2.census.gov/prod2/statcomp/documents/1916-04.pdf).

Wiedenhoft, W. A. 2002. 'The Politics of Consumption: A Comparative Study of the American Federation of Labor and the National Consumers' League during the Progressive Era.' PhD dissertation, Department of Sociology, University of Maryland, College Park, MD.

Worker Rights Consortium. 2010. 'Factory Database.' Washington, D.C.: Worker Rights Consortium. Retrieved August 5, 2010 (http://www.workersrights.org/search/index.asp?search=results&licensee=NIKE+USA+Inc%2E).

Part II
Social Labels
in Comparative Perspective

Part II

3 Ethical Branding In Sri Lanka
A Case Study of Garments without Guilt

Annelies Goger

In recent years, the Sri Lankan apparel industry has staked a prominent position on the ethical sourcing map.[1] Its ethical-branding project, called *Garments Without Guilt (GWG)*, is comprised of a certification scheme and a diverse set of company-specific projects that have won international recognition, such as the Nike Green Award, the American Apparel and Footwear Association's Award for Excellence in Social Responsibility, and the International Green Apple Environmental Gold Awards. In addition, Sri Lankan companies have been featured in several 'best practice' case study reports (IFC et al. 2007, Paavola and Chattopadhyay 2008, Story and Watson 2006).

At the heart of this development, however, lies a contradiction: within Sri Lanka, the garment industry has had the longstanding reputation of being *un*ethical. In the media and political discourse, jobs in the industry are considered 'bad' jobs, female workers are stigmatized and considered promiscuous and the lingerie products that the country has developed a specialization in producing are considered by many to be dirty and morally wrong (Hewamanne 2008, Lynch 2007, Shaw 2004). In Sri Lankan society, it is the 'amoral' (but not economic or technological) aspect of foreign/Western capital that is perceived to threaten local norms and the stability of Sri Lankan national identity. In this chapter, I argue that the origins of *GWG* lie in a response to these local and national articulations of ethical concern. Because of these origins, the Sri Lankan ethical-branding case can make novel contributions to the debate in this volume about how social labeling and branding might address the challenges of globalization.

Specifically, the existence of a well-articulated set of ethical norms at the local level in some production locations made it beneficial for Sri Lankan entrepreneurs to invest in programs and upgrades that enhanced working conditions and contributed to community development. These programs later became incorporated into *GWG*, which combined a certification scheme and a variety of community investments and programs for workers. Although the program is not without problems and challenges, it emphasizes the possibilities that arise from moving beyond the Export Processing Zone (EPZ) model of development and having strong, well-organized, local industry leadership supportive of implementing certain forms of ethical trade practices. The Sri Lankan case suggests that social labeling may be more successful if ethical priorities are not assumed and imposed from the start, if such initiatives look beyond the space of the factory, and if they take power dynamics within global production networks (GPNs) and the local community more seriously.

This chapter draws from qualitative field research in Sri Lanka that was carried out in 2008, 2010 and 2011. I conducted 90 key informant interviews with industry representatives, worker organizations, government officials and trade unions in Sri Lanka. In addition, I visited nine factories in EPZs and rural areas, as well as worker boarding houses near the Katunayake EPZ. I also observed five events on ethical trade: a multistakeholder workshop on ethical trade in London in 2009, a conference on Social Labeling in the Global Fashion Industry in Newcastle (UK) in 2010, the Sri Lankan Design Festival in Colombo (Sri Lanka) in 2011, Business for Social Responsibility 2011 in San Francisco and the International Labour Organisation (ILO) Better Work Conference 2011 in Washington, D.C. Additionally, this chapter draws from secondary sources, especially apparel-industry ethnographies by Lynch (2007) and Hewamanne (2008).

I will first situate the GWG case in academic debates about global value chains and ethical trade initiatives, including social labeling. Then, I will describe the conditions that led to the emergence of GWG and the factors that led to industry leaders making community-oriented investments. Next, I will present the core features of GWG and analyze how its principles compare with two of the most widely used labor standards globally. Here, I will show that a focus beyond monitoring (on giving back to and building rapport with the community) is the key component that sets GWG apart. Finally, I will analyze some of the main challenges and limitations for enhancing and sustaining GWG. Although I will identify strengths and weaknesses of this initiative, this chapter is not intended to be an evaluation of GWG or an assessment of its performance. Instead, my focus is on understanding how the GWG project can contribute to contemporary debates about the conditions that make more-ethical production favorable and how local concerns can shape the governance of global production networks. Conceptually, I am interested in how this initiative challenges established understandings of what it means to behave ethically in the garment industry.

1 THEORETICAL FRAMEWORK

Since the early 1980s, trade liberalization and the subsequent globalization of production networks have generated widespread concerns about the weakness of international regulation (Appelbaum et al. 2005; Dicken 2007). In a seminal work, Gary Gereffi argued that governance in a globalized economy could be better understood using a global commodity-chain approach, which analyzes geographically dispersed inter-firm networks that exist for transforming a commodity from inputs to final product (Gereffi 1994). Moreover, he argued that certain types of commodity chains, such as apparel, are buyer-driven rather than manufacturer-driven, meaning that lead firms govern by focusing on product development and design activities and externalizing the actual production process to independent suppliers. In a later, coauthored paper, Gereffi elaborated on the governance of these networks, now referred to as global value chains (GVCs). Gereffi and colleagues argued that characteristics of the production process, including the codifiability of information to be exchanged between the lead firm and supplier, the complexity of the transaction, and the capabilities of suppliers shape the patterns of governance (Gereffi, Humphrey and Sturgeon 2005). In apparel, one could argue that 'ethical' GVCs, or those produced for consumers and buyers concerned about excessively exploitative working conditions, have higher transaction costs due to the difficulties of coordinating supplier compliance, and that codifying information through standards helps reduce transaction costs.

Other scholars have critiqued the GVC approach for being too firm-centric, arguing that other institutions, such as the state or the labor market, also shape production practices in significant ways (Coe et al. 2004, Henderson et al. 2002) These scholars argue instead for a global production network approach that incorporates firm networks, as well as these other institutions, into the analysis of globalization. For example, the GVC approach often overlooks labor markets, but they are very important for influencing prevailing wages and the bargaining power of workers. In the higher-value apparel segments that Sri Lanka competes in, having more skilled and experienced workers (and reducing labor turnover) is important for staying competitive and enhancing productivity.

Jennifer Bair argues that the GVC and GPN approaches can be used in a complementary fashion, each with unique contributions to the study of globalization and uneven development (Bair 2009). This case study of *GWG* responds to the call from the GPN scholars to focus more on governance relations beyond firm networks, at the same time acknowledging that buyers (i.e., multinational brands and retailers) are still very influential in shaping how apparel suppliers behave. Specifically, the case demonstrates how local norms articulate with globalized phenomena (e.g., the influx of foreign capital for the production of apparel), and how those norms have shaped suppliers' ethical priorities and incentives.

While the GVC/GPN approaches provide a more theoretical understanding of why certain governance patterns emerge in global economies for particular kinds of products, the ethical trade literature has focused on the effectiveness of codes of conduct and monitoring in achieving the goal of raising labor standards and preventing a 'race to the bottom.' Because stakeholders such as consumer groups and global brands conceived of the 'ethical' problem of sweatshop conditions as one that results from the absence of a homogenized, global regulatory structure, the solution they offered was a privatized system of standardized codes (Pearson & Seyfang 2001; Barrientos et al. 2011). They were an attempt to homogenize expectations (establishing a 'floor' of decent working conditions) and reduce the transaction costs of collecting information about which suppliers were in compliance. This system of codes and monitoring programs to ensure compliance with them make up what I refer to herein as the global or conventional understanding of 'ethical' in the phrase 'ethical production.'

With more than 15 years of implementation, evidence has converged on the strengths and weaknesses of the codes-and-monitoring approach. This approach has been widely implemented in apparel GVCs since the mid-1990s. Although achieving compliance alone is insufficient to be considered 'ethical,' codes and monitoring are typically a minimum requirement for access to export markets in the United States and Europe. The achievements of codes and monitoring include improvements in meeting easily quantifiable measures such as health and safety standards, learning about more ethical practices among buyers and suppliers, and increased technical sophistication of codes and monitoring (Barrientos and Smith 2007, Gereffi and Mayer 2006, Hughes 2006, Jenkins 2001, Mamic 2003).

Despite these achievements, codes and monitoring approaches generally have not met the objective of raising the floor of standards due to several challenges (Barrientos and Smith 2007, Esbenshade 2004, Locke et al. 2007, Mamic 2003, O'Rourke 2003). First, enabling or process-oriented measures, such as freedom of association and discrimination, have been much more challenging to address than outcome-oriented measures like health and safety (Barrientos and Smith 2007, Jenkins 2001). Second, home workers, undocumented workers and contract/temporary laborers have benefited much less than permanent workers have from code implementation (Barrientos and Smith 2007, Rodríguez-Garavito 2005). Other challenges include the lack of awareness of codes among workers, the proliferation of multiple and sometimes contradictory versions of codes, the lack of transparency and independence in monitoring, and the lack of coordination of compliance systems with state and/or worker organization efforts (Barrientos and Smith 2007, Jenkins 2001, Locke et al. 2007, O'Rourke 2003). In addition, the tension between the higher costs of implementing compliance and downward competitive pressure on unit values in apparel has resulted in squeezing suppliers such that they are often asked to do more for less money (Oxfam 2004). Finally, some argue that suppliers are 'standards takers' rather than 'standards setters' within global production networks because of the level of market power that some retailers have, meaning that standards have become a disciplinary technique to which suppliers are subjected (De Neve 2009, Nadvi 2008). Because compliance codes are a basic requirement for inclusion in many social-labeling initiatives, social-labeling initiatives often struggle with similar challenges.

In addition, social-labeling efforts aimed at national-level branding may bring about unique opportunities and challenges. So far, there is a limited body of research on this type of social-labeling initiative because it is a relatively recent phenomenon. This chapter and some of the other contributions in this volume constitute an effort to begin to close this gap. The Sri Lankan case is important because *GWG* is an industry-led initiative. Because most ethical-trade initiatives struggle with getting industry support, the Sri Lankan case can be helpful in showing under what conditions buy-in has been possible to achieve and what the challenges are for sustaining and enhancing it.

2   CONDITIONS THAT LED TO SOCIAL LABELING IN SRI LANKA

The prominent role of the concerned Western consumer and the resulting anti-sweatshop movement of the 1990s are well documented in the literature on ethical trade (Esbenshade 2004, Jenkins 2005, Klein 2000). Less well studied and understood are the ethical concerns of local or national stakeholders in producing countries such as workers, factory owners or state officials (Raynolds et al. 2007). The focus has largely been on raising 'standards,' which are understood to be universal rather than contested, contextual, and political. In this section, I will review the most important local and national factors that shaped business practices in Sri Lanka to support my argument that these local and national articulations of 'ethical' attempted to address the challenges of globalization and ultimately led to the emergence of the *GWG* social label.

Sri Lanka is a multi-ethnic society with a complex set of religious, class, caste, ethnic, and regional identities. Two-thirds of Sri Lankans are Sinhalese, and Sinhalese Buddhism is the dominant religion shaping local norms. Ancient Theravada Buddhism emphasizes '10 good deeds': 'generosity, morality, mental development, transferring merit, empathizing in the merit transferred, doing service (to elders), respectful behavior, teaching, listening (to religious teaching), holding right views' (Gombrich and Obeyesekere 1988: 24). The most important of these principles for lay people are generosity and morality. Generosity is interpreted broadly to include material support of the monastic order, and morality is understood as observance of the so-called 'precepts,' which are, 'not to kill, steal, be unchaste (not further defined), lie, or take intoxicants that may lead, through carelessness, to infringing the first four' (Gombrich and Obeyesekere 1988: 24).

Protestant Buddhism emerged in the late 1800s as an anticolonial reform movement that criticized what was considered to be the moral depravity of 'the West,' led by a popular ideologue named Dharmapala: '. . . Dharmapala used the same logic as colonial writers to discredit colonialism by claiming that Buddhist society had upheld [moral] values until the colonial influence destroyed them' (Hewamanne 2008: 31). Dharmapala promoted specific moral codes for women, and Protestant Buddhism places more emphasis than precolonial forms of Buddhism on sexual purity, cleanliness, and domesticity (De Alwis 1998, Gombrich and Obeyesekere 1988).

Based on these roots in Theravada and Protestant Buddhism, therefore, the ethical norms in Sri Lanka emphasize giving back to the local community (sharing wealth), respectable and abstinent behavior (especially for women), and education (which implies a prohibition against child labor). Due to colonial legacies, the village is considered the authentic site of 'pure' and 'virtuous' Sri Lankan identity, whereas the former colonial port cities, including the capital Colombo and the EPZs, are considered Westernized and morally inferior (Hewamanne 2008). 'Good' women in this context are portrayed as passive, submissive, obedient and sexually chaste until marriage. 'Bad' women are portrayed as Westernized, aggressive and morally loose (Abeyesekera 1989, Hewamanne 2008).

Another legacy of colonialism was increased conflict, especially between the Sinhalese majority and the Tamils of the north and east. Because the Sinhalese perceived the colonial policies to have unfairly privileged Tamils, postcolonial, Sinhalese-led governments sought to reverse these privileges through various policies such as making Sinhala the official language (disadvantaging those who spoke other languages). Rising tensions led to large-scale emigration and conflicts, especially after liberalization in 1977. These conflicts included a 25-year civil war between the government and the Liberation Tigers of Tamil Eelam (LTTE) that started in 1983 and the violent insurrection of the *Janatha Vimukthi Peramuna* (People's Liberation Front) from 1987 to 1989. These instabilities siphoned resources away from development projects and constrained economic-growth opportunities on the island (Gunatilaka et al. 2009). In addition, the civil war imbued a nationalist tone to ethical norms, meaning it became more important to be 'virtuous,' disciplined, and dutiful as a way of supporting the national effort to conquer terrorism and uphold the righteousness of the nation (Lynch 2007).

The civil war officially ended in 2009 when the government defeated the LTTE, involving a highly controversial standoff with hundreds of thousands of civilians acting as human shields. The events at the end of the war continue to strain Sri Lanka's relations with Europe and the United Nations. Europe withdrew its Generalized System of Preferences Plus (GSP+) trade preferences program in Sri Lanka in 2010, alleging that the government committed war crimes. Meanwhile, the Sri Lankan government has denied these claims, strengthened ties with Asian donor countries and pursued the president's *Mahinda Chintana* national development vision (Rajapaksa 2010). This vision emphasizes a strong state, rural industrialization, entrepreneurship, and a disciplined society.

In addition to Buddhism, colonialism, and conflict, the combination of trade liberalization and protection of apparel exports under the Multi-Fibre Arrangement (MFA) quota system had major effects on Sri Lankan society and ethical debates therein. Although the liberalization process was gradual, it generated major social and economic changes, including rural unemployment, new gender roles as women entered the industrial labor force and migration flows to the Colombo area for employment (Jayaweera 2003). Because of the quota advantage and other factors, the garment sector grew rapidly in the 1990s and became a rare source of industrial employment. Since the 1990s, the garment sector has been the most significant export industry in Sri Lanka, making up 44.8 percent of exports in 2006 and 42.2 percent in 2010 (Central Bank of Sri Lanka 2007 and 2010). Young women migrated to the EPZs to work, which was a significant departure from the previous labor practices of women (Jayaweera 2003).

As a result, the garment industry was a key site of public controversy over the changing roles of women and the influx of global capitalism (Hewamanne 2008, Lynch 2007). For example, the spaces around the EPZs that workers live in, such as Katunayake, are commonly referred to as 'city of women,' 'love zone' and 'the zone of prostitutes' (Hewamanne 2008, Lynch 2007). In part, it was the moral panic over the so-called destruction of the virtuous, innocent village female subject that inspired the Sri Lankan government to depart from the EPZ model and move factories to rural villages through the 200 Garment Factory Programme (200 GFP) in 1994. Because these factories opened in rural villages, employers came face to face with community resistance to globalization because it threatened the moral integrity of female workers and, with it, the moral standing of the nation.

It was not long before domestic factory owners realized the potential benefits of implementing practices to demonstrate to the 200 GFP villages that, despite the fact that they were producing for foreign markets and were capitalist, they were also morally responsible and upstanding (according to local norms). For example, they built community centers, contributed to schools, built housing, and ran 'empowerment' workshops for female workers. They found that these programs improved relations with the community, increased productivity, reduced labor turnover and increased the size of the labor pool. In other words, these responses to local concerns translated into economic benefits and increased trust. As a sustainability manager in one major Sri Lankan garment company said, '[i]n the beginning [corporate social responsibility (CSR)] was put in place mainly to build community loyalty with the company. [Factory owners] found that the benefits from the community were very high because there were fewer labor issues, riots did not affect factories and they were well respected in the community.'[2]

Another CSR representative in a major garment company explained how Buddhist beliefs underwrote initial CSR efforts:

> CSR is very recent, but in Buddhist culture it is very common to give a lot back to the community. The tradition was to give charity to the schools and temples. The general feeling is not to hold money, but to

share the wealth. In Sri Lanka there is also a culture of putting a high priority on education and having high expectations.[3]

Therefore, these Buddhist values increased the emphasis of early Sri Lankan CSR practices on sharing wealth and promoting education. When the Boxing Day tsunami struck in December 2004, apparel companies were very engaged in tsunami relief efforts and sponsored several projects for rebuilding the affected communities. The scale of the disaster strengthened the will of company owners to 'give back' for both altruistic and self-interested reasons (i.e., improving the local image of the garment industry), and it strengthened ties between the apparel industry and development NGOs.

Due to these circumstances, Sri Lankan industry leaders seriously bought into CSR practices, even though, at first, they were not labeled as such or driven by global buyers (Perry 2012). With a moral panic, communities and citizens put pressure on the state to change its development strategy and maintain Sinhala Buddhist ethical values; these values had been strongly influenced by colonial (British Victorian) notions of female sexual purity, cleanliness and domesticity. At a local level, they put pressure on factory owners to share wealth, invest in the community and protect the virtue of 'our girls.'

3   GARMENTS WITHOUT GUILT

In 2005, the MFA quotas that had been in effect since the 1970s were phased out. Sri Lanka benefited under the quota system because larger countries such as China were limited in the amount they could export. In anticipation of the phaseout, several Sri Lankan apparel-industry associations came together in 2002 to figure out how the industry could stay competitive. Under the name JAAF, they released a five-year strategic plan identifying the strengths, weaknesses, opportunities and threats to the industry at that time. Among the opportunities, the plan listed the promotion of Sri Lanka as a socially responsible manufacturer of apparels (JAAF 2002). They had observed that consumers increasingly demanded more socially responsible products, and they had received feedback from buyers that Sri Lanka's lack of child labor, high health and safety standards and ratification of ILO conventions put them in a strong position relative to competitors. To take advantage of these strengths, JAAF recommended continued progress toward meeting global standards and suggested an accreditation scheme to recognize plants that do so. Thus, the idea of marketing the country as 'ethical' through a certification scheme first emerged in JAAF's 2002 strategic plan. A survey of buyers provided further fuel to the fire of formalizing an ethical label, because buyers considered Sri Lanka among the best in the world for ethical production.

The *GWG* branding effort officially started in 2006, with funding for marketing from the Sri Lankan government and for other operations from industry contributions (Loker 2011). Technically speaking, *GWG* can be considered a social label because it is an effort to brand the country's industry as 'ethical' and create a baseline of standards with the certification; however, it does not currently involve putting actual labels on finished products because buyers have, thus far, refused to do this.[4] Moreover, *GWG* does not yet have the bargaining power to secure a price premium from buyers (or end-consumers), which several industry leaders noted as a serious problem during a forum on ethical fashion at the 2010 Sri Lankan Design Festival. Because of the lack of a direct benefit, such as a price premium, *GWG* has had trouble retaining factories in the certification. Factories that seek to be *GWG* certified are required to pay for an annual audit, ranging from $500 to $2,000, depending on the size of the factory.[5] A Swiss-based, third-party auditing firm, SGS, conducts annual audits (the only auditing firm for the program).

Although standardized compliance codes are at the root of the label, there is also a focus on 'best practice' stories that document community-oriented initiatives. In this way, the initiative balances a set of standards with a story-telling approach that emphasizes unique strengths and innovations that specific companies have been implementing since the 200 GFP. These stories are prominently featured on the program's website.

A comparison of the *GWG* principles with the ILO Core Labor Standards and the Ethical Trading Initiative (ETI) Base Code, which are two of the most commonly used foundations for compliance standards, indicates some interesting areas of overlap and divergence.

Eliminating forced labor, discrimination and child labor figures prominently in all three. ETI and *GWG* focus more on working conditions, with ETI breaking that down into more specific focus areas such as working hours, safety, regular employment, humane treatment, etc. However, one of the standards is conspicuously absent from the *GWG* principles, namely, the provision for freedom of association and collective bargaining. Although *GWG* charter does recognize freedom of association, the absence of a core principle supportive of it is an indicator of the contentious atmosphere of unionization in Sri Lanka. Indeed, NGOs and trade unions that I interviewed criticized the apparel industry for being anti-union and, historically, substituting management-appointed committees for independent unions. As in many countries, this is an ongoing political struggle in the apparel industry.

Consistent with its origins, what stands out about the *GWG* principles is the focus on broader development themes rather than compliance standards alone. The mission of *GWG* is '[t]o employ ethical practices thereby contributing to the economic development of the country while improving the quality of life of our apparel industry's workforce and their communities. Our core values, combined with enlightened legislation, makes Sri Lanka a truly socially responsible and preferred destination for apparel sourcing' (JAAF 2009a). Themes such as 'economic development,' 'quality of life,'

Table 3.1   Comparison of Garments Without Guilt and Other Social Standards

Garments Without Guilt Guiding Principles	International Labor Organisation Core Labor Standards	Ethical Trading Initiative Base Code
Protection	1. Elimination of forced and compulsory labor	1. Employment is freely chosen.
1. Ethical Working Conditions	2. Abolition of child labor	2. Freedom of association and the right to collective bargaining are respected.
2. Free of Child Labor	3. Elimination of discrimination in respect of employment and occupation	
3. Free of Forced Labor		
4. Free of Discrimination on Any Grounds		3. Working conditions are safe and hygienic.
5. Free of Sweatshop Practices	4. Freedom of association and collective bargaining	4. Child labor shall not be used.
Progression		5. Living wages are paid.
1. Rural Poverty Alleviation		6. Working hours are not excessive.
2. Women's Empowerment		7. No discrimination is practiced.
3. Education		8. Regular employment is provided.
4. Environmental Initiatives		9. No harsh or inhumane treatment is allowed.
5. Better Quality of Life		

Sources: JAAF, 2009b; ILO, 1998; ETI, 2010.

and 'communities' emphasize the importance of extending the scope of ethical initiatives beyond the factory and the immediate employment relation. It is, as Polanyi (1957) would say, a more embedded understanding of ethical responsibility. In fact, the program's materials state explicitly:

> One cannot better lives of people without a clear understanding of the key issues that confront them, both professionally and personally. That is why our mission has progressed beyond the work place to the community to include pro-people initiatives like women's empowerment and poverty alleviation in rural areas. These are two issues that have a profound impact on the quality of life of our people and the development of our society (JAAF 2009b).

Although the mission incorporates abstract concepts, such as 'empowerment,' the mission statement alludes to specific projects that companies started in response to local concerns over the location of export-oriented factories in rural villages under the 200 GFP program. Companies initiated these projects to build loyalty with the local community and share wealth according to the local expectations of what a 'good' employer should do.

MAS Women Go Beyond was one of the 'best practice' initiatives that brought attention to Sri Lanka as an innovator in ethical production. MAS Holdings is one of the largest domestic apparel companies on the island, and the CEOs have been active in JAAF. MAS Women Go Beyond started in 2003, and it focuses on 'empowering' women through career advancement, skills development, work-life balance initiatives and rewarding excellence. Gap, Inc. cosponsored Women Go Beyond for several years, but does not do so any longer. MAS Holdings defines an empowered woman as, 'One who is secure in the knowledge of herself, her abilities, and is able to tread the balance of fulfilling her career aspirations with the demands of personal life' (Jayasuriya 2011). The main programmatic elements are training workshops in soft skills, such as making presentations, and technical skills, such as computer programs, financial management and English. There are also workshops on gardening, sports activities and other artistic interest groups such as singing or dancing. For promoting work-life balance, counselors are available on site certain days of the week, and there are workshops on sexual and reproductive health, domestic violence and stress management. The program was written up as an INSEAD case study, an IFC Market Movers case study, and in several UN Global Compact publications (IFC et al. 2007, Jinadasa 2007, Story and Watson 2006).

Another community-oriented initiative is the Brandix Care for Water: Care for Women program. Started in 2004 (with a different name), this initiative was based on the realization by company owners that many workers were spending a great amount of time walking to get water before and after work. They reasoned that if they could help improve access to water for their workers ('associates'), then the workers would come to work less tired, more healthy, and more satisfied with their employer. Every year, Brandix invites applications from workers for water infrastructure, interviews workers, short-lists them and then visits the locations before making a decision on which projects to fund. More than 500 water projects have been completed so far, with more scheduled in future years. Brandix sees this as a way to contribute to development and the state's pledge to provide access to clean water to all Sri Lankans, as well as a way to build loyalty with communities and its workforce. Brandix also collaborates with other NGOs on various projects, often related to water. The projects have received support from buyers and intermediaries such as Gap and MAST.

In other communities that hosted garment factories (but not near EPZs), I observed that garment companies led other community-oriented CSR projects, such as funding an after-school tutoring program for children of garment workers, creating a partnership with local farmers to supply food to the canteen, and building housing for tsunami victims and disabled war veterans. I also commonly found small-scale features, such as a company funding workers a free meal for every shift, comprehensive bus-transportation networks, family days (for workers to bring their families to work), onsite gyms (even a boxing ring in one canteen), and competitive sports programs for workers. Even many small and medium-sized factories that I visited had some sort of program for 'giving back' to the local community or offering workers special assistance, such as when flooding damaged their house. Finally, several managers and line supervisors prioritized establishing good relations between workers and their direct managers and supervisors, because they found that it helped with worker retention, recruitment and productivity.

> Factory Director: We have a lot of competition [for labor]. . . . So, what we concentrate, mainly, on is the working environment. Because, even if the salaries are high, if you don't have the correct working environment, they will leave. So, number one, that is what we are looking into—to create a better environment for the employees.
> Goger: So, what does that mean to you, to create a better working environment? What elements are there?
> Factory Director: The relationship between the supervisor and the employee, and helping them wherever necessary, and work—by keeping a certain mentality without upsetting them. . .. I take a main role in that, developing the culture—this is the environment that we should have. And when an employee comes in, he or she should come in with a happy face and with a free mindset, and they should go also the same way. That's the motto that we expect, and that's the motto that our managers also get. And what we discuss is that we will do that for the worker level also. So, that's one thing that keeps others away, competitors away, because some of the factories pay more than us, but the working environment is not good. So, that's one thing that we can do.[6]

Obviously, healthy manager-worker relations are challenging to assess and measure, but for several managers, human-resource training and respectful treatment of workers was one of their highest priorities. Although management style is something that is extremely important for whether workers feel their job is 'good' on a day-to-day basis, global codes and monitoring systems have not prioritized these aspects of industrial relations and manager training very much.

Although it is now common in global ethical-trade debates to emphasize the importance of going 'beyond monitoring,' in Sri Lanka, these projects have been happening for a long time. Therefore, understanding the conditions under which such initiatives came about, what made them viable from a business perspective in the Sri Lankan context (at least in some places), and what some of the challenges and limitations are could be very useful for guiding future efforts to go 'beyond monitoring.' I am not assessing whether or not Sri Lanka Apparel has achieved the lofty goals set out for *GWG*, nor am I arguing that replicating this model will guarantee 'success.' Instead, I am asserting that by positioning local concerns and national development as one of several priorities in the first place, they are changing what we understand 'ethical' to be and challenging the notion that ethical trade can be reduced to universal standards. Furthermore, by analyzing Sri Lanka's more embedded approach to ethical labeling, I am not suggesting that buyer-driven codes and compliance systems are not important in Sri Lankan apparel factories. Indeed, Sri Lankan apparel companies participate in a wide range of certification schemes and have invested large sums in global compliance of various sorts—including building an international reputation for 'green' manufacturing. What I am saying is that GWG is a culmination of efforts by manufacturers to respond to a global audience of buyers and consumers, on one hand, and a local and national audience, on the other. Both forms of ethical authority are shaping factory practices in important ways.

Therefore, my argument is twofold. First, local and national concerns about globalization matter for what it means to be an ethical manufacturer, and these local and national understandings of 'ethical' can never be completely overwritten by external ethical priorities. In other words, ethical standards are always already situated, embodied, and emerging relationally through space-time and place (Hart 2006). By situating Sri Lankan apparel manufacturing in the context of colonialism and domestic ethical-political debates, it is easy to see why many Sri Lankans perceive the moral authority of the West to be more ethically questionable than the domestic industrialists do. Second, largely because of the tight labor market, the relevance of these concerns to the workforce and the surrounding community is what makes them more meaningful, valid and self-sustaining than compliance codes. Because the factories made efforts to 'share wealth' with the local community and 'take care' of young women who worked there, families were more willing to send daughters to work there, turnover decreased, and productivity increased. At the same time, I am not arguing that these initiatives in Sri Lanka are without problems or tensions. I will analyze some of the most significant tensions and problems in the next section.

4 CHALLENGES AND LIMITATIONS OF GARMENTS WITHOUT GUILT

> . . .[MAS Holdings has] always worked with customers who have always been able to give us sufficient amount of cash—enough to invest in how we do business. We invested in ethical manufacturing because we had the margin to do that. As the interest moved from ethical manufacturing to sustainability, we stepped on that bus as well. But, working with that customer base gave us the opportunity to invest. We needed that additional margin. If we were working with customers at the value end of the market, I don't know if we would have had the resources to be able to do that.[7]

As Mahesh Amalean suggests, a focus on the high-quality market has enabled Sri Lankan suppliers the breathing room to invest in more ethical and sustainable manufacturing. With the onset of the global economic crisis and the end of safeguards on China, those margins began to shrink. This led to cutbacks in CSR and human resources staff in several companies; and, for many, it was a serious test of just how integrated compliance and CSR practices were with the core business model. These pressures also brought a major challenge for social labeling and ethical trade generally into sharp focus: the increasingly uneven power dynamics in global production networks and the growing market power of large, global buyers, retailers and first-tier suppliers. Under these circumstances, it is increasingly difficult for suppliers to capture value added, even in high-quality niches.

The Chairman of JAAF, A. Sukumaran, further illustrated the growing sentiment of frustration and anxiety among Sri Lankan suppliers:

> We don't see that all the other partners in the value chain are equally contributing as what we are contributing: brands, retailers, consumer, input suppliers. We don't see there is much contribution from the end consumer. . . . When it comes to brands, we have seen some progress but it does fall far short of our expectations. We embarked on ethical initiatives five to six years ago. It came from our efforts in the village. Unfortunately, the rewards from our partners were not meeting our expectations.[8]

GWG suppliers are starting to question whether buyers have sufficiently rewarded and valued their efforts. There is a concern that the burden of paying for ethical trade falls unevenly on suppliers (Ruwanpura and Wrigley 2011). According to industry representatives, the cost of the GWG audit, the onset of the global recession, and 'audit fatigue'[9] has contributed to an erosion of support for the GWG certification. In fact, the number of certified factories listed on the GWG website declined from 121 in June 2010 to 39 in June 2011 (JAAF 2009c). Ultimately, this suggests that raising the nation's entire sector to a baseline standard, which GWG aimed to do, did not increase competitiveness, as they had hoped.

These challenges are not unique to GWG, and the ethical trade debates have increasingly focused on promoting ethical buying practices (Oxfam 2004, Traidcraft and Impactt, Ltd. 2008). Still, because Sri Lanka Apparel has invested so much in the ethical label, Sri Lankan suppliers are justifiably concerned about whether participation has become a liability in the ultra-competitive, cost-conscious state of the global apparel market today. Moreover, JAAF's attempt to brand Sri Lanka at a national scale with the nomenclature, 'GWG' by 'Sri Lanka Apparel' makes it difficult for the industry as a whole to diversify risk without threatening the brand's validity. In other words, the validity of a national ethical label will be called into question if a large segment of the industry were to abandon ethical apparel and pursue a lower-cost approach instead. As it is, only roughly 20 percent of factories were certified under *GWG* in June 2010.[10] Industry representatives also reported that buyers were unwilling to substitute the *GWG* certification for their own audits, as JAAF had hoped, because buyers wanted to maintain tight control over the monitoring process. Therefore, *GWG* became an additional audit, which is a big reason why many factory managers decided not to get the *GWG* certification. For example, one company with 22 factories was audited 183 times in 2011, an average of more than eight audits per factory (almost once a month). Thus, national ethical-labeling initiatives, while offering the promise of increased orders from more ethically conscious buyers, also face the danger of constraining the industry's capacity to diversify and adding to an already onerous auditing load.

A second challenge for *GWG* is the lack of emphasis on freedom of association, collective bargaining and living wages. These issues are very high priorities for European and American ethical trade NGOs, but industry representatives at all levels are generally very resistant to them in Sri Lanka and elsewhere. Therefore, it is not a surprise that there is a very limited landscape of independent unions and a scant number of collective-bargaining agreements in the Sri Lankan apparel sector. Although the country has ratified the ILO conventions related to freedom of association and collective bargaining, enforcement is weak at best (Sivananthiran 2009).

The lack of progress on these issues severely limits possible alliances between *GWG,* ethical-trade NGOs and unions locally in Sri Lanka, and international consumer-oriented activist groups that could help promote the label and enhance its reputation. Instead, these groups position themselves as adversaries to the industry in Sri Lanka (and vice versa), and dialogue and trust are limited. For example, one NGO respondent said that the JAAF did not engage workers or worker organizations in the drafting process of the *GWG* principles, argued that the *GWG* principles on working hours do not comply with national labor laws and criticized the fact that *GWG* makes certification decisions rather than a tripartite body. Meanwhile, several industry respondents counter-argued that most apparel labor unions were very small, politically affiliated, unwilling to compromise on extreme positions, and pursuing their own interests rather than worker interests. There is a long history of adversarial relations between the industry and unions, as well as between unions and local NGOs (a small group with strong personalities) that serves as an additional barrier to forging new alliances (Biyanwila 2011). On the world stage, these adversarial relationships and dialogue failures limit the capacity of *GWG* to gain credibility in American and European ethical-trade circles.

A third challenge to *GWG* stems from the dual focus on standardization and customization in the principles. Having a certification scheme focused on common elements helps unify the *GWG* program and establishes a baseline for participation. At the same time, it may be cost-prohibitive for some factories, which gives larger suppliers an advantage. It may also divert resources away from other CSR projects that are a higher priority for workers, community leaders or owners themselves. In addition, it may divert resources away from meeting the compliance standards of a global buyer (assuming they are not always overlapping), which may be more important in terms of generating orders in the short run, as opposed to having the more abstract potential of increased orders in the long due to certification by *GWG*. Also, there is a free-rider problem, meaning that there is an incentive to reap the benefits of what *GWG* does for Sri Lanka's international reputation without paying for the certification or participating in the audits and other activities. Overall, the *GWG* certification component seems quite sensitive to business cycles, market fluctuations, and other factors that compete with it for resources.

A fourth challenge to *GWG* lies in the unevenness of the geographies of ethical concern and authority. Although the customization of CSR in Sri Lankan factories has become one of the greatest strengths of the label, this can also be a weakness when it means that some communities get a lot more investment than others do. Comparing EPZs and villages, the problems EPZ workers face are different from the problems workers in villages face (many respondents also said EPZs have more problems). Specifically, the social problems for EPZ workers include safety, theft, malnutrition, and unsanitary living conditions, whereas the social problems for village workers tend to be about domestic violence and struggles over changing income-earning roles in the household. Despite what seems to be a higher level of problems in the EPZs, industry respondents indicated that community-oriented investments (as opposed to workshops and programs for workers) were more prevalent in village-based factories than in the areas surrounding EPZs. Many respondents said that some ethically conscious buyers also preferred to source from village-based factories because they felt they had more control over the ethical-trade programs there (whereas the government had more control in EPZs), and in villages, they did not have to worry about the problems associated with having boarding houses. Therefore, the factory location shapes the predominant form of ethical authority (e.g., the state, buyers, community leaders) and the degree to which programs extend into the community or not. That makes it difficult to represent the *GWG* label as a consistent entity that guarantees a certain measure of equality across production sites such that all workers' and communities' concerns matter to the same degree. It also suggests that the industry could ostensibly hold up certain 'model' factories as symbols of ethical commitments, while maintaining less-ethical, lower-cost facilities elsewhere.[11]

A final danger lies in assuming that the concerns and priorities of workers are always aligned with those of the surrounding community. Although these often overlap, there could be substantial instances in which the interests of the communities conflict with those of the workers themselves. There is a risk in village-based factories, in particular, that *GWG* practices could reinforce certain forms of patriarchal control over the young women who typically work in the garment factories. Sandya Hewamanne (2008) found that even though the EPZs have bad reputations and the jobs are considered 'bad,' many workers decide to work there to take advantage of a higher degree of independence than is possible in the village setting, which is characterized by higher levels of surveillance and control over young women's activities. One could interpret the CSR practices of *GWG* as ways of mitigating what would otherwise be an untenable situation in which a worker is constantly under surveillance and expected to behave in a disciplined manner.

CONCLUSION

Local and national ethical concerns about globalization mattered for the conceptualization and practice of *GWG*. Specifically, Sinhalese Buddhism, colonialism, the government's 200 GFP program, and other factors led to the prioritization of sharing wealth with local communities, investing in infrastructure, and being mindful of the need to protect the virtue of young, female workers. These ethical norms are not the same everywhere, not even everywhere in Sri Lanka, but they were articulated strongly enough in the national industry context to manifest in some new forms of CSR. The Sri Lankan case suggests that no matter how much buyer demands change or which global ethical trends prevail at a given time, local and national concerns always contribute in some way to how ethical-trade programs are understood, how important they are considered to be, and how they are practiced. This is because ethical standards are political, unstable, embodied, historical and contextual.

Hence, this *GWG* case study contributes to the GVC/GPN literature in several ways. First, it helps elucidate the role of nonfirm institutions in GVC governance, specifically, the role of local and national actors in making ethical demands of globalizing agents (export-oriented garment firms). Second, the case confirms Bair's (2009) assertion that GVC and GPN frameworks can be used in a complementary fashion, because despite the importance of local and national actors in Sri Lanka, buyer-driven governance is still very powerful. Specifically, firms have to constantly juggle ethical priorities, appease different audiences and make wise short and long-term decisions to sustain production in a given location. Finally, more embedded forms of CSR provide opportunities for unconventional alliances between firm and nonfirm actors around particular forms of ethical governance (but not necessarily all).

The *GWG* case can also inform ethical-trade debates. It highlights the importance of questioning the assumption that standards are universal and that the boundaries of ethical trade and responsibility end at the factory gate. Second, it suggests that going 'beyond monitoring' is very complex and that it can be hard to juggle multiple concerns and priorities at the same time. Third, growing competition in the global apparel market has decreased the bargaining power of suppliers, and evidence from Sri Lanka suggests that this has constrained the capacity of suppliers to implement higher ethical standards, even when they are already engaged in doing so. Fourth, more embedded ethical trade practices bring new opportunities, but also new dangers and risks for the firm and the community. Finally, being able to reap benefits from addressing local and national concerns (e.g., these programs secured a larger supply of labor, higher productivity, lower labor turnover) helps increase firm-level buy-in for CSR, which has been a struggle to achieve elsewhere in the world.

There are also some specific insights that the *GWG* case can offer to the debate in this volume about the potential for social labeling to address concerns about globalization. The national orientation of this social labeling initiative has brought about some important challenges for *GWG*. The free-rider problem may be a disincentive for firms to participate, getting and sustaining membership seems to be a challenge, and the piecemeal approach to programming makes it difficult to assess the overall commitment to more ethical practices. In addition, the initiative struggles with the lack of credibility among more conventional ethical-trade advocates due to the absence of emphasis on components such as freedom of association, collective bargaining and living wages. Finally, Sri Lankan industry representatives have expressed concerns about how to share the burden of paying for ethical apparel, not getting a price premium from buyers, and buyers' reluctance to use the *GWG* audit in place of their own audits. The challenges that I have analyzed above are not confined internally to *GWG* or to Sri Lanka, but rather, they reflect power struggles, opportunities, and constraints arising at multiple scales simultaneously—global, regional, national and local. Overall, it is clear from the complex set of strengths and weaknesses of *GWG* that the process of becoming more 'ethical' is long, unstable, costly and fraught with risks.

Considering that *GWG* is still in the early stages, there may also be other significant challenges that I have not identified. Further research is needed to understand the ways in which embedded CSR projects—beneficial as they may be—also may place new constraints and obligations on populations that have few alternatives. Additionally, more research is needed on the degree of variation in ethical practices throughout the industry. For these reasons, it is important not to romanticize embedded CSR projects and to learn more about their dangers as well as their opportunities. As the *GWG* case demonstrates, making ethical trade interventions, like other innovations, is a political process of creative destruction and social change. It is always a struggle, always carries risks and is never complete.

NOTES

1. Research for this article was generously supported at different phases by the American Institute for Sri Lankan Studies, the UNC Center for Global

Initiatives/Carolina Asia Center, the National Science Foundation Doctoral Dissertation Research Improvement Grant, Fulbright IIE, the UNC Chapel Hill Department of Geography, and the Social Science Research Council International Dissertation Research Fellowship. I am indebted to Sapna Elizabeth Gardner Thottathil, Jennifer Bair, Liz Hennessey, John Pickles, Banu Gökariksel, and two anonymous Sri Lankan industry respondents for helpful comments and suggestions.

2. Interview with CSR representative, Sri Lanka, 2008.
3. Interview with CSR representative, Sri Lanka, 2008.
4. Sri Lankan industry respondents say buyers are reluctant due to multicountry sourcing for the same products.
5. Financial assistance was available for small and medium-sized enterprises.
6. Interview with a factory manager, Sri Lanka, 2011
7. Mahesh Amalean, CEO MAS Holdings, Ethical Fashion Forum, Sri Lankan Design Festival.
8. A. Sukumaran, JAAF Chairman, Ethical Fashion Forum, Sri Lankan Design Festival 2010.
9. 'Audit fatigue' is the perception among suppliers that they are overburdened by audits due to the need to be certified in numerous schemes so they can access export markets.
10. This doesn't necessarily mean that 80 percent of the factories are out of compliance or not as 'ethical.' JAAF representatives cite an overabundance of (costly) audits as the explanation.
11. I do not have evidence to make this claim about *Garments Without Guilt*. I am only identifying this as a danger.

REFERENCES

Abeyesekera, S. 1989. 'Women in Sri Lankan Cinema.' *Framework* 37:49–58.
Appelbaum, R., E. Bonacich, and K. Quan. 2005. 'The End of Apparel Quotas: A Faster Race to the Bottom?' Working Paper No. 35, Institute for Social, Behavioral, and Economic Research, University of California, Santa Barbara, CA.
Bair, J. 2009. 'Global Commodity Chains: Genealogy and Review.' Pp. 1–34 in *Frontiers of Commodity Chain Research*, edited by J. Bair. Stanford, CA: Stanford University Press.
Barrientos, S., F. Mayer, J. Pickles, and A. Posthuma. 2011. 'Decent Work in Global Production Networks: Framing the Policy Debate.' *International Labour Review* 150(3/4):297–317.
Barrientos, S. and S. Smith. 2007. 'Do Workers Benefit from Ethical Trade? Assessing Codes of Labor Practice in Global Production Systems.' *Third World Quarterly* 28(4):713–729.
Biyanwila, S.J. 2011. *The Labour Movement in the Global South: Trade Unions in Sri Lanka*. New York: Routledge.
Central Bank of Sri Lanka. 2007. 'Annual Report 2007.' Colombo, Sri Lanka: Central Bank of Sri Lanka. Retrieved June 30, 2011 (http://www.cbsl.gov.lk/pics_n_docs/10_pub/_docs/efr/annual_report/Ar2007/content.htm).
Central Bank of Sri Lanka. 2010. 'Annual Report 2010.' Colombo, Sri Lanka: Central Bank of Sri Lanka. Retrieved June 30, 2011 (http://www.cbsl.gov.lk/pics_n_docs/10_pub/_docs/efr/annual_report/AR2010/English/content.htm).
Coe, N.M., P. Dicken, J. Henderson, M. Hess, and H.W. Yeung. 2004. 'Globalizing Regional Development: A Global Production Networks Perspective.' *Transactions of the Institute of British Geographers* 29(4):468–484.

De Alwis, M. N. 1998. 'Maternalist Politics in Sri Lanka: A Historical Anthropology of Its Conditions of Possibility.' PhD dissertation, Department of Anthropology, University of Chicago, Chicago, IL.

De Neve, G. 2009. 'Power, Inequality and Corporate Social Responsibility: The Politics of Ethical Compliance in the South Indian Garment Industry.' *Economic and Political Weekly* 44(14):63–71.

Dicken, P. 2007. *Global Shift: Mapping the Changing Contours of the World Economy.* 5th ed. New York: Guilford.

Esbenshade, J. 2004. *Monitoring Sweatshops: Workers, Consumers, and the Global Apparel Industry.* Philadelphia, PA: Temple University Press.

Ethical Trading Initiative. 2010. 'ETI Base Code.' London, United Kingdom: Ethical Trading Initiative. Retrieved June 22, 2011 (http://www.ethicaltrade.org/eti-base-code).

Gereffi, G. 1994. 'The Organization of Buyer-Driven Global Commodity Chains: How U.S. Retailers Shape Overseas Production Networks.' Pp. 95–122 in *Commodity Chains and Global Capitalism*, edited by G. Gereffi and M. Korzeniewicz. Westport, CT: Greenwood.

Gereffi, G., J. Humphrey, and T. Sturgeon. 2005. 'The Governance of Global Value Chains.' *Review of International Political Economy* 12(1):78–104.

Gereffi, G. and F. Mayer. 2006. 'Globalization and the Demand for Governance.' Pp. 39–58 in *The New Offshoring of Jobs and Global Development.* Geneva, Switzerland: International Labor Organization.

Gombrich, R. F. and G. Obeyesekere. 1988. *Buddhism Transformed: Religious Change in Sri Lanka.* Princeton, NJ: Princeton University Press.

Gunatilaka, R., S. Chatterjee, and G. Wan. 2009. *Poverty and Human Development in Sri Lanka.* Mandaluyong City, Philippines: Asian Development Bank.

Hart, G. 2006. 'Denaturalizing Dispossession: Critical Ethnography in the Age of Resurgent Imperialism.' *Antipode* 38(5):977–1004.

Henderson, J., N. Coe, P. Dicken, M. Hess, and H. W. Yeung. 2002. 'Global Production Networks and the Analysis of Economic Development.' *Review of International Political Economy* 9(3):436–464.

Hewamanne, S. 2008. *Stitching Identities in a Free Trade Zone: Gender and Politics in Sri Lanka*: Philadelphia, PA: University of Pennsylvania Press.

Hughes, A. 2006. 'Learning to Trade Ethically: Knowledgeable Capitalism, Retailers and Contested Commodity Chains.' *Geoforum* 37(6):1008–1020.

International Finance Corporation and SustainAbility. 2007. 'Case Study: MAS Holdings: An Excerpt from Market Movers: Lessons from a Frontier of Innovation.' Washington, D.C.: International Finance Corporation and Sustainability. Retrieved April 1, 2009 (www.sustainability.com/marketmovers).

International Labour Organization. 1998. 'ILO Declaration on Fundamental Principles and Rights at Work.' Geneva, Switzerland: International Labour Organization. Retrieved October 2, 2011 (http://www.ilo.org/declaration/thedeclaration/textdeclaration/lang—en/index.htm).

Jayasuriya, S. 2011. 'MAS Women Go Beyond-Women's Empowerment Program.' New York: United Nations. Retrieved October 2, 2011 (www.unglobalcompact.org/docs/issues_doc/human_rights/WEPs/2011/Jayasuriya.pdf).

Jayaweera, S. 2003. 'Continuity and Change: Women Workers in the Garment and Textile Industries in Sri Lanka.' Pp. 196–226 in *Tracking Gender Equity Under Economic Reforms: Continuity and Change in South Asia*, edited by S. Mukhopadhyay and R. Sudarshan. Ottawa, Canada: International Development Research Centre.

Jenkins, R. 2005. 'Globalization, Corporate Social Responsibility and Poverty.' *International Affairs* 81:525–540.

Jenkins, R. 2001. 'Corporate Codes of Conduct: Self-Regulation in a Global Economy.' Programme Paper No. 2, United Nations Research Institute for Social Development, Geneva, Switzerland.

Jinadasa, K. 2007. 'MAS Holdings: Championing Women's Empowerment in the Apparel Sector.' *Compact Quarterly* 2007(1). Retrieved June 29, 2011 (http://www.enewsbuilder.net/globalcompact/e_article000776336.cfm).

Joint Apparel Association Forum. 2002. *Five Year Strategy for the Sri Lankan Apparel Industry*. Colombo, Sri Lanka: Joint Apparel Association Forum.

Joint Apparel Association Forum. 2009a. 'About GWG.' Colombo, Sri Lanka: Joint Apparel Association Forum. Retrieved June 8, 2011 (http://gwg.garmentswithoutguilt.com/about-gwg/36).

Joint Apparel Association Forum. 2009b. 'Brand Guidelines.' Colombo, Sri Lanka: Joint Apparel Association Forum. Retrieved June 10, 2011 (http://gwg.garmentswithoutguilt.com/about-gwg).

Joint Apparel Association Forum. 2009c. 'SGS Certified Plants.' Colombo, Sri Lanka: Joint Apparel Association Forum. Retrieved June 2, 2011 http://gwg.garmentswithoutguilt.com/sgs-certification?view=category).

Klein, N. 2002. *No Logo*. New York: Picador.

Locke, R., T. Kochan, F. Quin, and M. Romis. 2007. 'Beyond Corporate Codes of Conduct: Work Organization and Labor Standards at Nike's Suppliers.' *International Labor Review* 146(2):21–39.

Loker, S. 2011. *The (R)Evolution of Sustainable Apparel Business: From Codes of Conduct to Partnership in Sri Lanka*. Ithaca, NY: Cornell University Press.

Lynch, C. 2007. *Juki Girls, Good Girls: Gender and Cultural Politics in Sri Lanka's Global Garment Industry*. Ithaca, NY: Cornell University Press.

Mamic, I. 2003. *Business and Code of Conduct Implementation: How Firms Use Management Systems for Social Performance*. Geneva, Switzerland: International Labor Organization.

Nadvi, K. 2008. 'Global Standards, Global Governance and the Organization of Global Value Chains.' *Journal of Economic Geography* 8(5):323–343.

O'Rourke, D. 2003. 'Outsourcing Regulation: Analyzing Nongovernmental Systems of Labor Standards and Monitoring.' *Policy Studies Journal* 31(1):1–29.

Oxfam International. 2004. 'Trading Away Our Rights-Women Working in Global Supply Chains.' Oxford, United Kingdom: Oxfam International.

Paavola, N. and A. Chattopadhyay. 2008. *MAS Holdings: Leveraging Corporate Responsibility*. Fontainebleau, France: INSEAD.

Pearson, R. and G. Seyfang. 2001. 'New Hope or False Dawn? Voluntary Codes of Conduct, Labour Regulation and Social Policy in a Globalizing World.' *Global Social Policy* 1(1):48–78.

Perry, P. 2012. 'Exploring the Influence of National Cultural Context on CSR Implementation.' *Journal of Fashion Marketing and Management* 16(2):141–160.

Polanyi, K. 1957. *The Great Transformation*. 1st ed. Boston: Beacon.

Rajapaksa, M. 2010. 'Mahinda Chintana: Vision for the Future.' Colombo, Sri Lanka: Ministry of Technology and Research. Retrieved September 13, 2012 (http://www.motr.gov.lk/web/pdf/mahinda_chintana_vision_for_the_future_eng.pdf).

Raynolds, L. T., D. Murray, and J. Wilkinson. 2007. *Fair Trade: The Challenges of Transforming Globalization*. Oxford, United Kingdom: Routledge.

Rodriguez-Garavito, C. A. 2005. 'Global Governance and Labor Rights: Codes of Conduct and Anti-Sweatshop Struggles in Global Apparel Factories in Mexico and Guatemala.' *Politics Society* 33(2):203–333.

Ruwanpura, K. and N. Wrigley. 2011. 'The Costs of Compliance? Views of Sri Lankan Apparel Manufacturers in Times of Global Economic Crisis.' *Journal of Economic Geography* 11(6):1031–1049.

Shaw, J. 2004. 'Decent Work or Distress Adaptation? Employment Choice and Job Satisfaction in the Sri Lankan Garment Industry.' Pp. 50–64 in *Women and Work: Current RMIT Research*, edited by S. Charlesworth and M. Fastenau. Melbourne, Australia: RMIT.

Sivananthiran, A. 2009. 'Promoting Decent Work in Export Processing Zones (EPZs) in Sri Lanka.' Geneva, Switzerland: International Labor Organization. Retrieved March 22, 2009 (www.ilo.org/public/french/dialogue/download/epz srilanka.pdf).

Story, J. and N. Watson. 2006. *MAS Holdings: Strategic Corporate Social Responsibility in the Apparel Industry*. Fontainebleau, France: INSEAD.

Traidcraft and Impactt, Ltd., 2008. *Material Concerns: How Responsible Sourcing Can Deliver the Goods for Business and Workers in the Garment Industry*, London, UK. Retrieved April 29, 2013 (http://www.traidcraft.co.uk/Resources/Traidcraft/Documents/PDF/tx/policy_report_material_concerns.pdf).

4 Is There a Business Case for Improving Labor Standards?

Some Evidence from Better Factories Cambodia[1]

Drusilla Brown, Rajeev Dehejia and Raymond Robertson

'Sweatshop' conditions in developing countries have received considerable attention over the last decade. Reports of high temperatures, excessive noise, poor air quality, unsanitary conditions, verbal and physical abuse, and especially, the combination of low wages and long hours are often used to support the claim that 'sweatshops' are prevalent in developing countries. Growing international concern has prompted several organizations to apply pressure or develop programs designed to improve wages and working conditions. Recent evidence suggests that anti-sweatshop agitation has improved wages in global supply chains. Harrison and Scorse (2010) find that workers in Indonesia's apparel, textile and footwear global supply chains earned less than workers who supplied the domestic sector prior to the early 1990s anti-sweatshop campaigns. By 1997, however, these workers' earnings surpassed the comparison group. Studies of nonwage working conditions, however, are rare.

As one of the lowest-wage apparel producers, Cambodia emerged early on as a focal point for concerns about human resource practices in apparel supply chains. This focus resulted in a unique trade agreement between the United States and Cambodia. The U.S.-Cambodia trade agreement, which went into effect in 1999, offered Cambodian firms the incentive to improve working conditions in exchange for increased access to the U.S. market (Berik and van der Meulen Rogers 2010). Such access was important because apparel trade was restricted by the Multi-Fibre Arrangement (MFA) and the Agreement on Textiles and Clothing (ATC). Monitoring was tied to an innovative program called Better Factories Cambodia (BFC), which was administered through the International Labor Organization (ILO). The apparel industry's record of compliance was a factor the U.S. government used in determining Cambodia's apparel-export quota allocation. The resulting improvements in working conditions were anecdotally credited with Nike's decision to resume production in Cambodia. The BFC program has received considerable attention in policy circles, where it is generally considered an effective model that could be, and consequently has been, applied to other countries.

Several factors contribute to BFC's apparent success. One of the strategies BFC employed to control free-riding was to disclose noncompliant factories publically. Public disclosure has been identified as effective at least as early as Brandeis (1913). In the Cambodian case, such disclosure occurred in the periodic synthesis reports BFC issued and publically disclosed (Polaski 2004 and 2006). Polaski also suggests that universal participation was another critical factor because the BFC program made participation in the program a condition for export under the terms of the agreement.

One additional hypothesis is that improving working conditions enhances productivity in such a way as to make such improvements beneficial for firms (similar to an 'efficiency wage' explanation that dates back to Alfred Marshall). In other words, a 'business case' might be made for improving working conditions. A direct test of this hypothesis would involve comparing productivity levels of firms both in and out of the BFC program, which is not possible given available data. The goal of this paper is to review the growing body of literature that analyzes the BFC program, describe characteristics of compliance and noncompliance and evaluate some of the underlying factors that seem to have contributed to the program's success.

Several important lessons emerge from this analysis. First, since several dimensions of working conditions exhibit very different patterns over time and across plants, the term 'working conditions' may be too broad to describe accurately a given factory's experience. Nonetheless, recent research finds considerable support for several hypotheses at work in the program. In particular, public disclosure and reputation sensitivity (of buyers) play a critical role. Nevertheless, in the absence of public disclosure and other external changes, firms still maintain a significant record of compliance and rising market share, which is consistent with the possibility that additional factors—such as productivity improvements—may also contribute to Cambodia's success.

1   BETTER FACTORIES CAMBODIA

The International Labor Organization (ILO) established the Better Factories Cambodia program in 2001. The program covers Cambodian apparel exporters. One unique aspect of the program is multistakeholder participation that includes government, labor, factory owners and international buyers.[2] By bringing these stakeholders together, the program strives to improve working conditions with a combination of monitoring, remediation and training. ILO-trained Cambodian monitors enter factories on unannounced visits and assess the factory's compliance on various working conditions and wage requirements. Each monitoring team contains at least two people, and the same team rarely assesses the same factory twice in an effort to minimize monitor bias. The monitors' findings are evaluated relative to national law and international standards. Factories then can receive feedback and suggestions to help them address concerns uncovered in the factory visits. The factory's second BFC visit is followed by inclusion in an annual synthesis report that includes each factory's name and progress on improving working conditions. The BFC program shares these reports with the factories' buyers.

Cambodian law specifies that all exporting factories participate in the program. The original wave of visits from 2001 to 2002 included 119 factories. For the next three years, monitors did not carefully record results because their goal was to address specific concerns raised in the initial reports. As a result, factory-level data are unavailable for this three-year period. The launch of the improved Information Management System (IMS) survey in December 2005 initiated the next wave of documented visits with a goal of visiting factories once every eight months, on average.

2 COMPLIANCE PATTERNS

Several recent papers focus on the BFC program to analyze working conditions in Cambodia. Shea et al. (2010) combine interviews with key stakeholders and observations of relevant activities with synthesis reports provided by the BFC. They conclude that Cambodia succeeded in both improving labor standards and preventing their deterioration. While identifying some specific concerns about the monitoring process (such as the difficulty in detecting mandatory overtime and a perception that changes are not implemented quickly enough), they find a strong correlation between the issues identified in the BFC reports and those identified in personal interviews. Shea et al. (2010) also note that 'the availability of information could provide a way for factories to become more competitive, even after the positive incentive of the bonus quota has been eliminated.'

Becoming more competitive is important because the 2000–2009 period was characterized by rising international competition. The rise of China and the end of the MFA/ATC meant that buyers were able to seek the most profitable relationships. Beresford (2009), however, finds that working conditions did not fall in response to an increasingly competitive environment.

These papers rely on aggregate synthesis reports. The aggregate synthesis reports provided a very rich picture of changes in behavior of the industry as a whole, but they may mask important changes at the factory level. Factory-level data reveal several interesting dimensions of compliance; several recent studies employ these data, including Oka (2010a and 2010b) and Brown et al. (2011 and 2012).

Using the factory-level data from these previous studies, Table 4.1 describes the number of factories by both visit number and year. The analysis here is limited to visits that occurred in 2008 or earlier because the global financial crisis and subsequent 'Great Trade Collapse' (Baldwin

Table 4.1   Factory Counts over Time

			Visit Year				
Visit	2001	2002	2005	2006	2007	2008	Total
1	85	34	7	187	30	20	363
2	0	0	18	121	136	20	295
3	0	0	0	48	185	22	255
4	0	0	0	0	80	108	188
5	0	0	0	0	12	39	51
6	0	0	0	0	0	2	2
Total	85	34	25	356	443	211	1,154

Notes: Factory-level data are not available for 2003 and 2004. See text for details.

2009) significantly changed the environment facing Cambodian factories. Table 4.1 clearly shows that the factories can be divided into two 'waves,' one starting in 2001 and the other in 2005. Perhaps not surprisingly, there was significant turnover (exit and entry) of factories even prior to the crisis.[3] Of 363 factories with an initial visit, only 51 had a fifth visit by 2008. One possible explanation for the lack of fifth-visit observations may be that the second 'wave' is relatively large. In some cases, the goal of visiting factories every eight months may not have been realized, leaving some factories to be visited annually. As a result, it may not be surprising that only 188 factories had four visits by 2008.

Factory monitors use a tool that includes 405 specific questions designed to capture various aspects of working conditions. Of these 405 questions, 62 show no variation across both factory and visit. These questions are dropped from the analysis. We aggregate the remaining questions into 27 categories.

Figure 4.1 illustrates broad improvement in working conditions over time by measuring compliance as an average across all firms and across all questions within each visit. Table 4.2 summarizes the average compliance of each of the 27 different categories. Each factory's compliance measure is calculated by taking the average of all of the 0/1 compliance questions (1 indicates compliance) in each category. The averages in Table 4.2 are the average of these factory-level values across all factories and across all questions within each group.[4] Therefore, a 1.000 indicates that all factories are fully compliant with all questions within that category. A 0.860 indicates that the average compliance value for that category is 86 percent.

Several aspects of compliance emerge from Table 4.2. First, a wide range of average compliance occurs across groups—especially in the first visit. The standard deviation is 13 percent, and average values range from 0.996 (suggesting high compliance with the prohibition on forced labor) to 0.544

Figure 4.1   Overall Compliance by Visit

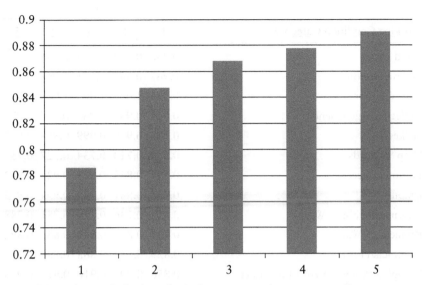

Note: Visit number on the horizontal axis. Bars represent the average compliance rate across all plants and across all questions within each visit number.

(indicating lower compliance in terms of guidelines regarding Occupational Safety and Health Assessment, Recording, and Reporting). These differences conform to preconceptions of the costs and benefits of each category. Forced labor, for example, may be considered more serious than scheduled checks for needle guards on sewing machines.

The second main point is that, on average, compliance improves across visits. The average values increase in nearly every category with additional visits. Third, the correlation between average values in the first and fourth visits is only 0.78, which suggests that an uneven improvement in groups occurs across time. Figure 4.2 shows compliance over time for those categories with the lowest compliance rates in the first visit. These were generally the categories that demonstrated the greatest improvement.

To show this pattern for a wider range of conditions, Figure 4.3 graphs the relationship between changes in working-group average (between the first and second visits) and the initial values. The clear negative slope shows that working conditions with the lowest initial averages showed the greatest improvement. The same relationship emerges between changes between the first and fourth visit, as the correlation between first-to-second visit averages and first-to-fourth visit averages is 0.97. This result suggests that most improvement occurs between the first and second visits and then performance remains relatively stable over time.

To evaluate the changes in compliance over time, Table 4.3 shows how firms evolve from different compliance groups over time. Using a cluster

Table 4.2   Compliance in Aggregated Working Conditions, Indicators by Visit

Working Condition Category	Visit				
	1	2	3	4	5
Child Labor	0.800	0.734	0.745	0.746	0.750
Discrimination	0.967	0.967	0.971	0.966	0.961
Forced Labor	0.996	1.000	1.000	1.000	1.000
Collective Agreements	0.904	0.933	0.966	0.977	0.976
Strikes	0.975	0.999	0.999	0.998	0.987
Shop Stewards	0.599	0.713	0.734	0.727	0.753
Liaison Officer	0.594	0.862	0.905	0.926	0.953
Unions	0.935	0.981	0.985	0.994	0.995
Information about Wages	0.613	0.736	0.775	0.781	0.788
Payment of Wages	0.769	0.805	0.840	0.861	0.896
Contracts/Hiring	0.829	0.833	0.868	0.886	0.924
Discipline/Management Misconduct	0.856	0.902	0.910	0.915	0.913
Disputes	0.933	0.955	0.958	0.974	0.967
Internal Regulations	0.896	0.956	0.971	0.981	0.986
Health/First Aid	0.570	0.690	0.710	0.746	0.778
Machine Safety	0.838	0.873	0.895	0.914	0.929
Temperature/Ventilation/Noise/Light	0.767	0.782	0.787	0.766	0.788
Welfare Facilities	0.767	0.837	0.856	0.867	0.874
Workplace Operations	0.697	0.757	0.775	0.786	0.804
OSH Assessment, Recording, Reporting	0.544	0.726	0.765	0.793	0.820
Chemicals	0.783	0.749	0.767	0.762	0.773
Emergency Preparedness	0.863	0.915	0.920	0.938	0.930
Overtime	0.588	0.662	0.709	0.723	0.762
Regular Hours/Weekly Rest	0.756	0.860	0.887	0.892	0.898
Workers' Compensation for Accidents/Illnesses	0.813	0.968	0.972	0.984	0.990
Holidays and Annual/Special Leave	0.842	0.850	0.890	0.901	0.923
Maternity Benefits	0.724	0.837	0.863	0.881	0.922

Notes: Values in tables are unweighted averages across all factories and questions within each group. 1.000 indicates that all factories are compliant with all subquestions for a given period. OSH represents Occupational Safety and Health. An example of a question in the OSH category is "Does the factory have a written health and safety policy?" An example of a question in the Workplace Operations category is "Are access paths wide enough to allow for two-way traffic?"

Figure 4.2　Lowest First Visit Compliance

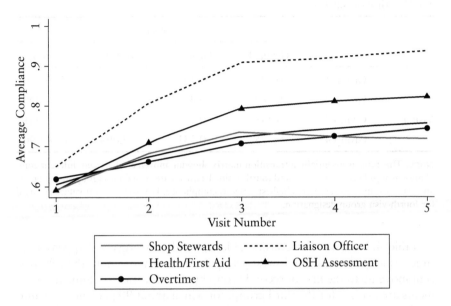

Figure 4.3　Change in Average Compliance Relative to First Visit

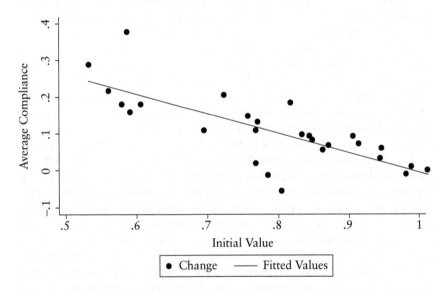

analysis, firms are grouped into four different categories based on the first-visit compliance. Group one represents those factories with the highest compliance (most compliant), and group four represents those firms with the least compliance. The rows show how firms in each group based on their visit moved between groups by their fourth visit.[5]

Table 4.3 Compliance Graduation Rates by Compliance Group between the First and Fourth Assessments

		Visit 4			
		Group 1	Group 2	Group 3	Group 4
	Group 1	0.839	0.161	0.000	0.000
	Group 2	0.560	0.413	0.027	0.000
Visit 1	Group 3	0.449	0.449	0.061	0.041
	Group 4	0.375	0.531	0.094	0.000

Notes: This table is essentially a transition matrix showing movement between different compliance groups between the first and fourth visits. Factories are sorted into groups using factor analysis. Group 1 (4) represents highest (lowest) compliance. First-visit cut-off values are used for fourth-visit group designation.

Table 4.3 shows that considerable upward convergence happens over time. Among those in the lowest group in the first visit, more than 90 percent move up to the first or second group by their fourth visit. Similar movements are evident for the third group, for which about 90 percent move into the first two groups by the fourth visit.

The incentives to remain in compliance that were linked to the trade agreement diminished over time. Growing international market pressures, such as the end of the Agreement on Textiles and Clothing (ATC) in 2004 and the recession in 2008, as well as the BFC's decision in 2006 to stop publicly reporting compliant factories, may have led some firms to become less compliant. Brown et al. (2012) define *regression* as the decision of a compliant factory to become noncompliant for each compliance point and *retrogression* as the decision to move from noncompliance to compliance and then back to noncompliance. They then use factory-level data to analyze factors that contribute to a factory's decision to become noncompliant.

One of the main results from Brown et al. (2012) is that, even with falling external incentives, regression in the absence of any reputational consequence of labor-code noncompliance is not inevitable. Factory managers who uncover production process efficiencies while attempting to come into compliance will retain efficiency-enhancing compliant behavior, even in the absence of public disclosure of noncompliance. Furthermore, in any event, a factory's labor-law compliance record will still be known by the buyers who subscribe to the compliance reports. Factories supplying reputation-sensitive buyers that require a minimum record of labor-law compliance, whether publically disclosed or not, may still have a business incentive to remain in compliance. Perhaps most importantly, labor union activity may also deter regression.

Table 4.3 shows some evidence of regression. Of those in group 1 in the first visit, 16.1 percent fall into the second group (although none fall into groups three or four). Less than five percent of the factories in groups two and three fall into lower groups by the fourth visit. To analyze regression more formally, we generate a bivariate indicator equal to one if the factory's compliance falls in any given area. The mean of this dummy variable is 0.035. This 3.5 percent of the question-plant-period observations can be decomposed to reveal falling rates of regression as the visit number increases. Between the first and second period, the regression rate (which is across all questions and factories) is 7.1 percent, but that rate falls to 2.6 percent between the fourth and fifth visit. Part of this may be explained by a selection bias in which the least successful firms, being most likely to regress, drop out of the sample.

There is very little regression in core labor standards and union activity. Core labor standards, such as the prohibition against child labor, are *zero-tolerance* points of compliance from the perspective of reputation-sensitive buyers and the U.S. government. Thus, it is not surprising to see low probability of regression. By contrast, regression in compliance points that involve more complex factory organizational change is considerably higher. The probability that BFC enterprise advisors would observe non-compliance on a visit following a visit where the factory was found to be in compliance in Communication and Workplace Systems, Occupational Safety and Health and Modern Wage Practices, are all close to 0.05.

It is clear that significant, although not universal, improvement in working conditions occurs over time. If poor conditions are profit maximizing, then improvements in working conditions should have hindered the prospects of success for the Cambodian apparel sector. On the other hand, improvements in working conditions may bring benefits to firms that outweigh the costs. The next section reviews several dimensions that might provide evidence relevant for evaluating the 'business case' for improving standards.

4 PERFORMANCE MEASURES OF CAMBODIAN APPAREL FACTORIES

There are several potential measures of the effects of working conditions on the Cambodian apparel sector. In this section, we review five of these: survival, changes in apparel exports (using post-crisis data), wages, the trade-off between wage compliance and working conditions, and productivity.

Survival

One of the main arguments against improving working conditions, especially in developing countries, is that such improvements increase costs. The logic behind these arguments is very strong: for factories operating in a perfectly competitive environment, increases in costs, holding all else constant, would almost necessarily induce factory closures. If working conditions were purely cost-increasing and had no other benefits, one would therefore expect to find a strong relationship between improvements in working conditions and an increased probability of factory closure.

Brown et al. (2011) evaluate this hypothesis by comparing improvements in working conditions against the probability of factory survival using survival analysis. They find very little, if any, evidence suggesting that improvements in working conditions increased the probability of factory closure and, in fact, find evidence suggesting that improvements in some areas increase the chance of survival. These results are inconsistent with the hypothesis that improvements in working conditions are purely cost-increasing.

Apparel Exports

The importance of apparel in Cambodia's economy has been well documented (see, in particular, Beresford 2009). Apparel accounts for 16 percent of GDP and 88 percent of exports. Between 2001 and 2008, Cambodia's share of total U.S. apparel imports increased from 1.3 percent to 3.1 percent (a nominal increase of nearly $1.7 billion). Figure 4.4 shows several interesting features of U.S. imports from Cambodia over time. First, there is a clear and steady increase in the share of U.S. apparel imports coming from Cambodia. This increase in share is clearly driven by the increase in total value from Cambodia (as opposed to falling values from other countries).

Berik and van der Meulen Rogers (2010) compare Cambodia to Bangladesh and suggest that the incentives tied to Cambodia's trade agreement

Figure 4.4   U.S. Apparel Imports from Cambodia

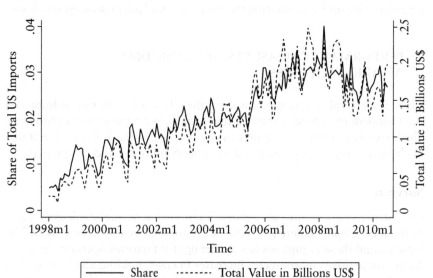

explain the improvements in working conditions. Without disputing this point, it is important to point out that both exports and working conditions continued to improve after MFA/ATC incentives disappeared, suggesting that perhaps additional factors explain improved compliance. Adler and Woolcock (2010) make this point specifically, noting that improved financial performance 'had financial benefits' (from increased quota access) but that these benefits were 'only part of the story in terms of its long term attractiveness' (543).

The second main feature of Figure 4.4 is the drop that occurred during the global financial crisis, also known as the 'Great Trade Collapse' (Baldwin 2009). This drop was more symptomatic of a drop in global demand than in Cambodian supply. Nevertheless, the drop during this period caused a great deal of concern among Cambodian producers, especially regarding perceived buyer shifts to other lower-cost destinations (e.g. Bangladesh). Figure 4.4 shows, however, that U.S. imports of apparel from Cambodia recovered and were nearly at pre-crisis levels by early 2011.

This recovery is important because it shows that Cambodia remains an important (and seemingly increasingly important) source of U.S. apparel imports after both the end of the MFA/ATC in 2004 and the end of China-specific safeguards that limited that country's apparel exports in 2008. While other countries (perhaps most notably Mexico) have been losing U.S. apparel market share, Cambodia's Better Factories Program does not seem to have deterred buyers. Beresford (2009) in particular makes this point, noting that 'the application of labour standards has not imposed a cost disadvantage on Cambodian producers.'

Wages

Wages of Cambodian apparel workers are very low by international standards. Workers earn a base salary of $55 per month, and senior workers earn $61 per month. In March 2011, the Labor Advisory Committee (the body that arbitrates apparel sector issues) approved an increase in attendance bonuses from $5 to $7 per month, an increase for meals, and a 'seniority' wage increase from $2 to $11 per month (Sothanarith 2011).

Powell and Skarbek (2006) suggest that apparel wages in many countries are often *higher* than domestic alternatives. Using aggregate data, they compare buyer-reported wage rates to national-level wages and find that, in many cases, the apparel wages are higher by a factor of two or more. Robertson et al. (2009) estimate these wage premiums directly using household data that control for demographic characteristics, such as age, education, gender and industry. They find positive wage premiums in apparel in all five countries examined (Honduras, El Salvador, Madagascar, Indonesia and Cambodia).

Among these five countries, however, Cambodia stands out in that it is the only country with an operating Better Work program (Better Factories

Cambodia) at the time covered by the analysis. Cambodia also stands out as having the highest apparel-specific wage premium—nearly 35 percent higher than the average domestic wage—after controlling for other demographic characteristics.

Robertson (2011) expands this analysis and compares the change in the wage premium over time with the U.S. import unit value of apparel from Cambodia. The apparel wage premium follows the unit values over time, which is not surprising. The increase in apparel exports is credited by the United Nations Development Program with reducing the income gap between men and women, and the drop in poverty rates from 34.7 percent in 2004 to 30.1 percent in 2007.[6] Using household surveys, Robertson (2011) finds that the female wage differential falls in absolute value from –25.4 percent in 1996 to –8.2 percent in 2007. This is significant because it represents a closing of the gender wage gap throughout the economy—not just in apparel.

What is surprising is that measures of working conditions do not follow the unit value of apparel. After rising sharply around 2001, apparel unit values fall and then stabilize. Working conditions, on the other hand, improved and continued to improve while the apparel unit values fell. If the unit values represent price pressure on the firms, it seems likely that their fall would put pressure on firms to regress on working conditions. But the opposite seems to be the case. This is consistent with the idea that either firms realized that the improvements in working conditions were somehow beneficial, or the Better Factories Cambodia program was a binding constraint that kept working conditions from worsening.

Did Factories Sacrifice Wage Compliance to Improve Other Measures?

Warren and Robertson (2010) use the factory-level reports to evaluate the possibility that factories faced a trade-off between working conditions and compliance with national wage laws that has roots in the extensive 'compensating differential' literature in economics. That literature suggests that workers will accept lower wages in exchange for improved conditions, and therefore, firms have the ability to choose optimally along a frontier that represents the trade-off between working conditions and wages.

Warren and Robertson (2010), however, find no evidence of such a tradeoff when comparing compliance with wage law with other measures of working conditions. This result is consistent with the idea that either factories were not operating efficiently along their frontier and therefore were able to increase both wages and working conditions, or improvements in working conditions improved productivity in a way that allowed firms to also increase wages (at least in the form of compliance with minimum wage laws) at the same time.

Productivity Growth

Ichniowski et al. (1997) finds that improvements in human-resource practices can improve productivity much like improvements in capital or process technology can. While a direct analysis of a link between working conditions and productivity remains elusive, Asuyama et al. (2010) conducted firm-level surveys designed to analyze productivity changes in the Cambodian garment industry. By comparing 2002/2003 with 2008/2009, they find significant increases in productivity at the industry level. Their firm-level data allow them then to decompose industry-level productivity measures into the contributions that arise from entry and exit and those that arise from changes within firms. This distinction has become increasingly important since the contribution of Melitz (2003), who shows that firms within industries can have very different experiences following trade reforms. Although they do not specifically address changes in working conditions, Asuyama et al. (2010) find that both entry (and exit) and within-firm improvements contributed significantly to improvements in productivity.

They argue that within-firm improvements in productivity were correlated with rising profitability and rising wages. Of course, it is important to point out that there is no established link in this study between working conditions and improvements in productivity, but it would be very difficult to suggest that improvements in working conditions were beneficial to firms in the absence of factory-level improvements in productivity.

5   KEY ELEMENTS OF SUCCESS

There seems to be a general consensus in the literature that the BFC period in Cambodia included improvements in many areas, including working conditions, exports, wages and productivity. As noted earlier, many researchers and policy makers have concluded that together these factors are indicative of BFC success. But, exactly what elements of the program have been the most important for this perceived success? Several possibilities have been identified in the literature. Three of the most prominent include public disclosure, reputation sensitivity and unions/industrial relations.

Public Disclosure

As noted earlier, one of the characteristics of the BFC program involves audits in which monitors enter the plants and record observations. These observations were the basis of BFC synthesis reports that were publically available on the internet. These reports named factories and linked them directly to working-condition violations. The policy of posting these reports

82   *Drusilla Brown, Rajeev Dehejia and Raymond Robertson*

changed in November 2006, at which point synthesis reports stopped naming specific factories and only published aggregate compliance data.

This change in policy provides an opportunity to investigate the possible role that public disclosure has on plant manager behavior. Robertson et al. (2011) investigate this change formally in several ways. They first apply a Chow-type test for a structural break in compliance. The results suggest that a structural break occurred during the 2002–2003 period that is consistent with the lull in BFC reporting during that period. Limiting the analysis to the period in which reporting was resumed, however, suggests a break occurred in October 2006.

The fact that the data suggest a structural break at approximately the same time as the policy change supports the hypothesis that public disclosure matters. The fact that the break appears one month before the policy change would be consistent with some advance notice of the change occurring or a change in the program that caused the break that then induced the policy change.[7] Discussions with ILO/BFC management, however, suggest that the former is a much more likely explanation.

They follow the structural break with a more formal regression analysis of the effect of public disclosure on compliance. They find that after the elimination of public disclosure of factory-level noncompliance, the rate of improvement in compliance slowed and, for some factories, declined. Even for factories and compliance points with falling compliance measures, however, compliance did not return to the baseline, even after the threat of public disclosure was eliminated.

Reputation Sensitivity

The role of reputation-sensitive buyers in promoting compliance with local labor law has strong support in both academic and popular literature. The impact on reputation is central to the effectiveness of the exposé and is not limited to sweatshops in developing countries. Weil (2005) finds that the potential loss of reputation-sensitive buyers was more effective than monetary fines the government levied in maintaining compliance with labor law in the U.S. apparel industry. Ferraz and Finan (2008) find a positive effect of disclosure of public audits on the re-election prospects of corrupt politicians in Brazil.

The weakness of the exposé as a strategy for improving conditions of work in apparel factories is that it may depend on the presence of a reputation-sensitive buyer. Brand-name firms are concerned with protecting brand value from the adverse effects of an exposé of work conditions in its vendor base. The corollary, of course, is that an exposé may have no effect in the absence of a reputation-sensitive buyer. Failing another mechanism, credible enforcement, if it exists, derives exclusively from labor rights organizations or the police power of a local labor authority.

Oka (2010a and 2010b) focuses specifically on the role of buyer's reputation sensitivity using factory-level BFC data and finds very strong effects of reputation sensitivity on factory-level compliance: factories that are as-sociated with more reputation-sensitive buyers are associated with higher compliance. Brown et al. (2010) extend this analysis to focus on regression. To measure reputation sensitivity, they use buyers' commitment to corpo-rate social responsibility (CSR), as indicated by publishing CSR reports in print or online.[8] This measure is combined with other measures found in Inter-Brand's Best Global Brands Ranking and *Fortune*'s 'Most Admired Companies' scoring system. Buyers are also classified according to buyers' primary sales strategy (an apparel retailer or mass merchandiser). Apparel retailers are primarily in the business of selling apparel (although they may sell other related but non-apparel goods). Mass merchandisers refer to large chain stores that sell a wide range of products, with apparel being only one subgroup. This distinction is important because the demand for quality is often higher among apparel retailers.

Classifying buyers in this way produced four broad categories. The first includes apparel retailers with significant evidence of corporate social re-sponsibility. The second consists of apparel retailers with little evidence of a policy relating to corporate social responsibility. The third includes mass merchandisers with significant evidence of corporate social responsibility (no buyers fell into the category of mass merchandiser without evidence of CSR). The last category consists of buyers that were not accessing BFC com-pliance reports. Note that the buyers in the first three categories did access BFC compliance reports.

By interacting the reputation-sensitive variable with indicators for these four factor categories, they find results consistent with Oka (2010a): a reputation-sensitive buyer clearly inhibits regression in all factors. The probability that a firm with a reputation-sensitive buyer retrogresses is smaller in all four of the broad categories identified in the factor analysis. Reputation-sensitive buyers often express chagrin at their inability to affect permanently the behavior of their vendors. These results, however, suggest that these buyers are having a distinct effect on the conditions of work in their supply chains. On the other hand, factories supplying reputation-sensitive mass merchandisers are just as likely to regress as other factories.

It is interesting to note, however, that together, these papers suggest that the threat of public disclosure of noncompliance and the presence of a reputation-sensitive buyer are not perfect substitutes in the firm's decision to comply and remain in compliance. Two obvious hypotheses suggest why direct public disclosure and disclosure mediated through a reputation-sensitive buyer have different impacts on the decision to com-ply. First, reputation-sensitive buyers may also be providing technical as-sistance that helps factories stay in compliance, as hypothesized by Sabel et al. (2000) and Fung et al. (2001). Alternatively, name-brand apparel retailers require high-quality workmanship. Such quality may be most effi-ciently provided in factories that have aligned the interests of the workers with the buyer. Properly aligned incentives may involve paying workers as promised (modern wage practices), controlling excess hours and a positive work environment.

Unions and Industrial Relations

One of the key concerns raised about the BFC program is union development. Beseford (2009), for example, suggests that unions are considered separate from working conditions in a World Bank survey of buyers. Miller et al. (2009) echoes this point, noting that factory owners continue to present 'dogged resistance' to collective bargaining, even while improving working conditions as part of the BFC program. Indeed, the union protests in Cambodia in July and September 2010, and the outcomes of those actions, have raised concerns about the prospects for collective bargaining. Even in this environment, however, analysis of the factory-level data suggests improvements in several key areas of industrial relations. For example, Rossi and Robertson (2011) find that compliance in the areas of collective agreements, disputes, and liaison officers were either high initially or improved dramatically between the first and fifth visits. Compliance in the area of shop stewards, however, remains relatively low, raising concerns about worker-elected representation within factories.

Overall, they conclude that BFC's monitoring and advisory services aimed at remediation have helped create an environment conducive to improving industrial relations. These improvements in industrial relations (especially in the case of improved communication between management and workers), seem to have facilitated improvements in other working conditions, such as occupational safety and health, wages, working time, and weekly rest.

6   CONCLUSIONS

The BFC program has been considered successful in improving working conditions in Cambodia's garment sector. Several recent papers that focus on the BFC program highlight some of the key program features. This paper reviews the results of these recent papers and adds some additional results using factory-level data. Overall, the results seem to suggest that the BFC program successfully improved working conditions. Analysts from a wide range of perspectives agree that working conditions have improved.

These improvements did not seem necessarily to require quota access, reputation sensitivity, public disclosure, or a significant trade-off with wage compliance (although the first three of these did affect compliance). Considerable evidence suggests that public disclosure plays an important role, but it does not explain all of the improvement in working conditions. In fact, working conditions still improved when these factors were removed or controlled for in empirical analysis. Furthermore, regression is limited, but it is affected by factors that also affect initial compliance. Productivity in the industry as a whole and within factories improved, although this has yet to be specifically linked to improvements in working conditions. While far from definitive, these results are consistent with the hypothesis that improvements in working conditions may bring real gains to factories, perhaps in the form of productivity improvements. Of course, other hypotheses are also possible, and continued research is critical to differentiate further between the various hypotheses.

NOTES

1. The authors thank participants at the September 2010 Social Labeling Conference (Debra Ang, Jenn Bair, Amy Luinstra, Doug Miller, Arianna Rossi, Cael Warren), and participants at seminars at the International Labor Affairs Bureau (ILAB) of the Department of Labor. The opinions expressed herein do not necessarily reflect those of the institutions the authors represent.
2. More information about the Better Factories program can be found at http://www.betterfactories.org/.
3. Asyama et al. (2010) use a different dataset of Cambodian factories and find significant turnover as well.
4. All questions within each category were weighted equally. All factories were also weighted equally. One might suggest an alternative weighting scheme, but any such weighting scheme (including equal weights) would necessarily be subjective. The equal weighting scheme is chosen simply because it may be less controversial (closer to a default) than alternatives.
5. The fourth-period groups were defined using the first-period cut-off values.
6. These data are taken from the World Development Indicators (WDI) online and are the only years for these statistics that are reported in the WDI for Cambodia for the 2001–2008 period. Technically, these statistics represent the national poverty rate, which is the percentage of the population living below the national poverty line. National estimates are based on population-weighted subgroup estimates from household surveys.
7. The policy change was explained at least in part by concerns raised by factories that did not want to have their compliance publically revealed.
8. CSR has been receiving increasing attention in the literature and popular press. For one prominent example, see Diara and McGuire (2004).

REFERENCES

Adler, D. and M. Woolcock. 2010. 'Justice without the Rule of Law? The Challenge of Rights-Based Industrial Relations in Contemporary Cambodia.' *Human Rights at Work: Perspectives on Law and Regulation,* edited by Colin Fenwick and Tonia Novitz. Oxford, United Kingdom: Hart.
Asuyama, Y., D. Chhun, T. Fukunishi, S. Neou, and T. Yamagata. 2010. 'Firm Dynamics in the Cambodian Garment Industry: Firm Turnover, Productivity Growth, and Wage Profile under Trade Liberalization.' Discussion Paper No. 268, Institute for Developing Economies, Chiba, Japan.
Baldwin, R., ed. 2009. *The Great Trade Collapse: Causes, Consequences and Prospects.* London: Centre for Economic Policy Research.

Beresford, M. 2009. 'The Cambodian Clothing Industry in the Post-MFA Environment: A Review of Developments.' *Journal of the Asia Pacific Economy* 14(4):366–388.

Berik, G. and Y. van der Meulen Rodgers. 2010. 'Options for Enforcing Labour Standards: Lessons from Bangladesh and Cambodia.' *Journal of International Development* 22(1):56–85.

Brandeis, L. 1913. *Other People's Money and How the Bankers Use It.* New York: Stokes.

Brown, D., R. Dehejia, and R. Robertson. 2011. 'Working Conditions and Factory Survival: Evidence from Better Factories Cambodia.' Discussion Paper No. 4, International Labor Organization, Geneva, Switzerland.

Brown, D., R. Dehejia, and R. Robertson. 2012. 'Retrogression in Working Conditions: Evidence from Better Factories Cambodia.' Discussion Paper No. 6. International Labor Organization, Geneva, Switzerland.

Ferraz, C. and F. Finan. 2008. 'Exposing Corrupt Politicians: The Effects of Brazil's Publicly Released Audits on Electoral Outcomes.' *Quarterly Journal of Economics* 123(2):703–745.

Fung, A., D. O'Rourke, and C. Sabel. 2001. *Can We Put an End to Sweatshops?* Boston: Beacon.

Harrison, A. E. and J. Scorse. 2010. 'Multinationals and Anti-Sweatshop Activism.' *American Economic Review* 100(1):247–273.

Ichniowski, C., B. Prennushi, and K. Saw. 1997. 'The Effects of Human Resource Management Practices on Productivity: A Study of Steel Finishing Lines.' *American Economic Review* 87(3):291–313.

Melitz, M. J. 2003. 'The Impact of Trade on Intra-Industry Reallocations and Aggregate Industry Productivity.' *Econometrica* 71(6):1695–1725.

Miller, D., C. Aprill, R. Certeza, and V. Nuon. 2009. 'Business as Usual? Governing the Supply Chain in Clothing-Post-MFA Phase-out: The Case of Cambodia.' *International Journal of Labor Research* 1(1):10–33.

Oka, C. 2010a. 'Accounting for the Gaps in Labour Standard Compliance: The Role of Reputation-Conscious Buyers in the Cambodian Garment Industry.' *European Journal of Development Research* 22(1):59–78.

Oka, C. 2010b. 'Channels of Buyer Influence and Labor Standard Compliance: The Case of Cambodia's Garment Sector.' *Advances in Industrial and Labor Relations* 17:153–183.

Polaski, S. 2004. 'Cambodia Blazes a New Path to Economic Growth and Job Creation.' Working Paper No. 51, Carnegie Endowment for International Peace, Washington, D.C.

Polaski, S. 2006. 'Combining Global and Local Forces: The Case of Labor Rights in Cambodia.' *World Development* 34(5):919–932.

Powell, B. and D. Skarbek. 2006. 'Sweatshop Wages and Third World Living Standards: Are the Jobs Worth the Sweat?' *Journal of Labor Research* 27(2):263–274.

Robertson, R. 2011. 'Apparel Wages before and after the Better Factories Cambodia Program.' Discussion Paper No. 3, International Labor Organization, Geneva, Switzerland.

Robertson, R., D. Brown, G. Pierre, and L. Sanchez-Puerta, eds. 2009. *Globalization, Wages, and the Quality of Jobs: Five Country Studies.* The World Bank: Washington, D.C.

Robertson, R., D. Ang, D. Brown, and R. Dehejia. 2011. 'Labor Law Compliance and Human Resource Management Innovation: Better Factories Cambodia.' Discussion Paper No. 1, International Labor Organization, Geneva, Switzerland.

Rossi, A. and R. Robertson. 2011. 'Better Factories Cambodia: An Instrument for Improving Industrial Relations in a Transnational Context.' *Practices and*

Outcomes of an Emerging Global Industrial Relations Framework, edited by Konstantinos Papadakis. Geneva, Switzerland: Palgrave McMillan.

Sabel, C., A. Fung, and D. O'Rourke. 2000. 'Ratcheting Labor Standards: Regulation for Continuous Improvement in the Global Workplace.' Working Paper No. 00–010, Kennedy School of Government, Harvard University, Cambridge, MA.

Shea, A., J. Heymann, and M. Nakayama. 2010. 'Improving Labor Standards in Clothing Factories.' *Global Social Policy* 10(1):85–110.

Sothanarith, K. 2011. 'Council Approves Wage Bumps for Factory Workers.' Retrieved March 7, 2011 (http://www.voanews.com/khmer-english/news/Council-Approves-Wage-Bumps-for-Factory-Workers-117513018.html).

Warren, C. and R. Robertson. 2010. 'Globalization, Wages, and Working Conditions: A Case Study of Cambodian Garment Factories.' Working Paper No. 257, Center For Global Development, Washington, D.C.

Weil, D. 2006. 'Public Enforcement/Private Monitoring: Evaluating a New Approach to Regulating the Minimum Wage.' *Industrial and Labor Relations Review* 27(357):357–376.

5 The Impact of the Fibre Citoyenne Label on the Moroccan Garment Industry and Its Workers

Arianna Rossi[1]

Global production networks (GPNs), characterized by lead firms in the industrialized world that outsource their production process to suppliers in developing countries, have become a distinctive feature of the global economy in the last decades. Involvement in GPNs has important implications in both economic and social terms for developing country firms and their workers, and it is crucial to understand under which conditions participation in GPNs leads to *social upgrading*, in other words, to improvements in the well-being of the workers operating in them.

Parallel to the emergence of GPNs, the recent decades have witnessed a dramatic growth of social compliance initiatives based on codes of labor practice aimed at improving labor standards in global production. These initiatives have been established and promoted by a variety of different actors, most notably multinational corporations, as well as industry associations and NGOs. This chapter explores a locally conceived social compliance initiative, the Fibre Citoyenne (FC) label in the garment industry in Morocco, and its impact on social upgrading.

In 2003, the Moroccan government backed a strategic plan for the repositioning of the textile and clothing industry in preparation for the phaseout in 2005 of the quota system regulated by the Multi-Fibre Arrangement. The plan stressed the importance of preferential access to the European Union market and aimed at targeting high-end market niches and strengthening flexibility and reactivity to buyers' demands. As part of this overarching strategic plan, the Moroccan textile and garment industry association (AMITH) adopted a charter for the promotion of ethical trading that encompassed environmental and social values for sustainable development in the garment sector. This code of conduct, which, according to its foreword, is based on the principles of civism and compliance with legal requirements, social ethics, protection of the environment and sustainable development, is associated with the label 'Fibre Citoyenne' that is awarded to enterprises in compliance with the code, based on independent monitoring.

In 2006, the FC initiative gained momentum because of the involvement of the MFA Forum Morocco, a multistakeholder initiative bringing together the government, the three main unions (CDT, UMT, and UGTM), and the main international buyers active in Morocco (Inditex, Levi Strauss & Co, Mango, Marks & Spencer, and Next). This initiative gave a higher profile and media exposure to the FC, and at the same time, it brought about significant questions concerning its scope, coverage, and monitoring system, and especially its interaction with buyers' own corporate codes of conduct. At the time of the field research in 2008, there was hope that the FC would become a standard not only for the local industry but also for international buyers, who may agree to stop their own audits. A turning point seemed to take place in conjunction with the signing of the first international framework agreement in the textile and garment sector between Inditex, the Spanish owner of the Zara brand, and the International Textile, Garment, and Leather Workers' Federation (ITGLWF) in October 2007 (Miller 2008). Inditex agreed with the AMITH to source exclusively from FC-labeled firms in Morocco and rely on FC audits for its own social monitoring. This commitment from one key global buyer has had an enormous impact on the spread of the FC among factories in Morocco, but the extent to which it is actually implemented remains questionable.[2]

Social upgrading, defined as the process of improvements in the rights and entitlements of workers as social actors by enhancing the quality of their employment (Barrientos et al. 2011), emerges as a key challenge because of participation in GPNs by Moroccan garment factories. In particular, there are findings of poor working conditions and long working hours, informality, extensive use of temporary and casual labor, gender disparity and low wages (Amri 2005, Arco 2008, Belghazi and Baden 2002, Clean Clothes Campaign 2003, Joekes 1985, Intermon Oxfam 2004). Freedom of association and collective bargaining are problematic issues (Amri 2005, Clean Clothes Campaign 2003, ICFTU 2006, ITUC 2009), due to relatively low unionization rate and a mismatch between union representatives (mostly male) and the largely female labor force in the sector.[3]

One of the obstacles to improvements in working conditions and labor rights is directly related to the commercial embeddedness of the garment industry in GPNs and the contradicting pressures suppliers receive from their global buyers. This obstacle is particularly relevant in the Moroccan context, which is characterized by the fast-fashion segment of the garment industry (Plank et al. 2012). Fast fashion requires fast delivery times, reactivity to market needs, and the ability to work on very small orders on a short notice. Thanks to its proximity to Europe, Morocco offers an ideal platform for this kind of 'quick response' orders. The main buyers active in Morocco are emerging Spanish brands that pioneer fast fashion, such as Inditex (Zara) and Mango; large French companies, such as Decathlon; and British buyers with a consolidated history of attention to quality and labor standards, such as Marks & Spencer.

Due to its characteristics, fast fashion poses specific challenges for economic and social upgrading, and it exacerbates the tension between commercial embeddedness on one side and considering workers as social actors, and not only as productive factors, on the other. The FC is therefore located in the midst of a challenging environment in which global buyers exert contradicting pressures: they follow the fast-fashion strategy, imposing low wages and short lead times, while at the same time, they require full compliance to labor standards. The aim of this paper is to understand to what extent the FC has contributed to fostering social upgrading for workers in garment supplier factories.

1   METHODOLOGY

This paper uses a qualitative approach based on a case study. Firm-level, semi-structured interviews and focus-group discussions were conducted during fieldwork in Morocco from January to June 2008. A sample of 19 enterprises was selected based on geographical location, type of buyer, and adherence to the Fibre Citoyenne.

The selected enterprises are located across four industrial areas characterized by significant garment exports and employment: Casablanca, Rabat-Salé, and Fez and Tangier. Table 5.1 presents the geographical distribution of the sample.

Table 5.2 illustrates the enterprises' participation in the FC initiative and whether they had already received the label, were in the process of obtaining it or were not participating.

Representing the predominance of small and medium enterprises in the Moroccan garment sector, the sample is constituted of nine factories with fewer than 400 employees, seven factories with between 400 and 1,000 employees, and three factories with more than 1,000 employees. In terms of their positioning within the GPN, all factories are engaged in cut-make-trim production, eight supply a finished product, three are developing design capabilities and two are developing their own brand for the domestic market.

Table 5.1   Geographical Distribution of Study Sample

Casablanca	Rabat	Fez	Tangier
1. C1	1. R1	1. F1	1. T1
2. C2	2. R2	2. F2	2. T2
3. C3	3. R3		3. T3
4. C4	4. R4		4. T4
5. C5	5. R5		5. T5
6. C6			
7. C7			

Table 5.2   Sample Participation in the FC Initiative at Time of Interviews

FC labeled	FC in progress	No FC
C1	C2 (later obtained)	C3
C4	F1 (later obtained, then suspended)	R2
C5 (later suspended)	F2 (later obtained)	R3
C6 (later suspended)	R4 (later obtained)	T4
C7	T1 (later obtained)	T5
R1	T2	
R5	T3	

Note: the suspension of the FC label is not necessarily imputable to a failure of passing the audit, but also to a decision not to renew the yearly subscription fee.

General managers and human resource managers were interviewed in all factories, and in 11 factories, small focus-group discussions with workers were organized, with a total participation of 53 workers. Members were chosen randomly on the factory floor, among workers operating sewing machines, cutting machines, serigraphy, finishing, ironing and packaging. All the interviewed workers were female, and both senior workers (with more than 15 years of experience) and recently hired workers were interviewed.

2   FIBRE CITOYENNE AS AN INSTRUMENT FOR SOCIAL UPGRADING?

This section analyzes in detail the impact of the FC initiative on social upgrading. The investigation focuses on the opportunities that this initiative has brought about for all types of workers, be they regular (with permanent contracts and all the benefits) or irregular (casual, contract, or temporary workers) (Barrientos et al. 2011). The impact is analyzed both in terms of improvements in measurable standards, such as health and safety, wages, and contract types, and in terms of enabling rights, such as freedom of association, nondiscrimination, dignity, and respect. This section underlines the aspects that characterize the initiative at the local level, as well as the issues that remain challenging and problematic in the wake of buyers' demands and pressures, in terms of both labor compliance and production.

The Content of the FC Code and the Labeling Process

Umbrella codes, such as the FC code, promoted by industry associations have been defined as 'second party certification' mechanisms (Gereffi et al. 2001). They largely originated in the north as a response to media exposés pointing out labor rights violations or to stricter codes proposed by unions or labor organizations (Pearson and Seyfang 2001). From this viewpoint, the FC initiative is an example of an umbrella code generating from the south without specific media pressure. Similar to buyers' codes of conduct, the AMITH issued the FC code unilaterally without a tripartite discussion with government and workers representatives. For this reason, local unions and NGOs have criticized it.

While union representatives have praised the initiative as a step forward for awareness of social responsibility in the garment sector, they have also underlined that the FC should not act as a substitute for the national labor code, which has specific provisions in terms of freedom of association and collective bargaining, although their implementation at the factory level is debatable. Describing the challenges for unions in Morocco, a representative from one of the main unions in Morocco, CDT, says:

> The Ministry of Labor does not play the role it should play when it comes to monitor and enforce the Labor Code. They do not have sufficient means to enforce it, especially in the field of freedom of association. The labor code here in Morocco is very good, among the best in Africa and the Arab world, because it was negotiated with the unions, the government and the patrons; it covers very well social protection and freedom of association. The problem is its application and implementation.

One representative from another union, UGTM, pointed out that the FC code does not devote enough attention to freedom of association and collective bargaining, and therefore, does not encompass all the basic rights outlined by the ILO:

> The reason why we are not satisfied totally with [the FC] is that there is not enough attention to freedom of association. The FC to be really 'citoyenne' [citizen] should encompass all aspects of decent work as described by the ILO.

Indeed, in reference to the ILO core conventions, the FC code explicitly covers the bans on child labor, forced labor, and discrimination in its first three chapters, as well as the right to freedom of association, but an important omission is the mention of collective bargaining. This lack of social dialogue represents a serious obstacle in the achievement of enabling rights for workers, as discussed further in this section.

Civil society has also been critical of the FC in terms of its scope, because at best, it applies to firms that are AMITH members, and therefore does not cover a large number of informal enterprises that still act as suppliers for international buyers through intermediaries. The tendency of a number of international buyers to equate the FC code to the labor code, or even to rely on the FC as the prime mechanism for social compliance, is a very controversial move. This sentiment is present also among managers, as the manager of the factory identified in my study as T5 argues:

> I don't like this term 'citoyenne' [citizen] because we are all citizens in Morocco. Corporatism is not an obligation, it is not compulsory to be part of AMITH. And you cannot have the FC certification if you are not part of AMITH. So I think it is not correct. What does it mean, that if you are not member of the AMITH then you are not a proper citizen? I fear that this initiative of AMITH is a substitute for the state. These things should be dealt [with] by the Labor Code.

The FC code provisions[4] in terms of health and safety, working hours, disciplinary measures, and harassment are based on the Moroccan Labor Code and are in line both with the ETI base code[5] and standard buyers' codes of labor practice. In terms of remuneration and social benefits, the FC code refers to a 'fair' remuneration at least equal to the minimum wage. The chapter on regular employment is aligned to the ETI base code, being detailed in its provisions to avoid misuse of temporary and apprenticeship contracts aimed at keeping the employee in precarious employment situations. The last three chapters of the FC code contain provisions concerning subcontracting of services, handling of chemicals and environmental protection, and implementation of the code. As with buyers' codes, the monitoring system of the FC code is based on social audits. When the label was established in 2003, a first group of enterprises was accompanied through a support program and certified by an external audit company. In the following years, new applicants were audited after the completion of the FC support program, which consists of a preliminary audit, followed by a plan of corrective actions aimed at achieving full compliance with the code. The enterprise is accompanied by a support cabinet, selected from a roster of external consultants, that assists it in the implementation of an action plan over a period of six months, covering issues of health and safety, minimum working age, wages, working hours, discrimination, freedom of association, forced labor and environmental protection. After this period, the enterprise is audited again. The FC label is issued based on the outcomes of the final audit. Interestingly, the support program of the FC is financed by the National Agency for Small and Medium Enterprises (ANPME), which is a government agency within the framework of the national Mise à Niveau program.[6] The ANPME is not associated with the Ministry of Employment and is therefore a separate entity from labor inspectorates. The ANPME covers 80 percent of the costs of the support program, and the enterprise pays the remaining 20 percent.

Management Perspectives on the FC Initiative

What is the impact of the FC on economic and social upgrading, according to factory managers? This section addresses this question highlighting the different opportunities created by the FC, as well as the challenges that it brings about for different types of factories. It emphasizes the tensions between complying with the FC provisions and responding to buyers' commercial demands.

All the interviewed managers who are involved in the FC agree that it has been a positive experience. The overall judgment on the FC labeling initiative, as well as on the support program, largely depends on the characteristics of the enterprise.

For most of the enterprises originally labeled in 2003, the FC represented an extra certification on top of its already-established efforts in the field of social compliance. These managers state that they had already made most of the investment before they were FC-labeled, because of the initiatives carried out bilaterally with their clients (especially American and British buyers). In these cases, managers felt they were already in compliance, and they did not take advantage of the support program. Because of these circumstances, it was more difficult to assess and isolate the changes in social upgrading brought about by the introduction of the FC. Similarly, those factories that have been involved in the FC for a longer time see hardly any inconvenience with it because they have observed that disadvantages in the short term—especially in terms of costs—turn into advantages in the medium and long term.

The experiences of the enterprises that have only recently joined the FC or are in the process of being labeled radically differ from those of the first group. Indeed, these managers recognize a very impressive change on their factory floors thanks to the involvement in the FC, and especially thanks to the consultancy of the cabinets carrying out the support program. These changes touch upon both economic and social upgrading, and highlight the relationship between the two.

Managers appear enthusiastic about the advantages pertaining to the economic performance of the enterprise, in terms of both increased business opportunities and process upgrading. Factory owners have started, or are planning, to venture into different export markets besides their traditional trading partners, such as the United States, Germany and Italy. They also suggest that they do not have to struggle to approach clients to have more orders, but instead are actively pursued by clients. Overall, managers of the FC-labeled firms recognize that their enterprises have become more reliable, and therefore, that clients are keener on entrusting them with larger or more complicated orders. They have been able to expand their client base toward more demanding, prestigious clients that value social-compliance efforts. The advantages in terms of new clients and export markets have been by far the most highlighted issue by managers, who perceive the FC primarily as a competitive advantage useful for their business, embedded in the commercial dynamics global buyers dictate.

In terms of process upgrading, defined as the improvements in the efficiency of the production process, through the introduction of new technology and/or through increased productivity (Dicken 2003: 107), managers of firms that have recently joined the FC support program are very impressed by the significant changes taking place on the factory floor. Specifically, they report that the FC certification and especially its support program have been instrumental for a complete restructuring of production, resulting in process upgrading. Many managers credit the support cabinet with helping them to improve their management system, rationalize their production and sustain their learning process. Through the support cabinet, they have changed their working methods to be more efficient and more productive to counterbalance the heavy investment to obtain the label. This shows that the FC initiative, besides its main objective of improving working conditions and complying with international labor standards, also has positive implications for the firm's productivity and economic upgrading.

To attain the FC label, factory managers often have to undertake significant investment. This investment is often seen as a substantial difficulty stemming out of the FC initiative. The extent to which firms perceived this problem largely depends on how far the firm was from compliance, and therefore, on how high the required investment was. In the majority of the visited factories, the investment has been very substantial in physical terms and especially in terms of wage and social security. Health-and-safety requirements, such as establishment and improvement of the factory canteen and additional toilets separated for women and men, account for large sums, but they are a one-off investment. The main long-standing cost that supplier firms encounter is paying all employees the minimum wage and registering the totality of the workforce with social security (CNSS). On average, the cost of compliance in terms of minimum wage and CNSS for a medium enterprise of around 300 employees can amount to between 100,000 and 150,000 dirhams (about US$15,000 to $20,000). The highest expense is registration with the CNSS and the penalties for delays in payments, which can reach millions of dirhams. Indeed, CNSS registration has emerged as one of the most pressing concerns: several managers, especially in Tangier, have lamented the very high charges connected with CNSS registration, because the status quo before their involvement in the FC was to register around 60 percent of the workers.

Hence, compliance with the FC requires a very significant investment, especially for larger firms. This issue highlights the intrinsic contradiction in buyers' demands for labor standards: compliance directly results in higher costs and poses additional limitations (e.g., in terms of lead times, if one is not to abuse overtime), automatically rendering the compliant factory less competitive and less cost efficient. This situation constitutes a disincentive for managers to embark fully in social-compliance initiatives. Nevertheless, while being aware of the high cost of compliance, several managers point out that the costs are justified when looking at the long term, when costs become a productive investment and are balanced by enhanced organization, improved stability on the factory floor, and stronger motivation of the workforce.

Given that the FC initiative is directed in great part to improving working conditions, its success is measured against its impact in this realm. This research investigated in detail how the introduction of the FC has influenced social upgrading. Literature shows that the introduction of a code of labor practice has primary impact on measurable standards, such as health-and-safety standards and contracts, because these are most easily addressed and observed, and changes are most easily quantifiable (Barrientos and Smith 2006, 2007, Oxfam International 2004, Raworth and Kidder 2009). The empirical research carried out in Morocco confirms these findings. The most observable improvements the FC has brought about have been recorded in measurable standards, and in particular, in safety and hygiene issues, as underlined by the manager of factory R1:

[The FC] brought a new conception of work in the factory, because everyone from workers to the management and also the clients realize the impact it has had, especially for safety issues. The difference is very palpable.

Through the FC, managers have a higher awareness of their factory's conditions. The manager of F2 factory states:

We have changed working methods and we have learned many things that we didn't know before. For example, concerning safety, I always thought we were doing well, but there were many things we had to change.

Other managers commend the progress in terms of keeping track of workers' dossiers, legal documentation and medical files. The reason why the introduction of the FC is particularly effective in improving measurable standards is easily found. These aspects are relatively easy to address and tackle, even when they require substantial investment (such as the renovation of a canteen or the installation of new ventilation systems), and changes are evident. As with private monitoring initiatives by global buyers, the success of the initiative is measured mainly according to measurable standards.

The impact of the FC on enabling rights is by definition much more challenging to assess. From the managers' perspectives, it is possible to identify what aspects of enabling rights they value (i.e., a good climate in the factory) and what aspects they intrinsically oppose (i.e., unionization). These perspectives offer insights into the way in which managers relate to their workers.

Mostly, managers identify the improvements in social climate within the factory as an important advantage. The relationship between management and workers seems to have improved greatly with the introduction of the FC, mainly thanks to the support cabinets, which initiated communication groups and health-and-safety committees in companies that had no workers representatives. In Morocco, due to its past as a French colony, the labor code follows a 'French model' of workers' representation based on the role of the *délégués du personnel* (workers' representatives) who may or may not be union members. These representatives have a seat in a committee that, according to the law, meets every month in the factory and is presided over by the factory owner. The improved representation described by managers refers to these representatives. Managers describe how the FC has advanced communication with their workers, improved clarity and simplified their relationship with workers' representatives. Underlining how the FC support program has shed light on the Moroccan legislation and raised awareness among workers of their rights and benefits, managers believe that workers are more motivated in their jobs, and therefore, more productive, because they know their rights and feel secure and respected. In factory C1, the manager stated:

> Also, [the FC] has built trust in workers, now that they know the rules they develop loyalty to the company, and there is a better climate in the factory. FC is a guarantee of impartiality, transparency, and equity so workers are more satisfied. Psychologically it makes them understand that they are better off in a firm like ours, and they become more motivated, improving their performance.

In reality, the extent to which this improved communication with workers' representatives actually translates into enhanced enabling rights and increased negotiating power for workers is questionable. Very often, the workers' representatives are not elected but are appointed by managers, who avoid 'troublemakers' and, as a rule, discriminate against the few unionized workers.

Confirming this crucial problem with unions, in several instances, factory owners have explicitly expressed their negative attitude toward unions and unionized workers. When discussing the reality of adherence to the FC code, they mentioned freedom of association as an unrealistic expectation. Among managers, there is a widespread suspicion toward unions,[7] and there seem to be a belief that allowing unions in the factory will mean going out of business because of strikes. An AMITH officer interviewed in Tangier was very candid about this fear, actually praising the fact that social dialogue in the FC code does not make explicit reference to the ILO core conventions concerning unionization:

> Unions are not objective toward workers, they don't really defend them but they are just about politics. The mentality is different and that is why employers are annoyed by unions. It is then good that the FC code does not foresee unions explicitly but just social dialogue, which means good communication with workers.

Factory T2 manager also confirms:

> [The presence of unions] is a mentality issue. The reality is that if you
> let unions in the factory you are sure to close because there is no dia-
> logue. It can reach a deadlock and it's not the fault of the workers but
> of the unions. They want it their way and if not, they go on strike and
> the factory closes. So, we are against unions because they jeopardize the
> business and we don't let them in the factory.

This excerpt is one of many examples in which managers have mani-
fested their mistrust of, or plain opposition to, unions. In most cases, they
have referred to the lack of maturity of industrial relations in Morocco and
the need for a change in mentality in unions. In particular, they believe that
unions are not open for discussion and do not have the workers' best interest at heart. It has emerged that several managers believe that the commercial success of the factory will automatically benefit workers, and therefore,
there is no need for unions. This idea links back to the expectation, unsup-
ported by evidence, that economic gains will automatically trickle down
to workers. From this point of view, a change in mentality is needed to
ensure that at least the provisions of the FC in terms of social dialogue are
implemented.

Going more in depth into the implications of the opposition to unions on
enabling rights, there is an important gender dimension to consider. In the
visited factories, an average of 78 percent of workers were women. According to the NGO Alliance des Droits des Travailleuses:

> Freedom of association is not existing at all. Women are afraid to join
> unions, because most of times, they come from very poor backgrounds
> and they absolutely need the job to sustain the family. Patrons (bosses)
> are totally against unions. In the case of demonstrations or strikes, they
> appeal to the Penal Code at the art. 288 that says that patrons can sue
> workers when they engage in activities that disrupt the normal func-
> tioning of the working day. Since the strike is an interruption of the
> working day, everyone that is associated with unions or goes on strike
> is likely to end up in prison.

The lack of freedom of association for women is also stressed by a representative from the CDT union:

> The large majority of patrons are against unions. In the clothing sector,
> there is very large majority of women workers, sometimes the totality.
> Women cannot afford losing their jobs, so they would rather say noth-
> ing in order not to upset the patron. They want to keep a good rela-
> tionship with the patrons, to gain premiums and have time off during
> festivities, so there is a lot of competition among the workers. This

makes it impossible for them to get together and aggregate, so it is very difficult for them to think of unionization.

Thus, despite the presence of the workers' representatives and the improved communication and social climate on the factory floor, it is debatable whether these changes have a deep impact on workers' (especially women workers') enabling rights. This is due to the desire of managers to maintain a status quo in which workers do not have negotiating power and can therefore be treated in certain circumstances as a factor of production, ignoring the social functions that workers hold as social agents. Furthermore, the aversion toward unions is explained by the tension that managers face between providing workers with rights and good working conditions, while at the same time constantly reducing production costs. Knowing that allowing unions in factories would automatically provide workers with stronger negotiating power, and therefore increased costs for the firm, managers preempt this from happening by restricting access to unions in the first place. Hence, in this regard, the FC has so far been unsuccessful, given that it does not acknowledge the right to bargain collectively in its code and that it uses a rather vague language in describing freedom of association and unionization rights. Analytically, the attainment of enabling rights, and especially unionization rights, represents the social embeddedness of GPNs, that is, the recognition of workers as social actors and of labor as a human activity. The increased costs of social embeddedness are in stark contrast with the pressures to reduce costs deriving from commercial embeddedness. It is therefore the tension between these two aspects, created at the top layers of the GPN and transferred to its lower segments, which prevents at least one key dimension of social upgrading, enabling rights, from being achieved. By not having a direct impact on enabling rights, the FC falls short of affecting workers in a durable way.

Managers have identified other issues as disadvantages or constraints deriving from the introduction of the FC, in particular the unrealistic expectations to comply with working-time regulations in the wake of fast-fashion requirements, which do not allow suppliers to comply fully with the FC provisions, especially in terms of legal working hours and overtime. To fulfill clients' orders on a very short notice, enterprises are not able to follow the legal requirements concerning working hours and overtime because, if they did, they would not be able to deliver the products and they would lose their supplying contracts.

There is also an issue concerning the time frame of the FC labeling and its related support program. Managers underline that they, as well as their workers, need more time to assimilate the information provided by the support program. Since many of the adjustments required involve not only physical investment but also a behavioral change, implementation is rather slow.

This section analyzed managers' views on which aspects of social upgrading were positively influenced by the FC program. It also acknowledged which issues remain unaffected by the initiative and what managers view as some of the difficulties they confront in complying with the FC. Keeping in mind that the FC is a voluntary initiative, it is important to understand the motivations behind managers' decisions to join the initiative and obtain the label in light of the above analysis. The interviews show two main factors as sources of motivation, one external and one internal to the enterprise, as summarized by the manager of F1:

> There are two reasons why we have become involved in social compliance initiatives and we applied for FC. The first is to give assurance to our clients for good working conditions, something that we have started with audits from our clients. The second is the principle of civic education within the company and within society in general. Our workers have learned how to work safely in a good environment, and this has become the main motivation.

Hence, the first very strong motivational factor is external to the enterprise and strictly business- and client-related. Being FC-labeled is seen as a competitive advantage by managers, who view it as an opportunity to acquire a larger number of clients, diversify their client base by attracting more prestigious brand names, and expand their exports toward unexplored, and possibly more demanding, markets. Managers believe that having the FC label reassures their clients because it guarantees a minimum standard of compliance with international and national labor laws. Some see it as an obligatory move to continue to work with large orders in a sustained way. In some cases, especially for those enterprises that have recently joined the FC support program, their participation reflected the fact that their clients, and in particular Inditex, specifically required that they engage in the FC labeling process (Pfeiffer 2007). In the realm of commercial embeddedness, it has been suggested that the FC support program serves as an additional motivational factor for enterprises that may join the certification process in the future. A large number of managers stated that they recommended the program to other enterprises because of the benefits that they have drawn from the support program, not necessarily in terms of social-compliance issues, but in terms of increased competitiveness or performance. As the manager of T2 says:

> We realized that [the FC] is very good for the enterprise in terms of organization and quality, and that it is a necessity for the firm's competitiveness. We realize the difference even after a few months. The cabinet was very helpful not only for strictly social compliance issues, but in general for human resource management, restructuring, and reorganization of the enterprise.

Thus, the FC and the measures taken to achieve the label have been instrumental in the achievement of process upgrading, providing a business rationale for managers to invest in social upgrading.

Therefore, it emerges quite clearly that the motivation to apply for the FC label is strongly influenced by factors external to the Moroccan industry, such as the prospect of attracting more clients and expanding to new foreign markets, and the pressures to comply with labor standards. The FC, albeit being a locally conceived initiative, seems to derive a strong motivational push from the global context. This analysis is sustained by the exploration of managers' outlooks for the future. When asked about their expectations concerning the FC, most managers referred to economic and business opportunities, without explicitly mentioning social upgrading. Indeed, the improved social climate in the factory is considered as the new status quo and there are no expectations to improve labor-management relations further. From a business perspective, due to the nature of the FC code as a sector-wide code, at the time of the interviews, there was a widespread hope among managers that the FC label could become a unified standard consolidating all existing codes of conduct, setting a single implementation system to replace social audits from each client. In the meantime, managers recognize that the FC facilitates the buyers' audits because it helps improve knowledge and awareness of the labor law. This aspect is also important in terms of changing the reputation of Moroccan firms abroad toward a more socially conscious image.

Furthermore, in 2008, all managers were highly concerned with the priority/exclusivity that buyers have hinted (or officially stated, as in the case of Inditex) of giving preference to suppliers with the FC label. Several managers joined the FC initiative with the expectation that doing so would secure them more and bigger orders and help them establish a long-lasting sourcing relationship with buyers. They are therefore concerned that, despite their investment to bring their factories in compliance with the FC code, some buyers will continue to source from noncompliant firms that offer lower prices, especially in the busy times at peak season.[8] Some managers also expect, or rather hope, that buyers will reward their investment in social compliance by increasing their prices, thereby mitigating the tension between their business demands and their labor standards demands. Managers underline how social upgrading is a shared responsibility and emphasize that their efforts and subsequent costs should be compensated by an increase in the prices they are offered. However, most managers do not rely on this outcome, recognizing that most buyers are not willing to make this step. This reinforces the tension between buyers and suppliers in terms of reconciling the commercial and social embeddedness of firms in GPNs.

Several factory owners have engaged in the FC labeling initiative for reasons that are independent from external pressures they may receive. This motivation factor is deeply rooted in the local environment and is particularly important to analyze vis à vis the highlighted tension between economic and social pressures because it links directly to the social embeddedness of the GPN. The internal motivation to engage in the FC is embedded in the social context and refers to the concept of 'citizenship' and civic responsibility, not only at the enterprise level, but also in the larger context of the Moroccan society. From this perspective, managers' engagement in social compliance was a personal, voluntary choice driven by the awareness of human and labor rights and rooted in the realization that labor is part of social agency and human activity. In particular, some young managers point out that they have developed a higher awareness about these issues during their studies in Europe and North America, as opposed to more traditional, 'old fashioned' management approaches. They underline that being socially compliant is a necessary factor to be good citizens and advance the Moroccan society as a whole, and they agree that, while it might not have been their first motivation to start the labeling process, this awareness has become increasingly important in their efforts toward the obtainment of the FC. Thus, the FC is also seen as an opportunity to improve labor rights and standards, regardless of external pressures, and to advance the Moroccan society in general.

From this analysis of managers' perspectives of the FC, it has emerged that the FC has had significant positive impact on measurable standards, especially health and safety, and has been positively received by managers across Morocco, who highlight its role in creating new business opportunities, as well as in raising the profile of the country in the global market. The FC, however, does not deliver the promised benefits in terms of enabling rights, and in particular, does not support or guarantee collective bargaining. Management's hostile approach toward unions may be explained by the fact that, at the moment, a clear power imbalance allows managers to pressure workers in terms of working hours, wages, and social protection, and this ability would be eroded if the bargaining power of workers were strengthened through the exercise of their enabling rights, such as through freedom of association and collective bargaining. It is important to note that the power imbalance between managers and workers is not the only relevant one because managers themselves are in a power imbalance with their buyers. It is therefore due to this original tension imposed on managers in terms of cost reduction and efficiency on one side, and compliance with labor standards on the other, that a more meaningful outcome of social upgrading is prevented.

Workers' Perspectives

This section illustrates the workers' point of view on the FC, in particular focusing on the changes they may or may have not witnessed because of the introduction of the FC, in both measurable standards and enabling rights. Workers were aware of the FC label only in one factory (F2), which was applying for the label at the time of the interviews. Numerous signs on the factory walls proclaimed '*Tous solidaires pour l'obtention de la Fibre Citoyenne*,' a slogan inciting workers to be 'united' to obtain the label. Incidentally, this is also the one factory where workers were forced to lie in audits concerning their minimum wage (or lack thereof) with the threat of losing their jobs. In all other visited factories, workers were not aware of the FC name, but they usually did recognize significant improvements because of the label and its support program. Also from the workers' point of view, social upgrading largely has taken place in terms of measurable standards. The most noticeable areas of improvement are related to tangible issues, such as access to the canteen, having the possibility to store and reheat homemade food, availability of clean toilets separated between women and men, benefiting from a cleaner and safer environment, and an improved ventilation system that reduces heat and dust in the factory.

Due to the changes the FC has brought about in terms of process upgrading, workers believe that the factory now supplies for 'better' and more stable clients, which in turn brings benefits to them because it translates into a steady, continuous workflow. In former times, there were frequent layoffs and more temporary work because no security existed over the amount of orders received. More established clients ensure more regular working hours. For machine workers and cutters, overtime has reduced. However, not all of the interviewed workers were satisfied with their situation. Especially among packaging and finishing units, where workers tend to be in more irregular working arrangements, they often work long hours and feel discriminated because they are told that they have a lower status on the factory floor when compared to machine workers.

In terms of social security and wages, interviews show that workers in serigraphy and quality control and sewing machine workers were already paid the minimum wage before the introduction of the FC. However, in certain occasions, they underline that they used to be paid a fixed wage, no matter the hours worked, whereas nowadays, they are paid on an hourly basis. In terms of CNSS registration, all the interviewed workers in the departments mentioned above were registered. Some of them notice an improvement due to the FC because the registration to the CNSS takes place when they are hired by the enterprise, whereas before, there was a six-month probation period, during which they were not covered. Finishing and packaging workers once again have a different experience. Describing the situation in the factory in the wake of the investment for social compliance, they say that the head of the enterprise cannot afford to bring every salary to the minimum wage. Since operators at the sewing and cutting machines are believed to be worth more than those at the packaging and finishing units, the manager chooses to raise their salary first. Workers interviewed in the packaging and finishing units were not paid the minimum wage.[9] As mentioned above, in one specific circumstance in factory F2, workers were instructed by their supervisor about what to say to pass the labeling audit, and they were threatened with layoffs if they did not comply. Their salary is often calculated on a fixed-time basis, regardless of how many hours of overtime they work.

As crucial components of social upgrading, enabling rights have emerged as a priority from the focus-group discussions with workers. While, in the same factory, certain groups of workers (mostly senior machine workers, i.e., regular workers) have direct access to the factory owner and they feel that they are listened to, many others (especially finishing, packaging, and warehouse workers) can only talk to their direct supervisor, who is often not interested or not helpful in listening to their concerns, taking advantage of the strong hierarchical structure and establishing a rather hostile climate. These workers are the same ones raising the problem of discrimination, pointing to the fact that they are not considered as worthy as other workers in the factory because their tasks are believed to be less complicated and skill-intensive. Discrimination takes place not only in terms of workers receiving harsh treatment and feeling undervalued, but also has direct repercussions over wages, contracts and occupational safety.

In terms of representation, workers' representatives have been mentioned in the discussions as a source of information to the management and as a reliable counterpart for the negotiations on deadlines and order volumes with managers. However, as mentioned above, registered unions are usually met with a high degree of mistrust and opposition. We must note that no unionized workers were among those interviewed, and although not explicitly asked,[10] it seems highly unlikely that unions were present in any of the visited factories. Workers did not raise the issue of unionization during the discussions, and none of the interviewed workers were elected representatives.

CONCLUSIONS

The empirical analysis of the garment industry in Morocco allows us to draw some important conclusions about the impact of the FC on workers' well-being. In particular, it has emerged that the impact of the FC on social upgrading is greatly connected to the global context, being unmistakably interconnected to the tension global buyers generate on suppliers in terms of pressure on cost, efficiency, and delivery times on one side, and pressure to be in compliance with labor standards (which inherently increases costs) on the other. Therefore, as analyzed in this paper, the FC has had a considerable impact on social upgrading in terms of measurable standards, but unless this tension is dissipated at the global level, the FC would fail to deliver social upgrading, and especially enabling rights, to regular and irregular workers alike.

Unquestionably, the introduction of the FC code and label has had positive impacts on increasing awareness of the implications of global production networks for social and labor aspects. It has increased the understanding of corporate social-responsibility initiatives by Moroccan enterprises and has provided workers with improved knowledge about their rights and entitlements. More specifically, the introduction of the FC code has had a number of visible effects on measurable standards. The most significant changes have been recorded in terms of health-and-safety standards. Improvements have also been made in terms of wages and social security, in particular, paying wages correctly by the hour and registering workers with the CNSS from the moment of recruitment. However, we must note that challenges remain, and managers should continue to pay the minimum wage to all workers and register the totality of the workforce with the CNSS. In many cases, excessive overtime, especially for regular machine workers, has been reduced, although both managers and workers still recognize this as a problematic issue. While improvements in measurable standards are easy to observe and were the first priority for managers to tackle once they joined the FC initiative, enabling rights are considerably more difficult to address. Notwithstanding the improved social climate on the factory floor that both managers and workers have witnessed, and the increased worker representation provided by nonunionized workers' representatives, a number of fundamental issues remain unaddressed. Discrimination toward certain categories of workers continues as well as a hostile attitude toward trade unions that undermines the rights of freedom of association and collective bargaining.

A crucial aspect emerging from the analysis of the impact of the FC code on social upgrading is that the advantages, disadvantages, and expectations that the FC brings are very tightly connected to global buyers, and in particular, to the commercial embeddedness of GPNs. In particular, most managers mentioned the priority to be given by buyers to FC-labeled enterprises and highlight the importance of the role played by the AMITH in negotiating and securing commitment from international buyers to prioritize FC-labeled suppliers. Because of the FC label, managers also expect to have regular orders from their clients, involving larger quantities. Since the competitive advantage of Moroccan enterprises largely involves their ability to deal with very small quantities, suppliers sometimes find themselves accepting orders consisting of just a few pieces of a certain size. This arrangement hinders the management's possibilities to invest in technology, materials and even further improvements on the factory floor, strongly undermining the opportunities for economic upgrading. Several managers believe the expectation for more and larger orders will be realized, since certain clients are already repeatedly asking them to increase their productive capacity. It remains to be seen how the global economic crisis has affected this forecast. The vast majority of managers see the FC certification primarily as an opportunity to attract more clients. They believe that the label attracts big retailers and brand-name companies that are especially concerned with the social compliance of their supplying base.

Hence, in managers' discussions, the emphasis is greatly placed on the global level and in particular on the FC as a competitive advantage to attract more and 'better' clients. It is crucial to stress that while the FC is a locally conceived initiative, it most likely would not have existed without the rising pressures on labor standards in the garment industry, and in particular, without the media and civil society pressures on multinational enterprises to comply with labor standards along their supply chain. However, the local identity of the FC has a clear role to play in explaining how and why it has been embraced with more enthusiasm than buyers' codes of conduct. Indeed, the local origin of the FC and the fact that it is rooted in the Moroccan milieu are crucial aspects that differ from other social-compliance initiatives at the global level, such as buyers' codes of conduct; the FC label is often seen as a source of prestige and pride for the enterprise and is considered instrumental to raise the profile of the recipient enterprises and promote the image of Moroccan firms abroad, reassuring buyers in their investment. Managers expect the AMITH to publicize the label widely if they are to reap the expected benefits in terms of business opportunities.

At the time of the research presented in this paper, there was cautious optimism about the increased business opportunities, the establishment of a competitive advantage based on social compliance, and the reduction in audit duplication associated with the FC. However, due to the economic crisis and the rather faltering commitment of global buyers with respect to the label, the FC has not yet fulfilled its promises. This issue raises significant concerns about its effectiveness in the long run, especially as a key instrument for social upgrading in the garment industry in Morocco.

NOTES

1. Arianna Rossi is Research and Policy Officer with the ILO/IFC Better Work Programme. This paper is based on her Ph.D. dissertation at the Institute of Development Studies at Sussex University. The views expressed in this paper do not necessarily reflect those of the institutions or programs with which she is affiliated.
2. Follow-up interviews carried out in April 2010 suggest that the exclusive sourcing relationship that was promised to FC-labeled factories has not been implemented and that Inditex continues to perform its own social audits in parallel to the FC audits.
3. Women constituted 83.6 percent of the workforce in 2007, and men are usually found in specific segments of the production chain, such as the cutting department, or in supervisory roles, highlighting an intrinsic gender imbalance. Women workers are usually very young and relatively unskilled, and they work in garment factories to contribute to their household subsistence. They often live at home with their parents or their married siblings, waiting to save enough money to get married and retire from waged work (Joekes 1985, Mellakh 2007).
4. For the full text of the FC code, see: http://www.textile.ma/NR/rdonlyres/667F1996-B880-4F4A-8565-22D7E31991A7/391/REFERENTIELan.pdf
5. The Ethical Trading Initiative (ETI) base code can be found here: http://www.ethicaltrade.org/eti-base-code
6. The Mise à Niveau Fund was established by a public-private partnership between the Moroccan government and the AMITH to modernize and upgrade firms prioritizing the textile and garment sector. The AMITH saw its membership radically increase during this process and it became a more 'developmental' business association (Cammett 2007).
7. Specific examples of trade unions rights violations can be found in ICFTU (2006).
8. Anecdotal evidence collected in April 2010 suggests that this is indeed taking place.
9. A total of 53 workers took part in the focus groups. Of these, 10 workers worked in the packaging and finishing units, and were not paid the minimum wage.

10. The question of unionization was not explicitly addressed during focus-group discussions following the suggestions of Moroccan academics, who advised against raising the topic directly. Unions and union members are regarded as troublemakers, not only by managers, but often also by workers.

REFERENCES

Amri, A. 2005. *Economic and Social Performance Indicators of the Textile and Garment Industry in Morocco: 1988–2000* (in French). Casablanca, Morocco: International Labour Organization.
Arco, S. 2008. 'Workers at Less Than One Euro Per Hour' (in Spanish). *El Pais*, February 17.
Barrientos, S., G. Gereffi, and A. Rossi. 2011. 'Economic and Social Upgrading in Global Production Networks: A New Paradigm for a Changing World.' *International Labour Review* 150(3/4):319–340.
Barrientos, S. and S. Smith. 2006. *The ETI Code of Labour Practice: Do Workers Really Benefit?* Brighton, United Kingdom: Institute of Development Studies.
Barrientos, S. and S. Smith. 2007. 'Do Workers Benefit from Ethical Trade? Assessing Codes of Labor Practice in Global Production Systems.' *Third World Quarterly* 28(4):713–729.
Belghazi, S. and S. Baden. 2002. 'Wage Discrimination by Gender in Morocco's Urban Labor Force.' Pp. 35–60 in *Women's Employment in the Textile Manufacturing Sectors of Bangladesh and Morocco*, edited by C. Miller and J. Vivian. Geneva, Switzerland: United Nations Research Institute for Social Development.
Cammett, M. 2007. 'Business-Government Relations and Industrial Change: The Politics of Upgrading in Morocco and Tunisia.' *World Development* 35(11):1889–1903.
Clean Clothes Campaign. 2003. *Working Conditions in Morocco*. Madrid, Spain: Clean Clothes Campaign.
Dicken, P. 2003. *Global Shift: Transforming the Global Economy*. 4th ed. London, United Kingdom: Sage.
Gereffi, G., R. Garcia-Johnson, and E. Sasser. 2001. 'The NGO-Industrial Complex.' *Foreign Policy* 125(July/August 2001):56–65.
Intermón Oxfam. 2004. *Squeezing Fashion: Precariousness of Garment Workers and Corporate Social Responsibility* (in Spanish). Madrid, Spain: Intermón Oxfam.
International Confederation of Free Trade Unions. 2006. *Annual Survey of Violations of Trade Union Rights 2006*. Brussels, Belgium: International Confederation of Free Trade Unions.
International Trade Union Confederation. 2009. *Report for the WTO General Council Review of the Trade Policies of Morocco*. Geneva, Switzerland: International Trade Union Confederation.
Joekes, S. 1985. 'Working for Lipstick? Male and Female Labor in the Clothing Industry in Morocco.' Pp. 183–213 in *Women, Work, and Ideology in the Third World*, edited by H. Afshar. London, United Kingdom: Tavistock.
Mellakh, K. 2007. *Study on the Context and Application Mechanisms of the Labor Law and Women Workers Protection in the Textile and Garment Industry in Morocco* (in French). Rabat, Morocco: Alliance des Droits des Travailleuses.
Miller, D. 2008. 'The ITGLWF's Policy on Cross-Border Dialogue in the Textiles, Clothing and Footwear Sector: Emerging Strategies in a Sector Rules by Codes of Conduct and Resistant Companies.' Pp. 161–189 in *Cross-Border Social Dialogue and Agreements: An Emerging Global Industrial Relations Framework?*, edited by K. Papadakis. Geneva, Switzerland: International Institute for Labor Studies.

Oxfam International. 2004. *Trading Away Our Rights: Women Working in Global Supply Chains.* Oxford, United Kingdom: Oxfam International.

Pearson, R. and G. Seyfang. 2001. 'New Hope or False Dawn? Voluntary Codes of Conduct, Labor Regulation and Social Policy in a Globalizing World.' *Global Social Policy* 1(1):49–78.

Pfeiffer, T. 2007. 'Zara Owner Lays down Ethics for Moroccan Suppliers.' *Reuters*, 27 June 2007.

Plank, L., A. Rossi, and C. Staritz. 2012. *Workers and Social Upgrading in Fast Fashion: The Case of the Apparel Industry in Morocco and Romania.* Vienna, Austria: Österreichische Forschungsstiftung für Internationale Entwicklung.

Raworth, K. and T. Kidder. 2009. 'Mimicking Lean in Global Value Chains—It's the Workers Who Get Leaned On.' Pp. 165–189 in *Frontiers of Commodity Chain Research*, edited by J. Bair. Stanford, CA: Stanford University Press.

6 From 'No Sweat Shop' Label to Ethical Clothing Australia

Patricia Brien

The Australian textiles, clothing and footwear (TCF) industry is at an inter-esting crossroads, with much production shifting offshore, consistent with the general trends of globalization and trade liberalization described else-where in this volume. However, a significant percentage of garments sold in Australia are still manufactured in the country, and a stubborn 70 percent of those items are made in people's homes. According to Michele O'Neil, the National Secretary of the Textile Clothing & Footwear Union of Aus-tralia (TCFUA), the vast majority of clothing work in Australia is done in workers' homes.[1] The last major study by the TCFUA into the industry was completed in 1995, since which time the number of workers in the formal sector and informal sector has dropped by around half.[2] The TCFUA now estimates the number of homeworkers to be 50,000 in the formal TCF sec-tor and around 150,000 in the informal sector.

Outworkers in Australia have traditionally worked on a piecework rate from their homes, which gives them the flexibility to combine wage work with family responsibilities. They do not have ready access to well-maintained machines and often are not at expert speed levels to gain the rates that factory workers do for the equivalent amount of work. They are only employed on a contract basis, do not receive holiday or sick pay, have poor occupational and safety standards, and are not covered by work-er's compensation insurance (Webber & Weller 2001: 141). According to TCFUA, in Australia the overwhelming majority are migrant women of Asian background—Vietnamese and Chinese predominantly—with poor English language skills. According to Michele O'Neil:

> The trouble is that the actual pay rates for outworkers have been on a downhill slide for many years and $4–5[3] per hour based on the piece work paying system, which is endemic in the area of TCF outwork, is all too normal. There are no overtime weekend rates but rather it is a flat rate way below the industry Award. Too many outworkers have slipped through the net.[4]

In the mid-1990s, when the TCFUA released a report on the *Hidden Cost of Fashion* (1995) as part of a broader National Outwork Information

Campaign, there was much publicity and lobbying by such groups as Fair-Wear and Asian Women at Work, alerting the public to the working conditions of Australian outworkers. This onslaught of publicity culminated in the establishment in 2001 of the joint industry and union initiative The Homeworkers Code of Practice (HWCP), and with it, The No Sweat Shop Label as a visible sign of 'proof' to consumers that a particular garment was made in Australia in compliance with legal rates and conditions.

However, uptake to the voluntary accreditation process has been slow. At the time of writing, there were only 36 signatory companies (and about nine of those came on board within the first six months of 2010, tying in perhaps coincidentally with the ECA rebrand discussed below). The HWCP and No SweatShop Label did not really capture the imagination of the business sector or the broader Australian public. In fact, Diviney and Lillywhite, in their paper *Ethical Threads* (2007), found a general lack of awareness of, or feelings of responsibility for, unethical working conditions of garment workers in Australia and abroad (Fletcher 2008). In addition, there seemed to be little consultation between companies and workers, and apart from a few of the larger companies, no monitoring or evaluation of factory conditions.

Nonetheless, it appears the zeitgeist is shifting, and the change is coming simultaneously from consumers, industry and the government. In May 2008, the Australian government 'committed to provide financial assistance over four years (2008 to 2011) to the Homeworker Code Committee Inc. to support the promotion of Ethical Clothing Australia (ECA) by increasing awareness and voluntary adoption of the accreditation program by businesses.'[5] In 2009, it was decided through consultation with industry and consumers that the existing 'carrot' approach needed to be updated—specifically, the 'No Sweat Shop' label and logo needed to be replaced by something that consumers and industry alike would find more attractive. This situation resulted in a shift from a negative assurance (no sweatshops) to a more affirmative label (ethical production). The inclusion of the term 'Australia' in the new label is further meant to mobilize consumer support for the domestic manufacturing sector.

1 POLICY RECOMMENDATIONS

In September 2008, *Building Innovative Capability*, a review of the TCF Industry in Australia was submitted. The author of this report noted that although 'Australia's TCF industries have a promising future, . . . this can only be achieved through a concerted effort to differentiate their products through uniqueness, product quality and design, branding, quick response and new approaches to supply chain management, with a *clear emphasis on corporate social responsibility in the application of labour and environmental standards* [emphasis added].'[6]

This TCF review contained 15 key recommendations, which were a further encouragement to the aims and specificities of the Homeworkers Code of Practice and its broader relevance within the TCF sector. These included the recommendation of a new Australian Ethical Mark (Conroy 2007) with a budget of AUS$8 million 'to reflect the incorporation of defined ethical standards relating to labour conditions, animal welfare and environmental sustainability. The review also recommended that '[b]etter protection should be provided to workers engaged in home-based manufacture of TCF products through both legislation and industrial awards, and steps should be taken to ensure that homeworkers whose work is performed for a single customer or business are deemed to be employees for the purpose of legislative and other entitlement' (Building Innovative Capability 2008). In essence, the report highlighted that the Australian TCF manufacturing sector must reposition itself for survival in the international arena (Webber & Weller 2001). If consumers and industry perceive the importance of clothing that is made ethically (and sustainably) in Australia, and if production is appropriately regulated, then the implications for Australian fashion and textiles workers are considerable.

2   FORMERLY KNOWN AS THE HOMEWORKERS CODE OF PRACTICE AND NO SWEATSHOP LABEL

The HWCP and No Sweat Shop Label was an initiative set up by union and business organizations and funded by the federal government in an attempt to eliminate the exploitation of textiles and clothing workers in Australia. The HWCP is a voluntary initiative that ensures legal compliance with Australian law. Businesses can participate in three different ways. First, businesses can become retail signatories to the code, which entails twice-yearly disclosure of suppliers of Australian-made products. It is mandatory in New South Wales only, and is also less rigorous than the other parts of the code. Manufacturers also can undergo an accreditation process (Part 2) for garments produced in Australia, which requires a transparent supply chain and award rates and conditions for workers. Becoming accredited with the HWCP was attainable through accreditation under the No Sweat Shop Label. It was the most 'public' face of the initiative.

The third way organizations can participate in the HWCP is by signing the Procurement Code of Practice. Similar to the Retail Code, it deals with organizations that have uniforms made in Australia—for example, sporting clubs, businesses, schools and councils.

3   INDUSTRIAL LAW IN THE AUSTRALIAN TCF INDUSTRY

The Homeworkers Code of Practice is a voluntary mechanism that helps companies comply with Australian law, and awards them for doing so. Annie Delaney (2007: 7) writes that the HWCP worked in conjunction with three different mechanisms that regulate the supply chain and, in particular, outworker's rights. These were The Clothing Trades Award 1999, the before-mentioned Homeworkers Code of Practice 1996 and Homework specific state legislation, for example, the Industrial Relations (Ethical Clothing Trades) Act 2001 (New South Wales) and the Outworkers (Improved Protection) Act 2003 (Victoria).

Under Australian law, outworkers are deemed employees and not contractors, legally entitling them to the same pay and conditions as factory-based workers. To avoid prosecution, any business giving work directly to an outworker must provide all employee entitlements, including superannuation and WorkCover (health insurance).[7] Businesses must also ensure that the contractor is award-compliant, and records of work they give to contractors must be kept, including the amount paid, time given for completion, and details of the complexity of the garment. The award also gives the TCFUA the right to enter workplaces to monitor conditions. While this 'regulatory pyramid' (Marshall 2007)[8] approach with sanctions at the top and more educative approaches at the bottom was set up to protect homeworkers, the reality is that the actual pay rates for outworkers have been on a downhill slide for many years.

4 SOFT LAW OR HARD LAW IN A VELVET GLOVE?

'In order to get companies to trust us, we couldn't be seen as the stick; we had to be seen as the solution' Emer Diviney (ECA National Co-ordinator).

While companies that did not become accredited with the HWCP and No Sweat Shop Label were not necessarily 'shady,' the TCFUA views unregulated production by outworkers as a strategy intended primarily to avoid or circumvent regulation (TCFU 1996). Companies that worked on transparency in their Australian supply chain were fewer than might have been anticipated, and it seems that the success rate of the 'regulatory pyramid' has been limited in cleaning up fashion outworkers' working conditions. Kirton and Trebilcock (2004: 23) consider soft law (voluntary regulation) to be a 'generative or at least permissive way to build the kind of hard law that the world needs, as opposed to a static, stand-alone superior substitute for hard law. Soft law at its best is complementary'. The Australian government, at the beginning of 2010, nationalized the TCF award and maintained its commitment to outworker protection, thus, in many ways, enhancing the role of the 'new' ECA as an easy and inexpensive step for industry to take in making supply chains transparent and compliant. As the director of ECA, Emer Diviney, explained, '[w]e sell ourselves to industry as a resource they can use to comply with regulations.'

So, how does Ethical Clothing Australia sit in terms of hard or soft law? First, it remains a voluntary system initiative designed to help businesses 'navigate the various mandatory legal obligations.' The union continues to have right of entry, and the employer has responsibility for all outworkers in their supply chain; while the processes for retail signatories and businesses gaining accreditation and using the ECA trademark have remained essentially the same, companies that are seeking government contracts in the TCF industry must now be accredited or be seeking accreditation with the Homeworkers' Code of Practice.[9] Self-regulation, it would seem, is the preferred business model.

5 MAKING 'ETHICAL' INTERESTING

Paula Rogers, the industry liaison from the Council of Textile and Fashion Industries of Australia (CTFIA), explains that 'the challenge for ECA is that in terms of ethics and sustainability businesses are still unwilling to come to the party but when they get to the party they find they enjoy it. Retailers need to be pushed into it at some level.'[10] However, it is imperative to find out how a government-funded organization like the HWCP and No Sweat Shop Label can be more essential to business (Harpur 2007). In 2009, research was carried out among TCF companies prior to the rebranding process, with 50 companies—both accredited and non-accredited—asked to participate in the online survey.[11] From the companies that responded, the majority supported the aims of the No Sweatshop Label but felt that the name and logo misrepresented the cause. When analyzed further, it seems that the connotations of 'No' and 'Sweat' were not appropriate for the fashion sector, that it was a negative approach. One respondent said, 'It has negative connotations and using the word 'sweat' does not sit well with designer products.'

Respondents also thought that a more 'neutral' logo like Woolmark or FairTrade might work better because these logos had less 'personality' of their own. The Australian Made logo was thought to be the most successful logo to influence customers at point-of-sale purchases. The Australian Made logo, with its symbolic kangaroo and green and yellow coloring, is likely to trigger responses in consumers that the products are 'Made in Australia, therefore well made.' Brioschi (2006: 204) cites the importance of Country of Origin code as an important factor in communicating brand-quality cues through advertising.

It wasn't only the logo and name that needed work, however. Most respondents thought that more work needed to be done to make consumers aware of the No Sweatshop Label and it purpose; the accreditation process, that is, paperwork, needed to be simplified; and connections to similar international organizations needed to be strengthened. Also, small producers perceived the costs associated with full accreditation to be exorbitant.

6 'NO' TO SWEATSHOPS OR 'YES' TO ETHICAL

Ethical Clothing Australia remains a multistakeholder and not-for profit initiative, and is financed by the Australian federal government, as No

Sweatshop Label was before it. The ECA is overseen by the Homeworkers Code Committee Inc., and current members of the Committee include the Textile Clothing and Footwear Union of Australia (TCFUA), the Council of Textile and Fashion Industries of Australia (CTFIA), New South Wales Business Chamber, the Australian Industry Group (AIG) and accredited business representatives, including Jets Swimwear, Pacific Brands, and Poppets Schoolwear. There is no direct representation from FairWear or Asian Women at Work on the Committee, and perhaps this is an area that needs redressing in the future for it to be a truly multistakeholder initiative. For Diviney, the ECA's current focus firmly rests on 'getting industry to join us.'[12]

Michele O'Neil from the TFCUA sees campaigns like FairWear that are free of government intervention as 'crucial in exposing exploitative workplace situations and in getting companies to change.' O'Neil believes that remaining separate from the ECA Committee is essential so that NGOs like FairWear won't become 'sanitized.' The TCFUA is a member and part of FairWear, and works closely with Asian Women at Work to educate and inform outworkers of their rights under the law, but also works in conjunction with the ECA in its Outworker Outreach program to inform workers of their rights and entitlements and offer English language classes.

To attract business, there is a new fee structure with a sliding scale, thus enabling start-up businesses and young designers an opportunity to have an accredited supply chain for a yearly sum of AUS$300. There are other fee scales, including 'value adding,' such as screen printing, embroidery, laundering, etc., and these vary depending on the number of full-time equivalent workers employed, starting at AUS $400 for small businesses and capped at AUS $2,000 for businesses that employ 41 or more full-time equivalent workers. If the business passes on any 'cut make and trim' work to other businesses, contractors, or individuals, the annual fee can range from AUS $1,000 up to a maximum of $6,000.[13] Paula Rogers, Industry Liaison with the CTFIA, commented:

> . . . the bottom line is that becoming accredited with the ECA means that businesses have better control of their supply chain. Fundamentally industry benefits from having better control of the supply chain and how to manage business; for what ECA is in terms of helping companies to better understand their supply chain, a consulting company hired to do this would cost a lot more.[14]

7   INITIAL REACTIONS

A recent study carried out by graduate students at the School of Fashion and Textiles RMIT in April 2010 found that 50 of 222 survey participants recognized the No Sweat Shop Label, while Ethical Clothing Australia was recognized by 49 of 222 participants (Choksi, Claudine & Pryor 2010). While recognition for both brand identities was fairly low in the sample, the ECA was already at the same level of recognition as the No Sweatshop Label. This may indicate that in its few months of establishment, ECA has already gained a foothold into the awareness of some segments of the Australian fashion-consumer psyche. Obviously, these are very early days.

However, some industry insiders aren't impressed. Just prior to the rebranding of the ECA, Jenni Bannister, who is a fairly well-known Australian fashion designer, quit the trade after a successful career in the fashion limelight for several decades, citing 'a shrunken and traumatised local fashion industry with a thin top layer of companies' such as hers, 'with all the right numbers and all the right paperwork and paying our taxes,' and a thicker, bottom layer of operators: 'oblivious of the [Textile Clothing and Footwear] union regulations, and all cash, no numbers, no papers, just a man with a van.'[15]

On the other hand, larger fashion enterprises like CUE Australia, who has been referred to as 'the largest manufacturer of women's fashion in Australia' have wholly embraced the ECA. CEO David Kesby saw the company's move to gain accreditation with the HWCP and ECA as a 'natural step because we'd been working closely with the TCFUA making sure they were happy with the supply chain. Two-thirds of our offer is Australian made. Our fashion pieces require speed to market and this is what differentiates our brand. We've got many makers who work exclusively with Cue and some have been working for us for thirty years.'[16] He is hopeful that Ethical Clothing Australia will get more notice in the broader consumer market.

Getting the fashion-savvy message out during Australia's two main fashion weeks has been an important part of the ECA's positive image change. The rebranding of the ECA was established only a few months ahead of the L'Oreal Melbourne Fashion Week and the Rosemount Sydney Fashion Festival, and in both cases, ECA had a presence. In Melbourne, ECA held an event during the March fashion week 'Growing Ethical Fashion,' with a specialist panel discussing the problems of sweatshop labor in the industry and the expected rise in demand for ethically produced garments. During the Sydney Fashion Festival, ECA had a stand showcasing the new logo and accredited fashion-forward labels. The reaction was definitely positive, according to Emer Diviney who said that several blog sites and newspaper articles all cast positive reviews of the organization and the fashion-forward emphasis during the fashion weeks.

8 FUTURE POTENTIAL AND SHIFTING SOCIAL PRIORITIES

Support for ethically or sustainably sourced goods has been slower in Australia than in Europe or the United Kingdom. However, Nicholas Bez from the Mobium Group sees eco-friendly and ethical purchases set to rise in Australia in the future. In 2009, the amount spent on sustainable products in six consumer categories including nutrition, mind, body, and home was $AUS19 billion, and it is predicted to rise to $AUS 27 billion in 2011.[17] Most people the Mobium group interviewed wanted to choose the right thing; however, there is a high level of skepticism in Australia, and Bez has attributed this skepticism to problems with the definition of what 'ethical' or 'green' is, but also to issues surrounding independent verification (Arnold 2009).

If the findings by the Mobium group are anything to go by, the Australian consumer will be actively pursuing products that are certified or accredited as eco/ethics-friendly products. Consumers as skeptical as they are in Australia will search out 'certified or accredited' products from reputable sources; if the rebranding of ECA is successfully put 'out there' in the public eye then when people are looking through the 'brand ecosystem lens' (Bergvall 2006: 190), they will know exactly what the ECA label stands for, and it will become a tool for purchasing decisions at point of sale. The new range of swing tags and 'care instruction' labels were to be released into the retail landscape for the spring/summer 2010–2011 collections.

There does appear to be light at the end of the tunnel in terms of a shift in industry attitudes to issues of ethics and sustainability. In May 2010, a discussion paper, the result of an initiative on product safety and safe chemical use by industry, educational institutes, unions, government representatives, and other stakeholders, was released to examine issues around 'inadequate product safety legislation' (CTFIA 2010). Seven key recommendations in the paper may encourage 'better protection for the health of workers and wearers, and deterring the dumping of substandard product in Australia.' This push to tighten up the supply chain for product-safety purposes might well help in ironing out issues related to workers' rights along that supply chain in Australia as well.

There is discussion at this point about where the potential growth areas of a 'successful' ECA rebranding campaign would be. There may well be expansion potential to supply chains internationally, and even an environmental component. However, at the moment, the real task for the ECA is to position the brand in the market as a trusted guarantee of ethical standards and to cultivate an appreciation for the value-added element of having an ethical supply chain in the Australian garment industry. Changes to legislation, an evolution of attitudes toward ethics and sustainability, and a more fashion-friendly branding may be the key factors in making ECA a positive and strong proponent in stamping out exploitation in the fashion industry in Australia. At this stage, the indications are good.

NOTES

1. In the Fair Work Act 2009, "an outworker is a contractor who works in the textile, clothing or footwear industry, or an employee who, for the purpose of business of his/her employer, that works at residential premises (e.g., in their

own home) that would not normally be regarded as being business premises."
http://www.fairwork.gov.au/Pay-leave-and-conditions/Conditions-of-employ
ment/Pages/Outworkers.aspx?role=employers

2. TCFUA (1995) 'The Hidden Cost of Fashion: Report on the National Outwork Information Campaign,' TCFUA, Sydney.
3. The then-current award rate for a Level 3 skilled worker is $AUS 15.68,
Lecture by Molly Williams (Ethical Clothing Australia), 2010.
4. Telephone interview with Michele O'Neil, National Secretary TCFUA, May
2010.
5. http://www.deewr.gov.au/WorkplaceRelations/Programs/Pages/Homework
ersCodeofPracticeProgram.aspx (accessed 9 May 2010).
6. 'Building Innovative Capability: Review of the Australian Textile, Clothing
and Footwear Industries,' Commonwealth of Australia (2008). p viii.
7. http://www.fairwork.gov.au/Pay-leave-and-conditions/Conditions-of-em
ployment/Pages/Outworkers.aspx?role=employers (accessed 10 May 2010)
8. Marshall, S. (2007). Australian Textile Clothing and Footwear Supply Chain
Regulation. In C. Fenwick & T. Novitz (Eds.), *Legal Protection of Workers'
Human Rights: Regulatory Change and Challenge*. Oxford: Hart. (Quoted
in Delaney, 2007)
9. Australian Government, Procurement Statement, July 2009.
10. Conversation with Paula Rogers, industry liaison (CTFIA), in conversation,
May 2010.
11. From a series of interviews with Emer Diviney (former ECA National Coordinator) in May 2010.
12. Interview with Emer Diviney (former ECA National Coordinator), May 2010.
13. http://www.ethicalclothingaustralia.org.au/business/fees-and-discounts (accessed 10 May 2010)
14. Conversation with Paula Rogers, industry liaison (TFIA),, May 2010.
15. Breen Burns, J. (2009) 'Red Tape the Clincher as Fashion Stalwart Closes,'
26 November 2009, *The Age,* Melbourne.
16. Telephone interview with David Kesby CEO of Cue, May 2010.
17. Telephone interview with Nicholas Bez, Mobium Group, May 2010.

REFERENCES

Arnold, C. 2009. *Ethical Marketing and the New Consumer*. Hoboken, NJ: John
Wiley and Sons.
Bergvall, S. 2006. 'Brand Ecosystems: Multilevel Brand Interaction.' Pp. 166–176
in *Brand Culture*, edited by M. Salzer-Morling and J. Schroeder. London, United
Kingdom: Routledge.
Brioschi, A. 2006. 'Selling Dreams.' Pp. 177–188 in *Brand Culture*, edited by
M. Salzer-Morling and J. Schroeder. London, United Kingdom: Routledge.
Choksi, M., N. Claudine, and F. Pryor. 2010. *Ethical Shopping Considerations and
Charity Engagement: Australian Consumer Insights*. School of Fashion and Tex-
tiles, Royal Melbourne Institute of Technology, Melbourne, Australia. Unpub-
lished research.
Commonwealth of Australia. 2008. Building Innovative Capability, Review of the
Australian Textile, Clothing and Footwear Industries. Canberra, Australia: Com-
monwealth of Australia. (http://www.teansw.com.au/Curriculum/Textiles%20
11-12/Resources/401_TCF%20review_vol1.pdf)
Conroy, M. 2007. *Branded!: How the Certification Revolution is Transforming
Global Corporations*. Gabriola Island, Canada: New Society.

Council of Textile and Fashion Industries of Australia. 2010. 'TCF Industry Submission on Product Safety and Safe Chemical Use.' Discussion Paper, Council of Textile and Fashion Industries of Australia, Collingwood, Australia.

Delaney, A. 2007. 'Fair Trade, Corporate Accountability and Beyond: Experiments in Globalising Justice, Corporate Accountability through Community and Unions: Linking Workers and Campaigning to Improving Working Conditions across the Supply Chain.' Retrieved August 4, 2011 (*http://www.celrl.law.unimelb.edu.au/ files/Annie_Delaney_paper.pdf*).

Diviney, E. and S. Lillywhite, S. 2007. *Ethical threads: Corporate Social Responsibility in the Australian Garment Industry*. Melbourne, Australia: Brotherhood of St. Laurence.

Fletcher, K. 2008. *Sustainable Fashion and Textiles: Design Journeys*. London: Earthscan.

Harpur, P.D. 2007. 'Occupational Health and Safety Duties to Protect Outworkers: The Failure of Regulatory Intervention and Calls for Reform.' *Deakin Law Review* 12(2):41–77.

Kirton, J, and M. Trebilcock, eds. 2004. *Hard Choices, Soft Law: Voluntary Standards in Global Trade, Environment and Social Governance*. Surrey, United Kingdom: Ashgate.

Marshall, S. 2007. 'Australian Textile Clothing and Footwear Supply Chain Regulation.' Pp. 555–584 in *Human Rights at Work: Perspectives on Law and Regulation*, edited by C. Fenwick and T. Novitz. Oxford, United Kingdom: Hart.

The Textile, Clothing, and Footwear Union of Australia. 1995. *The Hidden Cost of Fashion: Report on the National Outwork Information Campaign*. Sydney, Australia: The Textile, Clothing and Footwear Union of Australia.

The Textile, Clothing, and Footwear Union of Australia. 1996. *Supplementary Submission of the Textiles Clothing and Footwear Union of Australia to the Inquiry into Outworking in the Garment Industry*. Sydney, Australia: The Textile, Clothing, and Footwear Union of Australia.

Webber, M. and S. Weller. 2001. *Refashioning the Rag Trade: Internationalising Australia's Textiles, Clothing and Footwear Industries*. Sydney, Australia: University of New South Wales Press.

Part III

Consumer and Business Perspectives on Social Labeling

Consumer and Business Perspectives on Social Labeling

7 Identifying and Understanding Ethical Consumer Behavior

Reflections on 15 Years of Research

Marsha A. Dickson

Consumers are key to the development and use of a social label. Fundamental to the theme of this special issue is the assumption that by accessing and acting on information provided on a social label, consumers will seek out and support businesses that ensure that workers' rights are upheld in the production of their goods. A long history of scholarship and activism supports this assumption (Dickinson and Carsky 2005, Lang and Gabriel 2005). Powell (1969) equated consumers with voters, saying that 'Everyone who goes into a shop and chooses one article over another is casting a vote in the economic ballot box' (33). Closely related is the concept of consumer sovereignty, which addresses the idea that, through their purchases, consumers decide what products and services are available in the market—those that are made in sweatshops or those made with respect to workers' rights. Consumers do this by either rewarding companies and purchasing the goods of apparel brands and retailers that act socially responsible or punishing companies by withholding purchasing, sometimes due to organized boycotts (Dickinson and Carsky 2005). These are compelling ideas, but Ross, in Chapter 2, raised questions about whether the concept plays out as assumed, and evidence from research with consumers suggests that a majority of consumers are not putting theory into action in ways that those advocating for social labels would hope.

This chapter reviews research conducted over the last 15 years on what can be termed ethical or socially responsible consumer behavior with the aim of clarifying what has been learned, how the findings can best be interpreted, and how they inform social-labeling strategies and future research. Throughout the chapter, where propositions based on the findings can be made, they are. Most of the literature reviewed focuses specifically on apparel, although a small number of studies on other types of ethical consumer behavior (i.e., related to environmental issues or nonapparel products), as well as theoretical pieces, are drawn upon where relevant. Most research has focused on consumers in the developed countries of Europe and the United States, but recently, new studies extend to consumers in Hong Kong and India. For this chapter, ethical consumer behavior refers to market-related behaviors contributing positively to societal concerns, not solely the concerns of individuals. Ethical consumers are individuals who are 'concerned with the effects that a purchasing choice has, not only on themselves, but also on the external world around them' (Harrison et al. 2005: 2). Ethical purchasing is one aspect of consumer behavior and encompasses 'a broad expression embracing everything from ethical investment (the ethical purchasing of stocks and shares) to the buying of fair-trade products supporting small cooperatives of some of the most disadvantages individuals in developing countries, and from consumer boycotts to corporate environmental purchasing policies' (Harrison et al. 2005: 2).

Consumer behavior, however, is much broader than simply purchasing behavior, involving a variety of prepurchase activities, the purchase itself, and postpurchase behavior, any point at which ethical consumer behavior can take place. Much attention in the research literature has focused on purchasing, since this is where the ultimate decision is made—which product will be purchased, how much of it will be purchased, and from which brand or retailer it will be purchased. Nonetheless, ethical purchasing is but one component of ethical consumer behavior, and it warrants remembering that it is often preceded by prepurchase activities, including the search for information related to possible purchases. Postpurchase behavior includes the use, care, and discard of items, which also have relevance to ethical consumer behavior, especially environmental concerns.[1] At every point of consumer behavior—prepurchase, purchase, and postpurchase—consumers have the potential to support socially responsible business and ethical consumption.

The review of literature is organized around three research streams:

- Research involving self-reported response to simple rating scales on surveys and opinion polls.
- Research that models the relationships between values, attitudes, and other factors that influence ethical purchasing behavior, or at least consumers' intentions to purchase ethically.
- Research incorporating experimental or quasi-experimental methods that allow prediction of how consumers will behave if given the chance or actual behavioral outcomes in specific situations.

In addition to noting important results, in discussing the research in each of these three categories, theoretical foundations and/or methodological limits are highlighted to illuminate their implications to understanding ethical consumer behavior. The chapter concludes with a proposal for a fourth stream of research that could provide the critical next step for galvanizing consumer behavior in support of worker rights.

1   SELF-REPORTED SURVEYS AND OPINION POLLS

Over the last 15 years, numerous surveys and opinion polls using simple rating scales to self-report attitudes and behaviors have identified a large majority of individuals who claim to support socially responsible businesses. A series of widely cited telephone opinion polls conducted in the United States in the mid- to late 1990s by Marymount University found that between 75 and 79 percent of consumers would avoid shopping from retailers that sold garments made in sweatshops, and 83 to 86 percent would pay $1 more for a $20 garment guaranteed to be made in good conditions (Elliott and Freeman 2003). In the late 1990s, a mail survey of a national sample of consumers found that more than 81 percent desired to ban from sale apparel made by child labor and more than 72 percent thought governmental regulations should be in place to protect workers in the apparel industry. More than 76 percent of women surveyed professed interest in a hangtag (social label) on apparel informing them of a company's avoidance of sweatshop production. Yet, only 33 percent of the women indicated they would sacrifice their own requirements for price to avoid purchasing apparel produced in sweatshops (Dickson 1999). Many similar studies have been conducted over the years by market research firms, academic scholars, and others. This is not a comprehensive review of those, especially of studies that are very limited in scope;[2] rather, the focus here is on providing a sampling of findings from the range of studies.

Vogel (2005) in his book *The Market for Virtue* and Fliess et al. (2007) in an Organization for Economic Cooperation and Development report, review a number of polls published from the mid- to late 1990s through the mid-2000s. The findings compiled are fairly similar to what the previously mentioned studies had found, including that consumers would consider a company's commitment to corporate social responsibility when making purchasing decisions (70 percent of Europeans in 2000, 80 percent of British in 2005, and 92 percent of Canadians in 2005), want to specifically know about the conditions of production (64 percent of French in 2000), avoid purchasing products made in poor working conditions (75 percent of U.S. consumers in 1995), and pay more to purchase a product free of child labor (71 percent of French in 1997). Recent polls provide similar results and keep alive the hope that consumer demand for ethical products and socially responsible business actions will lead companies to pursue fair labor standards and safe working conditions for those making their apparel products. For example, a poll conducted by Hertel et al. (2009) found that 62 percent of consumers are willing to pay more for a sweater guaranteed not to be made in a sweatshop.

Taken together, these studies suggest that in the more economically advanced countries, there is relatively strong consumer support for companies assuring production is carried out in appropriate conditions and then marketing clothing based on that fact.[3] This support, however, will only affect companies if it reflects consumers' true buying decisions. Auger and Devinney (2007) caution that 'policy makers should be more careful about jumping to conclusions based solely on evidence from traditional survey instruments' (378). Based on research comparing the findings from a traditional survey with simple Likert-type rating scales replicating the Market &

Opinion Research International (MORI) surveys conducted out of the United Kingdom, and research involving more rigorous methods with constrained choices, Auger and Devinney (2007) concluded that the gap between what consumers say they will do in these polls and what they actually do may be an artifact of the survey instruments used, with much of the research overstating the importance of ethical issues. They contend that more-rigorous methods are needed to determine if indeed consumers would behave ethically. Specifically, Auger and Devinney (2007) explain that, 'The issue we have sought to highlight is that unconstrained survey instruments, the modus operandi of much of the empirical research on ethical consumerism, do not force consumers to reveal their true attitudes or intentions due to inherent weaknesses in survey design and the sensitivity of the issues under investigation' (377). Analyzing the research methods of many studies on consumers and social responsibility, Davis (2012) similarly concludes that 'Insufficient testing for validity, use of unsuitable measures, inadequate research designs or concentration on the small group of ethical consumers have led to a gross misrepresentation of the actual state of affairs' (10).

Seminal research from the field of social psychology supports the assertions made by Auger and Devinney (2007) and Davis (2012) and indicates that with topics having more socially desirable responses,[4] what people *say* they will do typically correlates about 30 percent of the time with what they will *actually do* (LaPiere 1934*)*. Since LaPiere (1934) carried out his study of U.S. innkeepers and their claimed attitudes and subsequent behavior when it came to accommodating Chinese guests, an extensive body of research has aimed at understanding the limited link between attitudes and behaviors and exploring ways to more accurately predict behaviors. Advances have been made, particularly with the discovery of the utility in measuring behavioral intentions instead of self-reported behaviors (Ajzen and Fishbein 1980). Additionally, studies have demonstrated that misleading information will be obtained by measuring attitudes and behaviors in vague or ambiguous ways that are inconsistent or unrestrained regarding their target, context, time and action (Ajzen and Fishbein 1980, Auger and Devinney 2007, Hill 1990). Attitudes and behaviors that are not measured consistently with each other have only low-to-moderate correlation (Hill 1990).

Applying this knowledge to the surveys previously described, it is easy to anticipate that the answer to 'would you pay $20 more for a garment not made in a sweatshop?' would likely be very different from the answer to 'would you pay $20 more for an Easter dress for your eight-year old daughter when shopping tomorrow?'. Any number of conditions could interfere with the intentions to buy the latter product, including that the young daughter is likely growing quickly and will get only limited wear from the garment, making the extra $20 more significant. Thus, while providing seemingly compelling statistics about consumer demand for socially responsible apparel production, a proposition related to knowledge gained from this type of research is as follows.

Proposition 1. Opinion polls and surveys relying on simple rating scales and unrestrained scenarios provide little true understanding of what consumers will actually do in support of improved working conditions; instead, they reflect little more than consumer recognition of some issues they *ought* to be thinking about when purchasing clothing.

To improve the validity of descriptive studies of consumer attitudes and opinions, future research could incorporate more-advanced methods requiring greater concurrence in results or more investigation of individuals' claims.[5] For example, Auger et al. (2007) used an innovative survey method that forced consumers from the United States, Germany, Spain, Turkey, India and South Korea to choose issues that were most and least important across a number of choices. Four issues were consistently rated highly—human rights, child labor, safe working conditions and good living conditions (i.e., dormitory housing for workers). From their more-rigorous survey, the authors had the confidence to suggest, 'that some universal beliefs about social issues do exist with respect to human and certain worker rights' (318). Likewise, Hertel et al. (2009), after carefully examining the correlations between self-reported willingness to pay $5 more for a $20 sweater and attitudes on human rights, were able to determine that it is actually whites with lower levels of education and those under 60 years of age who are willing to do so, and that the willingness is connected with the belief that a minimum standard of living is a human right.

2   MODELING VALUES, ATTITUDES, AND OTHER FACTORS INFLUENCING BEHAVIORS

A second stream of research on ethical consumer behavior involves modeling the relationships between factors that influence behaviors. It is helpful to begin with background in social psychological theory, including the difference between values, attitudes and behaviors. Values are principles that individuals use to assess situations and form social and ideological positions (Smith 1982). They can be classified in a variety of different ways based on whether they reflect desired end states (e.g., 'a world at peace') or a means of achieving those (e.g., 'loving'). Likewise, they can be classified on the extent they reflect individual concerns (e.g., an exciting life) or larger societal concerns (e.g., equality). Not every value is tapped for every situation encountered, but because they are centrally held and not easily changed, they provide a steady influence on an individual's attitudes and behaviors (Munson 1984, Rokeach 1973). Values, along with an individual's beliefs, knowledge and personal characteristics, provide a base from which attitudes are formed (Ajzen and Fishbein 1980, Hill 1990, Rokeach 1973, Smith 1982). As compared with values, attitudes are more specifically focused on objects or situations; it is easier for them to be changed (Smith 1982). Attitudes

126   *Marsha A. Dickson*

themselves have a continuum from less to more specificity, which also influences their relationships to behaviors (Hill 1990, Smith 1982).

Behaviors are quite simply what people do. Because it is difficult to obtain data on actual behaviors while still retaining the control necessary to isolate the factors influencing them, behavioral intentions are used as an indicator of future behaviors (Ajzen and Fishbein 1980). The predominant thinking of many social psychologists is that fairly abstract and general values influence more specific attitudes, which in turn influence behavior; thus, attitudes more specific to a given behavior are better predictors of that behavior than are more general attitudes (Ajzen and Fishbein 1980, Hill 1990). These relationships are reflected in behavioral models, including Ajzen and Fishbein's (1980) model of behavioral intention, also referred to as the theory of reasoned action, and the theory of planned behavior (Ajzen 1991). The theory of reasoned action illustrates the distinction between behaviors and behavioral intentions; the cause of behavior is the behavioral intention, and a number of situational factors in the context of specific behaviors may not make them possible, despite the intentions to act in a particular way. Behavioral intentions are a function of attitude toward a specific behavior or object and norms placed by important others (subjective norm, Fishbein and Ajzen 1975). The theory of reasoned action is commonly used and has been successful at predicting a great variety of behaviors (see Ajzen 1991), but some researchers have continued to experiment by adding additional variables in hopes of better predicting behavior or behavioral intention. Ajzen's (1991) theory of planned behavior expands the theory of reasoned action to include the variable of perceived behavioral control.

Some of the first studies examining relationships between variables associated with ethical consumer behavior focused on fair-trade consumers and those considering purchasing from the U.S. Department of Labor's Trendsetter list of companies voluntarily agreeing to monitor and remediate violations of labor laws found in apparel factories. Survey methods and a variety of statistical techniques (i.e., path analysis, discriminant analysis, and structural equation modeling) were used to examine the influence of, and relationships between, values, attitudes (i.e., support for socially responsible business or fair trade, concern about fair-trade or apparel manufacturing workers, beliefs about conditions workers faced, level of perceived knowledge about working conditions, and attitudes about the apparel products), and consumer purchase intentions (Dickson 2000, Dickson and Littrell 1996, 1997, Kim et al. 1999). A later study examined similar variables in relationship to use of a 'no sweat' label guaranteeing that apparel was made under good working conditions (Dickson 2001, 2005). Recent studies extend support for these findings to university students and consumers in Hong Kong and India. While limited in its inclusion of students from a single university, one study used structural-equation modeling to further examine the role of beliefs about social issues faced when manufacturing university logo apparel, concern for workers, and support for socially responsible business practices have on willingness to pay 5 to 20 percent more for the licensed apparel products (Pookulangara et al. 2011). A survey of shoppers in Hong Kong department stores found that concern, knowledge and beliefs about sweatshops positively influenced support for socially responsible business, and that support was associated with an increased willingness to pay a premium for garments made under socially responsible conditions (Shen et al. 2012). A flurry of recent qualitative studies claim to provide new knowledge on what factors interfere between attitudes/behavioral intentions and ethical consumer behavior (Bhaduri and Ha-Brookshire 2011, Bray et al. 2010, Oberseder et al. 2011, online first), but all rely on very small samples representing only narrow groups of consumers and make limited connections between their findings and previous research.[6]

Studies examining whether support for socially responsible businesses and business practices influenced an intended ethical consumer behavior have varied in their findings. This type of support was significant in distinguishing consumers who had actually purchased clothing from nonpurchasers for one fair-trade organization (Dickson and Littrell 1997) and users of a no-sweat label from nonusers in consideration of purchasing a shirt (Dickson 2001). It was also positively related to intentions to purchase from another fair-trade organization (Kim et al. 1999) with university students' and Hong Kong shoppers' willingness to pay more for non-sweatshop-made apparel products (Pookulangara et al. 2011, Shen et al. 2012). However, in the fair-trade study conducted by Dickson and Littrell, a second analysis revealed that support for socially responsible business was not directly related to intentions to purchase the fair-trade organization's clothing, although it was influential to attitudes about the clothing itself and the willingness to make potential purchasing sacrifices (Dickson and Littrell 1996). Support for socially responsible business did not influence the intentions to purchase jeans from the Trendsetters (Dickson 2000). Yet, given the findings that support was clearly related to actual behaviors or those identified in an experiment, the following proposition is asserted.

Proposition 2. Support for socially responsible business practices differentiates ethical consumers from those pursuing less ethical consumer behaviors.

Every study examining the relationship between concern about workers and the issues they face has found a positive relationship with support for socially responsible business and business practices, including purchase intentions and willingness to pay more for apparel products made under socially responsible conditions (Dickson 2000, 2001, Dickson and Littrell 1996, 1997, Kim et al. 1999, Pookulangara et al. 2011, Shen et al. 2012). Therefore, the following proposition is extended.

Proposition 3. Concern for workers is influential to ethical purchasing behavior.

Beliefs about issues associated with life in a developing country supported by fair trade have been found to be related to concern for fair-trade workers—the more consumers agreed that the workers faced issues regarding access to housing, basic education, adequate job, freedom of political expression, and other issues, the greater their support for fair trade (Dickson and Littrell 1996). Furthermore, these beliefs distinguished purchasers of fair-trade clothing and other products from nonpurchasers (Dickson and Littrell 1997). Similarly, the worse off consumers thought the working conditions were in foreign apparel-manufacturing facilities (i.e., wages, working hours, health and safety and use of child labor), the more supportive they were of socially responsible business (Dickson 2000, Pookulangara et al. 2011). While consumers' beliefs about these issues did not distinguish no-sweat-label users from nonusers, all the consumers in that survey agreed that the conditions were poor (Dickson 2001). Dickson (2000) also found beliefs about these issues to be negatively associated with an attitude of suspicion among jeans purchasers; the more negatively consumers perceived working conditions at foreign sites, the more likely they were to doubt the sincerity of business claims for social responsibility and agree that government regulations were needed. Indian consumers also raised concerns about trust, questioning whether businesses would actually use money from higher prices earned for social responsibility to benefit workers (Gupta and Hodges 2012).

Measuring these relatively specific beliefs about issues workers face seems to be more useful than general statements of how knowledgeable consumers are about the issues. The latter type of measure was positively associated with concern for workers (Dickson 2000), negatively associated with support for socially responsible business (Pookulangara et al. 2011), and not significant for distinguishing no-sweat-label users from nonusers (Dickson 2001). Yet, a recent qualitative study of a convenience sample of consumers in India, many of whom had experience working in the apparel industry, found that awareness of socially responsible business was associated with statements of support for those businesses and willingness to pay more for products made by these firms (Gupta and Hodges 2012). Additionally, personal travel experience in Latin American countries supported by one fair-trade organization's efforts distinguished purchasers from the fair-trade organization from nonpurchasers (Dickson and Littrell 1997). Two propositions about beliefs and knowledge are warranted.

Proposition 4. Consumer beliefs about issues workers face are more influential to ethical consumer behavior than the level of knowledge they might have.
Proposition 5. Direct personal experience with the relevant issues has a significant influence on ethical consumer behavior.

In the study of intentions to purchase jeans from Trendsetters, the influences of knowledge, belief, and concern about social issues, and support for socially responsible business practices, were not related to purchase intentions; the only factors related to those were past purchase of the brand (i.e., brand/store loyalty) and the desire for fashionable styles and colors (Dickson 2000). Likewise, for the majority of consumers considering purchase of a dress shirt, product attributes such as quality or price were more influential than the label in determining purchase likelihood (Dickson 2001). The early research on fair-trade consumer behavior identified the importance of having the right product; quality of a fair-trade organization's clothing was the variable most distinguishing consumers who bought clothing from those who did not (Dickson and Littrell 1997). Furthermore, attitude about the clothing products, derived from detailed assessment of quality and aesthetic attributes, was influential to fair-trade purchase intentions (Dickson and Littrell 1996).[7] Similarly, in a study interviewing consumers who buy from Gap, Inc. in Scotland, Ivanow et al. (2005) found that, despite being highly aware of ethical issues, consumers were more influenced by price, quality and style than with issues of social responsibility, including child labor, when purchasing apparel. Likewise, while Indian consumers believe that socially responsible business is important, they admit their purchase decisions and willingness to pay price premiums are more heavily influenced by price and quality (Gupta and Hodges 2012). However, unlike studies focused on apparel from mainstream companies, fair-trade consumers' willingness to sacrifice some desired product characteristics was positively related to intentions to purchase fair-trade clothing (Dickson and Littrell 1996).

Paharia and Deshpande (2009) shed light on the role of the product itself, as compared to variables associated with social issues and ethical business practices. Particularly, the authors provided a possible explanation for why consumers who seemingly cared about the conditions in which apparel was manufactured actually downplayed those concerns when products were highly desirable for other reasons. In experiments controlling product desirability, sweatshop labor conditions, and perceptions about brand use of sweatshop labor, the authors found that consumers increased their rationalization of sweatshop conditions (i.e., moral disengagement) when the product was highly desirable but made in sweatshop conditions or by a brand believed to use sweatshops.[8] Another indication of moral disengagement was reported by Dickson (2005) in qualitative findings from a survey of consumers' potential use of a 'no sweat' label. When asked to explain their intention to purchase a garment guaranteed not to be made in a sweatshop, several took the opportunity to explain why they would likely not follow through due to lack of information or other priorities (e.g., price). Given the importance of the product, it is valuable to consider Carrington et al.'s (2010) proposal that the 'proximity of competing products and accessible price comparison' (149) in the shopping environment may facilitate or hinder consumer intentions being translated into ethical purchasing. The research incorporating product characteristics as a factor leads to the following proposition.

> Proposition 6. The characteristics of apparel products being considered for purchase play a significant role in ethical consumer behavior.

While additional research has examined a few other variables and their possible influence and relationships, the discussion above covers the dominant ideas that have emerged over the last 10 plus years. It is beneficial to remember that the value of this type of modeling research is for its ability to identify the triggers for various attitudes and behaviors. By understanding the relationships between various attitudes and behaviors, it is possible to develop strategies for changing them. Specifically, these types of studies provide understanding of

- the various social-psychological influencers of ethical consumer behavior;
- the critical importance of offering apparel products that meet consumer demands for quality, price, aesthetics, and other features;
- how situational factors in the shopping environment, including availability of information during the prepurchase stage, will interfere with carrying out intended ethical behavior;
- and ultimately, what aspects of consumers' beliefs and attitudes might be manipulated to influence desired changes in behavior.

It would be beneficial to conduct additional modeling research to identify the role and best measurement of beliefs about issues, perceived knowledge and prior experience. Two recent manuscripts suggest ideas that could be researched in the future. Carrington et al. (2010) discuss a theoretical concept with the potential to explain, at least partially, the gap between behavioral intentions and ethical consumer behavior. Without 'implementation intentions,' whereby individuals form a plan of action, their intentions to behave may be inadequate to navigate the complexity of carrying out the intended behavior. For example, the authors contend that individuals who have decided to pursue a new behavior, such as purchasing ethical products, may forget to do so or may not know how to go about carrying out their intentions; they may simply not realize how difficult it will be to carry out their intentions to purchase ethically (Carrington et al. 2010).[9] Similarly, Oberseder et al. (2011) studied the process in which consumers utilize perceptions about corporate social-responsibility (CSR) initiatives in making decisions, having the 22 consumers interviewed in Western Europe discuss these in relationship to past purchases.[10] In focusing on process, the authors identified core factors that must be met if consumers will consider CSR issues in purchasing, factors including having information about the company's CSR position and being concerned about those issues. Once these conditions are met, additional factors central to moving forward are having the financial means and willingness to spend based on a company's CSR initiatives. Finally, peripheral factors come into play after core and central factors are met; these involve whether the CSR initiatives are credible by being aligned with the core business and not overcommunicated, and the influence of peer groups (Oberseder et al. 2011). Furthermore, Hyllegard et al. (2012) found that consumers evaluated hang tags containing information about labor practices more favorably when they reported making socially responsible purchase decisions in the past. While many of the factors presented as influential to carrying out ethical consumer behavior are not new, the process with which they are integrated into decision-making is worthy of further consideration.[11]

3   EXPERIMENTAL STUDIES OF BEHAVIOR

A third type of research on ethical apparel-consumer behavior can be classified as experimental or quasi-experimental, and it includes studies that allow us to see how consumers will behave—at least in controlled settings. These studies are invaluable to consideration of a social-labeling initiative because they provide a more valid understanding of the potential market for ethical fashion. A quasi-experimental study examined the potential use of a 'no sweat' label by consumers who were faced with the possibility of needing to trade off important attributes such as price, quality and others.[12] Consumers were asked to rate the likelihood of purchasing eight different shirts that were experimentally varied on key product attributes, including a label indicating that some of the shirts were not made in sweatshops. Rather than directly asking consumers about each of the attributes and potentially overinflating claims about the importance of the label, a statistical technique called 'conjoint analysis' enabled identification of those attributes most influential to the ratings of purchase intentions. For the majority of consumers, the no-sweat label was not prioritized as highly as price, quality, fiber content and other attributes. Yet about 16 percent did prioritize the no-sweat label over any product attribute when indicating purchase likelihoods (Dickson 2001). Obviously, this is a much smaller ethical consumer market than opinion polls have identified.

Using related quasi-experimental techniques, Auger et al. (2003) were able to calculate the dollar value of various product and ethical attributes in the hypothetical purchase of athletic shoes. Not surprisingly, the highest value came from the fit attribute—consumers would pay $14.49 for shoes that fit. But, the next attributes with the highest value to consumers were a variety of ethical attributes rather than ones increasing the function of the shoes, such as shock absorbers. While not directly observing actual consumer behavior, by using advanced methods to uncover factors influential to a series of constrained choices, both the Dickson (2001, 2005) and Auger et al. (2003) studies provide consumers with situations similar to what they would encounter when shopping and make choosing the 'correct' (i.e., most socially desirable) answer more difficult.

A more recent experimental study took rigor but also artificiality a step further by obtaining behavioral data through experimental auctions. Hustvedt and Bernard (2010) auctioned T-shirts labeled as being either (a) made in a factory that complies with international labor laws, (b) made in a factory that is independently inspected for compliance to international labor laws, (c) made in a factory that has an independent trade union, or (d) labeled with one of three more ambiguous terms: living wage, 100 percent union made, or sweatshop free. With the auction technique, researchers were able to determine a dollar amount for consumer willingness to pay, thus the findings are a vast improvement over surveys simply asking consumers if they would pay a certain dollar or percentage amount more. The study found that consumers who believed in social responsibility and fair trade were willing to pay extra for products labeled with information about labor conditions, regardless of whether the information provided was relatively vague/ambiguous or in contrast was more explicit and extensive. When recognizable brand names were added to the information provided consumers, willingness to pay increased even more, though there was no significant increase in willingness to pay for a brand with which few participants were familiar. The T-shirts varied in color, neck style and fabric weight; color was important, but not more so than the labor-related attributes, suggesting that all things being equal in terms of style, labor-related attributes would determine the purchasing outcome. Yet another experimental study focused on how consumers perceive the quality of message content, particularly the level of detail provided and the effect of a presumably credible third party being named on the label. Hang tags containing information about the use of fair labor practices were more favorably evaluated when they were more explicit and included the logo of a third party (Hyllegard et al. 2012). However, the study included message content that many apparel brands might refuse to adopt because of its absolute 'guarantee.' Specifically, the message stated that 'Fair labor practices were used in the manufacture of this garment. *No* exploitative labor practices including sweatshops, unfair wages or child labor were used to make this garment' (Hyllegard et al. 2012: 57, emphasis added). The value of a third party's endorsement of a company's labor practices was further supported in another experimental study involving university students who more greatly valued information about one apparel company's practices when it was delivered through a television news magazine instead of the company's own advertisements (Yan et al. 2010).

Uncertainties remain about the extent consumers would use a hang tag or advertisements to inform their purchase decisions. The findings of these studies more likely indicate consumers' desire for reassurance and simple answers rather than information about the complex reality of social responsibility and worker rights. The apparent consumer support for vague claims or ones that may be difficult if not impossible to support lead to this proposal:

> Proposition 7. There is need for governmental regulation of labeling to assure that information provided is credible and is supported with due diligence and independent verification.

A final experiment conducted in an actual retail setting combats problems with narrow/artificial settings, but creates a loss of control over situational factors potentially influencing behavior. Hiscox and Smyth (n.d.) carried out an experiment manipulating the labeling and price of towels offered for sale in the ABC Carpet and Home retail store in New York City. Sales of towels labeled as being made 'under fair labor conditions, in a safe and healthy working environment which is free of discrimination, and where management has committed to respecting the rights and dignity of workers' were measured (10). Consumer purchases of the towels increased after prices were increased 10 to 20 percent and labels were manipulated to reflect good working conditions.[13] Despite loss of some control, the results provided from this type of experiment will probably have the most influence on persuading other brands and retailers to attempt marketing products assured to be made under fair labor standards and good working conditions. As Robinson et al. propose in the following chapter, it may indeed be the market's failure to provide apparel that allows consumers to purchase ethical products that has led to their presumed disinterest in actually carrying out their claims. The next section of this paper proposes a fourth stream of research that builds upon the type of study conducted by Hiscox and Smyth (n.d.) but that aims to increase ethical consumer behavior.

4   TRANSFORMING ETHICAL CONSUMER BEHAVIOR WITH ACTION RESEARCH

Opinion polls and surveys of consumer attitudes have promised a large market that expects socially responsible business practices, yet more rigorous studies have suggested that the market of ethical consumers is much smaller. Questions about the market for ethical apparel have undoubtedly influenced brands and retailers that may have considered marketing their products as ethical, but that have decided that currently, the costs of ensuring an accurate label outweigh the benefits of increased sales. Despite the fact, brands and retailers have a responsibility to respect human rights, even when their consumers do not demand it (Ruggie 2008), many are driven by avoidance of risk (i.e., what is the minimum I have to do to stay out of trouble?) rather than taking a human rights approach to their global supply chains where there is work to be done if rights of workers have not been upheld.[14] Thus, it would be helpful if a clear ethical consumer market existed.

The research described here has unfolded over a 15-year period, accentuating that academic research is slow. It takes considerable time for academic studies to be conducted, for results to be published, and for additional research to build incrementally upon previous studies. Undoubtedly, the traditional academic research that has been done and will be done on ethical consumer behavior is important, but we need quicker action. As the years have passed while studies are carried out, workers have continued to be exploited and denied their rights, and brands and retailers, for the most part, have continued to hesitate to compete in a 'race to the top' for sales based on social responsibility. Consumer researchers, brands and retailers, and other stakeholders need to combine efforts in developing action research aimed at transforming consumer behavior. Bold steps are needed to conduct research that will *create and expand* markets for products that are made by workers whose rights are supported.

There is a somewhat new area of inquiry in consumer research termed 'transformative consumer research, (which) benefits consumer welfare and quality of life for all beings affected by consumption across the world.'[15] Transformative consumer research is related to action research, long conducted in the educational field but increasingly being pursued by activist scholars.[16] Action research is conducted in partnership with relevant stakeholders who are involved in the design and assessment of the research; an aim is to design interventions that create change, and, because of assessment and reflection, the researcher is able to determine the extent of change and the success of the intervention (Bradbury-Huang 2010). Action research is ideal for the present situation, where academic research has been slow to produced findings that compel brands and retailers to action because it pursues action and research at the same time. As explained by Learning for Sustainability in discussing action research, 'The focus is action to improve a situation and the research is the conscious effort, as part of the process, to formulate public knowledge that adds to theories of action that promote or inhibit learning in behavioural systems.'[17]

Adopting an action-research approach to ethical consumer behavior has the potential to make quick and significant improvements for workers toiling in the garment industry. What would this approach look like? Dickinson and Carsky (2005) argue that the action research might take an educational approach, stating that:

> teaching individual members of society that they should be responsible for the consequences of their action, if such consequences could be reasonably and steadily ascertained, should be integral to various levels of education . . . educators should be enlisted in an attempt to change the values and assumptions underlying the dominant approach in the

USA and in much of the developed world with respect to consumer purchasing (31).

Specific to ethical consumer behavior, there are a variety of ways that action research could focus on creating transformational experiences for consumers in both developed and developing countries.

- Building on the area of research on knowledge and beliefs about social issues impacting workers, there could be field-based experiments attempting to increase the knowledge or the salience of consumer beliefs and assessing the results of those experiments, including whether consumers in developing country (and garment producing) markets respond differently from those in developed countries,.
- In collaboration with brands or retailers, marketing campaigns could be developed, implemented and assessed, drawing on previously identified relationships between values, attitudes, and other factors that influence ethical or socially responsible purchasing behavior, while tracking potentially differing effects on consumers in developed and developing countries.
- Researchers skilled in designing experimental studies could engage with apparel brands and retailers in testing various labels for products made under socially responsible conditions. And, if early results suggest sales are promising, perhaps the companies can ramp up orders for these products, just as they would for the hot styles of the season, thus showing clear rewards to suppliers for their responsible actions.
- Researchers collaborating with brands and suppliers could test strategies for genuinely raising the wages of workers, not simply raising the price paid for those goods. This would allow comparative analysis of the merits of costing products appropriately for covering the needs of workers, instead of relying on consumer altruism to pay a premium, such as with the fair-trade model described in Chapter 11.

The Hiscox and Smyth study described earlier in this chapter resembles action research but without the focus on consumer education. Perhaps the positive findings from their study could be extended by having an informed sales associate talk with a subset of consumers about the social responsibility program as they consider the labeled and unlabeled products, then measuring whether this increased sales of the labeled products even further. Other chapters in this issue, when read from an action-research perspective, surely provide additional ideas for research that will make a difference. From the various disciplinary and practitioner vantages included here, we can together identify ways to creatively transform consumer behavior in support of worker rights, whether it be through action research with consumers or by constructing the necessary policies to support ethical consumer behavior.

NOTES

1. At the post-purchase stage of consumer behavior, consumers make determinations about a product's usefulness that impact whether they will wear a garment again and again or quickly discard it for a more serviceable item—one that is perhaps more fashionable, more durable, or more useful to the consumer's lifestyle. At the post-purchase stage, consumers also decide the best way to care for garments—for example, with dry cleaning or machine washing, line drying, etc. They also determine where the garment will go when it is discarded—with household waste headed for a landfill, or perhaps as a donation to an organization that will resell the garment or sort it into materials to be reprocessed as rags, recycled or donated for use by needy people in developing countries.

2. See, for example, Kozar and Hiller Connell (2010), a study that includes only a small sample of students from a single university pursuing degrees in the apparel field.

3. The assumption that companies wish to determine ways to market to segments of ethical consumers may simply be an academic assumption or apply only to entrepreneurial startups that have no idea what it would require to actually produce clothing warranting a social label. For example, I have counseled potential business entrepreneurs that they really cannot promote their products as fair trade without knowing what is expected of fair-trade organizations and that ethical fashion requires more than simply consulting a list of factories or a list of materials that are approved for use.

4. Social desirability relates to the condition where respondents want to give the 'right' response or the one that reflects most positively on them. Auger and Devinney (2007) assert that simple rating scales have social desirability issues because of 'the lack of any penalty for not revealing the "truth"' (363).

5. Auger and Devinney (2007) found illogical relationships in their correlation of responses to simple survey items with more constrained measures.

6. For example, Bhaduri and Ha-Brookshire (2011), in their interviews with 13 consumers who work at a single university, along with Bray et al. (2010) in their focus groups with 18 U.K. consumers 'discovered' that price and product quality interfere with ethical consumer behavior.

7. Note that another manuscript from the study provides product development information that could be used to increase sales of the fair-trade organization's products (see Dickson and Littrell, 1998).

8. Paharia, N. and Deshpande, R. (2009) Sweatshop labor is wrong unless the jeans are cute: Motivated moral disengagement. Working paper 09–079 downloaded from the Harvard Business School on September 5, 2011: http://www.people.fas.harvard.edu/~hiscox/Peharia.pdf.

9. Although not making the connection, Carrington et al. make similar assertions to the heavily cited work of Fishbein and Ajzen (1975) in their theory of reasoned action, which explains that individuals may lack the skills, resources, or opportunities to act on their behavioral intentions and that behaviors must be under the control of the individual to act on if attitudes and behavioral intentions are to predict them.

10. This approach may be valuable given the assertion of Auger and Devinney (2007) that past behavior is a better predictor of future behavior than are simple unconstrained rating scales.

11. Credibility of a company's CSR initiatives would likely be related to cynicism (see Bray et al. 2010) and trust (see Bhaduri and Ha-Brookshire); yet, as will be shown in the next section of this paper, trust appears to be a questionable

factor for explaining ethical consumer behavior given the perhaps unde-served trust given to ambiguous claims (see Hustvedt and Bernard 2010). Research on knowledge and concern has been discussed earlier in this chap-ter. The influence of peer groups is similar to the subjective norm concept included in Ajzen and Fishbein's Model of Behavioral Intentions (1980) and has been shown to be insignificant, after accounting for personal norms such as self-identity as an ethical consumer and perceived obligation to purchase ethically among fair-trade grocery consumers (Shaw et al. 2000) and organic-clothing consumers (Hustvedt and Dickson 2009).

12. Quasi-experimental studies have characteristics of controlled experiments without the artificiality of a lab setting.

13. Unpublished manuscript by Hiscox and Smyth (n.d.) downloaded from http://www.people.fas.harvard.edu/~hiscox/SocialLabeling.pdf on September 5, 2011. The authors did not explicitly point out, however, that the largest volume of sales for the store's towels were from unlabeled products.

14. Dickson, M.A. 'The growing gap within CSR in the apparel industry,' a paper presented in the "Prospects for the industry's recovery and opportu-nities for labour standards' session of the Fair Labour Organization's Stake-holder Forum, Washington, D.C., June 25, 2009 and Dickson, M.A. 'Social responsibility in the global apparel industry,' invited presentation to industry professionals in corporate social responsibility, hosted by Phillips-van Heu-sen Corporation, New York, NY, April 16, 2009.

15. See http://www.acrwebsite.org.

16. See Hurley, J., A. Hale, and J. Smith (2003) 'Action research on garment industry supply chains: Some guidelines for activists,' published by Women Working Worldwide and available online at http://www.women-ww.org/doc uments/www_action_research.pdf.

17. See http://learningforsustainability.net/research/action_research.php.

REFERENCES

Ajzen, I. 1991. 'The Theory of Planned Behavior.' *Organizational Behavior and Human Decision Process* 50(2):179–211.

Ajzen, I. and M. Fishbein. 1980. *Understanding Attitudes and Predicting Social Be-havior.* Englewood Cliffs, NJ: Prentice-Hall.

Auger, P., P. Burke, T. M. Devinney, and J. J. Louviere. 2003. 'What Will Consumers Pay for Social Product Features?' *Journal of Business Ethics* 42(3):281–304.

Auger, P. and T. M. Devinney. 2007. 'Do What Consumers Say Matter? The Mis-alignment of Preferences with Unconstrained Ethical Intentions.' *Journal of Busi-ness Ethics* 76(4): 361–383.

Auger, P., T. M. Devinney, and J. J. Louviere. 2007. 'Using Best-Worst Scaling Meth-odology to Investigate Consumer Ethical Beliefs across Countries.' *Journal of Business Ethics* 70(3): 299–326.

Bhaduri, G. and J. E. Ha-Brookshire. 2011. 'Do Transparent Business Practices Pay? Exploration of Transparency and Consumer Purchase Intention.' *Clothing and Textiles Research Journal* 29(2):135–149.

Bradbury-Huang, H. 2010. 'What is Good Action Research?: Why the Resurgent Interest?' *Action Research* 8(1):93–109.

Bray, J., N. Johns, and D. Kilburn. 2010. 'An Exploratory Study into the Factors Impeding Ethical Consumption.' *Journal of Business Ethics* 98(4):597–608.

Carrington, M. J., B. A. Neville, and G. J. Whitwell. 2010. 'Why Ethical Consum-ers Don't Walk Their Talk: Towards a Framework for Understanding the Gap between the Ethical Purchase Intentions and Actual Buying Behaviour of Ethically Minded Consumers.' *Journal of Business Ethics* 97(1):139–158.

Davis, I. 2012. 'How (Not) to Market Socially Responsible Products: A Critical Research Evaluation.' *Journal of Marketing Communications* doi: 10.1080/1352 7266.2012.696076.

Dickinson, R. A. and M. L. Carsky. 2005. 'The Consumer as Economic Voter.' Pp. 25–39 in *The Ethical Consumer*, edited by R. Harrison, T. Newholm, and D. Shaw. Thousand Oaks, CA: Sage.

Dickson, M. A. 1999. 'U.S. Consumers' Knowledge of and Concern for Apparel Sweatshops.' *Journal of Fashion Marketing and Management* 3(1):44–55.

Dickson, M. A. 2000. 'Personal Values, Beliefs, Knowledge, and Attitudes Relating to Intentions to Purchase Apparel from Socially Responsible Businesses.' *Clothing and Textiles Research Journal* 18(1):19–30.

Dickson, M. A. 2001. 'Utility of No Sweat Labels for Apparel Consumers: Profiling Label-Users and Predicting Their Purchases.' *Journal of Consumer Affairs* 35(1):96–119.

Dickson, M. A. 2005. 'Identifying and Profiling Apparel Label Users. Pp. 155–171 in *The Ethical Consumer*, edited by R. Harrison, T. Newholm, and D. Shaw. Thousand Oaks, CA: Sage.

Dickson, M. A. and M. A. Littrell. 1996. 'Socially Responsible Behaviour: Values and Attitudes of the Alternative Trading Organisation Consumer.' *Journal of Fashion Marketing and Management* 1(1):50–69.

Dickson, M. A. and M. A. Littrell. 1997. 'Consumers of Clothing from Alternative Trading Organizations: Societal Attitudes and Purchase Evaluative Criteria.' *Clothing and Textiles Research Journal* 15(1):20–33.

Dickson, M. A. and M. A. Littrell. 1998. 'Consumers of Ethnic Apparel from Alternative Trading Organizations: A Multifaceted Market.' *Clothing and Textiles Research Journal* 16(1):1–10.

Elliot, K. A. and R. B. Freeman. 2003. *Can Labor Standards Improve under Globalization?* Washington, D.C.: Institute for International Economics.

Fishbein, M. and I. Ajzen 1975. *Belief, Attitude, Intention, and Behavior: An Introduction to Theory and Research*. Reading, MA: Addison-Wesley.

Fliess, B., O. C. Agatiello, O. L. Dubruil, and H-J. Lee. 2007. 'CSR and Trade: Informing Consumers about Social and Environmental Conditions of Globalised Production.' Working Paper No. 47, Organization for Economic Co-operation and Development, Paris, France.

Gupta, M. and N. Hodges. 2012. 'Corporate Social Responsibility in the Apparel Industry: An Exploration of Indian Consumers' Perceptions and Expectations.' *Journal of Fashion Marketing and Management* 16(2):216–233.

Harrison, R., T. Newholm, and D. Shaw. 2005. 'Introduction.' Pp. 1–8 in *The Ethical Consumer*, edited by R. Harrison, T. Newholm, and D. Shaw. Thousand Oaks, CA: Sage.

Hertel, S., P. Heidkamp, and L. Scruggs. 2009. 'Human Rights and Public Opinion: From Attitudes to Action.' *Political Science Quarterly* 124(3):443–459.

Hill, R. J. 1990. 'Attitudes and Behavior.' Pp. 347–377 in *Social Psychology: Sociological Perspectives*, edited by M. Rosenberg and R. H. Turner. New Brunswick, NJ: Transaction.

Hiscox, M.J., & Smyth, N.F.B. (n.d.). 'Is There Consumer Demand for Improved Labor Standards? Evidence from Field Experiments in Social Product Labeling'; available at http://www.people.fas.harvard.edu/~hiscox/SocialLabeling.pdf.

Hustvedt, G. and J. C. Bernard. 2010. 'Effects of Social Responsibility Labeling and Brand on Willingness to Pay for Apparel.' *International Journal of Consumer Studies* 34(6):1–8.

Hustvedt, G. and M. A. Dickson. 2009. 'Consumer Likelihood of Purchasing Organic Cotton Apparel: Influence of Attitudes and Self-Identity.' *Journal of Fashion Marketing and Management* 13(1):49–65.

Hyllegard, K. H., K-H. Lee, J. L. Paff Ogle, and R-N. Yan. 2012. 'Socially Responsible Labeling: The Impact of Hang Tags on Consumers' Attitudes Ad Patronage Intentions toward an Apparel Brand.' *Clothing and Textiles Research Journal* 30(1):51–66.

Ivanow, H., A. Jeffrey, and M. G. McEachern. 2005. 'The Influence of Ethical Trading Policies on Consumer Apparel Purchase Decisions: A Focus on the Gap, Inc.' *International Journal of Retail and Distribution Management* 23(5):373–387.

Kim, S., M. A. Littrell, and J. L. Paff Ogle. 1999. 'Social Responsibility as a Predictor of Purchase Intentions for Clothing.' *Journal of Fashion Marketing and Management* 3(3):207–218.

Kozar, J. M. and K. Y. Hiller Connell. 2010. 'Socially Responsible Knowledge and Behaviors: Comparing Upper Vs. Lower Classmen.' *College Student Journal* 44(2): 279–293.

Lang, T. and Y. Gabriel. 2005. 'A Brief History of Consumer Activism.' Pp. 39–53 in *The Ethical Consumer*, edited by R. Harrison, T. Newholm, and D. Shaw. Thousand Oaks, CA: Sage.

LaPiere, R. T. 1934. 'Attitudes vs. Actions.' *Social Forces* 13(2):230–237.

Munson, J. M. 1984. 'Personal Values: Considerations on Their Measurement and Application to Five Areas of Research.' Pp. 13–33 in *Personal Values and Consumer Psychology*, edited by R. E. Pitts, Jr. and A. G. Woodside. Lexington, MA: Lexington.

Oberseder, M., V. Gruber, and B. B. Schlegelmilch. 2011. 'Why Don't Consumers Care about CSR?: A Qualitative Study Exploring the Role of CSR in Consumption Decisions.' *Journal of Business Ethics* 104(4):449–460.

Paharia, N. and Deshpande, R. 2009. 'Sweatshop labor is wrong unless the jeans are cute: Motivated moral disengagement.' Working paper 09–079 Harvard Business School; available at http://www.people.fas.harvard.edu/ hiscox/Peharia.pdf; accessed September 5, 2011.

Pookulangara, S., J. Mestres, and A. Shephard. 2011. 'University Community's Perception of Sweatshops: A Mixed Method Data Collection.' *International Journal of Consumer Studies* 35(4):476–483.

Powell, E. 1969. *Freedom and Reality*. Tadworth, United Kingdom: Elliot Right Way.

Rokeach, M. 1973. *The Nature of Human Values*. New York: Free Press.

Ruggie, J. 2008. 'Protect, Respect and Remedy: A Framework for Business and Human Rights.' *Innovations* 3(2):189–212.

Shaw, D., I. Clarke, and E. Shiu. 2000. 'The Contribution of Ethical Obligation and Self-Identity to the Theory of Planned Behavior: An Exploration of Ethical Consumers.' *Journal of Marketing Management* 16(8):879–894.

Shen, B., C. K.Y. Lo, M. Shum, and Y. Wang. 2012. 'The Impact of Ethical Fashion on Consumer Purchase Behavior.' *Journal of Fashion Marketing and Management* 16(2):234–245.

Smith, M. J. 1982. *Persuasion and Human Action*. Belmont, CA: Wadsworth.

Vogel, D. 2005. *The Market for Virtue: The Potential and Limits of Corporate Social Responsibility*. Washington, D.C.: Brookings Institution.

Yan, R-N., K. H. Hyllegard, and J. L. Paff Ogle. 2010. 'The Impact of Message Appeal and Message Source on Gen Y Consumers' Attitudes and Purchase Intentions toward American Apparel.' *Journal of Marketing Communications* 16(4):203–224.

8 The Strength of Weak Commitments
Market Contexts and Ethical Consumption

Ian Robinson, Rachel Meyer and Howard Kimeldorf

From the perspective of neoclassical economics, the marketplace is the realm of self-interested, utility-maximizing behavior.[1] Many consumers, however, claim to be guided by ethical and moral considerations when making purchasing decisions. Indeed, cross-national representative survey data indicate that a growing number of consumers, now reaching sizable majorities in several Western European countries and the United States, say that they would pay more for sweat-free clothing and other ethically desirable products (Devinney et al. 2010, Harrison et al. 2005, Hertel et al. 2009, Pietry-kowski 2008). But, while such claims of ethical concern are widespread, acts of ethical consumption are far less common. This leads to what we term the ethical *concern-action gap*. What explains this gap between consumers' expressed preferences and their actual behavior? Put differently, why do some consumers with ethical concerns buy things that they believe are ethically produced, at extra cost if necessary, while others do not?

Given the far-reaching implications of ethical consumption for conventional theories of market behavior, scholars in several fields have sought to answer these questions by probing the psychic, or subjective, state of prospective ethical consumers. They have employed a variety of concepts—from ranked 'preferences' to developmental 'identities' and internalized 'norms.'[2] The strength of these orientations, it is argued, determines how we participate in the market, such that ethical consumers can be distinguished from their nonethical counterparts by their subjectivity, pointing in particular to the greater strength of their morally inflected convictions. The concern-action gap thus represents a kind of *moral failure* in which ethical concerns for the majority of consumers are too weak, relative to other preferences, to motivate corresponding ethical action in the marketplace.

We argue, instead, that focusing on moral failure is inadequate for understanding the ethical dimension of economic transactions and thus for explaining the concern-action gap. This is not to deny that preferences, identities, norms and morality more generally influence consumer choices. But it is *not their strength* per se that determines the extent of ethical consumption, but rather how those subjective states *interact* with, and are shaped by, the wider social context as defined by the consumer markets in which purchasing decisions are made. Contrary to the existing literature, then, we argue that even weak ethical commitments can, under favorable market conditions, lead to ethical consumption. Specifically, we find that when markets provide a range of ethically desirable products, along with sufficient information to choose among them, many consumers who are not strongly motivated by ethics will nonetheless choose to purchase ethical products. In short, the market context both shapes (via information) and refracts (via the range of choices offered) consumer subjectivities in ways that largely determine the extent of the concern-action gap.

Many markets appear to be responding poorly, if at all, to consumers' ethical concerns, suggesting that the recent and dramatic surge in sales for various 'fair trade' products may reflect a latent demand for ethically produced goods that is only beginning to be met (Krier 2007). If, as our analysis indicates, the demand for such products greatly exceeds supply, we may be witnessing a large-scale failure, not of individual morality but of markets. Correcting this failure would benefit not only ethically inclined consumers but also the many suppliers who could begin tapping into the demand for ethical products. A more efficient market would also make it possible to return a portion of the higher earnings generated from the sale of ethical goods to their direct producers, many of whom are laboring under the worst possible conditions in the sweatshops of the global south.

To assess our market-centered theory of the ethical concern-action gap, we interviewed 169 customers emerging from American Apparel's Ann Arbor, Michigan, store. Of interviewees who had heard that American Apparel produced sweat-free clothing, 89 percent believed that this assertion was true. By contrast, in a parallel survey of University of Michigan students— American Apparel's main customer base in Ann Arbor—30 percent said they believed that almost all apparel is made under sweatshop conditions, while another 57 percent thought that some clothing is manufactured under sweat-free conditions, but indicated that it is very difficult to identify those items.[3] Equally important, most customers exiting American Apparel regard its clothing as stylish and high quality. This gives American Apparel unique standing as a research site: it is the only clothing retail outlet in the United States where we can directly observe what happens to the concern-action gap when consumers who care about sweatshops do not believe that they are forced to choose between ethics and style.[4]

1   THEORIZING THE CONCERN-ACTION GAP

For many—perhaps even most—U.S. economists, it is axiomatic that most people, most of the time, rationally pursue their economic self-interest (Becker 1986, Mueller 1985). Some, such as Olson (1965), took the more nuanced position that this claim is not valid for actions undertaken in other arenas, such as religion or politics, but he firmly embraced the consensus that competitive commodity markets are the natural home of rational egoism. From this mainstream perspective, the ethical concern-action gap, as it relates to commodities like clothing, exists either because people lie and say that they are motivated by moral duties when they know they are not, or because people, while honest, are confused about their motives. Either way, the concern-action gap arises because what people say they will do is at odds with their actual motivation.

Rational egoism has long had challengers within economics. One of the most elegant and forceful critiques was Sen's (1979) 'Rational Fools' essay. Sen argued that most people are motivated by two factors that regularly supplement or override egoistic preferences: 'sympathy' (i.e., concern for others' welfare) and counter-preferential 'commitments' that could be ethical in character but could have other sources as well. Sen argued that people who had no capacity to subordinate short-term preference-maximizing to broader, higher or longer-term commitments, would be rightly regarded as fools by ordinary people, and should be so regarded by economic theory as well.

Rational egoism has never been the dominant view among psychologists. The psychology of moral development, which has paid closest attention to questions of when and how moral concerns or commitments motivate action, has two important strands. One examines the processes through which we acquire the cognitive capacity to engage in complex moral reasoning (Gilligan 1982, Kohlberg 1981). The other focuses on how much we care about what befalls others and the degree to which following moral duties is integrated into our sense of who we are and aspire to be (Blasi1984, Colby et al. 2003). This second strand privileges the role of personal identity, suggesting that the more we embrace a conception of self that revolves around concern for others, the more likely we are to make and keep moral commitments (Monroe 1996). With few exceptions (Shaw et al. 2000), this literature has not been applied to ethical consumption. However, extrapolating from this perspective, the concern-action gap should occur when cognitive development is insufficient for the formation of moral commitments, or when moral commitments are not well enough integrated into one's sense of self to motivate ethical action.

Thus, despite their disciplinary differences, economists like Sen and psychologists like Colby converge around a common view that ethical behavior is determined by the strength of ethical commitments. Their position is that such commitments must be strong enough to override all competing preferences if they are to have a significant impact on behavior.

Sociologist Etzioni (1988), putting the moral dimension of human behavior at the center of his 'socio-economic' analysis, also grounds his theory on two categorically different kinds of motivations: a desire to do one's duty and a desire for pleasure. However, he stresses that these 'parallel utilities' are not necessarily hierarchically ordered, with ethical duty trumping all other concerns, if it matters at all. Instead, he distinguishes two ways that our choices can be affected by moral concerns: 'by heeding an absolute command in some areas or periods of time; and by preferring certain means, the moral means, over others, but not at all costs.' Etzioni calls the former 'absolute' and the latter 'expedient' morality, arguing that most people are affected by both (Etzioni 1988: 42). By definition, absolute duties—like Sen's counter-preferential 'commitments'—are supposed to trump all other desires. If they do not, moral failure occurs. But that is not true of the more common class of 'expedient' moral duties that give rise to limited or conditional commitments. Being conditional rather than absolute, these 'not-at-all-costs' commitments are subject to tradeoffs: they call for action but not at the expense of all other desires.

In recent years, a growing body of experimental economics has demonstrated that altruistic behavior is widespread—though far from universal—across a range of economic transactions simulated by means of different game structures and rules (Frank 1988, Henrich et al. 2001). In this literature, altruistic means acting contrary to the dictates of economic self-interest, as specified by the game situation (e.g., in the famous prisoners' dilemma game, rational self-interest dictates defection). Recent experiments have shown that altruistic behavior, so understood, is often best explained by fairness norms, but that sustained action governed by those norms is conditional on others doing the same. Thus, a key finding, very much in line with Etzioni's conceptualization, is that many people are *conditional* altruists. The social context, as shaped by the rules of the game and the group dynamics they generate, is therefore the key to both the scale and the sustainability of ethical action (Fehr and Fischbacher 2003, Fehr and Gintis 2007).

In the apparel market, the product choices firms offer represent the most important kind of social context affecting the incidence of ethical consumption. Because limited duties are situationally contingent, they will be poor predictors of behavior unless we can identify and control for the relevant contextual factors. But limited duties, while weaker than absolute duties, will often be much more pervasive, allowing them, under favorable market conditions, to exert a determining influence on the behavior of a large share of consumers. In other words, in the real-world context of conditional commitments and constrained choices, the *interaction* of markets and consumer subjectivity determines the extent of ethical consumption.

The literature that seeks to explain the ethical concern-action gap in the apparel industry tends to ignore the social context of the marketplace, often treating it as outside the scope of the literature's analytic framework. Dickson (2001), for example, focuses on the 16 percent of her survey respondents who were significantly more concerned about issues affecting apparel workers and more likely to use a sweat-free label. She then concludes that the market for ethical goods is destined to remain a small niche, limited to the minority of consumers who place such ethical considerations above all others. In a subsequent analysis of the same data, Dickson goes further, classifying everyone else as a 'self-interested consumer' even though most of them also indicated that the no-sweat label made them slightly more likely to purchase a shirt (Dickson 2005: 163–165). Vogel (2005: 6) argues similarly that most consumers do not rank ethical commitments above all other preferences, and that this is an important reason why ethical concerns seldom influence market choices.

Some scholars have acknowledged the importance of market context, but they reach a similarly limited assessment of ethical consumption because they take market *failure* for granted. For example, Paharia and Deshpandé (2009), whose title—'Sweatshop labour is wrong, unless the jeans are cute'—purports to capture the thinking of most consumers. Respondents in their phone surveys rationalized away the evils of sweatshop production when told that they would look really good in a pair of jeans made in a sweatshop. Given the limited sweat-free options available in most apparel markets, this experimental scenario faithfully reproduces a real dilemma facing many apparel consumers. But this dilemma would not arise in a more consumer-responsive clothing market that provides the option of purchasing sweat-free jeans that are also cute. Why take for granted the market's current failure to respond to consumers who want cute, sweat-free jeans? Paharia and Deshpandé never address this question.

Market failure is likewise the starting point of the provocatively titled recent volume *The Myth of the Ethical Consumer* by Devinney et al. (2010). They too assume current market conditions, taking into account realistic 'price premiums' for ethical goods, in addition to other kinds of trade-offs, such as style, quality, and functionality. For example, they find that more than 60 percent of their sample opted for ethically made athletic shoes when the price premium was $5 and the shoes' functionality was good, but that demand fell sharply to about 20 percent when the shoes' functionality was bad. At a higher price premium of $25, demand for ethical shoes fell to 25 percent when they were functionally good, and 7 percent when they were functionally bad (Devinney et al. 2010: 94–7).

Again, while such trade-offs correspond to current market realities, Devinney et al. do not acknowledge the corollary of this setup: an apparel market that eliminated nonprice trade-offs would yield levels of ethical consumption much closer to those found in national surveys (which only consider price premiums). In short, the importance of market context, which they rightly stress, cuts both ways: it can reduce or increase ethical consumption. There is no 'natural' level of ethical consumerism—limited by the moral character or development of human beings—that exists apart from social context. We will now show that, under the more favorable market conditions present at American Apparel, ethical consumption will occur on a much larger scale than analysts such as Devinney et al. expect.

2   RESEARCH DESIGN

American Apparel in Ann Arbor

American Apparel's arrival in Ann Arbor in Fall 2005 created what amounts to a natural experiment: from that point forward, local consumers had a choice between a retailer claiming that all of its clothing is manufactured sweat-free and all the other local retailers who make no such claim. American Apparel sells cotton T-shirts, 'hoodies,' buttoned shirts, simple slacks, dresses, skirts, and undergarments, none of which have a brand or label, in a range of attractive colors and styles. The types of clothing available are thus limited. But for the kind of casual clothes it sells, American Apparel gives customers a wide range of aesthetically attractive and well-made options. American Apparel thus offer a unique opportunity to assess our account of the ethical concern-action gap because it dramatically reduces the trade-off between ethics and style, enabling us to identify the conditions under which ethical concerns, even when weakly held by consumers, are strong enough to motivate ethical consumption.

Interviewing American Apparel customers was also an attractive option for a more pragmatic reason: because of its effective publicity campaign, the store attracts a disproportionately high share of customers with ethical concerns about their clothing purchases. Since our aim is to determine how ethical concerns translate (or not) into ethical behavior, American Apparel provides the ideal research setting because of its high concentration of customers for whom ethical considerations play a role of some kind in their purchasing decision. Although the store does not actually use the term 'sweat-free' in advertising, it promotes its products as American made (and promotes the Los Angeles location of its production facility) and boasts about its worker-compensation policy, which is much more generous than that of other apparel-industry manufacturers. Fully 89 percent of respondents who had heard that American Apparel produced its clothing by 'sweat-free' processes believed that claim. From the perspective of these customers, then, American Apparel offers an ethical alternative. For purposes of this analysis, it is what they believe that matters, not whether we agree with their assessment.[5]

3   CONCEPTS AND MEASUREMENT

Defining an Ethical Consumer

We develop a stringent definition of an ethical consumer by adapting Monroe's (1996: 6–7) conception of altruism to capture both the other-directed beneficial intent of action and the underlying sense of moral duty. Monroe conceives of altruism as:

a. Action: an altruist does not just talk about acting in a certain way; an altruist acts that way.
b. Goal-directed: an altruist acts to realize a conscious end.
c. Other-oriented: the goal of the altruistic act is to improve the welfare of one or more others.
d. Independence of extrinsic incentives: the altruist's willingness to help others must not hinge on anticipation of extrinsic rewards or penalties.

e. Cost to actor: to clearly distinguish altruistic acts from acts of self-interest, Monroe specifies that they must carry some risk of diminishing the altruist's welfare (material or otherwise), though that higher cost need not be a certainty, and so, need not prove to be the case.

Monroe's abstract altruistic conditions can be mapped onto our data, allowing us to operationalize a working definition of ethical consumers based on four criteria:

Altruistic Criterion 1: Consistent with Monroe's (a), ethical consumers must, *at some point*, actually purchase clothing that they believe is sweat-free. The phrase 'at some point' recognizes that some consumers will not buy anything on the day we interview them. That alone does not deprive them of their ethical-consumer status, provided they have made ethical purchases in the past. But, someone who has never bought sweat-free clothes when presented with opportunities to do so is not an ethical consumer. Our survey asked customers what, if anything, they purchased from the store on the day of the interview and whether they had ever purchased anything from the store. If they purchased something on either occasion, they satisfied this criterion.

Altruistic Criterion 2: Consistent with Monroe's (b), ethical consumers must purchase the sweat-free clothing at least in part *because* of its putative sweat-free status. This does not have to be the only, or even the highest, consideration guiding their purchasing decision, but it must be a factor. If someone buys a sweat-free shirt solely because of an attraction to the color and style, then any ethical concerns they may have are irrelevant to that purchase, which means they are not acting as an ethical consumer. Our survey asked respondents whether American Apparel's claim to be sweat-free had anything to do with their decision to buy clothes there. If they replied that it did, they satisfied this criterion.

Altruistic Criterion 3: Consistent with Monroe's (c) and (d), ethical consumers must care about the sweat-free status *because* they believe that buying sweat-free clothing will help protect the rights and/or improve the welfare of apparel workers, *not* because they think they will derive some personal benefit from wearing such clothes (e.g., impressing or gaining approval from others). Our survey explored a number of possible reasons why respondents might be willing to pay more for sweat-free clothing. Two of these options invoked or implied a moral duty: 'Better-off people like me ought to help people who are not doing as well' and 'Anyone who buys goods made in a sweatshop is taking advantage of the workers, and that's wrong.' If a respondent agreed with either or both of these statements, they satisfied the third criterion.

Altruistic Criterion 4: Finally, consistent with Monroe's (e), ethical consumers must be *willing* to pay a price premium for sweat-free clothing. It is not necessary actually to pay that higher cost—that is why Monroe refers to a 'risk' of paying more. And, from a practical perspective, this criterion may not be as important as the others may be since wages in the apparel industry typically represent less than 2 percent of the final sales price (Pollin, Burns, and Heintz 2004). Our survey asked respondents 'whether you would be willing to pay more for the clothes you bought [at American Apparel] today—or for the clothes you would buy here the next time you visit—if you knew that they were produced sweatshop-free?' A positive response satisfies this last criterion.

Operationalizing Moral Failure

Our measure of moral failure is based on how respondents ranked their most important sweatshop concern in response to a question that asked them to indicate how much their purchasing decision was affected by style, quality, price, three sweatshop factors—was child labor involved, were wages and conditions decent, and were workers represented by a union?—and whether the product was made in the United States or abroad. Respondents were allowed to assign the same rank to more than one factor. A rank of 1 for any of the three sweat-free factors indicates a very strong ethical commitment. Following Dickson and others who expect that only those who have such a strong commitment are likely to behave as ethical consumers, we regard as an ethical failure anything less than a top-priority ranking for at least one sweat-free factor.

Operationalizing Market Failure

Two different kinds of market failures could contribute to the concern-action gap: information failures and supply failures. Information failures occur when consumers are unaware of an opportunity to make an ethical choice when purchasing. This is a kind of market failure because whether or not consumers have such information very much depends on corporate advertising and effective marketing of sweat-free products. More consumers will know about their sweat-free options if such efforts are aggressive, widespread and successful. There is also the question of credibility. Given justified consumer skepticism regarding claims made by self-interested firms, the credibility of sweat-free claims depends on social-movement organizations—or, potentially, state regulations—that can validate, challenge, or (as in the case of American Apparel) remain largely silent regarding corporate sweat-free claims. Building on our previous work (Kimeldorf et al. 2006, Prasad et al. 2004), we operationalize the informational function of markets by stipulating that the consumer must:

1. be aware of the sweat-free claims the retailer makes, and
2. trust those claims (i.e., find them credible).[6]

A market-based information failure occurs if either of these conditions is not met. Our survey asked: 'Do you know anything about where American Apparel stands on the sweatshop labor issue?' If the respondent answered yes, two follow-up questions were asked: 'What have you heard, and where did you hear it?' and 'Do you trust this [i.e., American Apparel's] claim?' If respondents knew about American Apparel's sweat-free claim and trusted it, then both 'informational preconditions' are met.[7] Consumers who fail to meet either of these informational preconditions cannot act as an ethical consumer no matter how concerned they are about sweatshops. Such failure, therefore, could explain part of the concern-action gap.

The second kind of market failure—supply failures—occur when markets do not offer consumers the products they want (and can pay for). In the case of sweat-free apparel, supply failures occur either when ethical products not available or when choosing them requires major sacrifices regarding style, quality, or price preferences.[8] Our survey asked respondents how they compared the style, quality, and price of American Apparel clothing with those of the store that they thought carried the most similar type of clothing. If consumers responded that American Apparel's style or quality are inferior to this alternative source, or that its prices are higher, we regard this as a case of supply failure based on the assumption that the rival store is not—and makes no claim to be—offering sweat-free products.

4   ANALYZING THE CONCERN-ACTION GAP

Beginning in March 2006, student research assistants interviewed American Apparel customers as they exited the store, speaking with everyone who agreed to an interview. Customers were told that the interview would take 10 to 15 minutes, and they were paid $5 for their time. Nearly two-thirds of those approached agreed to be interviewed. Over the next year, we collected 169 interviews. Our interviews probed customers' knowledge of American Apparel's sweat-free claims, their reasons for visiting the store, whether or not they bought anything, the relative importance of various factors in deciding whether to buy anything, and their beliefs about whether they had a duty to buy sweat-free clothing when given an opportunity. A complete copy of our survey instrument is available upon request.

How Big Is the Gap?

What share of our respondents had ethical concerns about the way their clothing was made? We measured ethical concern by asking respondents to rank-order seven variables that might be relevant to their purchasing decision: style, quality, price, whether the item was made in the United States, and our three sweatshop variables. Respondents were asked to assign a zero to all factors that were 'not important at all' in their decision. Just 15 percent of our 169 respondents ($N = 26$) assigned a zero to all three sweat-free factors and so were deemed unconcerned about sweatshop conditions.[9] The remaining 85 percent (143 respondents) expressed some level of ethical concern about at least one of the three sweatshop factors. They comprise our pool of potential ethical consumers.

Of these 143 respondents, only 26 percent (37 respondents) met all four of our altruistic criteria and so were classified as ethical consumers. Thus, almost three-quarters of those with concerns about sweatshops (106 respondents) fell into the concern-action gap. Figure 8.1 indicates how many American Apparel customers failed each of the four criteria used to

Figure 8.1 Number of Respondents Failing Each Criterion in Definition of an Ethical Consumer

■ Failed Criterion 1 (i.e., bought nothing) – 35 cases

  Failed Criterion 2 (i.e., sweat-free reputation was not important to purchase decision) – 80 cases

■ Failed Criterion 3 (i.e., does not recognize a moral duty to buy sweat-free) – 22 cases

■ Failed Criterion 4 (i.e., not willing to pay a price premium for a sweat-free product) – 28 cases

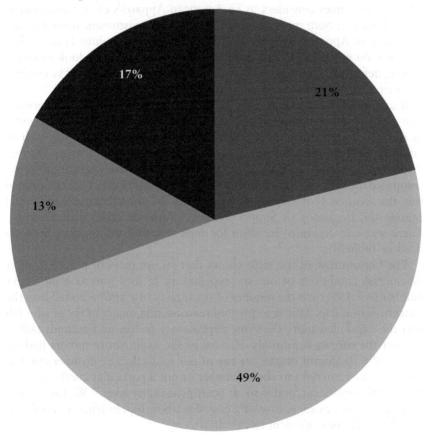

determine whether someone was an ethical consumer. Some individuals failed more than one criterion, so summing all failures for the four criteria gives us a larger number ($n = 165$) than the number of consumers who fell into the concern-action gap ($n = 106$). We see in this figure that nearly half (49 percent) of all ethical consumption failures were due to the failure to meet Criterion 2 (i.e., a knowledge of American Apparel's reputation for sweat-free products did not influence their decision to buy from that store).

What Explains the Gap?

Is the concern-action gap, as most scholars presume, largely attributable to moral failure, or is it due much more to one or more of the types of market failure discussed above? To answer this question, we examine six factors that could affect ethical-consumption levels. Three are types of supply failure: failure to provide sweat-free clothing that the customer considers stylish (Supply Failure 1), high quality (Supply Failure 2), or equal or lower pricing (Supply Failure 3)—all compared to the sweatshop products sold by what the customer considers to be American Apparel's closest competitor. We also look at both types of information failure: customers are not aware of American Apparel's sweat-free claim (Information Failure 1) or, if they are, they do not trust it (Information Failure 2). Finally, we look at moral failure, defined as failure to rank at least one of our three types of sweatshop concern as a top priority.

If any of these six factors have an impact on the size of the concern-action gap, it must be because it affects the likelihood of meeting one or more of the four criteria that define an ethical consumer. In principle, each of our four criteria could be affected by all six of our explanatory factors. This yields a matrix of 24 possible permutations. For each permutation, we computed a 2 × 2 cross tab. For example, one of the 24 cross tabs examined was the frequency of failure on Criterion 1 (no purchase; dichotomous) against the frequency of Supply Failure 1 (inferior style; dichotomous). There was one degree of freedom for each test. Our findings are summarized in Table 8.1.

The bottom row of the table shows that all instances of failure to meet the success conditions of our six explanatory factors sum to a far larger number ($n = 359$) than the number of consumers ($n = 106$) who fell into the concern-action gap. This is so for two reasons: first, many of those who fell into the gap failed more than one explanatory factor; and second, failure to meet the success conditions of some of the explanatory factors had no statistically significant impact on any of our four ethical consumer criteria. Table 8.1 uses asterisks to show whether or not a particular coefficient was statistically significant, and if so, at what probability level.[10] We take statistical significance as suggestive of a causal relationship, bearing in mind that correlation is not equivalent to causation.

Table 8.1 Distribution of Observed (and Expected) Number of Dual Failures of Ethical Consumer Criteria and Six Explanatory Factors

Ethical Consumption Criterion Failures (N=165)	Supply Failure 1 Inferior Style	Supply Failure 2 Inferior Quality	Supply Failure 3 Inferior Price	Information Failure 1 Don't Know Sweat-free Claim	Information Failure 2 Don't Trust Sweat-free Claim	Moral Failure Sweat-free Concerns Not a Top Priority
Criterion 1: Do not buy from American Apparel (n=35)	7** (3.2)	3 (3.8)	20 (16.5)	18* (12.2)	4*** (1.2)	10 (6.9)
Criterion 2: Sweat-free status did not impact decision to buy (n=80)	10 (8.1)	11 (10.1)	41 (42.9)	50*** (31.6)	4 (4.6)	74 (71.3)
Criterion 3: Do not recognize moral duty to buy sweat-free (n=22)	6*** (1.9)	2 (2.4)	14 (10.5)	7 (7.3)	1 (0.5)	17 (17)
Criterion 4: Not willing to pay price premium for sweat-free (n=28)	5* (2.4)	2 (3.1)	15 (13.5)	14* (9.4)	1 (1.0)	23 (21.7)
Total Explanatory Factor Failures by Type (n=359)	28	18	90	89	10	124

The number in each cell is the frequency of "dual failures" (i.e., did not meet the criterion in that row and also exhibited the type of failure in that column). These were drawn from 24 cross tabs [i.e., Criterion 1 failure (yes/no) by Supply Failure: Style (yes/no)]. Below each number, in brackets, is the expected number of failures. Asterisks indicate the levels of statistical significance for the Chi-square test conducted for each of 24 cross-tabs: *** =p<.001, ** =p<.01, * =p<.05.

Table 8.1 shows that Information Failures of Type 1 (do not know sweat-free claim) are associated with 18 Criterion 1 failures, 50 Criterion 2 failures, 0 Criterion 3 failures and 14 Criterion 4 failures. Postulating a causal relationship makes sense in this case: if consumers who care about sweatshop issues do not know about American Apparel's sweat-free reputation, then that reputation cannot affect their decision to buy there (hence, the impact on Criterion 2). As a result, they are less likely to buy there than are ethically concerned people who know about American Apparel's reputation (hence, the impact on Criterion 1). Similarly, if ethically concerned consumers do not know about American Apparel's sweat-free status, they will be less likely to pay a price premium for those goods (hence, impact on Criterion 4). On the other hand, there is no reason to think that ignorance of American Apparel's sweat-free reputation would affect whether or not one has an absolute or conditional moral duty to buy sweat-free. These beliefs come from different sources. Consistent with this account, we find no statistically significant relationship between Type 1 Information Failure and Criterion 3 failure.

Table 8.2 shows only the 'dual failure' relationships that are statistically significant. Figures in each cell of the table are the product of each type of criterion failure (as a percent of all criterion failures) and of each type of factor failure (as a percent of all factor failures). In this way, we can estimate what share of the concern-action gap is accounted for by each statistically significant instance of dual failure. For example, we see that almost two-thirds ($n = 50$, 62 percent) of the 80 customers whose decision to buy from American Apparel was *not* influenced by the store's sweat-free claim (thereby failing to meet Criterion 2) did not know about that claim (Information Failure 1). The 80 customers who were not classified as ethical consumers because they failed this criterion account for just under half (48 percent) of all 143 criterion failures. In sum, this particular dual failure accounts for (.62*.48), or almost 30 percent of all criterion failures, and by extension, an equal share of the concern-action gap.

The lower right-hand box in Table 8.2 sums these calculations for all of the statistically significant combinations reported. Together, they account for almost 60 percent of the concern-action gap, with most of this percentage accounted for by Type 1 Information Failures. Whether or not a consumer ranked his or her highest sweat-free issue as a top concern had no statistically significant impact on the likelihood of meeting any of our four ethical consumption criteria. In other words, as measured here, moral failure explains none of the ethical concern-action gap. The results reported in Table 8.2 are thus entirely consistent with our contention that, in an all-too-rare, real-world situation like American Apparel, where sweat-free supply failures are limited, moral failure will contribute little to the concern-action gap because weaker commitments are often sufficient to induce ethical consumption among those who are concerned about sweatshops.

At the same time, about 40 percent of the concern-action gap is not accounted for by any of our six factors. It is possible that some kind of moral

Table 8.2 Share of Concern-Action Gap Explained by Statistically Significant Instances of Each Type of Explanatory Factor Failure

Failure Impacts	Supply Failure 1 Inferior Style	Supply Failure 2 Inferior Quality	Supply Failure 3 Inferior Price	Information Failure 1 Don't Know Sweat-free Claim	Information Failure 2 Don't Trust Sweat-free Claim	Moral Failure Sweat-free Concerns Not a Top Priority	Totals
Criterion 1: Buy from American Apparel?	4.0%	0	0	10.3%	0	0	14.3%
Criterion 2: Did sweat-free status impact decision to buy?	0	0	0	30.3%	0	0	30.3%
Criterion 3: Recognize moral duty to buy sweat-free?	2.8%	0	0	0	0	0	2.8%
Criterion 4: Willing to pay price premium for sweat-free?	3.0%	0	0	8.5%	0	0	11.5%
Totals	9.8%	0	0	49.1%	0	0	58.9%

failure other than what we measure here could account for some portion of the unexplained gap. Still, even if it explained as much as half, that would mean that moral failure accounts for no more than one-fifth of the total gap—far less than conventional accounts suppose.

5　THE STRENGTH OF WEAK COMMITMENTS

While our statistical results are consistent with our theory, it is possible that the observed patterns are not caused by the market failures we highlight. How can we test for this assumption? We first need to elaborate a realistic model of how consumers make decisions when conditional ethical commitments are in play. Then we can predict the patterns that our data should exhibit if our model is accurate.

The central premise of our model is simple enough: if sweat-free clothing is available in the desired style, at affordable prices and good quality, then there is no necessary trade-off between wanting a particular style and purchasing sweat-free clothing. In the absence of such trade-offs, even those with relatively weak ethical commitments to sweat-free consumption can often be ethical consumers. We can illustrate the point less abstractly with the hypothetical example represented in Table 8.3.

Imagine that, as in the table, consumers consider just four factors when making their purchasing decisions, and that the factor to which everyone assigns top priority is style, followed by quality and price, in that order. Sweat-free production, while a genuine concern, is everyone's fourth-ranked priority. In this scenario, consumers decide among three stores offering products that vary on these four dimensions. Since style dominates the other three factors, Store 3 is eliminated in the first round of competition, owing to the inferior style of its product. Stores 1 and 2 are basically the same, not only with respect to style but also in price and quality. So the *decisive* factor in this example is the fourth-ranked criterion, the desire for sweat-free products. Consumers with this preference ordering, when faced with this array of choices, will all buy from Store 2 because it sells sweat-free clothing while also meeting their other three, higher-ranked preferences.

Table 8.3　How the Fourth-Ranked Factor Can Be Decisive

Considerations Rank Ordered	Store 1	Store 2	Store 3
1. Style	Excellent	Excellent	OK
2. Quality	Good	Good	Good
3. Price	Average	Average	Below average
4. Sweat-Free	No	Yes	No

If real-world consumer decision-making occurs in this way, two patterns should appear in data from a store like American Apparel. First, ethical consumers should not be confined to those who rank a sweat-free concern as a top priority; instead, many—perhaps even most—ethical consumers should be drawn from among those who assign a lower ranking to sweat-free production. Second, we should find that most—perhaps even all—ethical consumers who did not rank a sweat-free factor as a top priority believe that their higher-ranked preferences are satisfied by American Apparel products.

The interview data reported in Table 8.4 exhibit both patterns. First, ethical consumers extend far beyond those who are most concerned about the ethics of sweat-free production. Column (3) shows that the respondents with the highest probability of becoming ethical consumers were those whose highest ranked sweat-free factor was third in their preference ordering: fully 41 percent of this group became ethical consumers, as opposed to 32 percent and 27 percent, respectively, of those who ranked a sweat-free factor first or second. Column (4) indicates that nearly two out of three (65 percent) ethical consumers in our sample ranked sweat-free factors no higher than third. Put another way, looking at Column (2), almost three times as many ethical consumers did *not* rank sweat-free as their top priority compared to those who did. Thus, the strength of sweat-free commitments plays little, if any, role in determining the extent of ethical consumption, consistent with what we saw in Table 8.1 and Table 8.2.

Second, our ethical consumers reported that their higher-order preferences were satisfied by the products at American Apparel. Just over half

Table 8.4 Highest Sweat-Free Ranking and Share of Respondents Who Become Ethical Consumers

Highest Rank assigned to a Sweat-free Factor	(1) Number of respondents assigning each rank to their top sweat-free factor	(2) Number of those in Column (1) who are Ethical Consumers	(3) Share of those with moral concerns about sweatshops who are Ethical Consumers Col (2) / Col (1)	(4) Share of all Ethical Consumers in sample Col (2) / 37
1 (top priority)	28	9	32%	24%
2	15	4	27%	11%
3	27	11	41%	30%
4	61	11	18%	30%
5 (lowest)	12	2	17%	5%
Total	143	37	—	100%

(53 percent) ranked style as a top concern, 14 percent listed quality, and 31 percent said price was a top concern. Strikingly, not a single ethical consumer thought American Apparel's clothing style was inferior to its nearest competition. Similarly, 86 percent of our ethical consumers thought that the quality of American Apparel's products was as good as, or better than, its nearest competitor. That included four of the five who ranked quality as a top concern. Thus, shopping at American Apparel enabled consumers to act on their ethical commitments without having to subordinate their preferences for style and quality.

The story with price is more complex: 61 percent of our ethical consumers ranked price higher than their highest-ranked sweatshop factor. If price had the same role in consumer decision-making as style and quality, then only those who thought American Apparel's prices were about the same or lower than the closest competitor would be ethical consumers. In fact, however, 41 percent of those in this subset thought that American Apparel's prices were higher, but they became ethical consumers nonetheless.[11]

The different way in which price impinges on consumer decision-making can be traced to two sources. First, we built a willingness to pay a price premium into our definition (Criterion 4) of ethical consumption—something we did not do with style or quality. Thus, everyone who we classify as an ethical consumer has already indicated a willingness to pay a price premium for sweat-free apparel, though not everyone thought he or she actually paid extra. Second, our sample population—composed mainly of University of Michigan students—tends to come from affluent families. This means that higher prices are less of a deterrent to purchases—and so, to becoming an ethical consumer—than might be the case for less-affluent consumers. In a much poorer population, in other words, we might find price working in a way more analogous to how style works in this sample.

This raises the question of the representativeness of our sample. The 85 percent of customers with ethical concerns at American Apparel was considerably greater than the 68 percent who were willing to pay a 25-percent premium for a sweat-free version of a $20 shirt, as reported in the representative national survey conducted by Hertel et al. (2009). However, this difference affects the share of the population that has the potential to become ethical consumers, not the share that falls into the gap and fails to realize that potential. Our explanation for why potential ethical consumers fail remains valid, we believe, whether the share of those in the initial pool of potential ethical consumers is 85 percent or 68 percent.

The higher average family income of the respondents in our sample, relative to the national average, lowers the opportunity cost of agreeing with Criterion 4 (paying a price premium for sweat-free goods). However, capacity to pay is not the same thing as willingness to pay. Lower-income people, for example, tend to give a larger share of their incomes to charity (Piff et al. 2010), and most ethical-consumer studies find no relationship between family income and willingness to pay a modest price premium (Devinney et al. 2010).

Might the students who make up 80 percent of our sample be less subject to information failure than the general population? We find just the opposite: 67 percent of American Apparel customers who are not students knew of the company's sweat-free reputation, compared with 52 percent of university students. Of course, Ann Arbor is a university town, so nonstudents also have higher-than-average levels of education. But, more fundamentally, the main cause of information failure is not to be found in individual consumer attributes, but in the marketing behavior of the major apparel-production and retail firms. Together, these firms account for most of the supply side of the apparel market; by choosing whether or not to enhance consumer awareness of, and concern about, the production process, they also have a major impact on the demand side of the global apparel market.

CONCLUSION

The number of apparel consumers who profess ethical concerns, falling somewhere in the range of 60–80 percent in most surveys, dwarfs the current level of sweat-free apparel consumption in the United States. Most accounts from the fields of economics, psychology and sociology attribute this concern-action gap to the weakness of ethical commitments, whether the source of this weakness is conceptualized in terms of overriding rival preferences, underdeveloped moral identities, or undersocialized norms. In each case, ethical commitments, however genuine, prove too weak to dislodge higher-order considerations that determine what consumers purchase. It follows that the market for ethical consumption is destined to remain a specialized niche since it depends on the small minority of consumers for whom ethical commitments are strong enough to trump all other considerations that might influence purchasing behavior. As Devinney et al. (2010) conclude, the ethical (mass) consumer is a myth.

Our findings from American Apparel challenge this explanation for the concern-action gap. Given the store's reputation for marketing sweat-free clothing, it attracts a high proportion of customers with ethical concerns (about 85 percent of those we interviewed). Yet, nearly 75 percent of those with ethical concerns fail to satisfy one or more of the four criteria that we use to define an ethical consumer. The most important cause of this failure, accounting for almost half of those who fell into the concern-action gap—and more than 80 percent of the gap that can be explained with the variables examined in this study—is a type of market failure: not knowing about the store's sweat-free claim (in our terms, Information Failure 1). In contrast, moral failure—based on the strength of ethical commitments—explains none of the concern-action gap as measured here. In short, what matters is not the strength or weakness of ethical commitments per se, but rather the *interaction* between the strength of those commitments and market context.

The position of Devinney et al. and other scholars who dismiss ethical mass consumerism as a myth rests on an even greater myth: the impossibility of developing more efficient markets to capitalize on the latent demand for ethical products. When consumers have the information they need to act on their ethical concerns, and when they can do so without being forced to choose between desirable product characteristics and ethics, even weak moral commitments of the kind held by many consumers can lead to ethical consumption. Only in the context of systematic market failure are strong moral commitments required to motivate ethical consumption, leading to small niche markets that then reinforce the mistaken belief that widespread ethical consumption will never happen.

What explains the prevalence of market failure? In particular, why have so few firms taken the moral 'high road' in cultivating the market for ethical consumption? The answer is beyond the scope of our data and present analysis. But, it does deserve some comment, even if it is, at this point, largely speculative. We can imagine three plausible explanations. Corporate decision-makers may: (1) recognize that there is a large latent ethical consumer market but be unwilling to risk a fundamental change in their competitive strategy; (2) agree with Devinney et al. that large-scale ethical consumption is a myth, and conclude that the ethical consumer niche market is too small to warrant the major changes it would require to satisfy; and/or (3) believe (perhaps incorrectly) that they can best maximize shareholder value through sweatshop production.

The first kind of explanation may well account for American Apparel's reluctance to promote aggressively its clothing as sweat-free. CEO Dov Charney surely knows that the anti-sweatshop movement regards his company as falling well short of their ideals, given its history of union-busting and sexual harassment. But, most American Apparel customers assume—based on its U.S. production plant and its website statements about generous wages and benefits—that the company is a sweat-free producer. The anti-sweatshop movement has not challenged this belief because American Apparel's wages and working conditions are in fact much better than most sweatshops, even if it falls short in other respects. Why devote a lot of resources to attacking a company that treats workers better than most companies do? Still, an aggressive attempt by American Apparel to claim the mantle of 'sweat-free' might provoke the movement to challenge such claims more openly. In this context, the lower-risk strategy for American Apparel is to profit from the customers who believe it is a sweat-free operation, rather than making a stronger claim that would likely trigger an NGO mobilization that could change perceptions and jeopardize its current consumer base.

Parallel concerns could discourage major apparel brands from pursuing a bold sweat-free marketing agenda. It would certainly be possible to create a sweat-free line—as Knights Apparel recently did with its new Alta Gracia brand of college athletic clothing—that has the anti-sweatshop movement's endorsement (Kline 2010, Greenhouse 2010, Alta Gracia 2011). But, what would that imply for the ethical defensibility and resulting desirability of their other product lines? Would such firms be admitting, by implication, that they are all sweatshop products? Corporate decision-makers may feel that they face an all-or-nothing choice, in which case the latter option—doing nothing—is appealingly familiar and risk averse.

On the other hand, why have other companies failed to follow the lead of Knights Apparel? After all, ethical consumers could well comprise 17 percent of the entire market, even if information failures remain as widespread as they were in our sample.[12] If new firms followed Alta Gracia's example by producing clothing that meets the anti-sweatshop movement's standards, they could launch aggressive advertising campaigns, quite possibly with movement backing. A concerted attack on information failures should make it possible to expand the ethical apparel market by another 15 to 20 percentage points to perhaps 32–37 percent of the entire market.[13] This is a very large number of consumers, if divided among a small number of firms that pioneer this market.

Explaining the near-uniform failure of firms to respond to this potential thus seems to require that we go beyond risk aversion to one or both of the other types of explanation identified above. First, if decision-makers believe that most consumers would not pay a price premium for sweat-free apparel, they are not likely to switch to sweat-free production, which will surely raise labor costs. If they could be persuaded by arguments like those we make here, they might then decide to enter this promising, underserved market. In this scenario, there is considerable potential for market self-correction once the problems of false information and understanding are addressed. A credible system of sweat-free labeling could play a vital role in minimizing the information failures that we have found to be so important.

By contrast, the argument that maximizing 'shareholder value' requires the hyper-exploitation of labor implies that the market (i.e., the major firms that control production and retail) will never 'self-correct.' In that case, there is no alternative to building the combination of worker organization, NGO support and citizen mobilization necessary to move key nation-states to outlaw competition based on the hyperexploitation of labor. Social labeling could again play a role in such a government-led response, depending on the specific strategies that governments adopt.

Corporate strategy may be explained by different combinations of the above factors, and there may be other explanations that we have not considered. Given the uncertainties, this is a vital area for future research. In the meantime, we can say this much with confidence: our study suggests that market efficiency—that is, markets that really do supply what customers want, particularly when consumer preferences are informed by ethical concerns—is in the interests of most consumers as well as the workers who actually make the clothing. The only losers—and even here, it is not clear what share of this group would actually lose—are the tiny fraction of the world's population who are the major shareholders of the world's apparel manufacturing companies and retail brands. A commitment to efficiency, as well as to justice, requires that we pursue strategies that will help to realize the full potential of the ethical-apparel market. Success in this regard would mean driving sweatshops and their morally tainted products from the center to the margins of the global apparel market while lifting out of poverty the direct producers of the clothes we wear.

NOTES

1. Thanks to a succession of University of Michigan undergraduates who conducted our interviews, graduated, and went on to greater things: Sunil Joy, Caitlin Pahl, Jenny Lyons, Patrick Fodell, Brandon Thompson, Joanna Hartranft, Elise Herrala, Maggie Klein, Jeremy Levine, Ilan Brandvain, Nakia Kyler, Bryndis Woods, Lynn Lin, Zina Badri, Allison London, Elliot Jankelwitz, Jamie O'Malley, and Lauren Tenney. We are indebted to Larry Root, Bama Athreya, Trina Tocco, Bjorn Claeson, Don Wells, Gregor Murray, Scott Nova, Jeff Ballinger, Bruce Pietrykowski, Hank Greenspan, and Mayer Zald for their encouragement and support for this research, and to Shareen Hertel, Lyle Scruggs, David Vogel, April Linton, and Suzanne Loker for comments on a preliminary draft of this paper presented at the International Studies Association. Finally, our thanks to the participants in Michigan's Economic Sociology workshop, particularly Mark Mizruchi and Greta Krippner, for their excellent feedback on an earlier version of this paper, and to the editors of this volume for their detailed suggestions.
2. These core concepts derive, respectively, from the disciplines of economics, psychology, and sociology, although there is a good deal of borrowing across disciplinary borders.
3. The question to which these students responded was part of a larger survey of 159 University of Michigan students conducted in Robinson's Introduction to Sociology class in Fall 2010.
4. A few web-based businesses—see, for example, Ethix Merch (http://ethixmerch.com) and Justice Clothing (http://www.justiceclothing.com/thereis/justice/)—offer high-quality, sweat-free clothing, but the range of available clothing types and styles is very limited.
5. In fact, American Apparel violated U.S. labor law in its efforts to resist an attempt by UNITE! to organize its L.A. facility. As well, sexual harassment charges have been filed by several female employees against the founder and CEO of the company, Dov Charney (Baker 2003, Economist 2007, Hill 2010). For these reasons, we ourselves do not regard American Apparel as a sweat-free operation.
6. To be an ethical consumer of the sort we are discussing, consumers must also understand what a sweatshop is. Such knowledge is presumed to exist for our subset of consumers who express an ethical concern, which itself requires a basic understanding of sweatshops.
7. Unfortunately, we only added the trust question to our survey toward the end of our interviews. As a result, only 29 of the 143 American Apparel customers who expressed concerns about sweatshops were asked the trust question. These last 29 interviews do not seem to have been unrepresentative, however, so we are reasonably confident that we can extrapolate from them to our whole sample.

8. While regarding higher American Apparel prices as a type of supply failure, our definition of an ethical consumer requires that they be willing to pay a price premium. So, this type of supply failure could explain why some people do not become ethical consumers—that is, they are not willing to pay the requisite price premium.

9. We recognize that concerns about whether the clothing were made in the United States could also be construed as ethical, if they arise from a sense of responsibility for the employment and compensation of American workers. We do not include such concerns in this analysis because we want to focus on sweatshop conditions as the central moral issue. We note, however, that despite American Apparel's name and the "Made in L.A." slogan, many more customers indicated a concern about sweatshops than about the country in which the clothing was manufactured.

10. Statistically significant findings occur where there are substantially more ethical consumer criterion failures of a particular type than we would expect if there were no relationship between failure to meet that criterion and the type of market or moral failure under consideration.

11. Our survey asked respondents to estimate the price premium they were paying at American Apparel, relative to prices of the competitor selling clothing most like American Apparel's, if they believed they were paying a higher price at American Apparel. The mean price premium estimated by this subset was about 18 percent.

12. The 17 percent figure is derived from the share of concerned consumers in our sample who became ethical consumers (26 percent), and the share of all consumers in the general population who have ethical concerns about sweatshops (using Hertel's figure, 65 percent): $.26 \times .65 = 17\%$.

13. The 15–20 percentage-point figure comes from the share of the concern-action gap explained by Type 1 information failure: about 60 percent of the gap was explained, and this type of failure accounted for more than 80 percent of the explained gap. The gap, in turn, applied to the 85 percent of customers who had ethical concerns about sweatshops, which might be reduced to 65 percent for the general population. This yields $.6 \times .8 \times .65 = 31\%$ of the entire consumer population. Since no ad campaign can reach everyone, assume that between half (15 percentage points) and two-thirds (20 percentage points) of those with ethical concerns become aware of the sweat-free option they face.

REFERENCES

Alta Gracia. 2011. 'Alta Gracia: Living Wage Apparel.' Retrieved July 22, 2011 (http://altagraciaapparel.com/).
Baker, L. 2003. 'The Goal: Sweatshop Free. The Problem: Defining It.' *The New York Times*, December 14.
Becker, G. 1986. 'The Economic Approach to Human Behavior.' Pp. 108–122 in *Rational Choice*, edited by J. Elster. New York: New York University Press.
Blasi, A. 1984. 'Moral Identity: Its Role in Moral Functioning.' Pp. 128–139 in *Morality, Moral Behavior and Moral Development*, edited by J.L. Gerwutz and W.M. Kurtines. Hoboken, NJ: John Wiley and Sons.
Colby, A., E. Beaumont, T. Ehrlich, and J. Stephens. 2003. *Educating Citizens: Preparing America's Undergraduates for Lives of Moral and Civic Responsibility*. San Francisco, CA: Jossey-Bass.
Devinney, T., P. Auger, and G.M. Eckhardt. 2010. *The Myth of the Ethical Consumer*. New York: Cambridge University Press.

Dickson, M. 2001. 'Utility of No Sweat Labels for Apparel Consumers: Profiling Label Users and Predicting Their Purchases.' *The Journal of Consumer Affairs* 35(1):96–119.

Dickson, M. 2005. 'Identifying and Profiling Apparel Label Users.' Pp. 155–172 in *The Ethical Consumer*, edited by R. Harrison, T. Newholm, and D. Shaw. Thousand Oaks, CA: Sage.

The Economist. 2007. 'American Apparel's Unusual Flotation is Typical of Dov Charney, Its Founder.' *The Economist*, January 4.

Etzioni, A. 1988. *The Moral Dimension: Toward a New Economics.* New York: Free Press.

Fehr, E. and U. Fischbacher. 2003. 'The Nature of Human Altruism.' *Nature* 425:785–791.

Fehr, E. and H. Gintis. 2007. 'Human Motivation and Social Cooperation: Experimental and Analytic Foundations.' *Annual Review of Sociology* 33(1):43–64.

Frank, R. 1988. *Passions within Reason: The Strategic Role of the Emotions.* New York: W. W. Norton.

Gilligan, C. 1982. *In a Different Voice: Psychological Theory and Women's Development.* Cambridge, MA: Harvard University Press.

Greenhouse, S. 2010. 'Factory Defies Sweatshop Label, but Can it Thrive?' *The New York Times*, July 17.

Harrison, R., T. Newholm, and D. Shaw, eds. 2005. *The Ethical Consumer.* Thousand Oaks, CA: Sage.

Henrich, J., S. Bowles, R. Boyd, C. Camerer, E. Fehr, H. Gintis, and R. McElreath. 2001. 'In Search of Homo Economicus: Behavioral Experiments in 15 Small-Scale Societies.' *American Economic Review* 91(2):73–78.

Hertel, S., P. Heidkamp, and L. Scruggs. 2009. 'Human Rights and Public Opinion: From Attitudes to Action.' *Political Science Quarterly* 124(3):445–461.

Hill, A. 2010. 'The Rise and Fall of American Apparel: The Ethical Clothing Firm Founded by Controversial CEO Dov Charney is Facing Bankruptcy.' *The Guardian*, August 25.

Kimeldorf, H., R. Meyer, M. Prasad, and I. Robinson. 2006. 'Consumers with a Conscience: Will They Pay More?' *Contexts: Understanding People in their Social Worlds* 5(1):24–29.

Kline, J.M. 2010. *Alta Gracia: Branding Decent Working Conditions. Will College Loyalty Embrace Living Wage Sweatshirts?* Research Paper, Kalmanovitz Initiative for Labour and the Working Poor, Georgetown University, Washington, D.C.

Kohlberg, L. 1981. *Essays on Moral Development, Vol.1: The Philosophy of Moral Development.* San Francisco, CA: Harper and Row.

Krier, J. M. 2007. 'Fair Trade 2007: New Facts and Figures from an Ongoing Success Story. A Report on Fair Trade in 33 Consumer Countries.' Schin op Geul, Netherlands: European Fair Trade Association. Retrieved July 22, 2011 (http://www.european-fair-trade-association.org/efta/Doc/FT-E-2007.pdf).

Monroe, K. 1996. *The Heart of Altruism: Perceptions of a Common Humanity.* Princeton, NJ: Princeton University Press.

Mueller, D. 1985. *Public Choice.* New York: Cambridge University Press.

Olson, M. 1965. *The Logic of Collective Action: Public Goods and the Theory of Groups.* Cambridge, MA: Harvard University Press.

Paharia, N. and R. Deshpandé. 2009. 'Sweatshop Labour is Wrong Unless the Jeans are Cute: Motivated Moral Disengagement.' Working Paper No. 09–079, Harvard Business School, Boston, MA. Retrieved July 22, 2011 (www.people.fas.harvard.edu/_hiscox/Peharia.pdf).

Pietrykowski, B. 2008. *The Political Economy of Consumer Behavior: Contesting Consumption.* London, United Kingdom: Routledge.

Piff, P. K., B. H. Cheng, S. Côté, D. Keltner, and M. Kraus. 2010. 'Having Less, Giving More: The Influence of Social Class on Prosocial Behavior.' *Journal of Personality and Social Psychology* 99(5):771–84.

Pollin, R., J. Burns, and J. Heintz. 2004. 'Global Apparel Production and Sweatshop Labour: Can Raising Retail Prices Finance Living Wages?' *Cambridge Journal of Economics* 28(2):153–171.

Prasad, M., H. Kimeldorf, R. Meyer, and I. Robinson. 2004. 'Consumers of the World Unite: A Market-Based Approach to Sweatshops.' *Labour Studies Journal* 29(3):57–79.

Sen, A. 1979. 'Rational Fools.' Pp. 87–109 in *Philosophy and Economic Theory*, edited by F. Hahn and M. Hollis. Oxford, United Kingdom: Oxford University Press.

Shaw, D., I. Clarke and E. Shiu. 2000. 'The Contribution of Ethical Obligation and Self-Identity to the Theory of Planned Behavior: An Exploration of Ethical Consumers.' *Journal of Marketing Management* 16(8):879–94.

Vogel, D. 2005. *The Market for Virtue: The Potential and Limits of Corporate Social Responsibility*. Washington, D.C.: Brookings Institution.

9 Social Labeling on the Web

How Fashion Retailers Communicate Information about Labor Practices to Online Consumers

Llyr Roberts

The last decade has seen a rapid rise in online fashion retailing. A growing number of apparel retailers and clothing and footwear brands now retail on the web, and the market share of online clothing sales is growing every year. The period has also witnessed high-profile campaigns against global sportswear brands and media exposés of poor working conditions in factories supplying retailers in the United Kingdom and other Western countries (BBC 2008, Spar and La Mure 2003). Reports have identified major labor violations in garment supply chains, including low wages, excessive working hours, lack of freedom of association, dangerous working conditions, physical and verbal harassment, and child labor (Clean Clothes Campaign 2005). As a result, there is growing pressure on retailers to improve ethical traceability and disclose information about labor standards in their supplier factories. One of the traditional barriers to disclosure has been the practical difficulty of communicating information about working conditions to consumers in a meaningful way at the point of sale in retail stores. Information on traditional garment tags or labels has been limited to fabric composition, washing instructions and country of origin, and there is limited space on these labels to provide information on working conditions in complex supply chains. Online retailing spaces provide several opportunities to overcome this barrier. A large amount of information on working conditions can be shared with consumers on web pages, and decisions on the level of detail can be left to the individual user through links that enable customers to draw as much or as little information as they need, depending on their own individual information requirements. This study therefore seeks to explore how information about working conditions is currently communicated to consumers in online fashion pages and to assess the progress of social labeling on the web in the garment sector.

1 LITERATURE REVIEW

Online Fashion Retail

Online fashion is one of the more unexpected success stories of internet retail. Previous research had pointed to consumer reluctance to shop for garments by telephone (Cox and Rich 1964), catalogue (Gaal and Burns 2001), or other remote means because of the perceived risk of making a purchase without being able to physically inspect the merchandise or try it on. This concern was echoed in early studies of online retail, which suggested that, while consumers were happy to buy online products with primarily geometric properties, such as books and CDs, they preferred to purchase products with primarily material properties, such as clothes, in shopping environments that allowed for physical inspection (McCabe and Nowlis 2003). Concerns about online fraud and security were also identified as significant barriers to the growth of the market (Kwon and Lee 2003). Much of the subsequent research focused on how to improve the online shopping experience and reduce the perceived risk of making clothing purchases online by providing more verbal and visual product information (Kim and Lennon 2008, Seock and Norton 2007b). Studies have tested how the use of components such as virtual models (Fiore et al. 2005, Yang and Young 2009), product movement and rotation (Park et al. 2005), and personalization elements such as wish lists, personal shopping advice, and online chat functions (Lee and Park 2009) could help reduce uncertainty. Kim et al. (2007) have organized these components into high and low task-relevant information cues based on the findings of a content analysis of U.S. apparel websites and a survey of consumers. Of the 61 separate website components they identified, price, product photographs and assurances on payment security were found to have a high task-relevance in terms achieving utilitarian and shopping goals; and while personalization elements had a low task-relevance, they were found to enhance the hedonic value of online fashion websites by making the shopping experience more pleasurable.

Despite the pessimism of the early literature, online apparel sales have grown steadily over recent years. This growth can be explained in part by the growing sophistication of online retail websites and the increased availability and choice of clothing on the web. Park and Stoel (2005) have also found that previous experience of online clothing purchases significantly reduces uncertainty and the perceived risk of buying clothes over the internet, and in the United Kingdom, a quarter of all internet users now report having made clothing or footwear purchases online in the last three months (ONS 2009). In fact, clothing and sporting goods are now the second-most common item bought online by British consumers, after films and music (ONS 2009), and online clothing and footwear sales were valued at £4.3 billion in 2010, which equated to 10 percent of all U.K. spending on fashion (Mintel 2010b). This figure seems set to continue to rise as more and more consumers gain experience buying apparel online and become more confident about online shopping for fashion items as a result.

Another key trend over the last decade has been the emergence of multi-channel retailing. During the dot-com bubble at the turn of the millennium, some commentators forecast that internet pure-play retailers would overtake leading high-street names. But while the traditional bricks 'n' mortar stores were initially slow off the mark to enter cyberspace, they soon begun to fight back by adopting multichannel—or bricks 'n' clicks—strategies (Nicholson et al. 2002). They were able to capitalize on existing brand awareness and brand loyalty among consumers, and brand familiarity has been found to reduce the perceived risk of purchasing clothing online (Jones and Soyoung 2010, Kwon and Lennon 2009, Park and Stoel 2005). Hence, despite the success of some internet pure-play retailers such as Asos, an estimated 80 percent of all U.K. online fashion sales now go through the websites of established high-street or catalogue retailers (Mintel 2010b). Multichannel retail has also influenced consumers' information search behavior as shoppers increasingly use the internet to research products and brands prior to eventual purchase offline in traditional stores (Hyun-Hwa and Kim 2010, Sands et al. 2010). A number of consumers also engage in the reverse practice of sampling goods in a physical store before shopping remotely via a catalogue or online where there may be better deals and greater availability in terms of size and color (Nicholson et al. 2002, Seock and Norton 2007a).

Communicating Social Responsibility on the Web

The social and environmental performance of corporations has come under growing scrutiny over the last two decades. Activist organizations have used the internet and other mass-communication channels to highlight some of the negative consequences of globalization and corporate behavior (Smith 2001). This in turn has created a need for companies to disclose more information about their social and environmental records. It has now become the norm for large corporations to issue annual corporate social responsibility (CSR) or sustainability reports and to have CSR pages on their corporate websites (KPMG 2008, Lee et al. 2009). Most studies of CSR communication to date have focused on hard copy, formal CSR reports (Adams and Frost 2006). However, a growing number of studies have started to analyze social reporting on the web, and the internet has gradually established itself as the main channel of corporate communication with stakeholders (Bondy et al. 2004, Coupland 2005). Studies of CSR communication on the web have ranged from large-scale, web-content mining surveys of the web pages of hundreds of global companies (e.g., Pollach et al. 2009) to much more narrowly focused studies of a handful of companies in a single country (e.g., Kolk et al. 2010) or sector (e.g., Holcomb et al. 2007, Jenkins and Yakovleva 2006). Most studies have focused on quantifying the level of disclosure, identifying themes, and reporting trends (e.g., Lee et al. 2009), although a handful of studies have adopted a more interpretive approach and looked at the use of language and imagery to try and construct particular meanings and understandings (e.g., Coupland 2005).

While the origins of social labels can be traced back to the Co-op brand in the United Kingdom in the nineteenth century and the White Label for apparel introduced by the National Consumers League in the United States in 1899, most social labels as we know them today came into existence in the 1990s (Fliess et al. 2007, Zadek et al. 1998). The number of labeling schemes on social and environmental issues has since soared, and the global directory Ecolabel Index currently lists almost 400 labels in more than 200 countries spanning 25 industry sectors (Ecolabel Index 2011). Social labeling differs from social reporting and other forms of CSR communication in two key ways. The primary audience for social labeling is consumers, whereas other material is usually seeking to meet the information needs of a broader range of stakeholders, including pressure groups, investors, and the media. Social labels also usually take the form of words and symbols positioned on or alongside a product, and they aim to influence economic decisions at the point of sale (Zadek et al. 1998). Internet retail presents a number of new opportunities for social labels since space is not as limited as on traditional product tags and labels. Much more comprehensive labeling information can be provided on or alongside a product in online retail spaces and decisions about the level of detail can be left to the individual user through the use of links that enable customers to draw as much or as little information as they need. Yet despite the growing academic interest in the content and design of online retail spaces, surprisingly little research has been conducted into different approaches to social labeling on the web. Tang et al. (2004) have compared the use of visual and verbal communication in the design of environmental labels in a simulated web-based shopping environment and found a combination of words and imagery to be more effective than visual or verbal elements alone. A couple of further studies have looked at how social responsibility is communicated to consumers in actual online retail spaces (Caruana and Crane 2008) and how this compares with other types of material, such as product packaging and corporate publications (Karstens and Belz 2006). However, in general, there has been a dearth of research to date on the use of social labeling on the web.

Social Responsibility, Fashion and the Web

Fashion brands and retailers in affluent consumer countries have faced more criticism than companies have in most other sectors in relation to their records on social responsibility. A process of vertical fragmentation started in the 1970s has seen companies outsource most of the labor-intensive aspects of production to suppliers in developing and emerging economies due to lower labor costs and the removal of traditional barriers to international trade (Dicken 2007, Jones 2006). Different functions such as garment design, fiber production, fabric manufacture and garment assembly are now typically undertaken by completely separate companies, and retailers source from tens or even hundreds of independently owned garment factories scattered across the globe (Hines 2006, Rivoli 2005). The sector came under intense scrutiny in the mid-1990s for sourcing from suppliers with poor records on working conditions. Campaigning organizations, such as the National Labor Committee in the United States and the Clean Clothes

Campaign in Europe, highlighted cases of low wages, excessive hours, poor health and safety, child labor, and other labor violations in factories supplying the U.S. university athletic apparel sector and global retail giants such as Nike and GAP (Spar and La Mure 2003, Wight et al. 2007). These stories were picked up in turn by the media, and managers and investors became increasingly concerned about the potential damage to the reputation and value of their brands (Roberts 2003). What followed has been described as a 'code rush' as retailers hurriedly introduced codes of conduct and factory audits to answer their critics and protect themselves from further reputational harm (Sum and Ngai 2005). In some cases, this movement has led to some notable improvements in terms of working conditions and transparency, especially in cases where audits are undertaken by not-for-profit multistakeholder organizations and where the results are publicly reported (Dickson and Eckman 2008, Dickson et al. 2009). In other cases, the implementation of codes has been patchy, however, and many argue that weak social reporting and a lack of transparency about audit methodology and findings allows labor violations to remain hidden (Clean Clothes Campaign 2005).

Several studies have shown high consumer awareness of poor working conditions in garment-assembly factories due to the high-profile campaigns of the mid-1990s (Carrigan and Attalla 2001, Joergens 2006). Despite this awareness, social labeling for fashion is much less developed than labeling for food and other consumer goods (Fliess et al. 2007). In the United Kingdom, for example, fair-trade foods have gained a considerable market share over recent years, aided by the Fairtrade Foundation label and wide availability of products in mainstream outlets (Co-operative Bank 2010). But, the ethical-fashion market is much less developed, and while clothes made with Fair Trade Certified cotton are now available on the high street, no social label on working conditions at the garment-assembly stage is in widespread use (Fairtrade Foundation 2008, Shaw et al. 2006). Aspers (2008) argues that this is absence of labeling is because the garment sector is too complex and volatile for social labeling systems because fashion items are constantly changing and the number of links in clothing production chains are too complex to share with consumers. Other studies have suggested that consumers are simply not interested in how their garments are assembled. Joergens (2006), for example, found that her sample of young shoppers did not find information about labor violations in clothing factories in distant countries relevant because it did not have a negative impact on their own personal well-being. Dickson (1999) did find an appetite for some form of hang tag or label with information about a company's avoidance of sweatshop production among a much larger sample of U.S. consumers, however, and subsequently identified a market segment of 16 percent of consumers that would use a no-sweat label and place more importance on this than quality, color, and fiber content (Dickson 2001). Both Shaw et al. (2006) and Valor (2007) in turn have found considerable uncertainty among their respective samples of British consumers about the conditions under which their garments are assembled, and frustration about the lack of information available to them about working conditions and the origins of clothes.

Only a handful of studies have looked at how fashion retailers communicate information about social responsibility on the web. The broadest study is by Dickson and Kovaleski (2007) who surveyed the websites of the 119 largest clothing retailers in the United States to measure CSR disclosure. They found only 27 percent published their codes of conduct on their websites, and 72 percent did not report any information about their CSR programs; furthermore, while some well-known apparel companies provided detailed information and the option of downloading CSR reports, only 8 out of the 119 companies published the results of their code-implementation efforts. Similarly, a content analysis of the websites of the 10 leading clothing retailers in the United Kingdom found two continue to operate without publishing any code of conduct and only three disclose any findings from factory audits (Roberts 2010). A couple of other U.K. studies have explored how individual companies use their corporate websites and the social web to try and improve their corporate identity and reputation for social responsibility (Cheng et al. 2008, Jones et al. 2009). And Kim et al. (2007) found in their aforementioned study of apparel website components that information about social responsibility had a fairly low task-relevance among their sample, which suggests consumers do not feel this information is essential for making online-apparel purchases. Social responsibility is not the primary focus of this study, however, and the findings from Dickson (1999, 2001), Shaw et al. (2006), and Valor (2007) suggest that social responsibility may have a much higher task-relevance for some fashion consumers. And the Kim et al. (2007) study also implies that shopping experience may be enhanced and made more pleasurable for consumers by the inclusion of information on social responsibility.

No studies of how social labeling is used in online fashion retail pages were identified during the review of the literature. This study therefore seeks to address this gap by focusing on how information about working conditions is communicated to apparel consumers in online retail spaces. A sample of fashion retail pages was evaluated to identify what words and symbols relating to social responsibility are included alongside a product. The study also explored how elements such as the design and layout of web pages and systems of navigation shape consumer understanding and privilege some elements over others (Papson et al. 2007).

2 METHODS

Most of the studies of online-fashion retail to date have used content analysis (e.g., Kim et al. 2007), surveys (e.g., Kim and Lee 2008), and experimental methods (e.g., Fiore et al. 2005) to test a particular hypothesis or theory. The literature review highlighted that social labeling on the web is an underdeveloped area of research, however, particularly in the context of fashion. An exploratory design was therefore considered more appropriate because of the need to describe the phenomena in more detail and define the research problem (Schutt 2001). Qualitative content analysis was used as the main method of inquiry, and a sample of web pages was subjected to analysis in a similar fashion to the way texts and documents have been analyzed in previous studies (Bryman 2008). A critical hermeneutic analytical approach was adopted because of its emphasis on understanding texts from the point of view of the author(s) and within the context in which the texts were written (Forster 2006), and a formal critical hermeneutic framework for analyzing documents developed by Phillips and Brown (1993) was adapted for the study. The framework entailed considering the following five key aspects of the texts:

- Structural aspect: does the order in which different elements are arranged shape the meaningfulness of the text?
- Conventional aspect: does the text follow rules and conventions that can only be decoded and understood by members of a particular social group?
- Contextual aspect: is the meaning of text shaped by the historical and social context of its production and the position of the author within the organization?
- Intentional aspect: who is the intended audience and readership for a text, and how does this shape the content?
- Referential aspect: do the websites make symbolic references to elements outside of themselves?

A multiple-case-study approach was adopted to allow for the examination of all the major players in the sector, to gain an understanding of the range of social labeling that exists, and to identify norms and patterns that may have developed (Morhardt 2010, Yin 2003). U.K. multichannel retailers were selected because of the relative maturity of the online-fashion sector in Britain and the high proportion of online clothing sales channeled through the websites of these companies (Mintel 2010b). Discounters, sport shops and department stores were excluded because they retail other brands in the main and do not have direct oversight over garment assembly factories as a result. Supermarkets were also excluded, despite having a growing market share in terms of volume (TNS Worldpanel 2008) because the primary focus of their websites is food and items other than clothes. The top 20 U.K. fashion multiples were identified from a list of leading U.K. clothing retailers produced by the market-research company Mintel (2010a). Six of the companies were excluded because they did not retail clothes online on their U.K. websites (Primark, H&M, Gap, Zara, Dunnes Stores, and Ethel Austin), and TK Maxx was also excluded because it does not have its own label. The 13 retail groups in the final sample had 46.3 percent share of clothing retailers' sales in the 2008–2009 period, but no breakdown into offline and online sales was available (Mintel 2010b). Some of the retail groups have more than one high-street and retail brand (Arcadia Group, Peacock Group, Alexon Brands, and Auora Fashions), and one retail brand was used to represent the group as a whole in these cases (Dorothy Perkins, Peacocks, Alexon, and Oasis). A basic plain women's cotton T-shirt was selected as a constant attribute to allow valid comparisons to be made between the different cases. Four of the final sample of retailers (River Island, Monsoon, Alexon, and Oasis) did not sell a basic cotton T-shirt on their sites, however, so the least expensive T-shirt they sell online was taken as a proxy to allow for their inclusion in the remainder of the study. (See Table 9.1).

Retail pages are constantly being changed and updated, which presents a number of challenges in terms of the reliability, replicability, and validity of the study. Web pages are ephemeral objects and can be adapted, redesigned,

Table 9.1   Leading Clothing Retailers Share of U.K. Clothing Sales 2008–2009

Retail Group	% Share of Clothing sales 2008–09	Retail Online (Website Name)	Price of Basic Cotton T-shirt
Marks & Spencer	13.4	Yes	£5
Next	7.5	Yes	£4
Arcadia Group	6.3	Yes (Dorothy Perkins)	£5
Primark	5.2	No	
TK Maxx	4.7	No	
New Look	3.8	Yes	£4
Matalan	3.6	Yes	£3
Bhs	2.7	Yes	£6
Peacock Group	2.4	Yes (Peacocks)	£4
River Island	2.3	Yes	
Monsoon	1.9	Yes	
H&M	1.8	N	
Gap	1	N	
Zara	0.9	N	
Dunnes Stores	0.7	N	
Alexon Brands	0.6	Yes (Alexon)	
Mackays Stores Group (M&Co)	0.6	Yes	£5
The Edinburgh Woollen Mill	0.5	Yes	£7
Ethel Austin	0.5	N	
Aurora Fashions	0.5	Y (Oasis)	

Source: Mintel (2010a).

moved, or removed without warning, so proactive steps need to be taken to capture web pages and allow for future analyses (Schneider and Foot 2004). An electronic print was therefore taken of each retail page on 14 June 2010, and links and paths to information on working conditions were also logged on this date.[1]

3 FINDINGS

Structural Aspect

The sample online-retail pages all follow a fairly standard design template, which is illustrated in Figure 9.1. The header section at the top of the page always includes the logo of the retailer and a checkout or order total function in all cases except River Island. There are also links to other areas of the website in most headers. The main body takes up most of the available space; it is usually made up of an image of the product on the left and the product name, price, and description on the right. A number of the retailers also recommend complementary items and accessories in this area or list products that other browsers have bought. Some of the retailers include a navigational sidebar on the left-hand side of the page, with subheadings

Figure 9.1 Standard Template of Retail Pages

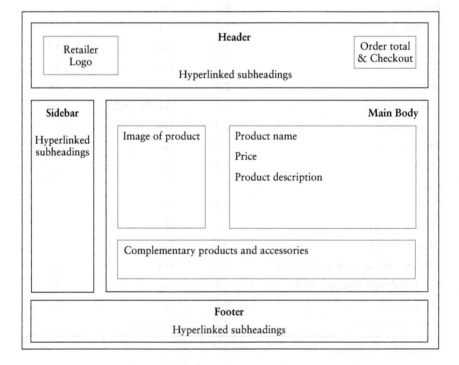

linking to other areas of the website. Finally, all the retail pages have a footer area with a range of hyperlinks to other areas of the site and / or external sites. The hypertext used in these links is invariably much smaller than the text used in the main body. (See Figure 9.1).

Table 9.2 presents a summary of where information about working conditions is positioned. There is no reference by any of the retailers in the main body of the retail pages to factory working conditions. Furthermore, while all provide detail about material content and garment care next to the product, none provide the country of origin. The only reference to any ethical concern in the main body is by M&S, who includes a Fairtrade logo and a link to a video about Fairtrade Cotton; this material focuses exclusively on terms of trade with cotton farmers and makes no reference to the garment-assembly stage. Three of the retailers (Bhs, Edinburgh Woollen Mills and Oasis) provide no link to any detail on working conditions from the product page, or indeed anywhere else on their websites. The remaining 10 retailers require the consumer to navigate away from the retail page to find this information. The information is accessed by clicking on hypertext that is included either as a footer at the bottom of the page or as a link from the navigational side bar. In six cases, users need to identify and follow a further link (Dorothy Perkins, Matalan, Peacocks, Monsoon, Alexion, and M&Co), while information on working conditions is three clicks away from the retail page in the case of Next and New Look and four clicks away in the case of Marks and Spencer. See Table 9.2.

Table 9.2 Positioning of Information about Working Conditions

Company	Positioning of link	Number of Clicks
M&S	Footer	4
Next	Footer	3
Dorothy Perkins	Footer	2
New Look	Footer	3
Matalan	Footer	2
Bhs		
Peacocks	Footer	2
River Island	Footer	1
Monsoon	Footer	2
Alexon	Sidebar	2
M&Co	Footer	2
Edinburgh Woollen Mills		
Oasis		

Conventional Aspect

Table 9.3 details what text the sample retailers use to link to information on working conditions, or in other words, what hypertext consumers have to click on to find out more detail. The first level is the product page itself, and three of the fashion multiples (New Look, Matalan and Peacocks) use the term 'about,' a very general and indefinite word with no obvious association with working conditions. Several other retailers use words that assume familiarity with business terminology, for example 'corporate responsibility' and 'culture & commitment,' or terms that assume an interest in business and corporate matters, such as 'the company' and 'corporate.' Marks and Spencer also provide a direct link to Plan A, an interactive sustainability

Table 9.3 Hypertext Linking to Detail on Working Conditions

Company	First Level	Second Level	Third Level	Fourth Level
M&S	The Company	How we do business	Our policies	Ethical trading
	Plan A	What we're doing	Fair partner	Progress so far
Next	The Company	Corporate Responsibility	Our suppliers	
Dorothy Perkins	Responsibilities	Ethical policy FAQs		
New Look	About us	Responsibilities	Ethical trading	
Matalan	About	Ethical workforce responsibility		
Bhs				
Peacocks	About Peacocks	Ethical Trading		
River Island	Corporate responsibility			
Monsoon	Culture & Commitment	Values that put people first		
Alexon	Investors click here to get access to the Alexon PLC site	Corporate Responsibility		
M&Co	Corporate	Ethical Policy		
Edinburgh Woollen Mills				
Oasis				

website that includes commitments on working conditions, although an assumption is made that the consumer will be familiar with the Plan A brand since no further detail is provided at the first level. The term 'responsibilities' used on the Dorothy Perkins website has a closer and more obvious association with working conditions than any of the other terms used. Once the consumer has taken the first step and navigated away from the product page, the language and terminology becomes more direct. A number of the retailers use the term 'ethical' at the second, third, and fourth levels, a term that is more familiar to consumers due to media reports about ethical fashion and ethical consumerism (Ethical Consumer 2009). Matalan also uses the term 'workforce' at the second level, but none of the other retailers use self-explanatory terms, such as working conditions, factory workers, and labor standards, to link to material on these topics.

Contextual Aspect

The key contextual aspect here is who within the retail companies is responsible for the content and design of web pages. Product pages will have been developed in all likelihood by online retail teams whose main focus and priority will be product sales. The content of pages detailing working conditions, on the other hand, will have been developed by corporate communication professionals or teams dedicated to dealing with ethical issues. These authors will be looking to protect the reputation of the retailer and position the company as a responsible retailer. Online retail and corporate communications are usually separate functions within large retail organizations and fall under different parts of the business. This helps explain the separation of ethical pages from retail pages and the absence of references to working conditions on product pages.

Intentional Aspect

The intended audience for product pages will vary to an extent from retailer to retailer, depending on the retailer's position in the market and the customers it is targeting. Retailers like Dorothy Perkins and New Look target younger consumers, while Alexon and Edinburgh Woollen Mills target an older demographic. Price competition between U.K. clothing retailers has become intense over recent years, and most of the fashion multiples in this sample appear to be targeting price-sensitive consumers in their product pages. This is particularly the case with a basic item like a plain T-shirt: 9 of the 13 brands retail a basic women's T-shirt, and these range in price from £3 to £7 and average £4.78. Price is given a prominent position in a bold, large font at the top of the main body of each page, and a number of further discounts are offered on multiple purchases (e.g., M&S, Next, Bhs) and delivery costs (e.g., Dorothy Perkins, Edinburgh Woollen Mill). The intended audience for the pages detailing working conditions is different.

The main target here is corporate investors, pressure groups, the media and stakeholders other than consumers. In fact, in four cases, this information is located on a completely separate corporate website, away from the retail pages (M&S, Next, New Look and Alexon), and Alexon states explicitly whom its intended audience is in the hypertext used: 'Investors click here to get access to the Alexon PLC site.' There is no attempt to encourage consumers to access these pages and engage with the material, with the exception of Marks and Spencer who have a separate interactive website for Plan A that is aimed at consumers.

Referential Aspect

Communication materials often refer to things outside themselves to condition the understandings of the audience, and marketers often make extensive use of images, colors and symbols to create positive associations with a product or brand; however, the retail pages of most of the fashion multiples in this study are surprisingly bare of such elements. Almost all have plain black, gray and white backgrounds and limit the use of bright colors in product images and price promotions, and the only images used are of the garments themselves. There are a couple of exceptions to this rule: Monsoon opts for a purple background and a purple ethnic-style print to highlight its use of hand-crafted materials and links with home-workers, and Edinburgh Woollen Mill includes an image of an old mill in the header to emphasize the company's heritage, a key element of its branding. Five of the retailers include logos for internet security-accreditation schemes such as ISIS (Marks and Spencer), VeriSign Secured (Oasis and Edinburgh Woollen Mill), PCI Compliant (M&Co), and MasterCard SecureCode (River Island and Edinburgh Woollen Mill) to both address consumer concern about online security and create the feeling of a safe shopping environment. However, as already discussed, only Marks and Spencer displays a logo for an ethical-accreditation scheme with its inclusion of a Fairtrade Foundation logo. And the general absence of referential aspects suggests that the web page producers wish to keep retail pages as simple as possible, to focus consumers' attention on the product and its price.

There is considerable variation between the retailers when it comes to pages detailing working conditions; they range in detail and design from very basic (e.g., River Island, Matalan) to highly sophisticated (e.g., M&S, New Look). The content of these pages and level of disclosure by the retailers has been explored in more detail elsewhere (see Roberts 2010). It is worth noting, however, that these pages make extensive use of referential elements, in marked contrast with the retail pages. Six of the retailers are members of the Ethical Trading Initiative (ETI). M&S, Next, New Look, River Island, Monsoon, and M&Co highlight this fact in their responsibility pages by providing links to the ETI website and the ETI Code of Conduct, detailing what ETI work streams they are participating in, and, in the case of New Look, including a quote from an ETI director endorsing its approach. Non-ETI member Peacocks, in turn, highlights its membership in the Supplier Ethical Data Exchange (SEDEX), Matalan points to fact that it retains 'independent auditors,' and Alexon announces its intention to work with 'organisations such as Labor Behind the Label.' By doing these things, the retailers are seeking to create associations between themselves and respected external organizations. Only minimal use is made of images, however, and only two retailers—Monsoon and Peacocks—include any images of a garment factory or factory workers. This absence of any visual representation of the garment-assembly stage suggests that retailers do not want to make associations between their brand and product and the factories where garments are made.

4 DISCUSSION

The main finding of this study is that information on working conditions and broader ethical issues is completely separated from the retail pages of the main multichannel retailers in the United Kingdom. There are a number of potential explanations for this approach. It may be that the retailers have decided to keep retail pages as simple as possible and limit the content to the components Kim et al. (2007) and others have shown to have the highest task-relevance for consumers, components such as price, product images and product descriptions. Another possible explanation is that the separation is simply a reflection of the fact that the content of retail and corporate parts of websites are produced by different functions within large retail organizations, and separating product and corporate information has simply become the norm. However, fashion multiples simply might not want to engage with consumers on these issues in retail spaces in case highlighting how garments are assembled has a negative impact on sales and the bottom line.

Many of the fashion multiples do in fact provide quite detailed information on their codes of conduct and labor policies somewhere on their websites; however, the hyperlinks to this material are usually in an extremely small font and located outside the main body of the retail page. The language used in the hypertext is either very indirect or corporate in tone, and the navigational path from retail page to ethical information is usually complex. As Papson et al. (2007) point out, these design and navigational elements shape the user's understandings and privilege some users over others, depending on their knowledge and web-search skills, and few consumers will realistically be able or willing to decode the path to the information on social responsibility most sample retailers currently provide.

The inclusion of the recognizable Fairtrade logo alongside the product by Marks and Spencer illustrates how information on social responsibility can be incorporated into retail pages without significantly altering the standard layout and design. As suggested by Tang et al. (2004), the combination of visual and verbal elements appears more effective than a visual- or verbal-only approach, and the inclusion of hyperlinks makes it simple for shoppers to access further information. The absence of a logo or symbol for working conditions that is well established and instantly recognizable to a broad range of consumers is undoubtedly a limitation on the growth of social labeling in relation to garment assembly. Even taking the simple step of replacing hypertext such as 'about' and 'corporate responsibility' with terms such as 'working conditions' or 'fair labor' would enable a wider range of consumers to decode the path to information on labor policies, however. The inclusion of information about country of origin with the details about material content and garment care is another simple step that would help inform consumers about the origins of garments.

The fact that five of the fashion multiples already include logos for internet-security schemes reflects an awareness of consumer concerns about online fraud, as highlighted by Kwon and Lee (2003). This also demonstrates how logos and labels can be included in retail pages. Kim et al. (2007) have shown that assurances on payment security have a much higher task-relevance for most online fashion consumers than information on social responsibility, and advocates of social labeling may face an uphill struggle getting more information on working conditions included in online fashion retail pages as a result. However, other studies have identified considerable concern among a significant proportion of consumers about sweatshop working conditions (e.g. Dickson 1999, 2001), and the findings of the Kim et al. (2007) study suggest shopping experience may be enhanced by the inclusion of this information. Improved social labeling could therefore potentially be a source of competitive advantage for an online or multichannel fashion retailer.

CONCLUSION

Online retailing presents several opportunities to improve the way fashion retailers communicate information about labor practices to consumers. Much more detail about working conditions can be shared at the point of sale in online retail environments than in traditional offline stores, and navigational tools such as hyperlinks and logos can be used to empower consumers by giving them the option of accessing as much or as little information as they need. Yet while online fashion has become much more established in recent years, this study reveals that social labeling is still very much it its infancy in the sector. No widely recognizable logo or form of wording has been developed to communicate information about working conditions to consumers at the point of sale. U.K. fashion multiples separate information on working conditions from product pages, and the way websites are structured makes it difficult for users to find details about social responsibility. The language used to link to this information is difficult for consumers to decode, and the material is targeted at pressure groups, the media, and stakeholders other than consumers. And retailers appear reluctant to engage with customers about labor issues in online retail pages.

The study contributes to the literature on social labeling in the global fashion industry by presenting the first evaluation of how information on working conditions is shared alongside products at the point of sale in online retail environments. Interest in this emergent field of research is likely to grow as the market share of online apparel continues to rise and the boundaries between the online and offline information search behavior of consumers becomes increasingly blurred due to the multichannel marketing strategies of retailers. The main limitation of the study is the exploratory design, and the findings are not generalizable to other markets and sectors. Future research should look in more detail at the information needs of consumers and at how they interact with information on social responsibility in online environments. Further research is also needed into the communication strategies of fashion retailers and the potential use of new mobile and interactive technologies to share information with consumers in a meaningful way at the point of purchase.

NOTE

1. A PDF copy of the final sample of web pages is available on request from robertsls1@cf.ac.uk.

REFERENCES

Adams, C.A. and G.R. Frost. 2006. 'Accessibility and Functionality of the Corporate Web Site: Implications for Sustainability Reporting.' *Business Strategy and the Environment* 15(4):275–287.

Aspers, P. 2008. 'Labelling Fashion Markets.' *International Journal of Consumer Studies* 32(6):633–638.

BBC. 2008. 'Primark Fires Child Worker Firms.' Retrieved April 8, 2010 (http://news.bbc.co.uk/1/hi/business/7456897.stm).

Bondy, K., D. Matten and J. Moon. 2004. 'The Adoption of Voluntary Codes of Conduct in MNCs: A Three-Country Comparative Study.' *Business and Society Review* 109(4):449–477.

Carrigan, M. and A. Attalla. 2001. 'The Myth of the Ethical Consumer-Do Ethics Matter in Purchase Behaviour?' *Journal of Consumer Marketing* 18(7):560–578.

Caruana, R. and A. Crane. 2008. 'Constructing Consumer Responsibility: Exploring the Role of Corporate Communications.' *Organization Studies* 29(12):1495–1519.

Cheng, R., I. Grime, and T. Hines. 2008. 'Desired and Perceived Identities of Fashion Retailers.' *European Journal of Marketing* 42(5/6):682–701.

Clean Clothes Campaign. 2005. *Looking for a Quick Fix: How Weak Social Auditing is Keeping Workers in Sweatshops*. Amsterdam, Netherlands: Clean Clothes Campaign.

Co-operative Bank. 2010. *Ethical Consumerism Report 2010*. Manchester, United Kingdom: Co-operative Bank.

Coupland, C. 2005. 'Corporate Social Responsibility as Argument on the Web.' *Journal of Business Ethics* 62(4):355–366.

Cox, D. F. and S. U. Rich. 1964. 'Perceived Risk and Consumer Decision-Making: The Case of Telephone Shopping.' *Journal of Marketing Research* 1(4):32–39.

Dicken, P. 2007. *Global Shift: Mapping the Changing Contours of the World Economy.* New York: Guilford.

Dickson, M. A. 1999. 'US Consumers Knowledge of and Concern with Apparel Sweatshops.' *Journal of Fashion Marketing and Management* 3(1):44–55.

Dickson, M. A. 2001. 'Utility of No Sweat Labels for Apparel Consumers: Profiling Label Users and Predicting Their Purchases.' *Journal of Consumer Affairs* 35(1):96.

Dickson, M. A. and M. Eckman. 2008. 'Media Portrayal of Voluntary Public Reporting about Corporate Social Responsibility Performance: Does Coverage Encourage or Discourage Ethical Management?' *Journal of Business Ethics* 83(4):725–743.

Dickson, M. A. and K. Kovaleski. 2007. 'Implementing Labor Compliance in the Apparel Industry.' Paper presented at the International Textiles and Apparel Association Annual Conference, November 8, Los Angeles, CA.

Dickson, M. A., M. J. Eckman, and S. Loker. 2009. *Social Responsibility in the Global Apparel Industry.* New York: Fairchild.

Ecolabel Index. 2011. 'All Ecolabels: Alphabetical Index.' Retrieved March 3, 2011 (http://www.ecolabelindex.com/ecolabels/).

Ethical Consumer Research Association. 2009. *Clothes Shops Undressed.* Manchester, United Kingdom: Ethical Consumer Research Association.

Fairtrade Foundation. 2008. *Questions and Answers about Fairtrade Certified Cotton.* London, United Kingdom: Fairtrade Foundation.

Fiore, A. M., J. Kim, and H. H. Lee. 2005. 'Effect of Image Interactivity Technology on Consumer Responses Toward the Online Retailer.' *Journal of Interactive Marketing* 19(3):38.

Fliess, B., O. Agatiello, O. L. Dubreuil, and L. Hyung-Jong. 2007. *CSR and Trade: Informing Consumers about Social and Environmental Conditions of Globalised Production.* Paris, France: Organisation for Economic Cooperation and Development.

Forster, N. 2006. 'The Analysis of Company Documentation.' Pp. 83–106 in *Documentary Research*, edited by J. Scott. London, United Kingdom: Sage.

Gaal, B. and L. D. Burns. 2001. 'Apparel Descriptions in Catalogs and Perceived Risk Associated with Catalog Purchases.' *Clothing and Textiles Research Journal* 19(1):22–30.

Hines, T. 2006. 'The Nature of the Clothing and Textiles Industries: Structure, Context and Processes.' Pp. 3–28 in *The Fashion Handbook*, edited by T. Jackson and D. Shaw. London, United Kingdom: Routledge.

Holcomb, J. L., F. Okumus, and R. S. Upchurch. 2007. 'Corporate Social Responsibility: What are Top Hotel Companies Reporting?' *International Journal of Contemporary Hospitality Management* 19(6):461–475.

Hyun-Hwa, L. and J. Kim. 2010. 'Investigating Dimensionality of Multi-Channel Retailer's Cross-Channel Integration Practices and Effectiveness: Shopping Orientation and Loyalty Intention.' *Journal of Marketing Channels* 17(4):281–312.

Jenkins, H. and N. Yakovleva. 2006. 'Corporate Social Responsibility in the Mining Industry: Exploring Trends in Social and Environmental Disclosure.' *Journal of Cleaner Production* 14(3/4):271–284.

Joergens, C. 2006. 'Ethical Fashion: Myth or Future Trend?' *Journal of Fashion Marketing and Management* 10(3):360–371.

Jones, B., A. Lima, and J. Temperley. 2009. 'Corporate Reputation in the Era of Web 2.0: The Case of Primark.' *Journal of Marketing Management* 25(9/10):927–940.

Jones, C. and K. Soyoung. 2010. 'Influences of Retail Brand Trust, Off-Line Patronage, Clothing Involvement and Website Quality on Online Apparel Shopping Intention.' *International Journal of Consumer Studies* 34(6):627–637.

Jones, R. M. 2006. *The Apparel Industry.* Ames, IA: Blackwell.

Karstens, B. and F. M. Belz. 2006. 'Information Asymmetries, Labels and Trust in the German Food Market: A Critical Analysis Based on the Economics of Information.' *International Journal of Advertising* 25(2):189.

Kim, J. H., M. Kim, and S. J. Lennon. 2007. 'Information Components of Apparel Retail Websites: Task Relevance Approach.' *Journal of Fashion Marketing and Management* 11(4):494–510.

Kim, J. and H. H. Lee. 2008. 'Consumer Product Search and Purchase Behaviour Using Various Retail Channels: The Role of Perceived Retail Usefulness.' *International Journal of Consumer Studies.* 32(6):619–627.

Kim, M. and S. Lennon. 2008. 'The Effects of Visual and Verbal Information on Attitudes and Purchase Intentions in Internet Shopping.' *Psychology and Marketing* 25(2):146–178.

Kolk, A., W. van Dolen, and P. Hong. 2010. 'Corporate Social Responsibility in China: An Analysis of Domestic and Foreign Retailers Sustainability Dimensions.' *Business Strategy and the Environment* 19(5):289–303.

KPMG. 2008. *KPMG International Survey of Corporate Responsibility Reporting 2008.* Amsterdam, Netherlands: KPMG.

Kwon, K. N. and J. Lee. 2003. 'Concerns about Payment Security of Internet Purchases: A Perspective on Current Online Shoppers.' *Clothing and Textiles Research Journal* 21(4):174–184.

Kwon, W. S. and S. J. Lennon. 2009. 'What Induces Online Loyalty? Online Versus Offline Brand Images.' *Journal of Business Research* 62(5):557–564.

Lee, E. J. and J. K. Park. 2009. 'Online Service Personalization for Apparel Shopping.' *Journal of Retailing and Consumer Services* 16(2):83–91.

Lee, M. Y., A. Fairhurst, and S. Wesley. 2009. 'Corporate Social Responsibility: A Review of the Top 100 U.S. Retailers.' *Corporate Reputation Review* 12(2):140–158.

McCabe, D. B. and S. M. Nowlis. 2003. 'The Effect of Examining Actual Products or Product Descriptions on Consumer Preference.' *Journal of Consumer Psychology* 13(4):431–439.

Mintel International Group. 2010a. *UK Retail Briefing-Clothing and Footwear Focus: January 2010.* London, United Kingdom: Mintel International Group.

Mintel International Group. 2010b. *UK Retail Briefing-Clothing and Footwear Retailers: July 2010.* London, United Kingdom: Mintel International Group.

Morhardt, J. E. 2010. 'Corporate Social Responsibility and Sustainability Reporting on the Internet.' *Business Strategy and the Environment* 19(7):436–452.

Nicholson, M., M. Blakemore, and I. Clarke. 2002. 'One Brand, Three Ways to Shop: Situational Variables and Multi-Channel Consumer Behaviour.' *International Review of Retail, Distribution and Consumer Research* 12(2):131–148.

Office for National Statistics. 2009. *Internet Access: Households and Individuals.* Newport, United Kingdom: Office for National Statistics.

Papson, S., R. Goldman, and N. Kersey. 2007. 'Website Design: The Precarious Blend of Narrative, Aesthetics, and Social Theory.' Pp. 307–344 in *Visual Research Methods: Image, Society, and Representation,* edited by G. C. Stanczak. Thousand Oaks, CA: Sage.

Park, J., S. J. Lennon, and L. Stoel. 2005. 'Online Product Presentation: Effects on Mood, Perceived Risk, and Purchase Intention.' *Psychology and Marketing* 22(9):695–719.

Park, J. and L. Stoel. 2005. 'Effect of Brand Familiarity, Experience and Information on Online Apparel Purchase.' *International Journal of Retail and Distribution Management* 33(2):148–160.

Phillips, N. and J. L. Brown. 1993. 'Analyzing Communication in and around Organizations: A Critical Hermeneutic Approach.' *Academy of Management Journal* 36(6):1547–1576.

Pollach, I., A. Scharl, and A. Weichselbraun. 2009. 'Web Content Mining for Comparing Corporate and Third-Party Online Reporting: A Case Study on Solid Waste Management.' *Business Strategy and the Environment* 18(3):137–148.

Rivoli, P. 2005. *The Travels of a T-Shirt in the Global Economy: An Economist Examines the Markets, Power and Politics of World Trade.* Hoboken, N.J.: John Wiley and Sons.

Roberts, L. 2010. 'Accountable Apparel? A Review of Corporate Social Reporting on the Web by UK Fashion Retailers.' Paper presented at the Fashioning an Ethical Industry International Conference, March 2–3, London, United Kingdom.

Roberts, S. 2003. 'Supply Chain Specific? Understanding the Patchy Success of Ethical Sourcing Initiatives.' *Journal of Business Ethics* 44(3):159–170.

Sands, S., C. Ferraro, and S. Luxton. 2010. 'Does the Online Channel Pay? A Comparison of Online Versus Offline Information Search on Physical Store Spend.' *International Review of Retail, Distribution and Consumer Research* 20(4):397–410.

Seock, Y. K. and M. J. T. Norton. 2007a. 'Attitude toward Internet Websites, Online Information Search, and Channel Choices for Purchasing.' *Journal of Fashion Marketing and Management* 11(4):571–586.

Seock, Y. K. and M. J. T. Norton. 2007b. 'Capturing College Students on the Web: Analysis of Clothing Website Attributes.' *Journal of Fashion Marketing and Management* 11(4):539–552.

Shaw, D., L. Hassan, G. Hogg, E. Shui, and E. Wilson. 2006. 'Fashion Victim: The Impact of Fair Trade Concerns on Clothing Choice.' *Journal of Strategic Marketing* 14(4):427–440.

Smith, N. C. 2001. 'Changes in Corporate Practices in Response to Public Interest Advocacy and Actions.' Pp. 140–161 in *Handbook of Marketing and Society*, edited by P. N. Bloom and G. T. Gundlach. Thousand Oaks, CA: Sage.

Spar, D. L. and L. T. La Mure. 2003. 'The Power of Activism: Assessing the Impact of NGOs on Global Business.' *California Management Review* 45(3):78–101.

Sum, N. L. and P. Ngai. 2005 'Globalization and Paradoxes of Ethical Trans-National Production: Code of Conduct in a Chinese Workplace.' *Competition and Change* 9(2):181–200.

Tang, E., C. Chow, and G. Fryxell. 2004. 'Visual and Verbal Communication in the Design of Eco-Label for Green Consumer Products.' *Journal of International Consumer Marketing* 16(4):85–105.

TNS Worldpanel. 2008. 'Retail Sector Shares.' Pp. 3 in *Fashion Focus.* London, United Kingdom: TNS Global.

Valor, C. 2007. 'The Influence of Information about Labor Abuses on Consumer Choice of Clothes: A Grounded Theory Approach.' *Journal of Marketing Management* 23(7/8):675–696.

Wight, C. M., M. E. Smith, and B. G. Wright. 2007. 'Hidden Costs Associated with Stakeholders in Supply Management.' *Academy of Management Perspectives* 21(3):64–82.

Yang, K. and A. P. Young. 2009. 'The Effects of Customized Site Features on Internet Apparel Shopping.' *Journal of Fashion Marketing and Management* 13(1):128–139.

Yin, R. K. 2003. *Case Study Research: Design and Methods.* Thousand Oaks, CA: Sage.

Zadek, S., M. Forstater, and S. Lingayah. 1998. *Social Labels: Tools for Ethical Trade* London, United Kingdom: New Economics Foundation.

10 Motivations and Concerns for Public Reporting about Corporate Social Responsibility and Compliance with Labor Standards

A Case Study of the Apparel Industry

Theodora Valero and Marsha A. Dickson

Over the past two decades, there has been a continuous and increasing call for corporate social responsibility (CSR). Primarily, this demand has occurred in response to the unprecedented globalization of business, leading to a new set of questions regarding the roles and responsibilities of multinational companies in the expanding global economy. This demand has not come solely from socially responsible investors, those individuals who wish to invest their time and money in 'responsible' or 'ethical' corporations; rather, stakeholders at all levels, ranging from employees, to nongovernmental organizations (NGOs), to society at large, are looking for and demanding greater transparency and accountability from the companies with which they conduct business (Broad 2002, Conroy 2007). While there is an increased demand for CSR across all industries, this demand leads to both specific and often controversial dilemmas and outcomes for the apparel industry.

Arguably, the globalization of business has had a greater effect on the apparel industry relative to many other industries due to the implications of an increasingly global and complex supply chain. As apparel brands have globalized their design, production and sourcing operations to remain competitive, an unparalleled number of labor issues has arisen regarding forced labor, low wages, excessive work hours, discrimination, health and safety hazards, psychological and physical abuse, lack of awareness of workers' rights, and, finally, lack of worker representation for negotiations with management (Dickson et al. 2009). In response to these significant issues, apparel brands' stakeholders are no longer solely concerned with the general marketing mix the company provides; rather, they are looking for a degree of social concern, awareness and action *within* the corporate structure. In fact, one could contend that a brand's success or failure in the apparel industry is significantly influenced by its stakeholders' perceptions of its overall corporate social responsibility.

Aware of the favorable impact that marketing campaigns and actions with a social dimension have for their firms, companies are increasingly providing evidence of social responsibility within the brand's infrastructure (Handelman and Arnold 1999). However, the 'evidence' companies choose to provide is notably variable across the industry. Despite empirical evidence that corporate reputation and corporate responsibility are becoming inseparable, most brands in the apparel industry are reluctant to voluntarily report to stakeholders—including consumers—any information regarding social performance (Dickson and Kovaleski 2007). Bennett Freeman (2006), an expert on CSR and communications strategies, explains,

> Not all [corporations] are comfortable with integrating these issues into their communications strategies and addressing the demands of stakeholders to demonstrate accountability and their commitment to sustainability. They are frankly challenged by the demands of credible, transparent reporting and by the dynamics of stakeholder engagement (17).

Research is needed on how companies build legitimacy as it relates to CSR (Castello and Lozano 2011).

The purpose of this study is to determine the primary motivations and concerns that promote or discourage a brand's public commitment to social responsibility. This goal is accomplished by addressing several questions that explore the link between an apparel corporation's reputation, the company's commitment to corporate responsibility and its level of transparency in the dissemination of CSR information.

1. What are a brand's motivations and concerns that promote or discourage public reporting about labor compliance; why do companies choose to, or choose not to, report this information?
2. What are the challenges of transparent reporting in the apparel industry?
3. How do corporations consider the demands and expectations of stakeholders?

1   REVIEW OF LITERATURE

In business, the term 'transparency' refers to the full, accurate and timely disclosure of information. Transparency in business is important because it requires companies to take responsibility for their actions and holds them accountable for the impacts of their activities. The demand for greater transparency and accountability of businesses is coming from all stakeholder groups, including consumers (Dickson et al. 2009). According to an MS&L Global Values study conducted in May 2008, the majority of consumers surveyed around the world agree that companies can succeed while maintaining a high level of transparency. In the United States, 72 percent of consumers surveyed believed that an organization could be financially successful when it is open and honest with the public about its business practices (Zerillo 2009).

In the apparel industry, transparency is intimately linked to social responsibility. According to Dickson et al. (2009), 'Transparency of actions is an important way that apparel brands and retailers demonstrate they are taking charge of social responsibility' (216). In many cases, an apparel brand's commitment to transparency is demonstrated through an increased level of stakeholder communications and public reporting. Transparent communication provides an information-link between a company and its stakeholders.

Transparent communications can be carried out in a variety of ways. A label detailing a company's social responsibility is one method of providing information to consumers and other stakeholders. When the Apparel Industry Partnership (AIP) was formed by President Bill Clinton in 1996, a 'no-sweat' hang tag was planned as a means for communicating that garments were made under safe and fair working conditions. The Fair Labour Association (FLA), however, that developed out of the AIP, has pursued transparency by publishing its reports of factory audits rather than encouraging participating companies to use a label (Dickson et al. 2009). In fact, there is at least some concern among large apparel companies about using a social label for fear that the labor standards and working conditions of their vast supply chains could not be guaranteed for each single item that would bear the label, and this shortcoming would raise the risk of lawsuits for false advertising.[1] Additionally, how to summarize the complexity of labor compliance work into meaningful 'sound bites' for use on garment hang tags also presents difficulties. Other mechanisms for sharing information about CSR programs, such as the public reports published by the Fair Labor Association, can be daunting as well because of the way the media have headlined the bad news from those reports (Dickson and Eckman 2008).

These deterrents, however, have not stopped all apparel companies from engaging with the public about their CSR programs on their corporate websites. The information content pertaining to CSR that is publicly reported on corporate websites is extremely diverse. For instance, the Gap Corporation has a separate website that is devoted entirely to its CSR-related activities, while the Abercrombie & Fitch company website makes no mention of CSR at all. A small percentage of well-known apparel companies have begun to provide information about their labor compliance programs on their websites and/or in more detailed 'annual CSR reports' that can be downloaded (Dickson and Kovaleski 2007). In an annual CSR report, apparel companies disclose information about how they have performed in the area of social responsibility, the challenges and setbacks they have faced, and their goals for the future.

Corporations may face considerable challenges addressing stakeholder demands for accountability and transparency due to the lack of standardization for reporting across the apparel industry. In recent years, however, several initiatives have emerged to tackle this problem; one such program is the Global Reporting Initiative (GRI). The GRI is a multistakeholder, network-based organization that works to advance sustainability reporting. With more than 1,500 companies voluntarily declaring a commitment to the GRI G3 guidelines, the initiative has become the 'de facto' global standard for reporting. The GRI framework for reporting establishes the principles and indicators that brands can use to both gauge and report their economic, environmental and social performance (see https:www.globalreporting.org/Pages/default.aspx). According to the GRI website, 'Sustainability reports based on the GRI framework can be used to benchmark organizational performance with respect to laws, norms, codes, performance standards and voluntary initiatives; demonstrate organizational commitment to sustainable development; and compare organizational performance over time' (2009).

While the GRI has pioneered the development of a sustainability-reporting framework worldwide, the volunteer basis and wide variety of competing standards specific companies and initiatives across the industry have developed has left the landscape cluttered (Freeman 2006). Freeman (2006) asserts that the most successful CSR and sustainability communications and reports provide stakeholders with a 'series of snapshots' that demonstrate the company's CSR commitment and progress over time. However, the question remains, what types of information can a company disseminate that will successfully demonstrate such a commitment? The answer to this question is variable and is also dependent upon the intended stakeholder audience of the communication, for example, consumers, shareholders and NGOs. The variable needs of stakeholders further complicate the process of communicating about CSR and contribute to a firm's apprehension in choosing to become transparent.

Freeman (2006) cites a 2003 study (NGO Perspectives on Corporate Reputation and Responsibility) released by global public relations and communications firm Burson-Marsteller that identifies several key components of credible reporting and communications from the NGOs' perspective. In the study, the top four factors for credible reporting the NGOs recognize were reporting on noncompliance, poor performance or significant challenges; comprehensive performance metrics; third-party verification by independent groups or assurance firms; and standardization of reporting across a company's businesses. While this may be the type of information that a company would choose to release in a report directed toward NGOs, a consumer-oriented report may require a different set of criteria and guidelines. Frostenson et al. (2011) suggest that CSR communications are geared toward specific stakeholder groups, such as investors and nongovernmental organizations that pressure companies for information on the topics; consumers are not targeted. The combination of competing standards for reporting frameworks and initiatives, in conjunction with the vast amount of information that a firm has to consider when forming a report and the needs of various audiences, has likely presented the industry's players with a significant series of challenges. With this research, we sought to understand the challenges apparel companies face when considering whether and what to report publicly about their CSR initiatives and what motivates greater levels of transparency.

2 THEORETICAL FRAMEWORK

The two conceptual frameworks consulted for this study were institutional theory and stakeholder theory. These theories predict how and why organizations take certain initiatives and make certain decisions regarding their actions, including those actions related to social performance. Institutional theory is an organizational theory that acknowledges the existence of an institutional environment in addition to the organization's task environment. Researchers Handelman and Arnold (1999) describe the task environment as a component of traditional organizational theory that focuses on a firm's attempt to meet day-to-day business demands, such as maximizing the return on investment for shareholders, making timely payments to suppliers and satisfying consumer needs. Alternatively, the institutional environment takes into account the influence of social and cultural meaning systems, or social norms, on an organization or business (Handelman and Arnold 1999). These norms are social constructions that arise from public opinion, educational bodies and others, and serve as standards for proper social conduct and behavior. These standards apply not only to individual members of a social group, but also to businesses and organizations operating within a particular society.

In this study, the demand for corporate social responsibility is viewed as a social norm that businesses are increasingly required to conform with if they wish to gain support for their activities. According to Freeman (2006), 'A growing proportion of stakeholders around the world think that companies share responsibility with governments across a range of social and environmental issues' (13). Businesses, through their organizational structure as well as their operational activities, must communicate their acknowledgment and commitment to this emerging social norm by including elements of CSR throughout their corporate strategies and agendas.

The acknowledgment of an institutional environment suggests that a business is judged by members of society not only on its economic performance but also on its ability to conform to a prescribed set of norms. This judgment process is referred to as the 'legitimation' process. Suchman

188   *Theodora Valero and Marsha A. Dickson*

(1995) describes legitimacy as, 'a generalized perception or assumption that the actions of an entity are desirable, proper, or appropriate within some socially constructed system of norms, values, beliefs, and definitions' (574). A business or organization must be willing to internalize these standards by allowing the firm's organizational structure and actions to reflect societal expectations. In return, through the legitimation process, the business will then be rewarded, in other words, granted societal support, or punished based on its ability to adopt and conform to these standards. As with the organizational environment, a company's ability to gain legitimacy is based upon both economic (market driven) and social factors. In the economic realm, it is important for a business to achieve 'pragmatic legitimacy' (Handelman and Arnold 1999). Recall that legitimacy refers to the perception that a business's actions and structures are aligned with the norms and standards for proper behavior society mandates. Pragmatic legitimacy, then, is a business's ability to satisfy the needs of customers through the traditional marketing mix; for instance, the right product, at the right place, for the right price, at the right time. In contrast, the social component of the legitimation process is referred to as 'moral legitimacy' (Suchman 1995). Suchman (1995) explains that moral legitimacy 'reflects a positive normative evaluation of the organization and its activities. . . . [based on a] prosocial logic that differs fundamentally from narrow self interest' (579). Essentially, a positive perception of an organization's institutional environment composed of actions, which are consistent with the norms and expectations of the community at large, leads to moral legitimacy.

While a company can survive in the short term by gaining pragmatic legitimacy, to endure in the long run, a company must earn moral legitimacy as well. Castello and Lozano (2011) explain that 'moral legitimacy is needed not only to get closer to new, salient stakeholder such as those coming from civil society but also to comply with new sustainability expectations among consumers, governments, and shareholders' (14). By earning both pragmatic and moral legitimacy, an organization has essentially earned the necessary support to justify the business's existence. This support manifests itself economically when a consumer chooses to purchase a product or service from a company because of that company's commitment to responsible business practices. In a social context, support created by the attainment of moral legitimacy results in a business's enhanced corporate reputation. For instance, if an apparel brand is known for its excellent treatment of workers and it can communicate this commitment to outsiders, this fact may spread throughout the community by word of mouth, resulting in a favorable evaluation of the company and, consequently, a favorable evaluation of the company's product or service.

Institutional theory asserts that for a business or an organization to gain legitimacy, it must adopt the norms of its social environment (Handelman and Arnold 1999). However, this task is much easier said than done because businesses face a large number of diverse stakeholders from which they must earn support. This wide range of stakeholders, which for an apparel business ranges from factory workers to the company's shareholders, has an even greater set of diverse demands and expectations for the business, and these demands and expectations are rarely in congruence with one another. Careful management is required, and leading businesses initiating new trends in CSR communication are attempting to engage their stakeholders in dialog through themes focusing on partnership and accountability (Castello and Lozano 2011). Robin and Reidenbach (1987) describe how an organization's decision to take any 'socially responsible' action in response to the demands of one stakeholder group will almost always lead to criticism or even retaliatory action from another stakeholder group. For instance, when the shareholders of an apparel brand demand a greater return on investment, this may lead the company's management to seek greater margins by demanding a lower cost of production, which, in turn, may lead to a decrease in workers' wages. While the shareholders may be satisfied with this decision, the apparel brand will indubitably become the target of backlash and criticism from workers' rights organizations and other concerned stakeholder groups. Islam and Deegan's (2010) study of topics covered in corporate reports issued by multinationals with supply chains in developing countries suggests a link between the content of the reports and negative media attention. This desire to meet the demands of a wide range of stakeholders in addition to meeting the demands of the company's shareholders is a primary discussion topic of stakeholder theory.

Stakeholder theory mirrors the basic concepts of institutional theory in that it asserts that an organization's long-term survival is dependent on its ability to satisfy both economic and social objectives dictated by the business environment, as well as to meet the expectations of a diverse group of stakeholders within that environment. According to Freeman (1984), a stakeholder is any individual or group of individuals that is affected by the operations and activities of a business. Donaldson and Preston (1995) clarify that stakeholders are 'persons or groups with legitimate interests in procedural and/or substantive aspects of corporate activity' (67). For the purpose of this study, stakeholders to apparel companies include factory workers, employees, NGOs, governments, shareholders, suppliers and the communities within which these companies operate. Pfeffer (2009) observes that 'shareholder capitalism,' the idea that shareholder interest is paramount, is losing traction in today's business environment. He asserts that this trend is a result of renewed CEO interest in balancing the expectations of various stakeholder groups. This renewed interest has surfaced in response to the growing importance of knowledge work, outsourcing, global supply chains and nongovernmental and activist organizations (Pfeffer 2009). Stakeholder theory recognizes a symbiotic relationship that exists between a business and various stakeholder groups. A company's stakeholders are viewed as having both cooperative and competitive interests in the business, interests that have the power to create or deplete value for the company. In fact, despite managements' lingering focus on the maximization of shareholder wealth, the companies that have consistently outperformed their competition are those that have renounced a purely economic stance in favor of one that attempts to embrace all stakeholders and their interests (Pfeffer 2009). This evidence suggests that various groups of stakeholders warrant consideration in a company's management decisions (Dickson et al. 2009).

From a theoretical perspective, Argandona (1998) argues that the foundation of stakeholder theory is based, in part, on the concept of 'the common good.' In a study that examines the correlation between stakeholder theory and the common good, Argandona (1998) asserts that the good of the individual does not conflict with the good of society; in fact, the two concepts are inseparable. From this perspective, one can argue that while an individual's first priority is to secure his own personal good, this attainment is not possible except in society. Therefore, in seeking the 'common good' of society, an individual is securing his own personal good. To apply this concept to the topic of this study, a company can only secure its own success if it can operate justifiably within society. This justification must be earned from all stakeholders that have a place in society, and by doing so, a company is able to protect its position and success. Yet, this does not necessarily mean that a firm's activities must be special or unique to earn stakeholder approval. Instead, Argandona (1998) points out that:

> a company that shows a normal ethical concern for the problems of the local community fulfills most of its duties towards that community in the ordinary run of its activities: hiring employees locally or subcontracting to local firms, avoiding pollution, paying local taxes, obeying the law and encouraging employees to behave as model citizens (1,100).

All of these activities recognize a goal beyond the accumulation of the greatest possible profit.

Stakeholder theory provides a compelling case for apparel brands to invest assertively in CSR programs and initiatives that promote socially responsible business activities while responding to the demands of stakeholders. The desire to meet the demands of stakeholders arises from the fact that such activities are imperative to ensure a firm's long-term survival, economic prosperity, and competitive advantage; even when targeted toward other stakeholders, providing detailed information about a company's CSR program can lead to acquisition of consumer trust and loyalty (Berrone et al. 2007, Pirsch et al. 2007). The theory suggests that firms will be motivated to incorporate into their corporate strategies objectives that go beyond the attainment of economic-oriented goals, or profit maximization. Based on this theory, it is possible to conjecture the motivations and concerns that arise as companies weigh the costs and benefits of a CSR program, and analyze the ways in which companies choose to communicate the results of these programs to interested stakeholder groups.

3   METHODS

This study utilized the long-interview method for qualitative data collection. An interview schedule was created to cover the following broad topics: the company's history in CSR and public CSR reporting; motivations and concerns that promote or discourage public reporting; benefits of public reporting; how the demands and expectations of stakeholders are accounted for; and the challenges of public reporting in the apparel industry, including experiences of other companies, difficulties of engaging with stakeholders, and the value of standardized reporting initiatives.

We invited CSR representatives from 10 apparel companies to participate, eight of whom were willing and able to be interviewed. The eight individuals represented apparel companies purposefully selected because of the varying amounts of content on labor-compliance infinitives they publish on their corporate websites—ranging from relatively little information to those that published detailed CSR reports. The sample was also a convenience sample in that we had CSR contacts for each company. We did not attempt to interview representatives of companies having no transparency in their labor-compliance programs because, from past experience with such companies, we knew they were unwilling to discuss their programs, even on conditions of anonymity. The interviews, completed in 2008, were conducted by telephone and lasted between 25 minutes and one hour. All answers were recorded by hand and were later typed and sent to the representatives for clarification, edits and final comments.

Responses were varied since each participant drew on the unique experiences of her/his own company in the development of its CSR program and its involvement with public reporting, making coding and counting responses of diminished value. Where topics were mentioned by numerous participants, we point that out. However, frequency data were of limited value since many topics were brought up only by one participant. Therefore, we chose to aggregate the data without regard to frequency counts into a summary case study about CSR and public reporting in the apparel industry. Subsequently, the case study likely does not exactly mirror the experiences of any particular company, but instead, it shares the experiences of eight apparel companies in launching their CSR programs and publicly reporting about that work.

Although some of the information presented in the case study that follows has been discussed in the media or in other research reports, since the information was developed from our primary data collection, we do not cite references in the case study unless references provide further clarification on a topic. We use a combination of quotations and paraphrasing to present the information provided to us and which represents the aggregated experiences of the eight participants.

4   A CASE STUDY OF CSR AND PUBLIC REPORTING IN THE APPAREL INDUSTRY

Evolution of CSR

Corporate social responsibility became a 'hot topic' in the apparel industry in the late 1980s and early 1990s. During this time, a wave of NGO and activist criticism regarding labor issues in offshore factories began to sweep the industry, leaving soiled corporate reputations and consumer concern in its wake. One highly publicized case in the mid-1990s was the Kathie Lee Gifford scandal.[2] The television personality was vehemently reproached by the media for the production of her Wal-Mart clothing line in 'sweatshop' factories in Honduras and New York where workers were reportedly underpaid, underage, and generally exploited and abused. These scandals, in conjunction with pressures from the U.S. Congress and the Clinton administration during the mid- to late-1990s, signaled to other companies in the apparel industry that something needed to be done to protect their businesses against similar media and NGO attacks.

According to several participants, apparel companies' first attempts to address social-responsibility concerns came in two primary forms. First, apparel companies involved in offshore and/or outsourced production created or updated 'supplier codes of conduct' to include terms of engagement with factories and their workers. Second, several of the larger apparel companies in the industry established separate departments such as 'social compliance departments,' and later, 'departments for social responsibility' to handle the engagement terms with suppliers and also to mitigate or preemptively address emerging supply chain and labor-related issues. The general consensus among the study's participants was that the primary trends affecting the apparel industry during this early call for corporate social responsibility included demands for greater supply-chain visibility, supply-chain management, increased social compliance, and in general, a gradual building of awareness for all of these issues.

After nearly two decades, these trends continue to affect the apparel industry; however, they are joined also by a growing concern for corporate transparency, greater reporting, work with communities, and environmental awareness. One participant explains,

> Corporate social responsibility first began to affect the industry in the early 1990s when it became apparent that there needed to be greater visibility in the supply chain. Recently the idea of social responsibility in the industry has expanded beyond social compliance to include

other areas such as environmental sustainability, employee inclusion and foundation work.

In response to the changing landscape of CSR in the apparel industry, participants reported that their companies have had to change their initiatives to accommodate these emerging trends, or what one participant described as the 'societal mind-shift' to the next CSR hot topic. One change that several participants indicated that their companies have made is the gradual sophistication of supplier codes of conduct to include higher standards regarding labor rights, as well as to include standards for environmental regulation in an international setting. This concept of a company's tripartite responsibilities (economic, social and environmental) is often referred to as the 'triple bottom line.' Additionally, participants cited that a significant change from the supplier codes of conduct of the early 1990s is the degree to which these codes are now enforceable and enforced. During their inception, supplier codes of conduct were more often than not 'paper codes,' meaning the codes and the standards that they set for suppliers merely existed on paper as a defense for companies to place between their offshore activities and the media.[3] In the past decade, however, several multistakeholder initiatives (MSIs), notably the FLA, have emerged to create processes by which corporations can provide greater assurance that their supplier codes of conduct are being enforced. Participants suggested that the MSIs help companies to set social-compliance policies, provide standards and guidelines for the formation of more demanding supplier codes of conduct, provide independent and/or third-party monitoring and auditing services, and, more recently, assist companies in making transparency and reporting decisions. One participant explains the benefits of MSIs, saying,

> When publicizing information, it is often a good idea to have a partnership with an organization such as the FLA to help guide a company . . . these types of partnerships lead to constructive reporting.

Because of emerging initiatives including MSIs, leading apparel companies are increasing both the scope and transparency of their CSR activities.

5 MOTIVATIONS AND CHALLENGES OF PUBLIC REPORTING AND TRANSPARENCY

The apparel industry's trend toward more sophisticated CSR programs and greater accountability has presented two significant challenges in the form of transparency and reporting. As participants explained their companies' early stages of public reporting and increased transparency, they revealed varied decisions that were made regarding when to become more transparent through reporting or other forms of engagement. They also identified the challenges of determining what information they would report publicly and how they could become more transparent without exposing the company to negative media speculation and scrutiny. Several participants explained that their companies began to publicly report and become more transparent due to outside responsibilities and commitments to a variety of stakeholder parties. For instance, the FLA requires its participating companies to become more transparent with their reporting. An excerpt from the 'What We Do' (2008) section on the FLA website states,

> Companies that join the FLA commit to establishing internal systems for monitoring workplace conditions and maintaining Code standards, being part of a rigorous system of Independent External Monitoring (IEM), and public reporting on the conditions in their supplier factories. To ensure transparency, the results of the IEM audits are published on the FLA Web site in the form of tracking charts.

In exchange for this transparency, the FLA provides third-party credibility to the company.

Other participants believed that they had an obligation to external stakeholders, such as the universities with which they conduct business, to begin to report the company's CSR activities and become more transparent about their operations.[4] University students, especially, have historically been concerned with and demand that the companies with which they transact are involved in socially responsible business activities. The shareholders of large apparel companies were also identified by participants as an important impetus for top management to begin to construct and issue public social-responsibility reports. This is not to say that apparel companies were simply succumbing to outside pressures when choosing to become more transparent. Participants explained that as it became clear that companies were going to have to nurture more 'long-term' relationships with suppliers to ensure that the company's guidelines and supplier codes of conduct were being followed, the companies found themselves in a better position to report, with both increased clarity and assurance, that the conditions in factories and other areas of social compliance were being addressed.

Additionally, several participants explained that as the industry's CSR leaders began to explore the realm of public reporting and transparency, several benefits to those companies' businesses began to appear. The emergence of these positive outcomes served as motivation for other companies to follow suit and further motivated the industry's leaders to continue such innovative initiatives. First, companies recognized that their increased accountability meant that they would no longer be able to ignore the demands of CSR. As a result, public reporting in the form of annual reports with a CSR section, and later, annual CSR reports, became a way for companies to 'showcase' the positive steps that they were taking to become more socially responsible in their business activities. Participants reported that their company's stakeholders like to see that problems, of any type, are being addressed. Public reporting became a way for them to earn greater support from a variety of stakeholders—including consumers.

Consumer engagement was a second benefit of public reporting and transparency that further motivated such activities. For instance, before CSR information was available on a company's website, or before a company chose to issue an annual report discussing such activities, consumers had nowhere to turn, apart from the media, to glean information about a business's activities. One participant commented on this rejuvenated consumer engagement saying,

> The introduction of a social responsibility section on the company website allowed a place for customers to consult this type of [CSR] information. The concern of customers keeps the relationship alive.

Further facilitating CSR reporting, the emergence of MSIs meant that companies had the opportunity to affiliate with organizations that could help them to design 'constructive' reporting. These initiatives, composed of a variety of industry stakeholders, assist companies in treading the fine line between reporting discretion and the sharing of pertinent information. Participants reported that they began to appreciate the connection between engaging in and communicating socially responsible business activities, and enhanced business reputation in the form of increased credibility among a variety of stakeholders.

In spite of the benefits and motivations that arise from a company's decision to become more transparent about its responsible business activities, an extraordinary number of challenges discourage companies from engaging in such practices. In fact, it is important to note that apart from the few industry leaders and followers, most apparel companies, including the hundreds of thousands of medium- and small-size businesses may not have a formal CSR program, and even fewer have a program for communicating efforts in this area.[5] Participants identified that one of the major deterrents for apparel companies is the shear cost of implementing a CSR program, let alone the costs associated with designing and executing a formal communication plan. As explained by several of the participants, the largest apparel companies have the financial resources necessary to implement CSR programs, affiliate with MSIs, pay for the cost of auditing and monitoring, and adopt the standards and guidelines of an international reporting initiative. For small- and mid-sized businesses, it is easier to remain 'under the radar' so to speak, allowing the larger companies to continue in the media spotlight whether for their positive efforts or shameful scandals. This mind set is regrettable, as one participant points out,

> Unfortunately it is the large companies that have the resources to take the necessary steps in social responsibility . . . smaller companies

without the major resources to both take initiative and combat the negative media, are the companies that are using off-beat factories that could really benefit from the improvement that comes with openly monitoring factory and worker conditions.

A second major deterrent that participants identified is the increased level of scrutiny from all stakeholder groups that emerges as a result of increased transparency—companies believe that they can never 'do enough' or 'report enough' to satisfy the demands of all of their stakeholders. In the past, for instance, large companies such as Nike issued reports that were misinterpreted and drew unwanted criticism. Participants elucidated that companies may choose to refrain from issuing reports prior to requests from outside parties, for example, through shareholder proxies or affiliation requirements, because there is a constant fear of negative publicity. Although implementing a formal CSR program created additional opportunities for transparency and reporting, several participants explained that it was often difficult to decide how to analyze the data related to the program. Furthermore, putting large amounts of CSR data into a readable and understandable format that would provide a meaningful message to stakeholders, particularly consumers, was an exceedingly daunting task.

Additionally, participants stated that situations arise more often than not when the demands of different stakeholder groups are: (1) different from one another, or (2) in opposition to one another. For example, shareholders may want a company to issue reports that give statistical facts and figures for the value creation of the CSR program, NGOs may want a company to issue reports that explicitly explain how companies are addressing labor concerns, and consumers may want a company to issue a report that summarizes the company's CSR program in layperson's terms. Each of these reports would require different information directed toward a different audience, a task that proves too intimidating for many apparel companies.

A third reason participants identified about why companies often choose not to become more transparent or issue CSR reports is due to the lack of a standardized reporting format across the industry. As explained, a standardized format for reporting is important for several reasons. First, companies would have a set of guidelines to follow, which would make the process of organizing large amounts of CSR data much less daunting. Second, and most important, a standardized format for reporting would make it possible to compare companies' CSR programs and initiatives across the industry, as well as to compare an individual company's year-to-year performance. A standardized format, such as that established by the GRI, would allow the industry to establish meaningful benchmarks by which to evaluate both the industry's and an individual company's CSR performance.

While reporting initiatives such as the GRI do exist and have led to some level of standardization, participants identified that these are not overwhelmingly effective for several important reasons. First, these initiatives are all voluntary reporting initiatives, meaning that companies must decide on their own accord to follow the guidelines and standards of the reporting format. Many companies, especially small and mid-sized businesses, are reluctant to do so due to the high costs and the extensive set of standards and guidelines that make it cumbersome and expensive to implement. Even for larger companies and corporations that can afford the associated costs, the lack of standardization across the industry means that a company may have to adopt several different frameworks for reporting to make comparability possible. In most cases, shareholders are not willing to justify the extra expenses. One participant discusses the costs involved in adopting the standards of the GRI, explaining,

> The GRI at first was becoming an industry-focused initiative. In recent years, however, it has faced some pushback. A lot of companies were invited to join the initiative however there were extensive costs associated . . . it is arguable if that standard is worth the monetary cost associated.

General consensus on the subject seems to be that while the benefits of an industry-wide standard are undeniable, until one framework is established and legally mandated, the competing standards across the industry will continue to undermine their effectiveness.

Finally, participants suggested that apparel companies might be too uncomfortable with the level of transparency required to earn an increased level of credibility. For instance, several of the largest apparel companies and leaders in CSR have made their factory lists publicly available. Most apparel companies are too fearful of any negative repercussions from NGOs, activists, and the media that they may face in committing to such a high level of transparency. One participant remarked,

> Despite any apparent challenges, it was always clear to the company that in order to be perceived as having a credible program it was necessary to be transparent. The company was not comfortable as to go as far as to share our factory list.

6   CHALLENGES OF ENGAGEMENT AND STAKEHOLDER DEMANDS

Apparel companies must be cognizant of the expectations of a wide range of stakeholder groups, both when designing an appropriate CSR program and when deciding what types of reports to release and what business activities should be more transparent. Increasingly, companies are beginning to consider the expectations and demands of both traditional and nontraditional stakeholders. When participants were asked to identify their 'key' stakeholders, the responses varied greatly. All participants included shareholders as primary stakeholders—as the owners of the company, they have the authority to pressure the current management if it fails to meet shareholders' expectations. In reference to a CSR program, participants cited that shareholders want to see reports that are presented in a manner similar to a financial report; in other words, numbers and statistics that show what the expenses of the program are, and how shareholder money is being spent to create value for the company.

While shareholders are important, participants also identified other groups as important stakeholders, particularly their employees. They explained that employees want to feel positively about the company that they work for and need to be empowered through the right kind of information to move the company forward. Elaborating on the importance of employee support, one participant noted,

> Employees are a very important stakeholder [group] as the company strives to become more socially responsible. Employee support of the company's social responsibility efforts leads to positive HR [human resources], greater contributions, and leads to better recruitment and retention.

When it comes to public reporting and transparency, participants acknowledged that consumers tend to be a tricky stakeholder group for several reasons. First, most consumers are unwilling to take the time to do their own research on the CSR activities of a company. At the same time, however, skepticism remains about whether the majority of consumers have the awareness or interest levels to read a CSR report targeted toward consumers should they have the opportunity. As one participant observes,

> It is not likely that the CSR reports, case studies, etc. are being read by the average consumer, so they are not necessarily targeted for the average consumer. Consumers have a large appetite for transparency, which is not necessarily the same thing as reporting. Consumers are less interested in statistics and more interested in the fact that the information is made available at all.

For this reason, engagement with consumers through reporting and transparency is especially difficult to address. Apparel companies want to do 'what is right' for their customers by making it easy for them to find the information that they desire and providing information that assures customers that the business is engaged in socially responsible activities. In general, consumers tend to be less interested in the 'nuts and bolts' of a company's CSR program and progress—hence, the reason why they are less interested in types of reports such as annual CSR reports—and are more responsive to reports that outline a company's philanthropy or charitable activities that are highly visible, such as Gap's involvement with Product Red.

In the past, NGOs have played a significant role in holding apparel companies accountable for their business activities. NGOs and activists are excellent campaigners and are quick to bring media attention and heavy criticism to companies when there is evidence that workers' rights have been violated. For this reason, most participants also identified NGOs as key stakeholders that are considered when their companies are designing and reporting on their CSR programs.

Apparel companies' relationships with NGOs have had a rocky past. In the early 1990s, NGOs were quick to criticize and condemn companies for their globalized business activities and tended to be highly antagonistic in their approach. While this has not changed entirely, in recent years, both companies and NGOs have recognized the value in working together to address issues of social noncompliance. Participants admit that NGOs are passionately involved and often do raise legitimate concerns—when NGOs are a source of constructive criticism, they are able to provide highly meaningful guidance. One participant laments, however, about the often-antagonistic relationship between NGOs and companies, offering,

> It is unfortunate that some relationships between companies and NGOs are negative because they can be a form of good guidance when their concerns are constructive and not aggressive. A lot of NGOs serve an important leadership role for companies to consider when dealing with various factory issues.

Another group of stakeholders that has recently been the source of meaningful guidance for companies is the collection of MSIs that have emerged in the past decade.[6] Participants indicated that MSIs are having a profound impact on the level of reporting and transparency across the industry. However, this pressure to report is offered in conjunction with support and guidance. Companies are now able to work with MSIs to address the challenges of stakeholder engagement and to get the appropriate information to the appropriate audience.

Participants admitted that the response and feedback from the stakeholder groups regarding their CSR-related activities varies, but that there is evidence that most of the groups are receptive to the information. Again, it is most difficult for companies to gauge consumer responses because, as a group, they provide minimal feedback; however, apparel companies assume that consumers are accessing much of the information from their company websites. Alternatively, NGOs have been highly responsive, providing copious feedback on the issues with which they are particularly interested. This assertion is summarized by one participant who, when asked about stakeholder feedback, stated,

We are assuming that people are accessing our web site and getting the answers that they are looking for. In general, we get very few e-mails or telephone calls from stockholders, customers, or the public in general. Most of the direct contact comes from NGOs who have a specific issue that they want to address.

Alternatively, many participants stated that their annual CSR reports have received excellent feedback. For instance, various industry awards have been granted to companies that produce particularly enlightening and elaborative CSR reports (Business Ethics Awards, for instance). Ultimately, apparel companies use a variety of forms of reporting—for instance, annual reports, CSR information on a company website—and various levels of transparency—for instance, divulging factory lists, making audit results publicly available—to take both responsibility and credit for being a 'good corporate citizen'.

7   DISCUSSION AND CONCLUSION

With this study, we sought to determine the primary motivations and concerns that promote or discourage a brand's public commitment to social responsibility. Our first and second research questions regarded an apparel company's motivations, concerns, and the challenges faced when choosing to report on CSR activities and become more transparent. The evidence collected supports the assumptions of institutional theory. In the past several decades, corporate social responsibility has evolved into a social norm of the business environment. Castello and Lozano's (2011) assertion that CSR is becoming a social norm and required for moral legitimacy is demonstrated through the evolution of CSR throughout the apparel industry from an emphasis on labor concerns and supply-chain management to 'hot topics' such as the environment. CSR as a social norm is being set by specific groups of interested stakeholders, including NGOs and investors, as suggested by Frostenson et al. (2011). The CSR controversies of the 1990s and apparel companies' subsequent responses to these scandals suggest that apparel businesses are being held accountable for their offshore activities as their global reach expands. As CSR has moved from the margins of business into the mainstream, apparel companies have had to adapt their policies (rewrite supplier codes of conduct), their organizational structure (create social compliance/social responsibility departments), and their stakeholder engagement strategies (allow increased transparency and greater reporting) to achieve consonance with the institutional environment. Apparel companies have made these efforts to gain support and earn credibility from a wide range of stakeholders. This increased credibility ultimately results in an enhanced company reputation, which supports some researchers' assertion that social legitimacy is necessary for a firm to survive in the long term (i.e., Berrone et al. 2007, Pirsch et al. 2007).

The convergence of corporate social responsibility and corporate reputation through the legitimation process serves as a motivating factor for apparel companies to become more transparent about their CSR activities and engage stakeholders in two-way communication. Apparel companies that are choosing not to become more transparent are fearful that they are unable to meet the normative expectations set forth by society. Despite a growing emphasis on the triple bottom-line, economic deterrents including increased expenses and unwanted risk have slowed the progression of CSR reporting across the industry. Until the specific norms are refined, which may require legislation on reporting standardization, a majority of apparel companies will be unwilling to incur the costs and risks associated with greater transparency.

The evidence collected for our third research question regarding the demands and expectations of stakeholders provides compelling support for the tenets of stakeholder theory. Stakeholder theory argues that an organization's success is contingent on its ability to satisfy both economic and noneconomic (social) objectives by meeting the needs of a variety of stakeholders. Apparel companies have identified several important stakeholder groups in addition to the company's shareholders, implying that these companies do have goals and expectations beyond satisfying profit-maximization objectives. But in contrast to Islam and Deegan's (2010) emphasis on the media, in recent years, the power of 'non-traditional' stakeholders, including MSIs and NGOs, has grown exceptionally from almost nowhere to challenging large, multinational corporations. As the theory acknowledges, stakeholders have both cooperative and competitive interests in the business, which have the power to create or deplete value for the company. This assertion is especially indicative of the relationship between apparel companies and NGOs. As described previously, both NGOs and apparel companies are recognizing the value in working cooperatively to further the interests of both parties; however, many NGOs and activist organization still rely on antagonistic approaches to further their agendas. With the help of MSIs, apparel companies are learning how to create and communicate the progress of their socially responsible business activities with a range of interested parties. Despite these positive steps, apparel companies do admit that engagement with consumers as a stakeholder group remains a challenge. The next step for companies is to determine a way to engage them that is both meaningful and interesting.

8 IMPLICATIONS AND FUTURE RESEARCH

This research implies that, in terms of transparency and reporting as well as stakeholder engagement, the industry remains on a path of continuous improvement with a long, rocky road ahead. Despite the fact that institutional theory is able to adequately explain the factors that motivate apparel companies to increase their CSR efforts by means of increased transparency and public reporting, it does little to explain why the majority of apparel companies choose not to take such initiative. The research does suggest, however, that a required industry-wide standard for reporting may provide the next 'big leap' in CSR reporting and transparency. Future research could involve an in-depth look at the costs and benefits associated with such a standard and the steps that would be required to make such an initiative possible.

Additionally, the research suggests that in terms of stakeholder engagement, apparel companies still face significant challenges when attempting to promote two-way communication of their socially responsible activities to the average consumer. Consumers want to be assured that the apparel companies from which they purchase products conduct their business activities in a responsible manner; however, their levels of interest and awareness are often not clear enough for a company to devise an effective engagement strategy. Future research could look more closely at *what type* of information and *how much* information is needed for an apparel company to assure its consumers of the company's positive progress, and what type of information and how much information is needed to earn credibility from its consumers.

NOTES

1. The second author has interacted in varied industry settings with representatives of large apparel companies who have expressed these fears.
2. For more information, see Associated Press (1997).
3. See Dickson et al. (2009).
4. Note that licensees of universities that are FLA members are required to make their factory lists publicly available.
5. Dickson and Kovaleski (2007) studied 119 large U.S. apparel brands and retailers and found that only 28 percent report any information about their CSR programs on their companies' websites.
6. Dickson et al. (2009) describe five of these respected MSIs, including the Ethical Trading Initiative, the Fair Labor Association, the Fair Wear Foundation, Social Accountability International and the Worker Rights Consortium.

REFERENCES

Argandona, A. 1998. 'The Stakeholder Theory and the Common Good.' *Journal of Business Ethics* 17(9/10):1093–1102.
Associated Press. 1997. 'Kathie Lee Faces More Sweatshop Allegations.' *Toronto Star*, December 6. p. A30.
Berrone, P., J. Surroca, and J. A. Tribo. 2007. 'Corporate Ethical Identify as a Determinant of Firm Performance: A Test of the Mediating Role of Stakeholder Satisfaction.' *Journal of Business Ethics* 76(1):35–53.

Broad, R., ed. 2002. *Global Backlash: Citizen Initiatives for a Just World Economy.* Lanham, MD: Rowman and Littlefield.

Castello, I. and J. M. Lozano. 2011. 'Searching for New Norms of Legitimacy through Corporate Responsibility Rhetoric.' *Journal of Business Ethics* 100(1):11–29.

Conroy, M. E. 2007. *Branded! How the 'Certification Revolution' is Transforming Global Corporations.* Gabriola Island, Canada: New Society.

Dickson, M. A. and M. Eckman. 2008. 'Media Portrayal of Voluntary Public Reporting about Corporate Social Responsibility Performance: Does Coverage Encourage or Discourage Ethical Management?' *Journal of Business Ethics* 83(4):725–743.

Dickson, M. A. and K. Kovaleski. 2007. 'Implementing Labour Compliance in the Apparel Industry.' Paper presented at the Annual Conference of the International Textile and Apparel Association, November 8, Los Angeles, CA.

Dickson, M. A., M. Eckman, and S. Loker. 2009. *Social Responsibility in the Global Apparel Industry.* New York: Fairchild.

Donaldson, T. and L. E. Preston. 1995. 'The Stakeholder Theory of the Corporation: Concepts, Evidence, and Implications.' *Academy of Management Review* 20(1):85–91.

Freeman, B. 2006. 'Substance Sells: Aligning Corporate Reputation and Corporate Responsibility.' *Public Relations Quarterly* 51(1):12–19.

Freeman, R. E. 1984. *Strategic Management: A Stakeholder Approach.* Mansfield, MA: Pittman.

Frostenson, M., S. Helin, and J. Sandstrom. 2011. 'Organising Corporate Responsibility Communication through Filtration: A Study of Web Communication Patterns in Swedish Retail.' *Journal of Business Ethics* 100(1):31–43.

Handelman, J. M. and S. J. Arnold. 1999. 'The Role of Marketing Actions within a Social Dimension: Appeals to the Institutional Environment.' *Journal of Marketing* 63(3):178–191.

Islam, M. A. and C. Deegan. 2010. 'Media Pressures and Corporate Disclosure of Social Responsibility Performance Information: A Study of Two Global Clothing and Sports Retail Companies.' *Accounting and Business Research* 40(2):131–148.

Pfeffer, J. 2009. 'Shareholders First? Not So Fast. . .' *Harvard Business Review* 87(7/8):90–91.

Pirsch, J, S. Gupta, and S. L. Grau. 2007. 'A Framework for Understanding Corporate Social Responsibility Programs as a Continuum: An Exploratory Study.' *Journal of Business Ethics* 70(2):125–140.

Robin, D. P. and R. E. Reidenbach. 1987. 'Social Responsibility, Ethics, and Marketing Strategy: Closing the Gap between Concepts and Application.' *Journal of Marketing* 51(1):44–58.

Suchman, M. C. 1995. 'Managing Legitimacy: Strategic and Institutional Approaches.' *Academy of Management Review* 20(3):571–610.

Zerillo, N. 2009. 'Profit, Transparency Top Consumer Study.' *PR Week US*, January 2009, p. 6.

Contemporary Debates
and Controversies

Part IV

Contemporary Debates
and Controversies

11 Providing Direct Economic Benefit to Workers through Fair-Trade Labeling of Apparel

The Fair-Trade USA Apparel and Linens Pilot Project

Heather Franzese

Fair trade is a broad social movement that uses the market to push for ethical and sustainable purchasing, historically from developing countries. Fair-trade certification, as a category of social labeling and subset of the broader movement, is a proven model of economic development and empowerment. More than one million small-scale farmers and farm workers have earned $77 million in community development premiums from fair-trade sales in the United States since 1998, mainly from food products.[1] In 2005, fair-trade certification was introduced in Europe for cotton, one of the first nonfood products. This prompted a debate about the feasibility of the extension of the fair-trade model to address the problem of the sweatshop in apparel. Can the Fair Trade Certified™ label applied in the apparel and fashion industry provide a mechanism to translate consumer demand for ethical working conditions into real dollars for garment workers and cotton farmers? In 2005, Bama Athreya and Ian Robinson wrote that 'the potential for selling fair-trade apparel to conscientious consumers [in the US] remains almost entirely unrealized.' Seven years later, that is still true, but not for lack of consumer demand. In a 2008 Globescan study of 1,000 U.S. consumers, when asked 'what product would you like to see Fair Trade Certified™?' the most common response (49 percent) was textiles, rated above toys, gold, and forest products.[2] Another study released by Harvard/MIT in 2012 found a 14 percent sales lift on clothing labeled 'socially conscious' at Banana Republic outlet stores (Hainmueller and Hiscox 2012). Fair Trade USA, the third-party certifier of Fair Trade Certified™ products in the United States, has developed a fair-trade standard for the cut-make-trim (CMT) facility (whether industrial factory or small sewing cooperative) to pilot test with U.S. companies. These companies are mainstream brands and mission-driven companies, sourcing cotton apparel, bed, and bath products from countries such as India, Liberia, Peru and Costa Rica to sell in diverse U.S. retail channels.

Extending the fair-trade model to cut-make-trim raises a number of questions related to the cost-benefit of fair trade for actors along the chain, especially consumers, companies, workers and farmers. For consumers, how strong is the demand, and how much more are they willing to pay for apparel labeled Fair Trade Certified™? Moreover, is there a certain type of consumer who is most attracted to such a product? For companies, is there a model for Fair Trade Certified™ apparel that can shift the purchasing practices of mainstream, global brands while also recognizing and rewarding smaller, mission-driven companies that have demonstrated a commitment to fair-trade values and to sourcing from higher-wage factories where working conditions are relatively better? For sewing workers, how can fair trade have a meaningful impact, particularly on core fair-trade pillars of income and empowerment, areas in which existing labor code-of-conduct initiatives have conspicuously failed? Furthermore, what is the scope for sewing cooperatives and artisan-apparel producers to participate in fair trade and what challenges are unique to their production environment? Lastly, can the economic, environmental and community benefits enjoyed by other fair-trade farmers extend to cotton farmers? The pilot aims to test these questions.

In the United States, the Fair Trade Certified™ label can be found on more than 20 product categories—from coffee, tea and cocoa to flowers, wine, and even sports balls—sold by 800 companies in 60,000 stores with a retail value over $1.2 billion. In the United Kingdom, sales of apparel, bed and bath products made with fair-trade cotton over the first five years of the program channeled over $1.5 million in additional income and $750,000 in social investment to subsistence farmers of cotton in Mali, Burkina Faso and India.[3] The label is a tool for consumers to vote with their dollars for social responsibility, seek more information about where their products are made, and forge a new and direct relationship with the farmers and workers that make and grow their everyday products. This chapter examines the features of this model and the challenges to implementing it in the apparel supply chain.

The Fair Trade USA pilot program design applies the fair-trade pillars of income and empowerment to a factory production setting through the following features:

- A fair-trade premium, structured as a percentage on the FOB (free/ freight on board) price, paid by brands directly to a worker-controlled fund. Workers choose democratically how to allocate premium funds, as a cash bonus, a collective social investment or a combination.[4]
- A commitment to progress toward a living wage that meets the basic needs of workers, including health care, education, housing, and transportation.[5]
- Empowerment through democratic worker representation, improved worker-management communication, grievance channels inside the facility, and a complaints mechanism outside the facility. Fair-trade training for managers and workers, with worker training through a peer-to-peer model and modules integrated into ongoing factory training programs.

- Worker-centric monitoring against Fair-trade standards, which cover core ILO labor standards and best practices from multistakeholder codes such as Jo-In (the Joint Initiative for Corporate Accountability and Workers Rights Consortium).[6]

The Fair Trade USA pilot program for Fair Trade Certified™ Apparel and Linens launched in late 2010 with diverse apparel products in U.S. retail stores carrying the fair-trade label. The pilot ended in 2012. During the pilot, a monitoring and evaluation program was put in place to measure baseline indicators and progress—on impact, cost and scalability. Early findings indicate that fair trade can indeed channel meaningful benefits to reduce poverty for cotton farmers and garment workers. Some labor-rights groups have expressed skepticism about the model's ability to achieve a living wage in a short time frame and about the limits of voluntary, consumer-driven initiatives, as detailed in Chapters 12 and 14 of this volume. However, the label is undoubtedly bringing a new and innovative tool to the fight against sweatshops.

1 PILOT DEVELOPMENT (2006–2009)

Monitoring in factories by brands and multistakeholder initiatives using codes of conduct over the last 15 years has not measurably increased workers' earnings or worker voice and participation in the workplace. Fair trade has an opportunity to fill that gap by applying core fair-trade principles—(1) higher earnings toward a living wage and (2) worker empowerment—to factories and artisan-apparel producers. Fair Trade USA is testing the potential of the Fair Trade Certified™ label to generate economic benefit for apparel workers, using a fair-trade premium and worker-centric certification model. During the first six months of 2006, Fair Trade USA undertook a study to determine the feasibility of launching fair-trade garments in the United States, consulting over 60 NGOs, companies, farmer organizations, unions and factories in Europe, Mali, the United States, India, Guatemala and Mexico. The conclusion drawn from the research and consultation affirmed that Fair-trade garments certification for the U.S. market could be the 'win' the anti-sweatshop movement and brands have been searching for, if certain criteria were met (Quigley and Opal 2006):

- **Wages:** A strong position on wages that moves measurably toward a sustainable livelihood for workers, such as transitioning from minimum wages to the concept of living wages.
- **Social premium:** Some form of social investment modeled after social premiums in other fair-trade products.
- **Freedom of association:** A worker-empowered standard that actively promotes worker voice and their freedom to associate and affiliate with worker representative groups such as labor unions.

- **Purchasing practices:** Terms of trade between buyers and suppliers that support good working conditions, such as long-term relationships and technical assistance.

Throughout 2008, Fair Trade USA consulted with NGOs, brands and suppliers to develop a two-part draft standard—Obligations of Buyers and Obligations of Factories—that met the above criteria and could be pilot tested with labeled products in the U.S. market. The next step in this exploration was actually to conduct the live pilot test with a small group of companies and factories to test the theoretical approach in practice.

Living Wage: from Campaigning to Experimentation

Since 1995, a time of strong anti-sweatshop campaigning, real wage growth has not kept pace with economic growth and a large proportion of apparel suppliers still fail to pay even the minimum wage. Among 31 suppliers surveyed by Daniel Vaughan-Whitehead, formerly of the ILO, '23 per cent reported a starting wage that was below the official province or city minimum wage.' These suppliers produce for companies accredited by the Fair Labor Association, and presumably should show better-than-average wage rates. Furthermore, when these companies were asked, 'Is the starting wage provided by your company sufficient to ensure workers a minimum living standard?,' 75 percent responded stating they did not know or simply failed to respond (Vaughan-Whitehead 2009).

While more than 15 years of campaigning for higher wages has failed to deliver meaningful wage increases, the debate has advanced our collective understanding of methodologies to calculate a living wage, the latest being the Asia Floor Wage. This research has illuminated paths for experimentation and has informed the development of Fair Trade USA's pilot, especially with regard to wages. The pilot aims to help workers find a voice in bargaining for higher wages, while protecting the competitiveness of their employers. To implement a living wage in the apparel value chain, the ITGLWF (International Textile Garment & Leather Workers Federation) argues that 'buying companies will need to not only monitor wages in their supply chains against available living wage benchmarks and engage in price negotiations based on a unit labor cost which is compatible with paying decent wages, they will also need to create an environment in which the core rights of freedom of association and collective bargaining can be observed' (Miller and Williams 2009). Fair Trade USA's apparel pilot proposes to do just that. Researchers at MIT also caution on the trade-off between wage increases and facility competitiveness. 'Paying living wages could involve wages as much as two or three times as high as those that currently prevail, potentially reducing by a significant amount the number of jobs available and threatening the competitiveness of local industries. Seeking out the conditions that allow such wages to be paid without driving producers out of business is a logical next step in the discussion of wage standards' (Setrini and Locke 2005).

The Fair Trade USA apparel pilot promotes mutual commitment and capacity building between buyers and suppliers. In this context, worker earnings can grow in tandem with fair-trade production. Actual wage calculations are explained in greater detail below.

Need for Empowerment to Sustain Economic Gains

Worker voice in setting wages is just as important as actual wage rates. Fair Trade USA seeks to use the tools of worker participation, rights training and grievance channels to protect freedom of association and strengthen the possibility for collective bargaining. Athreya, formerly of the International Labor Rights Forum (ILRF), wrote about adapting fair trade to apparel, 'The most fundamental criterion for sweat-free status should be that workers have a collective voice in the determination of their wages, benefits and working conditions—in other words, real power in their workplaces, and a democratic process for determining how to use that power' (Robinson and Athreya 2005). Fair trade seeks to promote this collective voice through democratic worker representation, training for all workers on their rights—in particular, the right to join a union—and channels to communicate concerns internally to factory management, or externally to local NGOs or Fair Trade USA. The hope is for fair trade to serve as an enabling environment through which workers can seek individual and collective empowerment.

Premium Impact in Other Fair Trade Products

Success of the fair-trade premium in benefiting producers of Fair Trade Certified™ agricultural products presents an opportunity to test if the same approach can work in apparel. Farmers and workers have earned $77 million in community-development premiums through fair-trade sales to the United States. In hired labor, the three largest categories of investment historically have been community projects, career advancement (including skills training, computers, and books), and education, covering primary or secondary school or scholarships for the children of fair-trade farmers and people in the local community. Workers on banana plantations in Uraba, Colombia, for example, have invested fair-trade premiums in scholarships to a technical school, micro-loans for small businesses such as chicken raising and a supermarket, improved housing in an area prone to flooding, and environmental education for high school students (FLO 2007). These are only a few of the examples of the benefits of fair trade to these communities.

Label Shifts Social Compliance Paradigm from Risk to Opportunity for Companies

The two primary drivers for company supply chain CSR (corporate social responsibility) initiatives have typically been (1) to mitigate reputational risk and reduce the likelihood of activist pressure or campaigns, and (2) to align with company values of doing the right thing. Both of these are inherently limited to a small segment of companies, those that are attractive targets for campaigns, and those that explicitly aim to generate social value alongside shareholder value and profit. Unless and until there's a mechanism for companies to derive positive business value from investing in improved working conditions in the supply chain, only a fraction of companies will ever invest in social compliance (Porter and Kramer 2006). This fair-trade pilot aims to realign incentives for social compliance so that companies can see a long-term business benefit from investing in farmers and workers.

Many companies have invested heavily in social compliance, but they are not deemed a credible source to make their own CSR claims on sweatshop issues. In the Edelman Trust Barometer, NGOs were cited as the 'most trusted institution' by 55 percent of respondents in North America, ahead of companies, media and government. In particular, this NGO category includes third-party certifiers, who are trusted by consumers to regulate claims and evaluate whether companies actually fulfill their promises of social compliance and corporate responsibility (Edelman 2011). Alongside this trend of declining corporate trust, consumers are increasingly becoming more socially conscious and demanding that companies demonstrate their CSR credentials; otherwise, consumers threaten to boycott their products. Yet there is an information asymmetry in apparel: consumers are unaware of the actual sourcing and manufacturing practices in the production of their clothing. More explicit social labeling could prove to be an important solution to a complex problem.

A consumer-facing label could be the key to realigning incentives for social responsibility, unlocking the 'supplier squeeze.' NGOs and trade unions have attacked brands for squeezing their suppliers, and factory certification programs have evolved to try to intervene. But consumers have a responsibility as well, and they have come to expect lower and lower retail prices as excess global labor supply has pushed down workers' wages (Schor 2005). Without a label to signal to the consumer at the point of purchase that a shirt was made in a factory where workers earn a decent wage and have a voice in the workplace, the supply-and-demand market for ethical apparel is incomplete. Consumers have no way to reward or punish companies with their purchases, and no way to share the costs of better working conditions. The Fair Trade Certified™ label could change these incentives for the consumers and the companies.

U.S. Consumer Demand for Fair-Trade Apparel

Consumers are still greatly concerned with sweatshop issues. In a 2008 Globescan study of 1,000 U.S. consumers, 83 percent cited a 'high level of concern' with worker exploitation. These consumers are willing to pay more for products that offer a solution to issues that concern them, as Harvard researcher Michael Hiscox found in the market for eBay purchases for ethically certified polo shirts with consumers willing to pay up to a 14 percent premium (Hiscox and Smyth 2008). His most recent study showed a 14 percent sales increase on clothing labeled socially conscious in mainstream stores (Hainmueller and Hiscox 2012). This data provides key support for the pilot program indicating that there is a strong interest in Fair Trade Certified™ apparel. Consumers are seeking more information to translate their concern into action, and there is a trend toward greater transparency through product labels and consumer sites like GoodGuide that provides 'information on the environmental and social impacts of the products in your home.' GoodGuide was named by *Fast Company* magazine as one of its most innovative companies of 2010 and was recently purchased by UL Environment, signaling a move to the mainstream. Its rating system incorporates fair-trade standards as a benchmark and companies with a strong commitment to fair trade rank high in its apparel rankings (GoodGuide 2010).

Fair trade in other products has set up the pathway for credible fair-trade apparel, because the Fair Trade Certified™ label has become a credible source of information on the social and environmental responsibility of products and is recognized by 33 percent of U.S. consumers. In the 2008 Globescan fair-trade study, 75 percent of the U.S. 'involved consumer' segment believe the 'best way to verify a product's social or environmental claims is an independent, third-party organization.' More than half of the consumer segment recognizes the Fair Trade Certified™ label, and 93 percent of 'involved consumers' who recognize the fair-trade label say they trust it.[7] The Fair Trade Certified™ label in apparel has the potential to translate consumer concern into real dollars and cents for farmers and workers, and address the market failure of incomplete information. By buying fair-trade products, consumers could support higher and sustainable earnings for the farmers and workers that make the products.

2 FAIR-TRADE USA PILOT STANDARDS

Fair Trade USA invested four years of intensive consultation with more than 100 organizations to develop the pilot standards for Fair Trade Certified™ apparel. The process followed recommendations of the ISEAL Code of Good Practice for Setting Social and Environmental Standards. In 2008, Fair Trade USA received external funding to draft pilot standards for Fair Trade Certified™ apparel. Working with Verité, the leading nonprofit social auditor, and the Cahn Group, a CSR consultancy, standards were drafted for sewing facilities (CMT or 'cut make trim' factories) and for buyers. They draw directly from ILO Conventions and from the highest-bar, multistakeholder initiatives such as the Joint Initiative on Workers Rights and Corporate Accountability (Jo-In) and from factory certifications such as SA8000.[8] The buyer standards, which were based on trade standards for other fair-trade products and from cutting-edge thinking on responsible purchasing practices from groups such as the MFA (Multi-Fiber Agreement) Forum, were revised in a stakeholder consultation process during 2009 with U.S.-based labor rights and international development NGOs, community-based organizations in the global south, factories, cooperatives, and companies that could potentially use the fair-trade label. Fair Trade USA representatives made field visits to India and Rwanda to solicit input from NGOs, trade unions, suppliers, and workers, and convened advisory groups for the program.

During a public comment period in November 2009, Fair Trade USA received input from 55 organizations in 15 countries and responded by further strengthening the standards. In many instances, however, input from artisans and their buyers conflicted with input by labor-rights groups. Stakeholders disagree, for example, on how standards should apply to home-based workers. Those who represent small-scale textile artisans and handicrafts producers want to see Fair Trade Certified™ apparel reach 'marginalized producers who would otherwise be excluded from markets.' However, labor rights advocates and activists maintain that regardless of whether an individual is a home-based worker or a worker in a factory, that worker is entitled to the same rights and benefits, a position that in practice may prove impractical for small co-ops and artisan groups thus excluding them from eligibility to make Fair Trade Certified™ products.

Fair-Trade Premium Requirements

To address the wage gap and promote social development for workers, the pilot is testing a sliding scale premium on top of the FOB price of the garment, to be paid by buyers and managed in a worker-controlled fund. The fair-trade premium is paid by the buyer into a separate fair-trade premium bank account. The premium for workers is a minimum of 1 percent and maximum of 10 percent of Free/Freight On Board (FOB), depending on the wage level assessed in the factory or cooperative.[9] Wages in the facility are assessed against living wage benchmarks using a market-basket methodology. Wage assessments are conducted by independent third-party organizations in the country of manufacture (Fair Trade USA 2009). Essentially, the aim of the fair-trade premium is to achieve a *product* that pays a living wage, so that incrementally, we can reach a *facility* that pays a living wage.

The fair-trade premium upper value of 10 percent of FOB was set in reference to several important benchmarks. First, the premium seeks to double the return to labor on a per-product basis, since labor costs are typically less than 10 percent of the FOB cost of a garment (Worker Rights 2005). This is achieved when the factory is exclusively producing Fair Trade Certified™ product(s) and supports progress toward the payment of a true living wage in countries where the living wage is estimated to be about double the minimum wage. In India, for example, the Asia Floor Wage estimates the living wage to be less than double the government minimum wage, 7695 rupees and 4238 rupees, respectively (Merk 2009). Second, the premium is intended to provide a financial incentive for brands to consider sourcing in higher-wage countries and facilities, since brands pay a 10 percent premium to source in a minimum-wage factory, but only a 1 percent premium to source in a living-wage factory. This is the sliding-scale concept. Third, the intention is to achieve an alignment with premium levels in other fair-trade products, which generally range from 5–10 percent in cases where the premium is a percentage rather than a fixed-dollar amount. Finally, the pilot is designed to test the hypothesis, put forth by Ashim Roy of the New Trade Union Initiative and Asia Floor Wage Campaign, that brands would need to add 6 percent on the FOB cost of a garment to cover the cost of labor compliance and pay workers a living wage (Roy 2009).

The pilot standard requires that facilities producing Fair Trade Certified™ apparel products, whether factory or artisan cooperative, pay workers a living wage. 'Wages shall be gradually increased to 'living wage' levels above the regional average and official minimum' (Fair Trade USA 2009). Depending on the specific type of facility (artisan/cooperative vs. traditional factory), the methodology to calculate living wage will be transparent and consistent for all facilities in the Fair Trade USA pilot. Facilities that are sewing cooperatives and producers and that could be considered 'artisan' will use the Fair Wage Guide developed by World of Good, with data input from wage studies by organizations like CREA (Center for Reflection, Education and Action). Traditional cut-and-sew factories will use a market-basket methodology similar to the one used by the Asia Floor Wage Alliance.

For Artisans: Fair Wage Guide

The Fair Wage Guide was developed by World of Good (now Good World Solutions) to translate the core value of a fair price into a fair wage for piece-rate workers, particularly artisans, in the developing world (World of Good Development Organization Fair Wage Guide). Since 2006, more than 60,000 workers have used the free online tool and 25,000 artisans report wage increases of about 20 percent (World of Good Development Organization 2010). The tool shows what change in price or production time would be required to achieve a fair-wage equivalent. World of Good offers this example: 'If a semi-skilled worker in Delhi, India is receiving 20 rupees per scarf, it takes that worker 2 hours to complete each scarf, s/he pays 1 rupee for material and 2 rupees for electricity, this worker is earning 42 percent below the local minimum wage and 74 percent below the SweatFree Communities non-poverty wage. To bring this worker to a fair wage,[10] either the price paid per piece needs to increase by 32 rupees or the time spent making each product needs to decrease by 51 minutes.'

For Factories: Market-Basket Approach

Pilot factories have wages assessed using a transparent market-basket methodology that incorporates real local data to determine a locally appropriate wage. The formula uses the Asia Floor Wage assumptions as a starting point and also draws from the widely used SA8000 Basic Needs Wage formula. The comparison can be seen in Table 11.1 below.

According to the Asia Floor Wage Alliance, a few key assumptions need to be established as the basis for any credible living-wage formula:

- Calorie level needed for a basic food basket: This pilot uses 2,200 calories (Anker 2005).
- Ratio between food costs and the costs of other basic needs, and rate of savings and discretionary income: This pilot uses the 1:1 ratio recommended by the Asia Floor Wage proponents. Note that this figure includes savings. The advantage of this simple formula is that it accommodates local differences in climate, culture, and other factors that determine spending habits. It also reduces the need for expensive household price surveys, though local data can be incorporated where available.
- Family size and number of wage earners per family: This pilot will use the 4-person family assumed in Asia Floor Wage calculations and take as a starting assumption a single wage earner per family. Again, local data can be incorporated where available.

This example shows a typical gap between minimum wage and the living wage. The pilot uses a combination of strategies to close this gap: the fair-trade premium to address short-term needs, democratic worker organization

Table 11.1 Calculating a Living Wage

Variable	SA8000	Asia Floor Wage	Fair Trade USA
Calorie Needs (adult)	2100	3000	2200
Food Cost	Actual	Actual	Actual
Non-Food Cost	Actual + 10% savings	1:1 with Food	1:1 with Food
Family Size	Actual	2 + 2	2 + 2
Number of Wage Earners	2 (or actual)	1	1 (or actual)

Formula:
[(Adult food cost × # adults) + (Child food cost × # children) + (Basic needs)] / # wage earners
The following example shows the formula in practice:

- Food cost (1 adult) = 50 Rupees / day
- Food cost (1 child) = 25
- Basic needs (non-food) = 150
- Family size = 2 adults, 2 children
- Number wage earners = 1

Using the formula from above = [(50 × 2) + (25 × 2) + 150] / 1 = 300
Actual Wage at Factory A (lowest paid workers) = 150
Living Wage Benchmark = 300

to support collective bargaining, and wage benchmarking against international standards to promote continuous improvement along the path toward living wage (described in more detail below). The ability to achieve living wage will also hinge on the proportion of a factory's production that is fair trade, with the goal being to increase a factory's fair-trade production over time so that it represents the majority of production. For fair-trade farmers first entering the system, it is common to sell a small fraction of their harvest on fair-trade terms, and then grow the proportion of production sold as Fair Trade Certified™ over time. We expect the same with factories.

Worker Participation and Representation Requirements

To ensure a worker-centric model and address the empowerment gap, the U.S. pilot will require mandatory training for all workers on freedom of association and collective bargaining, require the factory to have a functional grievance procedure where workers can raise concerns without fear of retribution, and have an external complaints channel for issues that cannot be adequately resolved by systems inside the factory. This is detailed in the next section.

3 PILOT IMPLEMENTATION (2010–2012)

Following the standards development process for the pilot, Fair Trade USA began the process of certifying the first facilities against these new standards. The certification process at the factory level consists of a capacity-building model to train workers and managers on fair-trade standards (including basic labor rights), a monitoring model to assess rigorously factory performance against fair-trade standards at regular intervals, and transparent tracking of worker income—both fair-trade premiums and regular wages. Brands are also asked to commit to responsible purchasing practices that support a factory's ability to meet fair-trade standards. The first pilot facilities are located in India, Peru, Costa Rica and Liberia, with several other locations in the pipeline. A diverse portfolio of Fair Trade Certified™ apparel and accessories is now available on retail shelves in the United States.

Capacity-Building Model: Training for Factory Workers and Managers

Fair Trade USA surveyed factory-training experts to solicit best practices from their experience on how to build an effective and sustainable training model[11] that promotes supplier commitment and worker participation. One of the key challenges identified was teaching workers how to communicate effectively—with each other and with management. Another success factor reported was that the factory must be committed to investing the time and resources necessary to internalize and institutionalize any training model for their employees.[12]

The pilot is engaging a network of local grassroots NGOs and trade unions in pilot countries to support training, grievance processes, and monitoring. Local partners can share information in real time about factory working conditions and work quickly to address issues that arise. This feedback loop will form a kind of immune system for the facility and its workers that diagnoses problems early, prescribes locally appropriate solutions, identifies preventative measures to keep the same problems from recurring, and sustains itself with minimal outside investment.

Monitoring Model

A second cornerstone of the certification process after capacity building is monitoring performance against fair-trade standards. As discussed above, a top-down policing model of factory auditing has some serious limitations and has failed to deliver long-term and sustainable improvements for workers, especially in the areas of wages and worker participation (Clean Clothes Campaign 2006). In this context, the monitoring model for the fair-trade apparel pilot aims to empower workers themselves to monitor the facility and alert appropriate staff or external organizations if they feel workers' rights are not being upheld. Assessment of factories will be carried out by credible, independent organizations[13] using highly qualified auditors who will assess workplace conditions and management systems, relying heavily on worker input and using the strictest protocols for social assessments. Worker interviews will be conducted both on-site and off-site in safe settings as deemed appropriate by factory situation and local context. Auditors consult with local unions and civil-society organizations dedicated to workers' rights prior to the onsite audit. The worker representative body (e.g., union) is consulted during the audit, participates in the opening and closing meetings along with factory management, and provides comments on findings. This approach builds on best practice in social auditing and, over the long term, may support workers themselves becoming the monitors of workplace conditions.

In an effort to reduce redundant auditing and enable factory managers to spend time and resources making meaningful improvements rather than hosting audits, Fair Trade USA has partnered with respected social auditors and factory certifications such as Social Accountability International (SAI) to conduct joint and collaborative audits of the factories participating in the pilot project.[14]

Fair-Trade Premium Administration

Administration of the fair-trade premium is aligned with the model in other fair-trade products, where funds are paid directly to a worker-controlled fund managed by a fair-trade committee, but with one important exception—workers can choose to allocate the premium as a collective social investment or disburse it as a cash bonus. This innovation acknowledges the challenges of migrant labor and high worker turnover in the apparel industry, and responds to input from workers, workers' rights NGOs, and trade unions. Migrant workers may not be settled in the community and thus may not have a strong incentive to invest in that community. Therefore, the workers can decide to allocate the premium to one or the other option or even some percentage to cash and some to community investment. A cash premium would allow workers the flexibility to spend on individual needs and enable those who change jobs to benefit fully from the premium.

Fair-trade premium funds are managed and spent as follows, per the pilot standards for CMT facilities:

- Workers decide democratically how fair-trade premium funds are allocated. They may be distributed to all production workers as a cash bonus, pooled in a collective fund for social investment, or a combination of the two. Where the premium is distributed as a cash bonus, the bonus will be divided equally among all workers who are employed at the time of fair-trade production, regardless of their position or whether they worked on the actual fair-trade product.
- Where the premium is used for collective investments, they are decided upon by the fair-trade committee[15] described below. Examples of collective investments include, but are not limited to: health initiatives, micro-enterprise loans, day care, literacy and life skills, housing funds, educational initiatives and schools. Where migrant populations exist, investments that meet their needs will be considered, such as legal aid, education on legal rights, travel assistance and/or a clinic to meet preventative health needs.
- A fair-trade committee manages the fair-trade premium account. Workers shall comprise a majority of members on the fair-trade committee and shall be elected independently of management influence. The fair-trade committee is responsible for jointly managing, investing and spending the fair-trade premium to achieve improvements in the workers' lives (Fair Trade USA 2009).

Lastly, the fair-trade premium must be completely transparent. Each time any premium funds are received, the fair-trade committee must post it visibly and publicly for all the workers to be aware that a certain amount of premium has been received on that date. This increases trust between the workers and the management, ensures that all workers participate in the process of deciding how premium funds are spent and promotes worker empowerment, one of the major goals of the pilot program itself.

Wage Benchmarking

In combination with the fair-trade premium, the pilot will support wage increases through benchmarking, through freedom of association and collective bargaining, and through consolidating fair-trade production to increase the leverage of fair-trade buyers. The pilot will benchmark wages at pilot factories using the 'wage ladder' tool developed by the Joint Initiative on Corporate Accountability and Workers' Rights and pilot tested in Turkey (Jo-In 2007). Fair Wear Foundation (FWF) and other multistakeholder initiatives have begun experimenting with this tool. The benchmarking system charts factory progress on wages against multiple benchmarks, with the objective of moving factories 'up the ladder' by increasing workers' wages over time. Benchmarks can include the country minimum wage set by the government, the prevailing wage for garment workers in the country or region, a wage negotiated at the facility level through a collective-bargaining agreement (CBA), a living wage calculated by a local NGO or trade union, such as the Asia Floor Wage.

Purchasing Practices

Given the critical impact of buying practices (Galland and Jurewicz 2010; Impactt/Traidcraft 2008; see also Chapter 14, this volume), the fair-trade pilot requires buyers to pay a fair price and to commit to a set of responsible purchasing practices, by which buyers are expected to set targets for fair-trade sales and where product sales are successful, to commit to continuing to work with the existing suppliers and repeat and/or increase fair-trade orders, consistent with demand for the product. The aim is to demonstrate that brands can remain competitive and also adhere to fair-trade practices by making a commitment in orders over a period to factories as an incentive to continue positive labor-standards practices (Burns 2010).

Pilot Companies and Supply Chains

The Fair Trade USA pilot will include various transparent, traceable supply chains in diverse regions (Latin America, Africa and Asia) and organizational structures (industrial factories as well as artisan and cooperative workplaces). Pilot companies—both mission-based companies and mainstream brands—will bring their own supply chains and will also be encouraged to assess whether already certified operators meet their production needs. Initial pilot companies are small-to-medium-sized, mission-driven brands. These companies are obvious first movers for their demonstrated commitment to fair-trade values and established consumer trust. It is expected that the pilot will also include at least one large, mainstream brand. Mainstream brands source the overwhelming majority of apparel production and affect the largest number of workers, so a test would not be complete without this segment of the market. Another important advantage of pilot testing with a mainstream brand is the purchasing power to place larger orders and raise the percentage of fair-trade production in a factory, which in turn deepens the per-worker impact.

As an example, the first facility approved by Fair Trade USA to make Fair Trade Certified™ products for this pilot is Rajlakshmi Cotton Mills Pvt. Ltd. Workers at Rajlakshmi are represented by CITU, the Centre of

Indian Trade Unions, and have a collective-bargaining agreement. The 500 workers at Rajlakshmi, located in Kolkata, India, produce knit and woven apparel products, bedding and bath supplies, and accessories such as bags and aprons. The progressive social investments and programs at Rajlakshmi have resulted in a range of benefits for the workers, even prior to the factory's involvement with the U.S. pilot of fair-trade apparel:

- Housing allowance of 5 percent of wages
- Free transportation to and from the factory
- Interest-free loans of up to six months' wages
- Three subsidized canteens
- Free eye treatment and surgery
- Ten percent annual bonus (regardless of factory profitability)
- Medical care (to subsidized national health insurance)
- On-site training center
- Funds for the education of workers' children up to university level

For each Fair Trade Certified™ garment sold, the factory workers earn a premium to be invested in a worker-controlled fund. Workers vote on whether to receive cash bonuses from the fund or to invest the funds into important social programs. The factory also has strong backward linkages to the fair-trade cotton farmers. The factory buys nearly the entire harvest of a fair-trade cotton producer group in Hyderabad and offers farmers shares in the profitability of the factory.

3   IMPACT MONITORING AND RESEARCH AGENDA

Fair trade has the potential to easily double workers' income in a facility where the majority or entirety of production is on fair-trade terms. At the first approved factory in India, workers have already earned a bonus of an additional week's worth of pay and are on track to achieve a month's bonus in the next year. These early findings, though modest because the scale of the pilot is limited, imply real potential to replicate and scale the model and to grow the benefit to workers and farmers exponentially. The Monitoring and Evaluation model of the pilot will enable Fair Trade USA, together with external stakeholders, to evaluate which aspects of the pilot are most impactful for workers and farmers, and which aspects need to be changed or strengthened beyond the pilot period to take it to scale.

4   CONCLUSION: FAIR-TRADE LABELING–DRIVING
THE RACE TO THE TOP

The U.S. fair-trade pilot is an ambitious and innovative project that seeks to extend a social labeling model with a proven track record in agriculture to the apparel supply chain, an area of manufacture notorious for poor working conditions. The purpose of the project is to utilize the power of the Fair Trade Certified™ label in compelling brands and retailers to commit to higher standards by providing the consumer with an assurance that their clothes were manufactured in a factory that has a strong set of labor standards where the workers are going to receive direct economic gain from their purchase of that item. If consumers react positively to the labels and there is an increase in the demand for the labeled apparel, it will create a financial incentive for many more firms to not 'race to the bottom,' but rather start a 'race to the top' that motivates companies and factories to seek competitive advantage through improving factory working conditions.

Early results of the pilot confirm strong consumer demand, community development and higher earnings for factory workers. Fair Trade Certified™ apparel products in the United States saw a 260 percent increase in sales from 2010 to 2011, indicating a very positive consumer reaction. Fair-trade premiums contributed to community development, including the construction of a school in post-conflict Monrovia, Liberia. Lastly, workers at the first approved factory earned a bonus equivalent to an additional week's worth of pay and are on track to earn much more through fair trade.

The multistakeholder group for the fair-trade apparel pilot is currently assessing the impact and lessons learned from the pilot, which will help answer key impact questions relating to wages and empowerment, as well as cost, scalability, and demand. For example, has the fair-trade focus on factory workers opened or restricted market access and higher earnings for fair-trade cotton farmers? What potential barriers have surfaced, and how might they be removed? What are the cost implications of the pilot approach for suppliers, brands and retailers? Specifically, how does fair-trade certification affect the wholesale and retail price of the apparel, and will supply-chain actors bear these new costs? To have a meaningful impact, the model must be scalable and work not only for mainstream companies, but also across geographies and production types, that is, from typical CMT factory to artisanal setting/sewing cooperative. Finally, what has been the reaction of consumers to Fair Trade Certified™ garments? How does this compare to demand for organic and other types of sustainable cotton and indeed other fair-trade-labeled products? Finally, how much more are consumers willing to pay for Fair Trade Certified™ garments at retail? This critical question, explored elsewhere in this volume, is central to the debate on the power of markets to bolster corporate social responsibility.

NOTES

1. Fair Trade USA 2011 Almanac. http://fairtradeusa.org/sites/default/files/Almanac%202011.pdf
2. Globescan 2008.

3. Fairtrade Foundation U.K.
4. Definition of Fair Trade Premium / Social Premium: A payment in addition to the price of the product that farmers and workers invest collectively in social-development projects (Quigley 2006). For apparel, it can also be distributed as a cash bonus and ranges from 1 to 10 percent of the free on board cost.
5. Definition of a living wage: A wage that meets the basic needs of workers and their families, including food, housing, education, transportation and health care. A living wage also provides for discretionary income and savings.
6. http://www.jo-in.org/pub/about.shtml
7. Available on request from Fair Trade USA (http://www.fairtradeusa.org).
8. The standards cover the following areas: prohibition of forced labor, freedom of association & collective bargaining, health & safety, child labor, wages & benefits, working hours, nondiscrimination, subcontracting, disciplinary practices, environmental management and women's rights.
9. If the wages assessed meet the living-wage benchmark, the fair trade premium is set at 1 percent. If the wages assessed are closer to the living-wage benchmark than to the minimum wage, the fair trade premium is set at 5 percent. If the wages assessed are closer to the minimum wage than to the living wage, the fair trade premium is set at 10 percent.
10. The fair-wage benchmark is set at 10 percent above the local minimum wage or the $2 per-day global poverty line, whichever is higher.
11. Fair Trade USA's model for fair-trade training includes the following elements:

   • Fair-trade basics—for all workers in the factory to have at least a basic understanding of fair trade and how they participate in fair trade
   • "Fair Trade University"—time-based modules of increasing complexity spread out over the course of several years and embedded in a factory's ongoing training plan

12. Training of Trainers—cadre of peer trainers trained on fair trade and trusted by workers to institutionalize the training model—this will directly refer to the commitment problem demonstrated by many factories.

   • Locally appropriate pedagogy and materials—local-language instruction, visual presentation for illiterate and low-literacy workers, illustrated workbook for retention
   • Management-Worker Dialogue—sessions will be combined with workers and managers to promote worker participation in the process, and promote ongoing dialogue between workers and managers about fair trade. This type of forum will open up communication between the workers and the management.
   • Fair trade committee—in-depth training for fair trade committee members on administration and financial management of fair trade premiums

13. "Independent" means an organization with expertise in monitoring factory working conditions that is not owned or controlled in whole or in part by any brand holder or production facility seeking certification against fair-trade standards.
14. Partnership with SA8000, etc: http://www.sa-intl.org/index.cfm?fuseaction=Page.ViewPage&PageID=986
15. In other fair trade products made with hired labor, this is known as a joint body.

REFERENCES

Anker, R. 2005. 'A New Methodology for Estimating Internationally Comparable Poverty Lines and Living Wage Rates.' Working Paper No. 72, International Labour Office, Geneva, Switzerland.

Burns, M. 2010. 'Fair Trade, Garment Manufacturing and Empowerment-What Would This Mean for the Fair Treatment of Workers?' Presented at the Women Working Worldwide Meeting, Utrecht, Netherlands. Retrieved March 30, 2011 (http://www.fairtrade.net/fileadmin/user_upload/content/2009/news/Fair_Trade__Linen_Manufacturing_and_Empowerment__Maggie_Burns.pdf).

Clean Clothes Campaign. 2006. 'Looking for a Quick Fix: How Weak Social Auditing is Keeping Workers in Sweatshops.' Amsterdam, Netherlands: Clean Clothes Campaign. Retrieved March 30, 2011 (http://www.cleanclothes.org/doc uments/05-quick_fix.pdf).

Edelman. 2011. 'Edelman Trust Barometer: Annual Global Opinion Leaders Study-2011.' New York: Edelman. Retrieved March 30, 2011 (http://www.edelman. com/trust/2011/uploads/Edelman%20Trust%20Barometer%20Global%20 Deck.pdf).

Fairtrade Labelling Organizations International. 2005. 'FLO Generic Fair Trade Standards for Hired Labour.' Bonn, Germany: Fairtrade Labelling Organizations International. Retrieved March 30, 2011 (http://fairtrade.net/pdf/hl/ english/Generic%20Fairtrade%20Standard%20Hired%20Labour%20Dec%20 2005%20EN.pdf).

Fairtrade Labelling Organizations International. 2007. 'The Benefits of Fair Trade: A Monitoring and Evaluation Report of Fair Trade Certified Producer Organizations for 2007.' Bonn, Germany: Fairtrade Labelling Organizations International. Retrieved March 30, 2011 (http://www.fairtrade.net/fileadmin/user_upload/con tent/2009/resources/Benefits_of_Fairtrade_2007.pdf).

Fair Trade USA. n.d. 'Fair Trade Certified Apparel and Linens FAQ from Public Comment Period on Draft Pilot Standards.' Oakland, CA: Fair Trade USA. Retrieved March 30, 2011 (http://www.fairtradecertified.org/certification/produc ers/apparel-linens).

Fair Trade USA. 2009. 'Fair Trade USA Pilot Program for Fair Trade Certified Apparel and Linens: Obligations of CMT Facilities.' Oakland, CA: Fair Trade USA. Retrieved March 30, 2011 (http://www.fairtradecertified.org/sites/default/files/ FTC_Apparel-Obligations_of_CMT_Facility.pdf).

Galland, A. and P. Jurewicz. 2010. 'Best Current Practices in Purchasing: The Apparel Industry.' Oakland, CA: As You Sow. Retrieved March 30, 2011 (http:// www.asyousow.org/publications/2010%20articles/Apparel_Report.pdf).

GoodGuide. 2010. 'Best Apparel Ratings.' Retrieved March 30, 2011 (http://www. goodguide.com/categories/277459-apparel##products).

Hainmueller, J. and M. Hiscox. 2012. 'The Socially Conscious Consumer? Field Experimental Tests of Consumer Support for Fair Labor Standards.' Working Paper No. 2012–15, Department of Political Science, Massachusetts Institute of Technology, Cambridge, MA.

Hiscox, M. J. and N. F. B. Smyth. 2008. 'Is There Consumer Demand for Improved Labor Standards? Evidence from Field Experiments in Social Product Labelling.' Kennedy School of Government, Harvard University, Cambridge, MA. Unpublished manuscript. Retrieved March 30, 2011 (http://www.people.fas.harvard. edu/~hiscox/SocialLabeling.pdf).

Impactt and Traidcraft Exchange. 2008. 'Material Concerns: How Responsible Sourcing Can Deliver the Goods for Business and Workers in the Garment Industry.' London, United Kingdom: Impactt and Traidcraft Exchange. Retrieved

March 30, 2011 (http://www.traidcraft.co.uk/publications_and_resources/traid craft_publications).

Joint Initiative on Corporate Accountability and Workers' Rights. 2007. 'Jo-In Explanatory Note on the Treatment of the Living Wage Common Code Element during the Jo-In Pilot Project in Turkey's Garment Industry-2006–2007.' London, United Kingdom: Joint Initiative on Corporate Accountability and Workers' Rights. Retrieved March 30, 2011 (http://www.jo-in.org/pub/docs/Jo-In-%20Ex planatory%20Note%20for%20Living%20Wages.pdf).

Merk, J. 2009. *Stitching a Decent Wage across Borders: The Asia Floor Wage Proposal.* Amsterdam, Netherlands: Clean Clothes Campaign.

Miller, D. and P. Williams. 2009. 'What Price a Living Wage? Implementation Issues in the Quest for Decent Wages in the Global Apparel Sector.' *Global Social Policy* 9(1):99–125.

Porter, M. and M. Kramer. 2006. 'Strategy and Society: The Link between Competitive Advantage and Corporate Social Responsibility.' *Harvard Business Review* 84(12). Retrieved March 30, 2011 (http://www.fsgimpact.org/ideas/pdf/Strat egy_and_Society.pdf).

Quigley, M. and C. Opal. 2006. 'Fair Trade Garment Standards: Feasibility Study.' Oakland, CA: Fair Trade USA. Retrieved March 30, 2011 (http://www.fairtrade certified.org/certification/producers/apparel-linens).

Robinson, I. and B. Athreya. 2005. 'Constructing Markets for Conscientious Apparel Consumers: Adapting the Fair Trade Model to the Apparel Sector.' Paper Presented at the Conference on Constructing Markets for Conscientious Apparel Consumers, April 1–2, Ann Arbor, MI.

Roy, A. 2009. 'Incorporating International Wage Standards in Fair Trade: The Asian Floor Wage Initiative.' Presented at the Fair Labor Association Forum for Wages, October 26, Washington DC. Retrieved March 30, 2011 (http://www.fairlabor. org/images/WhatWeDo/CurrentIssues/wages-and-csr.pdf).

Schor, J. 2005. 'Prices and Quantities: Unsustainable Consumption and the Global Economy.' *Ecological Economics* 55(3):309–320.

Setrini, G. and R. Locke. 2005. 'Wages in the Apparel Industry: What Constitutes a Decent Standard?' Paper Presented at the Forum for Exploring Common Approaches to Corporate Accountability and Workers' Rights, July 11–12, Cambridge, MA.

Vaughan-Whitehead, D. 2009. 'Incorporating Fair Wages into CSR.' Presented at the Fair Labor Association Forum for Wages, October 26, Washington D.C. Retrieved March 30, 2011 (http://www.fairlabor.org/images/WhatWeDo/Current Issues/wages-and-csr.pdf).

Worker Rights Consortium. 2005. 'The Impact of Substantial Labor Cost Increases on Apparel Retail Prices.' Washington, D.C.: Worker Rights Consortium. Retrieved March 30, 2011 (http://digitalcommons.ilr.cornell.edu/cgi/viewcontent. cgi?article=1206&context=globaldocs).

World of Good Development Organization. 2010. 'Fair Wage Guide Report-January 2010.' Oakland, CA: World of Good Development Organization. Retrieved March 30, 2011 (http://www.worldofgood.org/wp-content/uploads/2009/03/Fair-Wage-Guide-Report-20101.pdf).

12 No Access to Justice
The Failure of Ethical Labeling and Certification Systems for Worker Rights

Bama Athreya and Brian Campbell

Global human rights treaties and the United Nations bodies, established in the wake of World War II, were crafted with a view to establishing the accountability of governments to agreed-upon human rights norms. The global governance framework established in that period failed to predict the enormous influence and power, or behavior, of transnational corporations in subsequent decades. During the same postwar period, the Bretton Woods negotiations, establishing a new framework for trade and investment, are characterized by naïve optimism in the virtuous effects of market forces, and thus, failed to establish safeguards to regulate behavior of market actors[1] (Roosevelt 1945, Collingsworth et al. 1994). Following the drafting of the General Agreement on Tariffs and Trade (GATT), there was an effort to create an International Trade Organization (ITO), charged with ensuring that trade met specific social aims, including elimination of unfair labor conditions (MacShane 1996: 63–64). Despite its opposition to the ITO charter, the U.S. government consistently articulated a belief that through trade and investment, U.S. corporations would act as 'ambassadors' for democratic values.[2]

However, in response to the increasingly evident governance gap in the 1970s, as evidenced, for example, by the involvement of International Telephone and Telegraph and other U.S. corporations in the bloody coup against the Allende government, multilateral bodies sought to address the accountability of corporations and other private, nonstate actors through such voluntary mechanisms as codes of conduct. Unfortunately, companies and less-developed countries (LDCs) successfully resisted all efforts to incorporate binding dispute-resolution mechanisms that would provide workers with clear processes to ensure that companies abide by their public commitments to labor rights and clear remedies when violations occurred.

By the 1980s, the U.N. Commission on Transnational Corporations, for example, had abandoned its efforts to develop any enforcement mechanisms that would make its code of conduct relevant. The U.N. commission did not even have ability to effectively research the level of compliance with the code by companies or countries, and, by the early 1990s, with little political and financial support, the commission was dismantled under strong pressure from the U.S. government.

The International Labour Organization (ILO), working with its tripartite members, also sought to establish a set of binding principles for multinational corporations when it adopted the Tripartite Declaration of Principles Concerning Multinational Enterprises and Social Policy in 1977 (ILO 2006). To enforce the commitments, the declaration established an ILO Standing Committee on Multinational Enterprises, which would have the power to investigate and resolve violations of the declaration. Victims were provided a complaints process through which they could file cases seeking an investigation of a company's practices (ILO 2006: 19). However, when workers from a PepsiCo bottling plant in Guatemala filed a complaint before the standing committee in 1993, alleging serious labor abuses including threats and intimidation of trade-union members, the committee was blocked from opening an investigation by the employer representative to the committee.[3] Seeking to ensure that the tripartite agreement had no teeth, the employers repudiated outright the complaints procedures. According to the committee report, the employer vice-chairman stated "that the Employers did not perceive respect for human rights as a precondition for investment. If that were the case, she argued, employers would not have accepted the Tripartite Declaration" (ILO 1993).

The Organization for Economic Cooperation and Development endorsed its own set of guidelines in 1976 aimed at ensuring multinational corporations from OECD countries respected the rights of workers and the broader community of stakeholders when doing business globally, particularly in countries where rights were not enforced and rule of law was weak. The guidelines are a set of voluntary principles and standards covering a range of business practice, including workers' rights (OECD 2000).

Though designed as voluntary and not legally binding, the OECD governments committed to establishing national contact points (NCPs) that would not only educate companies on the guidelines, but would also provide complaints processes through which violations of the guidelines could be raised to the NCP, which is tasked with responding to the complaint and finding ways to work with the parties to find a solution (OECD 2000: 27).

Unfortunately, the weakness of the OECD guidelines and the NCPs has been the failure of many governments, including the United States, to implement the complaint mechanism envisioned by the procedural guidelines. Some countries have chosen to create NCPs that provide complaints processes backed by the power to investigate and issue determinations, such as the British OECD NCP. However, others, like the U.S. government, have chosen to leave NCPs weak and irrelevant, without meaningful complaints procedures. As a result, most U.S. cases have not resulted in any effective action or even findings (HRW 2010).

A new wave of civil-society activism in the United States attempting to strengthen the U.S. NCP and its complaint processes has met with resistance from the U.S. Council on International Business, which stated bluntly that businesses would not support reform of the U.S. NCP if they saw it as creating an alternate forum within the United States for worker disputes (CAP 2010). It bears noting that this stance is inconsistent with the business community's willingness to be bound by dispute resolution processes that often bypass national judicial systems to resolve trade and investment disputes (Anderson et. al. 2010). Logical inconsistencies notwithstanding, however, it is clear that political mobilization will be necessary to achieve the objective of ensuring that corporations engage in good faith in dispute settlement mechanisms related to enforcement of human-rights norms.

1   THE LIMITATIONS OF "HARD LAW" IN THE UNITED STATES

In many countries, including those that rely on investments into labor-intensive, low-wage jobs in industries such as apparel, local laws may offer adequate protections for labor rights, including minimum wages and regulations on overtime and health and safety. While these standards are assured on paper, they are often not applied in practice. Labor activists in developing countries are unable to use the law proactively, particularly when corruption, bad politics, and a lack of respect for rule of law combine to ensure that cases are not adjudicated fairly, thus discouraging activists' investment in a proactive legal strategy. Thus, when countries fail to ensure that workers can exercise their rights, workers are forced to seek alternatives to help ensure that their rights are respected and protected.

When multinationals are responsible, either directly or indirectly, for abuses in their supply chains, workers have increasingly turned to labor and human-rights organizations in the multinational's home country in the United States or Europe to seek recourse under their laws. Unfortunately, advocates' attempts to use 'hard law' approaches to address worker-rights violations in global supply chains have met with very limited success, and have only been able to access legal remedies in the most egregious violations of international labor law, those involving trafficking and forced labor. In the 1996 precedent-setting *Doe v. Unocal* case, the International Labor Rights Forum (ILRF), along with Earthrights International and others, represented Burmese forced-labor victims filing a suit under the Alien Tort Statute (ATS)[4] against the Burmese government's joint-venture partner in a pipeline project, Unocal, in California.[5] When Unocal challenged the right of Burmese nationals to sue them under U.S. and California state law, the court rejected Unocal's argument and ruled that Unocal could in fact be held liable for violating U.S. law for using forced labor to build its pipeline in Burma, setting a strong precedent that corporations could face significant liability for assisting and benefiting from forced labor.[6]

The Unocal case and its path-breaking settlement in 2005 set the precedent that corporations could be held liable under U.S. laws for violations of universal international labor norms resulting from their overseas investments and business deals. Unfortunately for many victims, subsequent efforts to hold multinationals accountable under the ATS for labor violations have met with little success (Hoffman and Quarry, 2010).[7] As a result, recourse to courts has become even more difficult for victims of human-rights abuses. For victims of common forms of labor abuses in global sweatshops, including nonpayment of wages, violations of overtime, workplace abuse, and health-and-safety violations, the ATS provides no avenue for relief at all (Athreya and Su 2010).[8]

In contrast, when sweatshop conditions were discovered within the U.S. jurisdiction, workers successfully held brands and retailers legally responsible for cleaning up their supply chains. In 1999, UNITE, Global Exchange, Sweatshop Watch, and a number of foreign workers in factories in the U.S. territory of Saipan filed suit against 18 U.S. clothing companies' violations of U.S. laws, including forced overtime, withholding wages, and, in a couple instances, bonded labor.[9] Facing liability for a class of thousands of workers in Saipan, the U.S.-based retailers agreed to settle the case in 2002 and compensate the workers.[10] As a part of the settlement agreement, the retailers agreed to establish a program, called the "CNMI Garment Industry Monitoring Program," that would conduct monitoring of the factory conditions. An Oversight Board (OB) was established to ensure independent oversight of the entire program and establish communication directly with the workers. To meet this responsibility, the Oversight Board was empowered to establish a process for two purposes: (1) "receiving, evaluating, and responding to claims of non-conformance with Program Standards from workers" and (2) "responding to claims to information from reliable sources regarding any imminent threat to workers health and safety."[11]

Recognizing the need to ensure that the monitors were also accountable to the workers, the OB was also empowered to receive complaints directly from workers concerning instances when the independent monitors themselves "varied from the Inspection Protocols or acted in a manner that is biased, unnecessarily disruptive of the Manufacturer's Operations, unreasonably intrusive of Worker privacy, or otherwise contrary to the letter or spirit of the Program."[12] Unfortunately, beyond this ambitious beginning, the settlement did not stipulate the authority of the OB to mediate in such cases to resolve disputes. Also, although the agreement protected confidentiality of workers making complaints, an important breakthrough at the time, the agreement did not go so far as to require monitors to consult with or inform workers of their procedures for developing remediation plans, nor to invite worker consultation in the development of such recommendations.

Though the foreign workers on Saipan successfully sued in U.S. courts, the case simply highlights the troubling policy gap that allows multinational companies to benefit from investing in countries with weak legal-enforcement regimes, like Bangladesh and Pakistan, without accountability for labor violations committed in their supply chains.[13]

Throughout the 1980s and 1990s, consumer awareness of the sweatshop conditions in supply chains grew due to concerted campaigns by NGOs in Europe and the United States highlighting the troubling governance gap that enabled corporations to undermine workers' rights globally with impunity. Through these campaigns, activists and consumers began to demand that companies ensure that workers manufacturing their products enjoy their full range of rights, as well as fair compensation. Fearing a consumer backlash against their brands, companies began to adopt codes of conduct, which they hoped would be enough quell the public outcry and assuage customers' concerns. To demonstrate their commitment to the codes, some companies incorporated their codes of conduct into their contracts with suppliers and exacted promises from suppliers that they would allow inspections by internal auditors.

Despite obtaining promises from suppliers to respect labor and human rights or risk losing orders, the companies never intended the promises to extend to the workers themselves to enable them to enforce their rights. Rather, as workers in Wal-Mart's supply chain discovered when they sought enforcement of the contract, the codes were simply intended to protect the multinational corporation's legal right to rescind contracts and remove their orders from a factory found in violation of its code.

In the early 1990s, Wal-Mart developed its "Standards for Suppliers" (Standard), which required its suppliers to comply with local laws regarding working conditions such as pay, hours, forced labor, child labor, and discrimination. Wal-Mart then incorporated the standards into all of its supply contracts and reserved the right to inspect its suppliers to ensure that the code was being met. According to the contract, if a supplier fails or refuses to comply with the standards, Wal-Mart has the right immediately to cancel all orders and return any shipment. According to Wal-Mart public relations and advertising materials, the company requires its suppliers to comply with its standard to improve the lives of workers by improving working conditions in foreign factories.

Yet, despite the public promise by Wal-Mart and its suppliers to ensure that minimum working conditions are maintained in its supply factories, workers continue to suffer from widespread abuses, including uncompensated forced overtime, pay below the minimum wage, and unsafe working environments. In 2005, ILRF assisted workers from Wal-Mart supply factories in China, Bangladesh, Indonesia, Swaziland, and Nicaragua to file suit against Wal-Mart in the United States, seeking to compel Wal-Mart to abide by its contractual obligations to ensure its code of conduct was implemented. In their suit, the plaintiffs argued that Wal-Mart developed and incorporated its standard into its supply contract to benefit the workers.[14] According to the common law of California, where the suit was filed, and many other U.S. jurisdictions, "A promise in a contract creates a duty in the promisor to any intended beneficiary to perform the promise, and the intended beneficiary may enforce the duty."[15] Therefore, Wal-Mart and its suppliers contractually agreed to ensure that the minimum working conditions required by the standards were met.[16]

Rejecting the plaintiffs' contention, Wal-Mart argued that by incorporating the standards into its supply contracts, neither it nor its suppliers actually intended the contractual provisions to benefit the workers. Rather, the contract was only intended to empower Wal-Mart to remove its orders from a supplier in the event a violation is discovered, thereby shielding the company from some of the negative publicity, as well as to contractually require the suppliers to submit to factory monitoring at Wal-Mart's discretion.[17]

The Ninth Circuit Court of Appeals agreed with Wal-Mart and dismissed the plaintiffs' claims.[18] In its 2009 decision, the court found that neither Wal-Mart nor its suppliers had adopted the standards to benefit the workers at the supplier factories; that Wal-Mart never intended to promise any worker that its suppliers would meet the minimum working conditions required by the contract; and that it did not actually promise to inspect its suppliers to ensure they maintained minimum working conditions. Therefore, Wal-Mart owed no duty to the workers in its supplier factories. Ultimately, the court's decision rested on the conclusion that codes of conduct themselves, even when incorporated into a legally binding contract with a supplier company, are not intended to protect the workers, just the company.

2   NEXT GENERATION OF CODES: ETHICAL CERTIFICATION AND LABELING

Ethical Labeling and Market Demand

Because legal systems and corporate codes have generally failed to curtail effectively labor-rights abuses in many export industries, consumers and investors are increasingly looking for alternatives to fill the human-rights governance gap. Consumer and company demand for ethically produced goods has grown rapidly over the past decade. Initiatives range from eBay's World of Good online marketplace to the socially conscious Edun clothing brand and the Red initiative working to end AIDS globally, both of the latter promoted by U2 front man Bono (WEF 2006). The trend toward ethical consumerism is real and well documented (Giridharadas 2009, Jensen and Webster 2008, Mustafa 2007).

As a result, businesses are increasingly turning to private-certification initiatives to provide consumers with assurances that workers' rights are being enforced in their global supply chains. Sustainable- and ethical-certification initiatives directed at U.S. and European consumers now proliferate, with certification available for wood and wood products, fish and seafood, fresh flowers, carpets, and numerous other products.[19] Some, like Fairtrade, provide a product label; others, like Social Accountability International, provide certifications of the companies and their supply chains.

The ultimate purpose of these programs is to provide public assurance to consumers that goods are produced in an ethical manner, including conditions of environmental stewardship and worker rights. However, for the programs to be successful in the long run, they will have to demonstrate to consumers that they provide reliable assurance that the standards are being implemented on an ongoing basis. In return, though, consumers are willing to pay a premium for that assurance (Hiscox and Smyth 2007).

For example, shoppers at a department store in the Detroit area were presented with two identical sets of white socks, one of which was labeled 'sweat-free.' The sock labeled 'sweat-free' was more expensive than the unlabeled sock. Researchers found that 30 percent of the shoppers were willing to pay a premium and chose the product with the sweat-free label. Even more tellingly, exit interviews by the research team revealed that of the 70 percent of consumers who did not make such a choice found that most consumers either did not notice the ethical label or did not understand the meaning of the label, which suggests that more effective communication with consumers might result in more sales of the sweat-free labeled product (Kimeldorf et. al. 2006). The authors also concluded that given the fraction of ethically labeled products in the U.S. market at present, these results suggest a significant potential for market expansion.

As consumers increasingly look to private initiatives for assurances unavailable elsewhere, ethical certification and labels that incorporate labor standards, like corporate codes before them, will continue to face increasing pressure to ensure that certified companies meet the standard in practice. According to the ISO 65 Standard for credible certification bodies, workers and other stakeholders must have access to an effective complaints mechanism where both the certifier and the company can be held accountable to the standard (ISO 1996).

In line with the ISO 65 mandate, many certifications and multistakeholder initiatives, such as Fairtrade, Forest Stewardship Council, Marine Stewardship Council, Fair Labor Association (FLA), and Social Accountability International (SAI) have implemented some process to handle complaints (ISO 1996: 7). However, because the ISO 65 standard is silent on how the mechanisms should work and for what purpose, many certification bodies have instituted basic complaints mechanisms that provide little opportunity for workers to engage actively to protect their rights. The mechanisms are simply intended to provide a location to lodge allegations but do not provide workers an avenue to ensure their rights are protected and that no harm will come to them from utilizing the process.

ILRF's recent experience representing workers attempting to utilize two certification-complaints mechanisms under SAI's SA8000 standard and Fairtrade's 'allegations' procedure illustrates the overall gap in access to justice. The cases, intended to bring certified companies into compliance with labor standards, exemplify both the role a robust complaints mechanism can play to ensure enforcement, but also the failures of the existing mechanisms to provide workers with meaningful resolution of their complaints that take into full account their views and concerns.

From the workers' perspective, the complaints processes can be an uncertain, risky process. They contain very little guidance for potential complainants on the process or potential outcome. Since certification bodies and their audit arms often agree to blanket confidentiality agreements with the companies they work with, without preserving the right to disclose information to the workers whose conditions are being certified, workers are either poorly informed or not informed at all as the complaint proceeds. When, upon investigation, a complaint is verified and violations are discovered, the certification body does not consider the workers' views toward resolution, but instead, leaves development of corrective action plans up to the company, without consulting with the workers and subject only to the supervision of the compliance auditors. Finally, none of the complaints processes provides access to or envisions the use of conciliation, mediation, or arbitration to resolve complaints.

ILRF cases have demonstrated that certification systems suffer from the same core weaknesses as the codes of conduct before them. Although, technically, many of these programs are 'multistakeholder,' in reality, the logic parallels that of the Wal-Mart case cited above, where programs and standards are intended to be, and contractually arranged for, the benefit of the certified companies, not the workers whose conditions they purport to certify.

FLO "Allegations" Process and the Hired Labor Standard

In 2009, ILRF worked with local workers' organizations in Pakistan to conduct an investigation into working conditions at two Fairtrade certified factories and their associated stitching centers that were producing soccer balls under FLO's Hired Labor Standard (ILRF 2010). During the investigation, ILRF partners found that the two companies, Talon and Vision, were violating the right to freedom of association, had failed to use permanent rather than casual labor, and were guilty of widespread wage violations.

In response to a request by the local worker organization, ILRF raised concerns directly with the Fairtrade Labelling Organization (FLO), as well as its audit arm, FLO-Cert, and with the provider of Fairtrade labels for the U.S. market, Transfair USA. ILRF indicated its interest in filing a formal complaint and in understanding the availability of procedures to remediate the violations and ensure standards were enforced. However, the complaints process, as detailed by FLO, did not provide adequate assurance either that the complaint would be addressed or that the complainants (or their representatives) would have a formal standing during the review or when developing the remediation plan.[20]

Under the Fairtrade program, if a FLO-Cert[21] auditor fails to detect a past or on-going violation of FLO's standards, workers may notify FLO's auditors

234 Bama Athreya and Brian Campbell

of their mistake through FLO's 'allegations' process. According to the FLO-Cert 'allegations' process, 'any person' can send information to FLO-Cert regarding violations at a certified facility. However, the process was not designed in a manner intended to protect workers since there is no meaningful 'whistleblower' protection in place. Nor are the complainants/victims provided any standing or meaningful voice in the complaints and remediation process. Rather, FLO's process requires only that FLO notify the complainant whether their complaint was accepted or not, and, if accepted, the "outcome of the evaluation and subsequent decision" (FLO-Cert 2010). FLO's process does not provide the complainants a right to engage in the investigative process or to appeal or contest FLO-Cert's findings or investigative process. Only the factory or stitching center managers have a right to see this information, and complainants are not provided any further information during the pendency of the complaint. Finally, victims are not provided the right to help develop the corrective-action plan to remedy violations committed against them. In sum, victims have no voice in the process, which may result in further harm, particularly if FLO-Cert decertifies a company and buyers withdraw orders without first ensuring that all efforts are made to directly involve the workers in the decisions that affect their lives and livelihoods.

In this respect, Fairtrade shares the fundamental weakness of codes of conduct: it envisions a primary duty to the supplier company ('producer'), not the workers in the supply chain. It is particularly notable that FLO maintains full and strict confidentiality while a complaint or a discovered violation is being remediated, providing full information to the supplier company, but not to the third-party complainant or any other stakeholder (FLO-Cert 2010). Through legally binding confidentiality agreements with employers, FLO and FLO-Cert are prohibited from discussing any specific findings stemming from an audit or a complaint with representatives of the workers or the complainants/victims, thus preventing the workers from sharing information during the review process about whether the standard is being violated.[22] Taking their commitment to the employer one step further, FLO-Cert has also obligated itself to keep the details of the complaint, the investigation, and the remediation plan confidential as well.

When ILRF sought assurances from FLO, on behalf of the Pakistani stitching center workers, that FLO would adequately consider the workers' views, including the workers' desire for Talon to maintain certification and remediate problems, ILRF were simply notified that these concerns had been lodged as an allegation and that ILRF would be notified of the outcome of the investigation by FLO audits and FLO-Cert after the process was concluded. When ILRF pressed for a more rigorous process that involved the complainants in the investigation and remediation stage, ILRF was informed that FLO was unable to provide the complainants with any further information pending resolution of the allegation due to strict confidentiality agreements it signed with the employer. Finally, FLO did not respond to ILRF's request that the employer waive the confidentiality requirement.[23]

Confidentiality agreements may have their place as a means to protect legitimate business secrets. However, they are inappropriate to audits of labor standards because they create significant obstacles to ensuring workers' voice in the Fairtrade system. By agreeing to an employer's requirement that the certification body maintain full confidentiality without exception, FLO and FLO-Cert have not struck the balance between the employer's right to protect legitimate business secrets and the workers' right to fair treatment under the standard.

For any ethical certification or labeling initiatives to work effectively, they must acknowledge that fundamental conflict of interest exists between employers and workers in most workplaces. 'Producers,' or suppliers of product, must be acknowledged to be employers in this equation, and the certification bodies must recognize the need either to acknowledge that their role is to represent employers, and seek fair and neutral mediation of disputes elsewhere, or to strike a balance between the interests of employers and workers. For FLO's part, it has perhaps failed to fundamentally understand this distinction in its procedures because certification began on small farms and agriculture cooperatives in the coffee sector, where the producer/farmer also provides the labor. However, as Fairtrade expands to plantations and industrial settings, it must alter its understanding of worker interests.[24]

In the end, for Fairtrade to deliver on its promise to improve conditions for workers in certified facilities, it must find credible ways to balance the employers' interests, including the interest in protecting legitimate business secrets, with the interests of workers to have access to enough information to ensure that they can monitor compliance with both the standard and the implementation of the corrective-action plans at the workplace. Otherwise, by continuing to represent to the public, and to workers, that the system protects **both** producer (employer) interests **and** worker interests without establishing any means to mediate between conflicts in such interests, Fairtrade necessarily must cheat on at least half of such market claims.

Social Accountability International and SA8000

In early 2009, ILRF was retained by a union representing more than 4,200 workers at agricultural plantation and processing plant owned and operated by Dole Foods Philippine-based subsidiary, Dole Philippines. With the plantation located in Mindanao in the heart of a conflict zone, the union was facing a concerted campaign by the Philippine government, particularly the armed forces of the Philippines, to dismantle the union, which they accused of being communist and supporting a communist group that has been waging a 40-year insurgency. Dole Philippines management allegedly seized the opportunity to support the military campaign, both directly and through supporting a group of workers who were also being supported by the military to replace the union (KMU 2010). The facility had been certified against a globally recognized standard for decent work, known as

236 Bama Athreya and Brian Campbell

SA8000®, developed and promoted by Social Accountability International—
a U.S.-based multistakeholder initiative.[25] The union alleged violations of
the SA8000 standard governing freedom of association, including (1) discrimination against union supporters because of their leadership or membership in the union and their political ideology, (2) support for another
labor organization and facilitating the group to operate freely within the
company Dole's facilities to conduct campaigns against the union with impunity; (3) assistance to the Philippine military in conducting anti-union activities against the workers' democratically elected union in clear violation
of the workers right to freedom of association, (4) systematic violation of
the collective-bargaining agreement (CBA) to undermine the union's ability to represent and protect the interest of Dole's workers, and (5) actions
in bad faith such as refusal to cooperate in resolving complaints raised by
union on behalf of workers.

Prior efforts by the union to secure mediation, arbitration, or other legal
settlement through the Philippine government's National Conciliation and
Reconciliation Board (NCMB) and Department of Labor failed when Dole
refused to participate. Therefore, in July 2008, the mediator gave up, issuing
the statement that Dole "refused to follow the agreed procedure on grievance under the CBA" and that "the Company are using the military . . . to
harass the union" (KMU 2010). Subsequently, the union decided to pursue
a complaint before SAI in the hopes that Dole Foods, which has a seat on
SAI's advisory board and had been a key partner for SAI for nearly a decade,
would respond to efforts to remedy the violations through the services of
SAI. The union hoped that that when faced with the possible sanction of
being expelled from the SA8000 program and from SAI's advisory board
would provide enough incentive for the company to come to the table for
mediation toward resolution of the violations.

At the outset, though, the union was faced with a difficult challenge. If
it complained and subsequent audits confirmed the allegations, Dole would
risk losing its certification. This loss of certification would open the union
up to more serious retaliation from management, who would blame the victims for the loss of the SA8000 certification. To avoid this scenario, and to
demonstrate the union's willingness for constructive dialogue and amicable
resolution of the violations, the union lodged its request through a special
Complaints Management System (CMS) developed specifically for SAI's
Corporate Involvement Program and advisory board members like Dole
Foods.[26] The union also sought to lodge a complaint against the company's
anti-union policies through the SA8000-accredited certifier for the Philippine facility, SGS Group.[27] Finally, the union lodged a complaint against
SGS itself with the accreditation body, Social Accountability Accreditation
Services (SAAS), alleging faults in SGS's audit protocols resulting in the auditors missing or outright ignoring violations (SAAS 2008). In other words,
the union had to launch three coordinated complaints simply to address
violations at one facility.

In response to the CMS complaint against Dole and the SAAS complaint against the auditor, SAI and SAAS sent a representative to witness Dole Philippines regularly scheduled SA8000 audit in July 2009. In addition to addressing shortcomings to the audit protocol, the witness auditor was also retained by SAI to conduct his own field investigation into the merits of the complaint in response to the union's complaint through the CMS mechanism. Unlike FLO, however, SAI recognized the need to issue a report to the union detailing the results of the investigation for the union and secured a voluntary agreement, or waiver of confidentiality, from Dole to allow the union access to a scaled-down version of the investigative report. Unfortunately, when time came to release the report, Dole sought to prevent SAI from releasing the findings for more than one year.[28]

At the same time, SGS auditors found Dole to be in noncompliance with the SA8000 standard in its actions to openly support another labor group (SGS 2009a). However, in a remarkable finding, the auditors deemed the freedom of association violation as only a "minor noncompliance," citing as their reasons (1) an intra-union conflict that allegedly precipitated company intrusion into union affairs, and (2) the auditor's subjective belief, or bias, that Dole and the Philippine government favored 'development' (a subject not auditable under the SA 8000 standard) while the union did not. Therefore, according to the lead auditor, the social accountability auditors "will definitely favor the government programs," referring to the military's anti-union efforts.

The union was never notified of the audit findings, nor could it dispute the auditors' determination that company's support for the other worker group was only a minor infraction of the standard. First, the union was not provided with a copy of the results from which it could base an appeal. Second, the SA8000 complaint process, as managed by the auditing company, SGS, did not provide the union any standing to appeal a determination or an ineffective corrective-action plan.[29] Yet, the process did allow the company to appeal any negative finding, thereby providing the company with a second bite at the apple without granting the victims any similar right. Following the SGS finding of 'minor noncompliance,' Dole was given broad leeway by SGS to design and implement its own corrective-action plan. Dole's corrective-action plan consisted only of two steps: (1) it will remind the union not to raise complaints to the NCMB or the Philippine Department of Labor and stick to the internal grievance processes, and (2) it will "organize a meeting or remind all parties to implement corrective actions" (SGS 2009b). Neither step required Dole actually to implement reforms to end the abuses. Amazingly, the auditors accepted this proposed corrective-action plan.

After several months, Dole still refused to engage with the union, believing that it had met the SA8000 requirements by implementing the self-imposed corrective-action plan. During that time, though, the union continued to complain that Dole was further deepening its ties with the company-backed workers' group seemingly in an effort to accelerate the anti-union campaign. Facing increasing pressure, the union requested an end to the informal process and lodged a formal complaint against Dole directly with SAI. However, the workers were still concerned that filing a complaint could harm their interests and lead to further retaliation, so the union again requested that SAI not remove certification unless all possible measures toward mediation had been exhausted. The union continued to hope that the SA8000 certification, and the related complaints processes, would provide them an avenue to engage Dole constructively where the local government processes had failed.

As designed, the CMS was intended to be a detailed and outcome-driven process that provided the union with certain procedural rights, including the right to information and a formal panel. Because of the CMS complaint, SAI decided to convene a formal board hearing and explore a final board determination about whether Dole Foods, due to the actions of its wholly owned and certified subsidiary, would be allowed to continue participation in the SAI program. In May 2010, the hearing panel, which included representatives of the union, Dole, and other corporate and NGO stakeholders on SAI's board, met and the parties negotiated a proposed agreement calling for a mediation and a legally binding arbitration process to resolve the ongoing dispute between the union and company management, and thereby extricate management from union affairs well in advance of the workers' union-certification elections, which were set for February 2011.[30] While this would have been a significant victory for workers, Dole's executive management outright rejected the proposed agreement by denying that it had provided any support to the workers campaigning against the union. Rather, Dole proposed instead to expedite the union elections, which the union perceived as a yet another tactic to undermine the union's leadership.[31]

After the union sought resolution of its case in a timely manner, citing the need to resolve the complaint after more the 18 months, SAI's advisory board, including the labor representatives on the board, voted to end the CMS process and dismiss the complaint without resolution, finding that the alleged violations at Dole Philippines were outside the jurisdiction of the CMS process and should be addressed through the SGS complaint process.[32] As noted *supra*, SGS had already notified the union that it would not be allowed to participate in a complaint against Dole Philippines nor appeal the findings. Repeated efforts by the union to continue the complaint have failed.[33] After dropping the complaint, SAI went even further and secured the services of one of its own board members to work as a consultant with Dole company management to advise to company on how to address the labor dispute. SAI's newly appointed representative never met with the union nor visited the facility in question.[34] Dole Philippines continues to enjoy SA8000 certification, and the workers have not been informed of any corrective actions that have taken place because of their complaint.

While the result was disappointing for the union, on paper, the CMS mechanism did offer a path to resolve disputes and required a commitment by the company to abide by the decision as a demonstration of good faith. In the end, though, when SAI chose to dismiss the complaint without resolution, thereby forgoing written commitment of its own complaints processes, the workers were left without any further recourse or any way to appeal the decision. Dole Philippines continues to enjoy the benefits of SA8000 certification.[35]

3 A WAY FORWARD: CREATING BINDING MECHANISMS IN SOFT LAW INITIATIVES

Workers and communities worldwide lack meaningful access to justice, even where in principle international norms are in effect, domestic laws are adequate, and investors have stated additional human-rights commitments through codes of conduct or participation in other nonbinding instruments. Private voluntary systems to monitor codes of conduct or human-rights policies have failed entirely to create effective sanctions for free riders or company failure to exercise due diligence regarding market claims. Importantly, such systems have without exception failed to create practical 'whistleblower' or grievance channels that would provide meaningful redress of violations for those parties whose rights are directly violated.

Labor rights are analogous to other resource rights and thus a project to push corporations, industries, and other relevant actors to enforce labor rights should coordinate work around interconnected challenges and strategic opportunities to promote access to justice for communities seeking protection of their resource rights. In both cases, the main challenge is holding nonstate actors accountable. These actors include not only direct investors but also traders, financiers, risk guarantors, and other related entities.

Activists must be empowered to bring real sanctions to bear when companies are found to be in violation of basic labor or other human-rights standards. To do this, ultimately, activists must push for the enforcement of laws that provide universal protection for universally recognized human rights. Creating demand for 'hard law' protection can be facilitated by the 'soft law' mechanisms suggested in this chapter, however, by creating communications between grassroots actors seeking to promote meaningful access to justice, creating some common targets, and raising the bar for accountability of nonstate actors.

Analogous thinking is developing among advocates working on community and resource rights. In drawing conclusions from the Unocal settlement, Lehr and Smith (2010) have commented on the responsibilities of extractive sector corporations for community rights;

> Indigenous groups are unlikely to have significant funds available to sue in court, courts are likely to be very distant, and such a process often is extremely lengthy. . . . Notably, non-legal grievance mechanisms should

not supplant the rights of individuals or communities to seek legal redress, but rather should provide a mediation-focused alternative. An effective and locally available grievance mechanism therefore should be described in the agreement to resolve disputes that arise.

Civil-society organizations seeking to hold corporations accountable for the range of economic and social rights have recently turned more attention to the OECD Guidelines for Multinational Enterprises, discussed earlier in this chapter. In some European countries, National Contact Points (NCPs) have been active in recent years, and the record on resolution of cases before European NCPs has not been altogether negative (OECD Watch 2010). Moreover, at a multilateral level, stakeholders within the system have begun to advocate for more uniformity among the NCPs and processes applied to cases. Recently, an advocacy campaign in the United Kingdom succeeded in greatly strengthening the U.K. NCP structure and process for case review (OECD Watch 2010). New cases filed after the reforms have had promising results. For example, a case filed against Unilever Corporation on behalf of workers at a tea-processing facility in Pakistan, regarding the use of contracts to undermine freedom of association, led to mediation accepted by both worker representatives and company representatives.

However, as workers continue to seek access to justice through the OECD NCPs or other mechanisms intended to enforce labor rights, companies will continue to seek ethical certifications to defend against the workers' public exposure of violations. Therefore, certification bodies that make any claim to cover labor rights must provide access to workers to raise and resolve complaints through a transparent process where workers are provided real standing and companies commit to resolution through mediation. Certification bodies must also demonstrate that they will abide by findings by sanctioning companies that find violations of the basic standards.

There is ample precedent for such mechanisms in other aspects of trade and investment law. Where corporate rights are at issue, mechanisms are strong and binding. The final draft concluding the Uruguay Round of negotiations and creating the WTO is several hundred pages of regulations setting the rules of trade and protecting market access for MNCs.[36] A 32-page Annex I C deals only with protecting intellectual property rights, and the U.S. government has pursued aggressively the claims of companies seeking redress for property-rights violations (Collingsworth et. al. 1999).

The global labor movement is not without its own precedents for effective and meaningful systems of industrial relations, complete with the necessary formal channels for resolution of disputes. The challenge of the new global sourcing context has been to provide equivalent access to workers in developing countries where transnational companies have a significant impact on the employment relationship. Global protections for corporate property rights reflect the power of multinational corporations to impose regulations that protect their interests globally and not merely nationally, addressing global governance gaps. Workers lack the same protections. This distortion will remain until advocates for worker rights and social justice unify to counterbalance the power of corporations in establishing binding cross-border systems for access to justice.

NOTES

1. In a message to Congress on the outcome of Bretton Woods, President Frank-lin D. Roosevelt (1945) stated, 'These proposals for an International Monetary Fund and an International Bank are concrete evidence that the economic objectives of the United States agree with those of the United Nations. They illustrate our unity of purpose and interest in the economic field. What we need and what they need correspond—expanded production, employment, exchange, and consumption—in other words, more goods produced, more jobs, more trade, and a higher standard of living for us all. . . .'
2. Letter from William H. Taft, IV, U.S. Department of State Legal Advisor to Hon. Louis F. Oberdorfer, United States District Court for the District of Columbia, *Doe, et al. v. ExxonMobil, et al.*, 01-CV-1357 (July 29, 2002), on file with the author.
3. Correspondence from the International Union of Food, Agricultural, Hotel, Restaurant, Catering, Tobacco and Allied Workers' Associations to the International Labor Rights Fund, on file with the author.
4. AlienTort Statute, 28 USC §1350. See also *Sosa v. Alvarez–Machain*, 542 U.S. 692 (2004).
5. Total was dismissed from the case when the U.S.-based court ruled that it did not have jurisdiction over the French company.
6. *Doe v. UNOCAL*, 248 F.3d 915 (9th Cir. 2001).
7. Following the Supreme Court's decision in *Sosa v. Alvarez-Machain* (542 U.S. 692 (2004) where the Supreme Court upheld the ATS but cautioned that it applies only to a limited cause of actions universally accepted by the international community as violations of the law of nations, courts have been reluctant to hear ATS cases involving labor violations not involving forced labor, the worst forms of child labor, and the murder of trade union leaders. While ATS continues to provide victims one possible but difficult avenue for legal relief against corporations in U.S. courts, as was most recently affirmed by the Seventh Circuit Court of Appeals in *Flomo v. Firestone Natural Rubber Company*, LLC. No. 10–3675 (7th Cir. 2011). Recent court decisions, however, have further restricted the ability of victims to pursue claims under the ATS, including the *Flomo* case in which Judge Richard Posner further restricted the scope of the ATS to exclude many of the worst forms of child labor.
8. The April 2013 US Supreme Court ruling in the case Kiobel v. Royal Dutch Petroleum, brought under the ATS on behalf of Nigerian plaintiffs, further restricts the scope for any future cases using this vehicle.
9. *Does I–XXIII v. Advanced Textile Corp. SA US CNMI*, 214 F.3d 1058 (9th Cir. 2000).
10. CNMI Settlement Agreement, September 24, 2002, on file at ILRF.
11. CNMI Garment Industry Monitoring Program, addendum to CNMI Settlement Agreement at 4 (September 24, 2002), on file at ILRF.
12. Ibid.
13. See *Doe v. Wal-Mart Stores Inc.*, 572 F.3d 677 (9th Cir. 2009).
14. See *Doe v. Wal-Mart Stores Inc.*, 572 F.3d 677 (9th Cir. 2009).

15. Restatement (Second) of Contract §304 (1981).
16. Restatement (Second) of Contract §302(1) (1981).
17. Def. Motion to Dismiss at 19, *Doe v. Wal-Mart Stores Inc.*, 572 F.3d 677 (9th Cir. 2009).
18. *Doe v. Wal-Mart Stores Inc.*, 572 F.3d 677 (9th Cir. 2009).
19. For example, Forest Stewardship Council, www.fsc.org; Marine Steward-ship Council, www.msc.org; VeriFlora, www.veriflora.com; Rugmark/ Goodweave, www.goodweave.org.
20. Letter from Trina Tocco, ILRF Deputy Director, and Ineke Zeldenrust, Clean Clothes Campaign Secretariat to the CEO Fairtrade Labeling Organization International, April 20, 2010.
21. FLO-Cert GmbH is the auditing arm of the Fairtrade Labeling Organization International. FLO recently incorporated FLO-Cert as a separate subsidiary company.
22. E-mail from FLO-Cert GmbH Certification Director, to, ILRF Deputy Director, May 26, 2010 (stating ' . . . our confidentiality requirements . . . are legal requirements, set out and agreed to contractually with each operator. A breach of that confidentiality provision could lead to a law suit against FLO-CERT.').
23. E-mail from ILRF Director of Policy and Legal Programs to the CEO Fairtrade Labeling Organization International, June 6, 2010, on file with the author.
24. Fairtrade has attempted to empower workers by requiring employers to es-tablish 'Joint Committees' made up of management and worker representa-tives, and provides that committee with a financial 'premium.' In observed cases, however, workers were not able to determine how the 'Fairtrade' pre-mium would be spent since the decisions were subject to approval by man-agement representatives and made with company business interests in mind.
25. SAI certifies facilities worldwide on behalf of its member companies and upon request of facilities themselves. The largest number of certified facilities are in apparel and textiles http://www.saasaccreditation.org/facilities_by_in dustry.htm cf. last accessed 8.12.2012.
26. Social Accountability International, CIP and AB Member Complaint Man-agement System Process Overview, on file with the author.
27. See http://www.sgs.com/about_sgs/in_brief.htm.
28. SAI did provide the union with a summary report of the field investigation.
29. E-mail from SGS Systems and Certification, to the ILRF Director of Policy and Legal Programs October 1, 2010, on file with the author.
30. Proposed Agreement between Dole Foods and ILRF, May 7 2010, on file with the author.
31. Letter from VP of Worldwide Corporate Responsibility and Sustainability Dole Foods to the ILRF Director of Policy and Legal Programs (May 21, 2010), on file with author.
32. Letter from President of Social Accountability International, to the ILRF Di-rector of Policy and Legal Programs (October 31, 2010), on file with the author.
33. Letter from ILRF Director of Policy and Legal Programs to President of So-cial Accountability International (Nov. 3, 2010).
34. SAI's Board representative contacted the ILRF, who were representing the union during the CMS process, to discuss the case, but the discussions broke down when the union insisted that SAI continue to implement the CMS pro-cess in good faith.
35. In February 2011, a certification election was conducted at Dole Philippines. The union slate, LEAD-PH, which is comprised of the workers whom the

union alleges are supported by Dole management and the Armed Forces of the Philippines, defeated Amado Kadena-NAFLU-KMU and now represent the hourly employees at Dole Philippines in Polomolok.

36. Final Act Embodying the Results of the Uruguay Round of Multinational Trade Negotiations, December 15, 1993.

REFERENCES

Amado Kadena-NAFLU-KMU. 2010. 'Memorandum in Support of Complaint to Commission on Human Rights in the Philippines.' Washington, D.C.: International Labor Rights Forum. Retrieved September 25, 2012 (http://www.laborrights.org/creating-a-sweatfree-world/changing-global-trade-rules/resources/12442).

Anderson, S., R. Dreyfus, J. A. A. Purcell, and M. P. Rocha. 2010. 'Mining for Profits in International Tribunals: How Transnational Corporations Use Trade and Investment Treaties as Powerful Tools in Disputes over Oil, Mining and Gas.' Washington, D.C.: Institute for Policy Studies. Retrieved September 25, 2012 (http://www.fpif.org/reports/mining_for_profits_in_international_tribunals).

Athreya, B. and J. Su. 2010. 'The Perils and Promise of the Alien Tort Statute in Practice.' *Los Angeles Public Interest Law Journal* 2(1): 203–209.

Center for American Progress and the Human Rights Institute. 2010. 'The OECD Guidelines for Multi-National Enterprises: Global Perspectives on an Opportunity for Greater U.S. Leadership.' Paper presented at Georgetown University Law Center, May 11, Washington, D.C.

Collingsworth, T., J. W. Goold and P. J. Harvey 1994. 'Time for a Global New Deal.' *Foreign Affairs* 73(1):8–13.

Collingsworth, T., B. Athreya, and P. Harvey. 1999. *Workers in the Global Economy*. Washington, D.C.: International Labor Rights Forum.

FLO-CERT GmbH. 2010. 'Allegation: Standard Operating Procedure.' Bonn, Germany: FLO-CERT GmbH. Retrieved November 4, 2011 (http://www.flo-cert.net/flo-cert/41.html).

Giridharadas, A. 2009. 'Boycotts Minus the Pain.' *The New York Times*, October 11.

Hiscox, M. J. and N. F. B. Smyth. 2007. 'Is There Consumer Demand for Improved Labor Standards? Evidence from Field Experiments in Social Product Labelling.' Kennedy School of Government, Harvard University, Cambridge, MA. Unpublished manuscript.

Hoffman, P. and A. Quarry 2010. 'The Alien Tort Statute: An Introduction for Civil Rights Lawyers.' *Los Angeles Public Interest Law Journal* 2(2009/2010):129–157.

Human Rights Watch. 2010. 'US: Review of the National Center Point for the OECD Guidelines for Multinational Enterprises.' New York: Human Rights Watch. Retrieved September 25, 2012 (http://www.hrw.org/en/news/2010/11/08/us-review-us-national-contact-point-oecd-guidelines-multinational-enterprises).

International Labour Office. 1993. *Report of the Committee on Multinational Enterprises*. Geneva, Switzerland: International Labour Office.

International Labour Office. 1998. 'Press Release: Report of the ILO Commission of Inquiry Reveals Widespread and Systematic Use of Forced Labour in Myanmar (Burma).' Geneva, Switzerland: International Labour Office. Retrieved September 25, 2012 (http://www.ilo.org/global/About_the_ILO/Media_and_public_information/Press_releases/lang—en/WCMS_007995/index.htm).

International Labour Office. 2006. 'Tripartite Declaration of Principles Concerning Multinational Enterprises and Social Policy.' Geneva, Switzerland: International Labour Office. Retrieved September 25, 2012 (http://www.ilo.org/empent/Whatwedo/Publications/lang—en/docName—WCMS_094386/index.htm).

International Labor Rights Forum. 2010. 'Missed the Goal for Workers: The Reality of Soccer Ball Stitchers in Pakistan, India, China and Thailand.' Washington, D.C.: International Labor Rights Forum. Retrieved September 25, 2012 (http://www.laborrights.org/sites/default/files/publications-and-resources/Soccer-Report2010.pdf).
International Standards Organization. 1996. *Guide 65: General Requirements for Bodies Operating Product Certification Schemes.* Geneva, Switzerland: International Standards Organization.
Jensen, P. and E. Webster. 2008. 'Labelling Characteristics and Demand for Retail Grocery Products in Australia.' *Australian Economic Papers* 47(2):129–140.
Kimeldorf, H., R. Meyer, M. Prasad, and I. Robinson. 2006. 'Consumers with a Conscience: Will They Pay More?' *Contexts* 5(1):24–29.
Lehr, A. K. and G. A. Smith. 2010. 'Implementing a Corporate Free, Prior and Informed Consent Policy: Benefits and Challenges.' Boston: Foley Hoag. Retrieved September 25, 2012 (http://www.foleyhoag.com/NewsCenter/Publications/eBooks/Implementing_Informed_Consent_Policy.aspx).
MacShane, D. 1996. 'Human Rights and Labor Rights: A European Perspective.' Pp. 48–99 in *Human Rights, Labor Rights, and International Trade*, edited by L. Compa and S. Diamond. Philadelphia, PA: University of Pennsylvania Press.
Mustafa, Nadia. 2007. 'Fair Trade Fashion.' *Time*, February 27.
Organisation for Economic Co-operation and Development. 2000. 'Guidelines for Multinational Enterprises. Paris, France: Organisation for Economic Co-operation and Development. Retrieved September 25, 2012 (http://www.oecd.org/document/29/0,3746,en_2649_34889_2439005_1_1_1_1,00.html).
OECD Watch. 2010. 'Assessing the Contribution of the OECD Guidelines for Multinational Enterprises to Responsible Business Conduct.' Amsterdam, Netherlands: OECD Watch. Retrieved September 25, 2012 (http://oecdwatch.org/publications-en/Publication_3550).
Roosevelt, F. 1945. 'Message to Congress on Bretton Woods Money and Banking Proposals.' *New York Times*, Feb. 12.
SGS. 2009a. 'Management System Certification Audit Summary Report for Dole Philippines for July.' Washington, D.C.: International Labor Rights Forum. Retrieved September 25, 2012 (http://www.laborrights.org/creating-a-sweatfree-world/changing-global-trade-rules/resources/12442).
SGS. 2009b. 'Management Systems Certification Follow-Up Activity Report for Dole Philippines for August.' Washington, D.C.: International Labor Rights Forum. Retrieved September 25, 2012 (http://www.laborrights.org/creating-a-sweatfree-world/changing-global-trade-rules/resources/12442).
Social Accountability Accreditation Services. 2008. 'Global Procedures Guidelines 304.' New York: Social Accountability Accreditation Services. Retrieved September 25, 2012 (http://www.saasaccreditation.org/docs/How%20to%20file%20a%20complaint,%20Procedure%20304,%20January.2008.pdf).
World Economic Forum. 2006. 'Press Release: Bono and Bobby Shriver Launch Product Red to Harness Power of the World's Iconic Brands to Fight Aids in Africa.' Geneva, Switzerland: World Economic Forum. Retrieved September 25, 2012 (http://www.weforum.org/en/media/Latest%20Press%20Releases/PRESS RELEASES66).

13 Are Social Labels Symbols of Resistance?

A Case for Sweatshop-Free Procurement in the U.S. Public Sector

Bjorn Skorpen Claeson

A social label on garments, guaranteeing socially acceptable labor standards and decent working conditions for workers who made them, would be a welcome development for consumers seeking to avoid sweatshop products. But in a free-market economy, social labels exist side by side with other labels and brands, as one consumer choice among myriad other choices, facing the same competitive pressures as its artificially low-priced shelf-mates. Ensuring decent working conditions and good wages for workers by appealing to the altruism of consumers willing to pay a premium for a 'good cause' is not an easy task with reliable outcomes. A century ago, the National Consumer League's White Label program attempted to bring consumer pressure to bear on U.S. sweatshops, but the standards for the label were low and its market share was small. Today's Fair Trade Certified apparel, recently introduced by Fair Trade USA, faces similar challenges to compete for market share and uphold high standards.

More fertile markets for a social label—where the label would not be just one more brand alongside others but the price of admission—do exist. These are markets that are subject to political pressure and democratic forces that can establish access rules that protect the rights of workers who make the products for those markets. The SweatFree Communities movement in the United States provides one example where cities and local elected bodies, moved by constituent demand, establish 'sweat-free' procurement policies that only allow the purchasing of goods made in decent working conditions and in compliance with international core labor standards.

While verification and enforcement of labor standards remains a challenge, a social label for uniforms, work wear, and other garments could be of great value to government purchasers seeking to identify and obtain goods made in nonexploitative conditions. At the same time, government purchasers could provide a reliable market and pay a fair price for decent working conditions, while accessing the information and investigative resources to ensure the integrity of a label with high standards. A social label for the government purchasing market is a project well worth exploring.

1   THE LOW-PRICE, LOW-ROAD APPAREL ECONOMY

The U.S. apparel economy may be characterized by three interconnected trends linked to the rise of the free-market global economy: declining consumer prices along with increasingly excessive consumer accumulation of disposable apparel products, increasing volume of imported apparel, and hemorrhaging of domestic apparel manufacturing jobs. These trends either began or accelerated in the mid-1990s as the North American Free Trade Agreement (NAFTA) entered into force (January 1, 1994), and the World Trade Organization was founded (1995) to liberalize international trade.

The apparel consumer price index for U.S. urban consumers, a measure of the average change of price over time, had been trending steadily upward for half a century, from the time of World War II, peaking at 133.7 in 1993. But, in 1994, the apparel consumer price index began declining, going as low as 118.9 in 2008, a drop of 11 percent in 15 years (Bureau of Labor Statistics, U.S. Department of Labor 2010a).[1] According to Schor (2005: 313–314) cheap prices do not necessarily mean American consumers spend cumulatively less on apparel because the overall trend is toward "excessive accumulation" of "disposable apparel" with high rates of discard, low rates of utilization of existing inventories of garments, rapid fashion cycles, and failure to wear garments throughout their useful life.

These inexpensive, disposable apparel products are increasingly (debt-financed) imports. In 1994, the United States imported $40 billion of apparel and textiles. Imports increased steeply to $93 billion in 2008 before dipping in the recent global economic recession (Office of Textiles and Apparel 2010). Declining prices and increasing imports have spelled disaster for the domestic apparel industry, as large manufacturers have closed factories in the United States and transferred their work overseas in search of cheaper labor and weaker regulations. In 1969, the U.S. clothing industry employed a high of 1.5 million cut-and-sew manufacturing workers; in 1994, that number had sunk to 940,000 workers (Murray 1995: 63). Fifteen years later, only 200,000 apparel-manufacturing workers remained in the United States, a loss of nearly 80 percent of the industry since the mid-1990s. Unionization in the U.S. apparel industry stands at a low 6 percent. There is no end in sight. According to the Bureau of Labor Statistics, employment in the textile, textile product, and apparel-manufacturing industries is expected to decline a further 48 percent through 2018 (Bureau of Labor Statistics, U.S. Department of Labor 2010b). Unions will no doubt struggle to hold onto their already miniscule share of the industry.

Low-priced imported apparel and loss of domestic apparel-industry jobs are the predictable outcomes of global economy rules, which have removed obstacles to the movement of goods and capital across borders while depressing the price and power of labor around the world (Schor 2005: 312). Harbingers of the new free-market economy, NAFTA and the WTO agreements protect foreign investments but not the workers who make the investments worthwhile. As of 2005, the WTO members have removed export quotas for apparel and textile products, allowing unlimited export flow of apparel and textile products from any region, but disallowing the governments from distinguishing between—or discriminating against—products based on process or conditions of production. For trade purposes, a shirt must be treated as any other shirt whether it is made in conditions that respect the inherent dignity and rights of workers or in conditions where workers are, in effect, disposable.

2 PRICE MACHINATIONS

The free-market price of apparel is not a natural price determined by super-human market forces and reflecting the intrinsic worth of a product, but a human artifice that hides the full economic and ecological cost of production and devalues the true worth of the product. Prices are just as much the product of human machinations and power relations as of abstract laws of supply and demand, which conceal the power behind the price.

Buyer Power

Since the 1980s, retailers have bought each other out, creating giants with tremendous power over the industry. By the late 1990s, the 10 largest retailers accounted for nearly two-thirds of all apparel sales in the United States (Bonacich 1998). Concentration of buying power among large brands and retailers at the top of supply chains and world-wide proliferation of 'cut-and-sew' and 'ready-made garment' factories on the bottom have allowed buyers to reap maximum advantage of trade rules that allow goods and capital to flow across borders unhindered, but do not protect the workers. Large brands and retailers define the terms of the contract with supplier factories, decreasing the price they pay for goods and dictating more stringent performance standards without regard for the workers. The result is a cutthroat apparel industry where contract shops compete relentlessly for customers by cutting costs and pressuring workers to work harder for less.

Apparel industry analysis of purchasing practices explains just how buyers flex their economic muscle to depress prices at the factory level. For example, according to research commissioned by the MFA Forum Bangladesh Buyers' Group (named after the now-expired Multi-Fibre Arrangement, which established export quotas for garment producing countries), "There is agreement among suppliers, brands, non-brand manufacturers and buying houses that prices have decreased in the last two years" (MFA Forum 2008: 9) and not just because supply is up and demand is down. Apparel buyers (large brands and retailers) require 'open book costing' from suppliers and use those figures to obtain competitive counter quotes from suppliers in different countries. One buying house reported getting quotes from

Bangladeshi manufacturers to negotiate lower quotes in Turkey and China, while a Bangladeshi manufacturer testified that a buyer requested he provide a 25-percent lower price than the cheapest price received from other manufacturers (2008: 10). At the same time, quality demands have increased, leading to increased costs for materials, production systems, and quality inspections that must be borne by suppliers, not buyers.

Compounding the price pressure on suppliers are longer and more advantageous payment terms for buyers. According to the MFA Forum research, "There is a widespread agreement that payment dates have been pushed back" from 30-day to 60-day agreements (2008: 10). Some manufacturers even offer 60- to 90-day payment periods. Delivery times, however, have not lengthened correspondingly, but instead, have contracted. Just-in-time production for high-fashion designs has decreased production times by 13 to 25 days from an average of 120 days to 90 or 100 days (2008: 14). Production orders are often unpredictable as suppliers go from one 'volume contract' to another rather than 'relationship contracts' with predictable and manageable orders (2008: 7). For example, Wal-Mart's automated system of 'continuous replenishment'—based on computer technology that tracks every sale in every Wal-Mart store and transmits consumer preferences down the supply chain—enables Wal-Mart to keep inventory at a minimum while forcing suppliers to make unpredictable, frequent, and quick deliveries of smaller lots. Wal-Mart's turnover is so rapid that it sells 70 percent of its merchandise before the company even has paid for it, yielding enormous savings in financing and inventory maintenance, but forcing suppliers to carry the risk and cost of inventory (Bianco 2006: 171–192).

In addition, frequent changes to orders undermine production planning and can further cut into factory resources. According to one manufacturer interviewed in the MFA research, changes to even 5 percent of orders can eliminate the entire profit margin. Even the cost of cancelled orders is not borne by brands. Only one buyer interviewed said that it was willing to negotiate the costs incurred by lost production time, loss of opportunity, and impact on production planning (2008: 16).

Employer and State Power

Buyers' uncompromising demands for quick and flexible production at ever-lower prices force factories to produce goods faster and cheaper to keep their customers. Relations between buyer and supplier are replicated on the factory floor between management and workers. If the buyers provide 'one-off contracts' at rock-bottom prices to suppliers, factory management will relate to workers the same way, as a casual or temporary workforce without rights that can be paid rock-bottom wages for long hours in abusive conditions. A SweatFree Communities study (2008) of a supplier in Bangladesh squeezed by Wal-Mart and other buyers found that "the factory manages the only way it knows or can: it cuts costs by paying (sometimes illegal) poverty wages and denying workers their legal right to organize through a workers association; and it speeds up deliveries by requiring excessively long hours, sometimes until 3 a.m. in the morning." Workers are often aware of this cycle of repression. "The supervisors are afraid of making mistakes because if they do their salaries are cut or they are beaten themselves," said a worker for Asda, Wal-Mart's U.K. subsidiary, interviewed for an ActionAid study (2007) on low apparel prices. "They are under so much pressure from higher authorities, which is why they force us to work harder and they discount our extra working hours" (ibid: 6).

The fact that downward pressure on prices and lead times negatively affects working conditions is hardly an industry secret. According to a code-of-conduct impact assessment conducted on behalf of the Ethical Trading Initiative, suppliers "in all countries and sectors . . . reported that [lower prices and shorter production times] limited their ability to make improvements in labour practices" (Barrientos and Smith 2006: 59). The MFA Forum reports that, "working on one-off contracts at rock bottom prices increases insecurity in the industry and undermines manufacturers' ability to invest in their business, plan production appropriately and support code compliance" (2008: 1). Sweatshops with poverty wages, forced overtime, and dangerous working conditions have become the industry norm worldwide. In the United States, too, apparel contract shops are often sweatshops, operating 'underground,' hidden from public view, and employing mostly poor immigrants of color who cannot safely speak out against injustices.[2]

Meanwhile, government authorities often use artificial means, ranging from the overt use of force and the criminalization of organizing and advocacy to bureaucratic maneuvers and policies, to attract foreign investors with labor prices below those required to maintain a decent livelihood and human dignity. In virtually all apparel-producing countries, the statutory minimum wage for garment workers does not come close to meeting the basic needs of workers and their families: it is a poverty wage, and sometimes, a stark poverty wage. According to Miller and Williams (2009), the legal minimum wage for garment workers is worth an average of about 30 percent of a living wage. For example, it is 22 percent of a living wage in Brazil, 34 percent in El Salvador, and 35 percent in Bangladesh. Increases in the statutory minimum wage rarely match overall inflation or even the rate of increase in the cost of essential consumer goods. For example, in Bangladesh the legal minimum wage remained constant during 1994–2006 while prices increased significantly. The recent worldwide food crisis has doubled the price of rice—a basic staple for many garment workers—but, in most countries, the minimum wage has not been raised accordingly.

Flaw in the Market

Artificially low-priced apparel is one manifestation of what some sustainability professionals, ecological economists, and other advocates for 'true cost accounting' term a "critical flaw in the market" (Bainbridge 2009). This flaw allows the social and ecological costs of production, termed 'externalities,' to be excluded from the price of goods and services. Those costs—pollution, disease, social impacts, and depletion of natural resources—are passed onto future generations, the poor, and communities, allowing consumers to be apparent 'free riders.' But, in the long run, all of us pay for artificially low-priced consumer goods. For example, according to a study by the garment workers' union UNITE HERE!, workers absorb part of the cost of the cheap uniforms purchased by the U.S. military by enduring poverty-level wages, wage-and-hour violations, little or no benefits, forced overtime, hazardous working conditions, and violations of their associational and collective-bargaining rights. Taxpayers also pay part of the cost of cheap uniforms because these workers—most of them women and African American—often must supplement their incomes with social-assistance programs, including Medicaid and food stamps. The report estimates the cost to federal taxpayers for every employee of a military contractor that pays below poverty-level wages is nearly $3,000 (UNITE HERE! 2006). Can this market flaw, which displaces the cost of production on those least able to pay, be corrected?

3   FAIR TRADE: AN ALTERNATIVE ECONOMIC PARADIGM

According to the World Fair Trade Organization, fair trade is "a response to the failure of conventional trade to deliver sustainable livelihoods and development opportunities to people in the poorest countries of the world" and promotes values not common in conventional markets (World Fair Trade Organization 2010). In fair trade, it matters where, how, and in what conditions a product is made, but in free trade, those distinctions amount to unfair 'discrimination,' barriers to trade. In fair trade, the social relations of production are inherent to the definition of the product. In free trade, the product may only be described in terms of its performance requirements; other considerations are, again, unnecessary obstacles to trade. Fair trade is premised on decent working conditions and workers who are organized to have control or influence over the process of production. In free trade, suppliers must be judged solely on their legal, technical, and financial abilities to fulfill the requirements and technical specifications of a contract. In fair trade, producer and buyer meet as equals; in free trade, relations of production are characterized by inequality and political exclusion. The fair trade price considers the full cost of production when workers are treated fairly and the earth protected from harm; the free-trade price hides the social and ecological costs of production and, in effect, calls on the poor to bear the cost of low-price consumer products. The fair-trade price is not any more artificial—and does not involve any more market interference—than the free-market price, but simply reflects different interests and values.

Historically, fair trade is not solely a political-economic critique and a movement in opposition to the dominant economic paradigm, but also a more moderate charity and development-oriented program (Jaffee 2007). Nevertheless, mainstream fair-trade institutions retain a critical edge. According to the governing body of the Fairtrade certification and labeling system, Fairtrade Labelling Organizations International (FLO), fair-trade standards are "designed to address the imbalance of power in trading relationships, unstable markets and the injustices of conventional trade" (Fairtrade Labelling Organizations 2010). Rather than negotiating prices between the powerful and the weak, fair trade seeks an "equal exchange," an equitable and fair partnership between consumers, mostly in the global north, and producers, mostly in the global south. Buyers must pay a stable minimum price for products; producers must be democratically organized; and, production methods must be environmentally friendly.

Fair trade is essentially an attempt to prevent exploitation of labor and natural resources by requiring consumers and buyers to pay a price that includes the full cost of production.

4 SHOPPING FOR A BETTER WORLD?

Consumers who are willing to pay the full cost of products and services may be cause for optimism. A wide range of labeling schemes has been developed to offer additional information about the environmental and social impacts of products and services to consumers who strive to shop for a better world. Some leading businesses, seeking to do the right thing while benefiting from this consumer market have established "the triple bottom line," economic, social, and environmental, while others seek to respect "the 3 Ps—people, prosperity, and planet" (Bainbridge 2009: 2).

There is also evidence of a sizable consumer market willing to pay a fair price to ensure decent conditions and wages for workers. U.S. consumer surveys conducted 5 to 10 years ago show that a majority of consumers was willing to pay more for products not made under sweatshop conditions. Results ranged from a low of 61 percent to a high of 86 percent saying they would pay $5 more for a $20 item labeled as not made in a sweatshop.[3] While these surveys measure consumer attitudes, a more recent behavioral study suggests that the market for 'conscientious consumption' is close to that reported in national surveys with well over half of all consumers actually paying more for products certifiably made under conditions where worker rights are respected (Kimeldorf et al. 2006). If these results are anywhere close to accurate, the untapped market for conscientious consumption could approach half of the $200 billion U.S. apparel-consumer market. Connecting the dots between ethical producers and conscientious consumers with a social label that helps consumers "vote with their dollars" could have potential for advancing the rights of global sweatshop workers.

252 Bjorn Skorpen Claeson

Yet, worker-friendly apparel producers and retailers face an uphill battle operating within the constraints of a market and policy structure that discourages responsible production processes. There is no shortage of valiant attempts worldwide among both producers and retailers to demonstrate that socially responsible production for conscientious consumers is a viable business model. Unfortunately, many of these attempts have failed, some are at risk, and others are unable to grow beyond a miniscule market share. On the producer side one of the best-publicized attempts at worker-friendly production, and perhaps one of the most instructional failures, was Just Garments in El Salvador, launched in 2003.[4]

Just Garments was born from a remarkably successful *maquila* union-organizing campaign in which workers won a new company with a board of directors comprised of one representative from the Taiwanese factory owners and one representing the workers. Distinguishing the new worker-led factory from competitors "through our unionized workforce, our commitment to pay a living wage, and our vision towards worker ownership," Just Garments attempted marketing to the conscientious consumer market, offering an alternative to sweatshops and identifying their products with the 'sweat-free—union made' label. Large numbers of concerned consumers, including fair-trade supporters, university students, and faith groups, did commit to purchasing Just Garments products, and even organized fundraisers for this new "model where workers' rights are respected and a more just global economy is possible." Small socially conscious retailers, also seeking to reach the conscientious-consumer market, sold or made plans to sell their products. Yet, there were simply not enough large-scale orders to meet Just Garment's financial commitments.

As a result, Just Garments was forced to take on subcontract work (making chef uniforms), the lowest-paid and the most unstable business in the garment world. This arrangement kept a small number of workers on temporary life-support while working on a plan to manufacture and market their own T-shirt label. However, when their buyer, a contractor for a U.S. uniform brand, slashed orders by half and cut prices at the same time as El Salvador raised its minimum wage, Just Garments could no longer hold out.

Just Garments was forced to reject an order of chef jackets for which they would be paid only 40 cents per piece, a sharp cut from the earlier 70 cents per piece, which was just about the cost of production. The new jacket was almost identical to the old one, requiring 45 operations to produce, rather than 47. Surprised at the lower price, Just Garments inquired with the brand. They were told the price for the older-style jacket had been 'grandfathered' 20 years ago. "The price for the new jacket reflects today's price structure." To remain competitive, the brand was offering nearly 50 percent less in actual dollars than it had paid 20 years ago for a nearly identical product. To stay in business, Just Garments would have had to become the sweatshop the workers had fought against in the first place.

5   A FAIR-TRADE LABEL FOR CLOTHING?

Perhaps the failures of Just Garments and similar apparel businesses are in part a marketing failure. A credible social label, such as the Fairtrade label, might have connected Just Garments to larger numbers of conscientious consumers willing to pay a fair price covering the full cost of production. But, can such a label help usher in a new economic paradigm of fair trade where workers' rights are nonnegotiable?

A century ago, the National Consumer League introduced the White Label to guarantee consumers that women's cotton underwear was made under decent working conditions. In 1899, the New York Times reported that "women will for the first time be able to purchase goods guaranteed not to be sweat-shop products and to have been made under satisfactory conditions." The label, adopted on a voluntary basis by manufacturers, required compliance with the minimal legal standards of the time, no overtime work, and no children working below the age of 16. But, it was mute on wage issues and did not require unionization. At its peak, there were 68 White Label underwear factories, representing only some 1–5 percent of workers in women's garment factories. At the same time, the labor movement pressured the National Consumer League to promote union rights, and in 1918, the League withdrew the White Label in favor of support for union labels (Ross 2006).

Fair Trade USA, a former member of the Fairtrade Labelling Organizations (FLO) and the fair-trade certifier in the United States, is now developing a Fairtrade label for garments, similar in intent to the National Consumer League's White Label. "For more than 15 years, we've heard the stories of U.S. companies sourcing from sweatshops, yet there's still no easy way for U.S. consumers to walk into a store and choose an ethical tee over one made in a sweatshop," Fair Trade USA (2010) writes. Its recently initiated three-year pilot program in Fairtrade garment certification (see Chapter 11), which already is producing fair-trade labeled garments on U.S. store shelves, is designed to offer companies and consumers "an unprecedented opportunity to positively impact the lives" of both the farmers who grow the cotton and the workers who sew the garments (TransFair USA 2010). However, this ambitious and pioneering program may also be hampered by a flaw in a model of economic transformation that relies on the political force of conscientious consumers; namely, that these consumers are poorly informed and have no way of looking behind the claims of the label and hold either the producer or the certifying agency accountable.

In Chapter 12, we saw how in soccer ball manufacture in Pakistan, a series of noncompliances in a Fair Trade Certified facility highlighted the risks in relying on information-deprived consumers to ensure decent working conditions. (See also International Labor Rights Forum 2010.) Counter to fair-trade principles and standards, these soccer ball workers had no voice and little influence over the production process. Even unionized workers feared speaking against the management and believed they would be fired if they requested contract negotiations to begin (International Labor Rights Forum 2010: 15). To a fair-trade consumer, these findings would be startling and concerning. Arguably, a Fairtrade label in these circumstances does more harm than good, creating a veneer of decency and fairness that covers up abuses consumers have no way of discovering or rectifying. Fairtrade consumers may believe they are 'voting with their dollars' to support a global economy based on different values and priorities than the free-market system when, in actuality, they continue to be complicit with the abuses of a free-market system that displaces the costs of production on those least powerful in the supply chain—the workers.

How can consumers be sure that conditions in a Fair Trade Certified garment factory are better than those in Fairtrade soccer ball factories and stitching centers? Without access to information, how can consumers express their discontent if the standards are not realized? Moreover, should the realization of workers' rights be tied to the choices of consumers who are information-deprived, lack power to sanction violations, and may choose Fairtrade products on a good day and low-priced sweatshop goods when times are harder?

Referring to a controversy about the absence of a binding living-wage standard in the pilot project,[5] Fair Trade USA argues that the burden of living wages lies squarely on the backs of consumers: "The success of the pilot in increasing worker earnings is contingent on U.S. consumers buying Fair Trade product. The best way to support higher wages for workers making Fair Trade Certified products is to buy and promote Fair Trade Certified apparel" (2010a). As has been argued in Chapter 11, every time a consumer buys a fair-trade product, the company that makes it pays a fair-trade premium to a worker-controlled fund. "Then all the workers that stitched the item get a choice, to earn a cash bonus or to invest together in a community need" (2010a). Theoretically, with enough consumer demand to enable a factory to produce only for Fairtrade buyers, the fair-trade premium could double workers' earnings if they chose to use it as a cash bonus.

Yet, workers have a right to a living wage, whether or not consumers choose the product with the Fairtrade label on the store shelf. Why should the realization of the right to a living wage and a decent standard of living be tied to poorly informed and often fickle consumer altruism, which may be a little less conscientious in hard times? As Dickson shows in Chapter 7 of this volume, we are some way off from consumer altruism providing a foundation for global economic transformation. This market-based voluntary approach to the progressive realization of the living wage and other fair-trade standards ultimately implies acceptance of worker exploitation and the free-market price. Rejecting the free market and replacing it with a fair market requires workers to have enforceable rights, independent of the good will of consumers. In the free-market place, what scope is there for genuine consumer power for economic transformation? Are there market enclaves where 'critical consumer mass' can influence the buying practices of key economic actors?

6 CONSCIENTIOUS SUPER CONSUMERS

Unlike ordinary information-deprived conscientious consumers, governmental purchasers can help usher in a new economic paradigm in which the inherent dignity and rights of workers are paramount and nonnegotiable. Governments are purchasers unlike any other. They buy large volumes, maintain ongoing contracts, and their suppliers are increasingly global. They have access to information. They can receive and act on complaints. They have investigatory capacity. They can impose civil and criminal sanctions on suppliers that violate standards or provide false information. In short, as 'conscientious super consumers,' governments have the capacity to make labor compliance a market-access criterion that is independent of consumer altruism.

Procurement in the United States accounts for 20 percent of the gross domestic product (GDP), two-thirds of which is state and local purchasing, and one-third of which is federal (OECD 2002).[6] The federal government procures more than $500 billion of services and goods annually, which is more than the GDP of all but 16 countries (Office of Federal Government Procurement Policy 2010). The international labor rights campaign, Sweat-Free Communities, estimates that combined U.S. federal, state, and local government apparel procurement alone at more than $10 billion annually. Though not immune to economic recessions, government purchasing is a relatively stable market and a force that governments can use responsibly to foster a fair and equitable global economy.

Governments are responsible for spending public funds prudently, using competitive procurement practices to ensure the best possible price or value for the money. However, they also have a responsibility to recognize that their purchasing policies influence labor practices and working conditions, for better or worse, along the supply chain.

In the United States, several legal precedents obligate governments to look beyond the low bid to ensure that workers who provide a service or a good to a government contractor are paid decent wages for work in lawful conditions. Laws that require government contractors to pay prevailing wages and prohibit unsanitary, hazardous, and dangerous working conditions date back at least 80 years. The 1931 Davis-Bacon Act for construction workers employed on federal contracts, the 1936 Walsh-Healey Public Contracts Act for manufacturing workers, and the 1965 Service Contract Act for service employees, all require federal contractors to pay at least the wages and benefits provided by better-paying employers in the industry and labor market.[7] More recently, in excess of 140 U.S. cities and counties have enacted living-wage laws requiring businesses that receive service contracts to pay a wage above the federal or state minimum. In 2007, the State of Maryland became the first state to require employers with state contracts to pay a living wage to its employees (Greenhouse 2007).

The globalization of supply chains may appear to complicate governments' role in promoting decent working conditions for workers that make the products they buy. For example, U.S. states and local governments purchase increasing amounts of apparel from suppliers that obtain products from factories located in China, Southeast Asia, Central America, Mexico, and the Caribbean. Yet, just as conscientious consumers can choose Fairtrade products, governments, as market participants, can use their purchasing power to address unjust conditions in these sourcing countries.

Anti-Apartheid procurement policies may be the first and most strikingly successful examples of states and local governments amassing their procurement power to further international human rights. By the end of the Anti-Apartheid campaign, 25 states and 164 local governments avoided purchasing from or investing in companies doing business in South Africa. According to the U.S. consulate in South Africa, municipal procurement power was the most significant external pressure on U.S. firms to disinvest (Rodman 1998). Anti-sweatshop government procurement policies are another example. These efforts date to 1997, when North Olmsted, Ohio, became the first U.S city to adopt a 'sweat-free' procurement ordinance in the wake of a wave of media revelations linking major apparel brands and stars like Kathy Lee Gifford and Michael Jordan to sweatshops and child labor.

Nationwide, an inspired grassroots movement emerged in a variety of places led by community organizations, people of faith, labor unions, high school students, and others. In 2001, Maine became the first U.S. state to commit to ending public purchasing from sweatshops as legislators joined a broad 'clean clothes' coalition of human-rights groups, small businesses, laid-off shoe workers, and others. In 2003, anti-sweatshop campaigns from around the country founded a new organization, SweatFree Communities, to support and coordinate this national movement. Eight years later, 8 states, 41 cities, 15 counties, 118 school districts, and one nationwide religious denomination have adopted similar procurement labor rights policies to ensure decent working conditions for the workers who make the products these entities buy.[8] Three states and 10 cities, that together represent over 40 million people and a combined $50 million apparel-purchasing market, formed the Sweatfree Purchasing Consortium in June 2010 to help them act with combined strength and transparency in meeting their goals for sweat-free purchasing. The consortium provides expertise and pools resources to monitor working conditions and enforce procurement labor standards.

These government purchasers and their vendors now have the mandate to use their purchasing power to promote an economy that allows factories that are willing to take the high road in the global economy to be successful.

In return for maintaining decent working conditions, supporting workers' right to organize, and paying a true living wage, this set of high-road factories could receive fair prices and long-term, reliable business contracts to supply a relatively steady and predictable market. A label identifying these factories' products as sweat-free would help government purchasers fulfill their responsibility to procure products that meet certain labor standards. At the same time, these government purchasers would have access to the information and investigative resources to ensure the integrity of the sweat-free label, and could ensure that maintaining sweat-free standards are market-access requirements. In these respects, government purchasers differ significantly from individual consumers.

Binding Standards

Whereas individual consumers can only provide incentives to companies to voluntarily adopt and implement the fair-trade standard by 'voting with their dollars,' government purchasers can require companies proposing to sell them products to adopt standards binding on all suppliers that produce goods under a government contract. In the United States, states and local governments have adopted standards that include the applicable laws and regulations in the country of production, the core labor standards defined by the International Labor Organizations (standards regarding freedom of association and collective bargaining, forced labor, child labor, and non-discrimination), and nonpoverty wages beyond the legal minimum wage. Contractors must provide a sworn statement that they will comply with these standards and that they have required subcontractors to do the same. To ensure payment of fair prices to suppliers, government purchasers can also require contractors to make a commitment to purchase the products offered under terms—including prices and delivery dates—that will support and enable the manufacturing of the products in decent working conditions by workers paid living wages.

Access to Information

In addition to establishing binding standards for suppliers, government purchasers can require relevant information prior to making a purchase or entering into a contract. For example, in the United States, some state and local government purchasers require that each bid or proposal submitted for a contract, purchase order, rental, or lease agreement includes a list of each subcontractor and production facility to be utilized in the performance of the contract, including company names, owners or officers, complete physical addresses, as well as specific information on wages, benefits, working hours, and overtime policies.[9] In addition, some government purchasers require contractors to inform workers of their rights under the contract and how to complain if their rights are violated.

Complaints and Investigations

Information access ensures that governments can undertake routine inspections of contract factories providing covered goods and that any person can complain that the procurement labor standards have been violated. The merits of each complaint can be investigated. For example, common sweat-free contract language in the United States requires contractors to ensure that production facilities allow independent monitors or other agents authorized to act on behalf of the governments to conduct unannounced inspections of any worksite where a contract or any subcontract is performed. It also prohibits contractors or subcontractors from engaging in any reprisal, coercion, intimidation or taking any other adverse action against workers for filing complaints, giving evidence, or otherwise cooperating with monitoring and enforcement activities. Some U.S. cities and states also prohibit contractors and subcontractors from reducing orders to a production facility to avoid participating in the remediation process or denying workers any right or standard protected by the code of conduct of the contracting agency.

Sanctions

Finally, U.S. sweat-free contract terms typically specify that upon determination of a violation, the government agency and contractor should seek remediation, the intent being improved working conditions. However, unlike individual consumers, governments have at their disposal criminal and civil sanctions and subpoena power to back up the requirement that suppliers provide accurate information and remediate violations. Refusal of a contractor to facilitate monitoring, cooperate fully in the monitoring process, or take all reasonable steps to ensure that violations are expeditiously remedied may result in disqualification for bidding, termination of a contract, monetary penalties, or other sanctions.

A Social Label for the Government-Purchasing Market

There are several benefits to a social label for the government-purchasing market. Government purchasers could more easily identify products made in accordance with certain labor standards that citizens and legislatures demand. Contractors would have incentive to achieve and maintain the standards needed to qualify for the label, knowing there is a measurable and stable market for decent working conditions, and material consequences for violations. Factories, paid fair prices for their products, would have incentive for compliance, facilitating the monitoring and investigatory work. Over time, factories that qualify to supply this government-procurement market could also produce for the individual-consumer market, allowing more workers to benefit from higher labor standards. At the same time, activists could use the example of the alternative government-procurement market as leverage to delegitimize free-market rules and propose new ones that respect the inherent dignity and rights of all workers.

CONCLUSION

A social label dependent on altruistic consumer choice carries inherent risks. The label is corruptible when individual consumers have no access to independent sources of information and no investigatory capacity. More importantly, a social label as a consumer choice implies acceptance and legitimacy of a free market seemingly capable of providing ethical options and giving consumers real freedom of choice. Just as free-market behemoths such as Wal-Mart and Starbucks benefit from offering a tiny fraction of Fairtrade products as a sheen to gloss over the abuses incorporated in their other product offerings, the free-market system gains legitimacy from displaying a Fairtrade logo here and there while continuing to extort the most heinous sacrifices from the vast majority of workers to provide cheap products in fantastic abundance for consumers. Rather than a symbol of resistance, a social label presented as one consumer choice among many possible choices may actually affirm the free market's inequities.

A social label used as a market permit requirement is a more effective symbol of and tool for resistance. It unambiguously rejects the free-market rule to treat all commodities alike, as though it does not matter whether they are made in conditions that respect the inherent dignity and rights of workers or in conditions where workers are, in effect, disposable. It calls attention to the fallacy of the free-market price, which requires that workers, powerless and pliable, absorb part of the cost by working excessively long hours for remuneration that does not allow an existence worthy of human dignity. Not just an ethical style—in vogue one day, out of date the next—this social label urgently proclaims the need for a fair market to replace the free market and not just to be incorporated within it.

NOTES

1. The broader department store price index compiled by the U.S. Department of Labor shows that prices have declined in all categories—soft goods, durable goods, and miscellaneous—since the early 1990s (Schor 2005).
2. Between 1995 and 2001, the U.S. Department of Labor repeatedly surveyed cutting-and-sewing shops in the major United States apparel centers: New York, northern New Jersey and Los Angeles in particular. Each of these surveys cited by Ross (2004) found that 50–60 percent of the shops failed to pay either the minimum wage, or overtime, or both. In 1996, California state labor investigators found that 72 percent of the garment firms in Southern California also had serious health or safety violations.
3. Marymount University's Center for Ethical Concerns commissioned National Consumer Sweatshop Surveys to measure consumer attitudes toward products

made under sweatshop labor conditions. See Program on International Policy Attitudes (2000 and 2004).

4. The following account of Just Garments is based on Just Garments publications, and the author's correspondence with the worker representative on Just Garments board and the CEO of the uniform brand referred to below.

5. While the only binding wage standard is the statutory minimum wage, the living wage is a 'progress requirement' with each factory setting its own individual targets and timelines to achieve a living wage gradually over time (2010a).

6. OECD estimates that European public authorities' procurement, on average, accounts for more than 20 percent of GDP. Worldwide, government procurement is roughly equivalent to 82.3 percent of goods and services exports (2002).

7. See http://www.dol.gov/dol/topic/wages/govtcontracts.htm (retrieved January 31, 2010). Modeled in part on these prevailing wage laws, the 1949 International Labor Organization Labor Clauses (Public Contracts) Convention (No. 94) was intended to ensure government contract employees enjoy the most favorable conditions of work for a certain locality.

8. Similar ethical public procurement campaigns are led by the Maquila Solidarity Network in Canada, the Clean Clothes Campaign in Europe and the FairWear Campaign in Australia.

9. Examples of publicly accessible garment supply chain information from public entities include the State of Maine (http://www.state.me.us/purchase/re ports/cocdata.htm), the City of Los Angeles (http://www.gsd.lacity.org/sms/ WRC/WRC_reports.htm), the City of Milwaukee (http://www.ci.mil.wi.us/ ApparelAffidavitforA339.htm), the City of Portland (http://www.portlandon line.com/omf/index.cfm?c=50342), the City of San Francisco(http://sfgsa.org/ index.aspx?page=390), and the City of Ottawa, Canada (http://www.ottawa. ca/business/bids_contracts/ethical_purchasing/supplier_en.html).

REFERENCES

Action Aid. 2007. 'Who Pays? The Real Cost of Cheap School Uniforms.' London, United Kingdom: Action Aid. Retrieved July 5, 2010 (http://www.actionaid.org. uk/doc_lib/who_pays_school_uniforms_report.pdf).

Bainbridge, D. 2009. 'Rebuilding the American Economy with True Cost Accounting.' Retrieved July 12, 2010 (http://www.sustainabilityleader.org/Sustain ability_Leader/About_me.html).

Barrientos, S. and S. Smith. 2006. 'The ETI Code of Labour Practice: Do Workers Really Benefit?' Brighton: Institute of Development Studies. Retrieved July 5, 2010 (http://www.ids.ac.uk/go/idsproject/ethical-trading-initiative-impact-assessment).

Bianco, A. 2006. *The Bully of Bentonville: How the High Cost of Wal-Mart's Everyday Low Prices is Hurting America*. New York: Doubleday.

Bonacich, E. 1998. 'Organizing Immigrant Workers in the Los Angeles Apparel Industry.' *Journal of World-Systems Research* 27(4):10–19.

Fairtrade Labelling Organizations International. 2010. 'About Fairtrade.' Bonn, Germany: Fairtrade Labelling Organizations International. Retrieved July 6, 2010 (http://www.transfair.org/bot/fairtrade-in-english).

Greenhouse, S. 2007. 'Maryland is First State to Require Living Wage.' *The New York Times*, May 9. Retrieved February 17, 2009 (http://www.nytimes.com/2007/ 05/09/us/09wage.html).

International Labor Rights Forum. 2010. 'Missed the Goal for Workers: The Reality of Soccer Ball Stitchers in Pakistan, India, China and Thailand.' Washington, D.C.: International Labor Rights Forum. Retrieved July 6, 2010 (http://www. laborrights.org/stop-child-forced-labor/foulball-campaign/resources/12331).

Jaffee, D. 2007. *Brewing Justice: Fair Trade Coffee, Sustainability, and Survival.* Berkeley, CA: University of California Press.

Kimeldorf, H., R. Meyer, M. Prasad, and I. Robinson. 2006. 'Consumers with a Conscience: Will They Pay More?' *Contexts* 5(1):24–29.

MFA Forum. 2008. 'Assessing the Impact of Purchasing Practices on Code Compliance: A Case Study of the Bangladesh Garment Industry.' Retrieved July 5, 2010 (http://www.mfa-forum.net/themicworkinggroups/PurchasingPractices.aspx).

Miller, D. and P. Williams. 2009. 'What Price a Living Wage? Implementation Issues in the Quest for Decent Wages in the Global Apparel Sector.' *Global Social Policy* 9(1):99–125.

Murray, L. 1995. 'Unraveling Employment Trends in Textiles and Apparel.' *Monthly Labor Review* 118(8):62–72.

New York Times. 1899. 'War on Sweat Shops. National Consumers' League Induces Manufacturers of Women's Goods to Use a Label.' *The New York Times*, August 28.

Office of Federal Procurement Policy. 2010. 'Mission.' Retrieved July 6, 2010 (http://www.whitehouse.gov/omb/procurement_default/).

Office of Textiles and Apparel. 2010. 'U.S. General Imports in U.S. Dollars.' Retrieved June 12, 2010 (http://otexa.ita.doc.gov/).

Organization Economic Co-operation and Development. 2002. 'The Size of Government Procurement Markets.' Paris, France: Organization Economic Co-operation and Development. Retrieved January 31, 2010 (http://www.oecd.org/document/63/0,3343,es_2649_34119_1845951_1_1_1_1,00.html).

Program on International Policy Attitudes. 2000. 'Americans on Globalization: Study of US Public Attitudes.' Washington, D.C.: Program on International Policy Attitudes. Retrieved July 6, 2010 (http://www.pipa.org/archives/us_opinion.php).

Program on International Policy Attitudes. 2004. 'Americans on Globalization, Trade, and Farm Subsidies.' Washington, D.C.: Program on International Policy Attitudes. Retrieved July 6, 2010 (http://www.pipa.org/archives/us_opinion.php).

Rodman, K. 1998. 'Think Globally, Punish Locally: Nonstate Actors, Multinational Corporations, and Human Rights Sanctions.' *Ethics and International Affairs* 12(1):19–41.

Ross, R. 2006. 'No Sweat: Hard Lessons from Garment Industry History.' *Dissent*, September 1. Retrieved April 20, 2011 (http://www.dissentmagazine.org/article/?article=698).

Ross, R. 2004. *Slaves to Fashion: Poverty and Abuse in the New Sweatshops.* Ann Arbor, MI: University of Michigan Press.

Schor, J. B. 2005. 'Prices and Quantities: Unsustainable Consumption and the Global Economy.' *Ecological Economics* 55(3):300–320.

SweatFree Communities. 2008. 'Sweatshop Solutions? Economic Ground Zero in Bangladesh and Wal-Mart's Responsibility.' Northampton, MA: SweatFree Communities. Retrieved July 6, 2010 (http://www.'sweatfree'.org/sweatshopsolutions).

TransFair USA. 2010. 'Apparel Program.' Oakland, CA: TransFair USA. Retrieved July 5, 2010 (http://www.transfairusa.org/content/certification/apparel_program.php).

Unite Here. 2006. *Conduct Unbecoming: Sweatshops and the U.S. Military Uniform Industry.* New York: Unite Here.

U.S. Bureau of Labor Statistics. 2010a. 'Consumer Price Index-Apparel.' Washington, DC: U.S. Government Printing Office. Retrieved June 20, 2010 (http://data.bls.gov/PDQ/servlet/SurveyOutputServlet).

U.S. Bureau of Labor Statistics. 2010b. 'Career Guide to Industries: 2010–2011 Edition, Textile, Textile Product, and Apparel Manufacturing.' Washington, DC: U.S. Government Printing Office. Retrieved June 12, 2010 (http://www.bls.gov/oco/cg/cgs015.htm).

World Fair Trade Organization. 2010. 'Charter of Fair Trade Principles.' Culemborg, Netherlands: World Fair Trade Organization. Retrieved April 25, 2011 (http://www.wfto.com).

14 Social Labeling and Supply Chain Reform

The Designated Supplier Program and the Alta Gracia Label

Scott Nova and John M. Kline

In 2005, the Worker Rights Consortium (WRC), a U.S. nonprofit labor-rights-monitoring organization founded by student anti-sweatshop activists and universities that maintain licensing agreements with sportswear-apparel brands, proposed a system by which licensees would be expected to enforce enhanced labor standards in the production of university-logo apparel and to pay prices to their suppliers sufficient to make compliance feasible. This initiative—known as the Designated Suppliers Program, or DSP—has been endorsed by several major U.S. universities and colleges; however, stiff opposition from the apparel industry and other obstacles have prevented the program's implementation. Recently, however, one apparel brand, Knights Apparel, working with a former sportswear-apparel factory in Villa Alta-gracia in the Dominican Republic, has launched the Alta Gracia brand of T-shirts and sweatshirts. This brand, designed for the U.S. collegiate market, embraces key principles of the DSP. Workers have a union and are paid a 'living wage' three times above the national minimum wage for the industry. Knights Apparel ensures that the factory is in an economic position to pay the living wage, meet all other labor standards, and employ workers full-time, year-round. The factory's labor conditions are integral to the marketing of the products, which bear hang tags explaining the meaning of a living wage and a union to workers. In the first part of this two-part chapter, Scott Nova of the U.S.-based Worker Rights Consortium makes the argument for initiatives such as the DSP and Alta Gracia, which are geared toward a reform of the industry-pricing and sourcing practices to make social compliance in apparel supply chains feasible. In the second part, John Kline, Professor at the Walsh School of Foreign Service, Georgetown University, considers the social labeling challenges that the Alta Gracia case poses for NGOs, corporations, and consumers.

1 HOW APPAREL-INDUSTRY PRICING PRACTICES UNDERMINE LABOR RIGHTS PROGRESS

After nearly two decades of corporate codes of conduct and monitoring programs, subpoverty wages and abusive working conditions remain the norm in global apparel supply chains. The basic problem is straightforward: the pricing and sourcing practices of brands and retailers in North America and Europe ensure that their contract-apparel factories operate in an environment of intense price pressure and debilitating economic volatility. Even as the brands and retailers have made a public show of exhorting their suppliers to improve their labor practices, they have refused to accept the increased production costs necessary for genuine reform and have held fast to a business model that employs short-term, buyer-supplier contracts and the constant shifting of production between suppliers to force the latter to accept ever-lower prices.[1] This approach to sourcing is anathema to the goal of achieving and maintaining respect for worker rights. As a result, labor-rights violations remain widespread, despite the proliferation of private codes of conduct and monitoring regimes.

To address this problem, the Worker Rights Consortium helped to design and promote a reform program for the university-apparel sphere, known as the Designated Suppliers Program (DSP).[2] Under this program, brands making university apparel would be required to pay fair prices and make long-term commitments to their suppliers. The program involves a list of compliant suppliers, backed up by a product label intended to indicate to university-apparel consumers that their apparel has been produced under enhanced labor standards including living wage and union rights. Although the program has been endorsed by several major U.S. universities and colleges, it has not yet been implemented and has met with stiff industry resistance. This article explains why the supply-chain reforms embodied in the DSP—most importantly, fair prices for contract factories—are essential if decent working conditions and wages are to be achieved in the global apparel industry.

Unfortunately, while the central role of price pressure in retarding labor-rights progress is well understood by most labor-rights advocates, it is often obscured in professional and academic discourse about corporate social responsibility. The apparel industry is wedded to the existing production model and eager to deflect blame; it cannot acknowledge that its own pricing practices are the primary obstacle to progress.[3] Industry spokespeople instead offer explanations for the persistence of sweatshop conditions that largely or completely ignore price issues and focus instead on managerial weaknesses at the factory level and/or ostensible flaws in the technical design of monitoring programs. An analytical approach that treats the economics of buyer-supplier relationships as incidental to suppliers' labor practices defies logic, but this has not prevented apparel brands from advancing the argument,[4] or some academic analysts from giving it credence (Locke and Romis 2007: 60).

These analyses—whether written by academics, industry-funded nongovernmental organizations, or brands themselves—either ignore price issues entirely or minimize their importance. Locke and Romis, for example, note that suppliers complain of the contradiction between brand requests for improved labor conditions and the brands' simultaneous insistence on lower prices; however, they dismiss this criticism as a misperception, a product of mistrust, and lack of communication between brands and suppliers. The parties, Locke and Romis argue, can escape this 'low-trust trap' through 'more collaborative and transparent relations' geared toward the improvement of 'management systems.' The trouble with this analysis is that the suppliers' perception is entirely accurate: the brands' refusal to relent on their demands for lower prices is a massive obstacle to labor-rights improvements. This problem will not be solved through better communication or trust building; it will be solved when the brands bring prices into line with the cost of producing under humane conditions—a strategy Locke and Romis do not discuss.

The most common argument is that abuses persist because factory managers lack the 'capacity' to manage their businesses in a responsible way and often chafe at efforts by their customers to coerce them into improving their practices. According to this line of reasoning, the core problem is a deficit of managerial competence and skill, and the absence of sufficiently robust 'management systems' at contract factories—under which circumstances, the brands' employment of coercive means to compel improvements leads only to frustration and a breakdown in communications. The solution is for the brands to provide more 'training' and 'capacity building' and to move away from 'policing' and toward 'partnership' with suppliers.

The Fair Labor Association (FLA), a nongovernmental monitoring organization whose members include Nike, Phillips-Van Heusen, H&M and other leading apparel brands, provides an illustrative example of this argument:

> [A]udits are often perceived as policing; factories know they will fail . . . This results in no trust between customers and their suppliers . . . FLA 3.0, the FLA's new sustainable compliance methodology . . . [is] designed to help factories assess their own level of labor compliance and build capacity to implement systems to fill compliance gaps by addressing root causes of labor violations . . . Factories work in collaboration with affiliated companies and the FLA to take increasing responsibility for the progress and sustainability of their labor compliance programs. FLA 3.0 shifts the monitoring emphasis from policing to partnership. In the partnership approach, the 3.0 assessment reveals substantive information about the factory's strengths and weaknesses and provides a roadmap for improve. The results . . . are used to develop a capacity building program.[5]

The FLA is by no means alone in expressing this view. Most of the prominent labor-rights organizations with industry membership and funding emphasize 'capacity building' at the factory level and ignore or downplay prices issues; these include, for example: Social Accountability International, Worldwide Responsible Apparel Production, Global Social Compliance Program, Ethical Trading Initiative and Business for Social Responsibility.

Company representatives offer similar explanations for the weakness of existing industry code-of-conduct programs. Bill Anderson, a senior labor-rights compliance official at adidas Group, is quoted in a publication of the nongovernmental organization Business for Social Responsibility (BSR): 'A policing model is not a sustainable approach. It only addresses the immediate concerns and cannot tackle the root causes of the problem.' BSR explains that 'six years ago adidas adopted a policy of partnering with suppliers, in place of policing, to help them develop the necessary management systems to address social and environmental issues.'[6] It is worth noting that this perspective, while unflattering to factory owners and managers in terms of their professional competence, largely exonerates them in moral terms, as it does the brands.

When knowledgeable people in and around the apparel industry opine about the 'root causes' of substandard working conditions, one might assume the reference is to the underlying economics of a price-driven business. Such is not the case. Missing from the above, and other kindred analyses, is any serious consideration of the relentless price pressure that continues to define industry-sourcing practices, how this pressure constrains supplier action on labor rights, and, of equal importance, what the remarkable continuity in industry-pricing practices tells us about the sincerity of brands' stated commitment to the well-being of the workers who make their clothes.

It is important to consider the ideas embedded in this line of argument. First, to aver that the primary obstacle to progress is the inability of contract suppliers to accommodate the brands' demands that worker rights be respected, it is necessary to assume that the brands have, in fact, made such demands—not just rhetorically, but in the real world of buyer-supplier relationships. It makes little sense to ask why the industry's labor-rights efforts are being stymied unless one assumes that genuine efforts are being made. Moreover, one must consider it plausible that a brand like Nike—with US$21 billion in annual turnover, operating a business that is predicated on precise control of events in the supply chain—lacks the managerial acumen and the financial resources to figure out how to bring its suppliers into compliance with internationally recognized labor standards, despite having had nearly 20 years to get the job done.[7] In other words, the argument the industry and sympathetic observers put forward, that the apparel brands and retailers have tried but failed to achieve their stated labor-rights goals, assumes that the brands are good-faith actors who have made a genuine effort to protect the rights of the workers in their supply chains and are just learning now, after two decades of earnest endeavor, that they have been going about their task the wrong way.

In considering the reasonableness of assuming good faith on the part of major brands and retailers, it is instructive to recall the history of labor rights and codes of conduct in the global apparel industry. By 1990, apparel brands and retailers in the United States were importing US$27 billion worth of apparel into the country; one-third of all apparel sold in the United States was being made overseas, most of it in developing countries (Ross

2002: 115). Yet, despite the labor-rights challenges inherent in a strategy of locating production where labor is cheapest, in countries where the rule of law is weak, as of 1990, not a single major brand or retailer had adopted a code of conduct, or a monitoring program, or any other formal plan for protecting the rights of workers in contract factories.[8] The brands chose to concentrate production in countries where they knew, or should have known, that worker rights' violations were certain to be widespread and then failed to adopt any prophylactic measures.

Moreover, even when publicly challenged over labor-rights violations in its supply chains, the industry was slow to respond. When exposés by human-rights activists began to generate outrage among consumers, the initial response of high-profile apparel brands was not to take action to protect workers; instead, the industry tried to deny responsibility, arguing that since the brands did not directly own the factories, the brands had few obligations to the workers. Only when this argument fell flat with consumers and opinion leaders did major brands finally accepted that they had a responsibility for the working conditions under which their clothing is made.

There was, and is, an economic basis for the industry's reluctance to address labor-rights issues: low wages, lax regulation and the absence of unions in a given locale make it inexpensive to manufacture clothing. *New York Times* columnist Bob Herbert captured this point in a column penned in 1998, with a rhetorical question concerning Nike's practices in Vietnam: 'Does anyone think it was an accident that Nike set up shop in human rights sinkholes, where labor organizing was viewed as a criminal activity and deeply impoverished workers were willing, even eager, to take places on assembly lines and work for next to nothing?' (Herbert 1998). This same question can appropriately be asked about virtually every major U.S. and European apparel brand and retailer.

Conversely, increasing wages, stiffening regulation, and respecting the right to bargain collectively raises production costs. If factories are going to start paying workers properly, protecting their safety in the workplace, providing legally mandated benefits that were previously denied, and allowing unions, factories' labor costs are going to increase. Their overall production costs will still be low because labor is inexpensive in the developing world, but prices are not going to be as low as they could be. Ending sweatshop conditions thus means an end to sweatshop prices. Brands and retailers, though compelled by public pressure to promise efforts to improve working conditions, have a strong economic incentive to ensure that their efforts are ineffective.

Given the economic realities of global apparel production, and the labor-rights track record of major apparel brands and retailers, any effort to explain the lack of progress achieved through industry labor-rights initiatives should begin by asking an obvious question: Have the brands and retailers pursuing these initiatives committed to factoring the cost of improved labor practices into the prices they pay to suppliers? The answer is that brands and retailers have not done so. This is where the system of codes of conduct and monitoring broke down. Even as the apparel corporations made, and continue to make, public pledges to protect the rights of workers, and even as they officially instruct their contract factories to make improvements that carry significant costs, sourcing companies continue to demand price *reductions* and/or greater efficiencies from the factories.

The advent of codes of conduct and monitoring has thus left factories with a Hobson's choice. They are asked to meet two mutually exclusive demands: improve labor practices and cut prices. Factories can either do what it takes to meet the labor standards, which means being unable to meet the price demands, or meet the price demands and continue to violate worker rights (while doing their best to cover up the reality when the monitors came to inspect).

As rational economic actors, most factories have responded to this dilemma in a rational way: by assessing the costs and benefits of each course of action. If factories fail to meet a customer's price demands, the consequences are severe and immediate: the order is lost. Enough lost orders, and the factory is out of business. If, however, factories fail to comply with the labor standards, punishment is less sure and less severe. Due to the superficial way in which brands and retailers generally monitor labor-rights compliance, it is often possible for a factory that is violating worker rights to avoid getting caught. When violations *are* uncovered, the factory is almost always given ample opportunity to correct the problem and can often get away with partial and short-lived improvements, returning to business as usual shortly after the monitors are gone. The choice for most factories has therefore been clear: meet buyers' price demands by continuing to operate as a sweatshop, while seeking to remain 'under the radar' of labor-rights inspectors. In some cases, factory owners employ 'any means necessary' to achieve this goal, including falsifying factory records, coaching workers on what to say to investigators, and other forms of subterfuge. (For an illuminating discussion of this dynamic, see Harney 2008).

Employing an alternative worker-focused approach to monitoring, the Worker Rights Consortium has been able to uncover labor-rights violations that industry monitors miss, and, in the process, has witnessed firsthand the extraordinarily destructive impact the industry's pricing practices have had on working conditions. In pressing factories to fully correct labor-rights violations, the WRC has faced intense resistance. Managers believe that if they actually have to comply with the labor codes, they will be undercut by competitors who can continue to run roughshod over worker rights because they have not had the bad luck to get caught. When improvements are achieved, it requires constant vigilance to prevent the factory from backsliding, and sometimes, even constant vigilance is inadequate, because the price pressure is still there. Moreover, WRC case files include many cases concerning factories that have been successfully persuaded to improve their practices, only to be punished in the marketplace as orders have been shifted to factories that are not constrained in their efforts to hold down labor costs by a policy of actually respecting worker rights.

The BJ&B factory in Villa Altagracia, Dominican Republic for example, which produced caps for Nike and Reebok, was among the first factories where the codes of conduct of WRC-affiliate universities were brought to bear to improve labor conditions. In 2002, BJ&B management recognized the union that a majority of workers had elected to join, and a few months later, signed a collective-bargaining agreement—the first in any free-trade-zone factory in the Dominican Republic to provide for wages above the legal minimum. However, beginning shortly after the agreement was signed, the major brands that previously had sourced from the factory began to reduce orders, while the Korean parent company shifted production to nonunion facilities in Bangladesh and Vietnam. The plant's steady reduction in personnel culminated in its closure. Similarly, at the Sinolink factory in Mombasa, Kenya, factory management responded constructively to the WRC's findings and undertook important improvements in working conditions, including becoming the first factory in the Mombasa export-processing zone to demonstrate respect for workers' associational rights by formally recognizing a union chosen by employees. However, these improvements were eroded due to the factory's inability to secure sufficient business. Despite the WRC's appeals to major licensees and other brands that had been producing in the factory prior to the improvements, none of the companies agreed to return. Finally, the Lian Thai factory in Bangkok, Thailand, made substantial improvements in its labor practices in response to efforts by its employees' union and a WRC investigation in 2003. The company focused significant investment of time and resources toward improving health and safety in the workplace (including significant improvements in the area of ergonomics, something very unusual in the industry) and engaged in constructive negotiations with the union, resulting in one of the only meaningful collective-bargaining agreements in the country's apparel sector. However, the major brands using the factory prior to these improvements—including Puma and Nike—declined to continue doing business at the facility, precipitating its closure.[9]

Any program designed to achieve and sustain good working conditions and wages in global apparel supply chains must require participating brands and retailers to pay prices to suppliers commensurate with the cost of producing in compliance with the applicable labor standards. Any program that does not place the onus on the participating brands and retailers to create financial conditions for suppliers in which compliance is feasible will fail to generate meaningful gains for workers. Fair prices are not a sufficient condition; aggressive independent monitoring is also crucial, although this function can and should be performed primarily by democratic labor unions inside the factory, rather than by monitors outside.

The costs of producing in a responsible manner are not prohibitive. The most costly element of decent labor conditions, by far, is the payment to workers of a living wage. Yet, as illustrated in Table 14.1 and Table 14.2, in developing countries, labor costs typically account for only 1–2 percent of the retail price of a garment. Thus, even assuming all costs are passed on to consumers, doubling labor costs (by doubling wages) would result in retail price increases of roughly 1–2 percent; tripling wages would result in price increases of 2–4 percent. To be sure, these costs are not negligible and increases may be higher as the increase at factory prices is passed through (Miller & Williams 2009); much depends on the pricing decisions of wholesalers and retailers, who may choose to set prices higher in an effort to maintain a certain gross profit margin. However, even assuming higher 'markups,' and a complete pass through of costs to consumers, the price impact of enormous wage increases is still very modest. Moreover, it is well within the means of many multinational apparel brands to absorb these costs without passing them on to consumers

Table 14.1 Consequences of Wage Increases on Apparel Production Costs: Men's Knit Shirt (Manufactured in Philippines)

Apparel Costs	Costs at current wage rate	Impact of 50% wage increase	Impact of doubling wages	Impact of tripling wages
Nonlabor costs of production (incl. fabric & other materials, factory overhead & profit)	$7.31	$7.31	$7.31	$7.31
Labor costs of production (incl. direct & supervisory labor)	$0.69	$1.03	$1.38	$2.06
Freight-on-Board (FOB) price (price to brand at factory door: includes all labor & nonlabor factory production costs)	$8.00	$8.34	$8.69	$9.38
Labor costs as a % of FOB price	8.6%	12.4%	15.8%	22.0%
Landed-Duty-Paid (LDP) price (final cost to brand: includes FOB price plus shipping, duty, delivery, insurance, & customs clearance)	$10.00	$10.34	$10.69	$11.38
Labor costs as a % of LDP price	6.9%	10.0%	12.9%	18.1%
Wholesale price	$20.00	$20.34	$20.69	$21.38
Labor costs as % of wholesale price	3.44%	5.07%	6.65%	9.65%
Retail price	$44.00	$44.34	$44.69	$45.38
Labor costs as % of retail price	1.56%	2.33%	3.08%	4.55%
% change in retail price	0%	0.78%	1.54%	3.03%

Source: Birnbaum 2000: 211, with additional calculations by the WRC.

Table 14.2   Consequences of Wage Increases on Apparel Production Costs: Embroidered Logo Sweatshirt (Manufactured in Dominican Republic)

Apparel Costs	Costs at current wage rate	Impact of 50% increase in wages	Impact of doubling wages	Impact of tripling wages
Nonlabor costs of production (incl. fabric & other materials, factory overhead & profit)	$5.89	$5.89	$5.89	$5.89
Labor costs of production (incl. direct & supervisory labor)	$0.45	$0.68	$0.90	$1.35
Freight-on-Board (FOB) price (price to brand at factory door: includes all labor & nonlabor factory production costs)	$6.34	$6.57	$6.79	$7.24
Labor costs as a % of FOB price	7.1%	10.3%	13.3%	18.6%
Landed-Duty-Paid (LDP) price (final cost to brand: includes FOB price plus shipping, duty, delivery, insurance, & customs clearance)	$7.89	$8.12	$8.34	$8.79
Labor costs as a % of LDP price	5.7%	8.3%	10.8%	15.4%
Wholesale price	$15.78	$16.01	$16.23	$16.68
Labor costs as a % of wholesale price	2.85%	4.22%	5.55%	8.09%
Retail price	$35.00	$35.23	$35.45	$35.90
Labor costs as % of retail price	1.29%	1.92%	2.54%	3.76%
% change in retail price	0.00%	0.64%	1.27%	2.51%

To put this in perspective, consider that the sale of Reebok to Adidas in 2005 generated a US$700 million payday for Reebok CEO Paul Fireman. Had Fireman been willing to make do with a mere US$200 million, the remaining funds would have been sufficient to double the wages of *every worker* assembling Reebok shoes and apparel in the company's global supply chain—for seven years.[10] As it happened, Fireman had other priorities for the money. Notably, he spent $250 million to build a private luxury golf course on the Hudson River, overlooking Manhattan, to 'create a legacy' for himself. Membership in Fireman's Liberty National Golf Course costs US$500,000, plus annual dues (Bertoni 2011).

The potential thus exists for a transformation of wages and working conditions in the apparel industry. The realization of that potential requires political action: although the cost impact would be modest, the most powerful actors in the industry, the brands and retailers, have a vested interested in resisting any change that would increase costs and narrow profit margins. Overcoming that resistance depends, in part, on combatting the industry's efforts to obfuscate the economic dynamics that perpetuate labor-rights abuses.

In an encouraging development, an initiative incorporating fundamental supply-chain reforms, and featuring a living wage for workers that is several multiples of the prevailing apparel wage, is now underway in the Dominican Republic. The initiative involves a new apparel brand, Alta Gracia, that is committed to respect for worker rights and to pursuing a marketing strategy that relies on social labeling. This initiative has already demonstrated that a living wage and respect for union rights can be achieved with minimal impact on the retail price of apparel,[11] although there are practical implications for the stakeholders. These are now discussed in the second part of this chapter.

2 THE ALTA GRACIA CASE: A SOCIAL-LABELING CHALLENGE FOR NGOS, CORPORATIONS AND CONSUMERS

Background

Alta Gracia apparel is cut and sewn at a factory in Villa Altagracia in the Dominican Republic (Kline 2010). Some 130 factory workers are all paid a 'living wage' nearly 350 percent above the legal minimum wage. The workers have organized a recognized union, SITRALPRO, and engaged in a collective-bargaining process. Factory health-and-safety operations conform to standards recommended after inspections by occupational health and safety professionals from a U.S. NGO, the Maquiladora Health and Safety Support Network (MHSSN). The Workers' Rights Consortium (WRC) closely monitors factory compliance with the provisions of an agreement on enhanced labor standards. Alta Gracia apparel is the only product that carries a label from the WRC verifying that the product was produced under these specific high labor standards. Alta Gracia can legitimately claim to be 'the only clothing brand in the developing world known to have achieved these standards.' (Kline and Soule 2011: 3)

One of the most notable victories of the campus anti-sweatshop movement occurred nearly a decade ago in Villa Altagracia's Foreign Trade Zone (FTZ). A Korean-owned factory, BJ&B, employed as many as 3,000 workers to make caps primarily for North American brands. After years of hard-fought efforts by workers, the company finally accepted a union and in 2003 signed the first collective-bargaining agreement in a Dominican Republic FTZ that set wages and working conditions significantly above the legal minimum. This achievement was aided by a decisive push from campus activists organized through United Students Against Sweatshops

(USAS) to convince BJ&B's brand clients to take more responsibility for the factory's work conditions, and specifically, the freedom of association standard (Ross 2006). The victory proved short-lived, however, as factory orders dropped, workers were laid off, and BJ&B abruptly closed in 2007 with all-too-typical controversy over severance pay (Adler-Milstein 2008). For Villa Altagracia, the closure meant the loss of the town's only remaining significant employer. Without job options, residents moved away, commuted to housework jobs in Santo Domingo, or simply tried to survive with periodic menial tasks while moving in with, or borrowing from, relatives.

The WRC, which had worked with BJ&B's union, engaged in discussions with Knights Apparel regarding establishing a factory with model labor conditions. Knights Apparel is a leading producer of licensed collegiate apparel but lacked its own brand to compete for university bookstores sales. The company worked with WRC, as well as local NGOs and representatives from the former BJ&B union (and the national union federation with which it was affiliated, known as FEDOTRAZONAS), to reach a framework agreement on enhanced labor standards for a new apparel factory in Villa Altagracia. The location offered the advantage of many skilled but unemployed apparel workers. While the workers' union history would cause many companies to avoid the town, Knights Apparel was not deterred since it had already agreed to respect the right of workers to organize. After a major capital investment to upgrade the old BJ&B facility and a hiring process overseen by independent NGOs, the Alta Gracia factory began to ramp up operations in April 2010. The Alta Gracia brand was progressively rolled out during the 2010–2011 academic year. The product enjoyed sales success, particularly in stores offering ample display space and on campuses with organized and active student support. However, initial year orders were insufficient to fill the factory's productive capacity, leading Knights Apparel to shift production from some of its contract factories to Alta Gracia to keep the workers employed. In the process, Knights Apparel was losing money on these lower-priced, non-Alta Gracia goods, due to the factory's higher labor-cost structure.

3　THE NGO EVALUATION CHALLENGE

The anti-sweatshop movement led most universities to adopt licensing codes of conduct designed to assure that apparel carrying the university's logo is not made under sweatshop labor conditions. Although the specific wording of university codes can differ substantially, no effective effort was made to assess the differences or seek common standards among university codes on specific items such as wage rates, hiring practices, safety conditions or how to evaluate whether the right to organize and bargain collectively was being respected. A minimal ethical standard had been established—'not a sweatshop.' As a result, attention shifted from workplace standards to monitoring and enforcement in the belief that effective monitoring would ensure that university-licensed apparel was not produced in sweatshops. Unfortunately, only the most egregious cases, usually involving severe violations of local law, gain significant enforcement attention. As long as blatant factory violations are not vocally protested by workers willing to risk their job, and often their safety, the 'not a sweatshop' standard is assumed, by many universities, to be both sufficient and effective, an assumption disputed by some labor-rights groups.

Alta Gracia challenges this minimal ethical standard by adopting a clearly much higher set of workplace conditions. Most notable is the commitment to a 'living wage,' calculated by the WRC on the basis of a transparent process and yielding a wage rate nearly 350 percent higher than the mandated legal minimum wage (WRC 2010). Any overtime work is paid an additional 35 percent for evenings with weekend or holiday hours drawing a 100 percent premium, consistent with Dominican law. Workers are employed year-round, without layoffs or furloughs, and employees even receive paid leave for work holidays that, under local law, are normally treated as unpaid leave. However, the predictable focus on Alta Gracia's 'living wage' provisions often misses the array of other unusually good workplace conditions. For example, in line with recommendations from MHSSN inspectors, the factory upgraded electrical connections for safety, added signage for emergencies, improved both ventilation and lighting and purchased ergonomic chairs for the workers.

The form and tenor of management-labor relations also plays a crucial role in shaping Alta Gracia's workplace. A modular team-based production system eliminates typical layers of oppressive supervisors, permitting workers to organize and manage their workloads, with a trainer available when needed. Management is both accessible and responsive to worker inquiries and suggestions, either individually or through union representatives. From the beginning, management permitted union representatives access to the factory for information sessions covering worker rights to freedom of association and then recognized the SITRALPRO union once it formed. Alta Gracia management and SITRALPRO have engaged in a collective-bargaining process.

When questioned (Kline and Soule 2011: 12) about the difference between their current jobs compared to other factories where they had been employed, Alta Gracia workers inevitably cited 'salario digno,' as 'living wage' is translated in Spanish. However, the English wording is inadequate to capture the more inclusive concept of 'salary with dignity' that is encompassed in the Spanish translation and embodied in Alta Gracia's workplace conditions. More than just a level of monetary compensation, 'salario digno' requires a standard of treatment and respect for workers that values them as true partners in the production process, recognizing not just their level of output but the quality of their input and the dignity of their person. For virtually all the workers at Alta Gracia, 'salario digno' includes a wage that meets normal family necessities and permits hope for future progress, a safe and healthy workplace, and a management-labor system that respects individual and collective worker rights. Alta Gracia's workplace conditions offer a new higher standard for an ethical global-apparel factory.

The question for NGOs and universities concerned about workplace practices in global-apparel factories is: how should Alta Gracia be evaluated and treated? The factory is clearly 'not a sweatshop,' so its apparel can be licensed and sold in university bookstores. But, do its higher ethical standards merit differentially better recognition and treatment? The WRC implicitly answers 'yes' in permitting Alta Garcia products to carry a hang tag with WRC's verification that the apparel was produced under conditions respecting worker rights, including a living wage and freedom of association (Kline and Soule 2011: 10).[12] The WRC may be willing to consider a similar verification and social-labeling arrangement for other factories prepared to meet the same enhanced labor standards. But, what should be the practical meaning of the WRC's action?

If Alta Gracia apparel is treated by universities and NGOs the same as other brands that at best meet current 'not a sweatshop' standards with problematic enforcement, there is little incentive for companies to improve workplace conditions further. But if Alta Gracia products embody significantly different and desirable standards with strict verification, they could be endorsed and supported preferentially, with universities embracing a goal to increase Alta Gracia sales. Certainly, such an endorsement is consistent with the self-proclaimed mission of many universities that promote individual rights and dignity and seek to better the human condition. If successful, such differential treatment of collegiate apparel might encourage a 'race to the top' as other brands move from minimal to enhanced ethical-workplace standards. The basic minimal floor of 'not a sweatshop' could even be raised by refining or revising the definition of university codes to reflect the proactive concept of 'salario digno' that provides respect now and hope for the future, rather than settling for current reactive standards designed primarily to limit only the worst forms of labor abuses in traditional sweatshops.

4   THE COMPANY COMPETITIVENESS CHALLENGE

Alta Gracia's example of higher workplace standards results in increased costs, placing the firm at a competitive disadvantage in a global industry where cost reductions generally come from pressures to lower labor costs, as reflected in poor wages and other working conditions. Critics have denounced footloose brands and retail stores that appear to place constant pressure on foreign suppliers to reduce costs, with the implied and real threat that orders can be shifted to other factories willing to accept a lower price. While the pressure is directed at factory owners, the burden of meeting cost-reduction demands inevitably falls on workers who often already suffer from the lower minimum-wage rates and fewer labor protections required in FTZs (Kline and Soule 2011: 28).[13]

Most economic analyses of the global apparel industry account for its low wages and poor labor conditions by citing the competitive market pressures facing apparel factories, particularly in labor-intensive cut-and-sew operations. Thousands of factories compete to fill overseas apparel orders, with price generally the determining factor if quality and reliability are satisfactory. Many cost factors are relatively fixed by location, such as transport or government taxes. Labor costs are treated as variable, subject to downward pressure where high unemployment exists and unions are banned or discouraged. These circumstances are often portrayed as simply the workings of impartial market forces, perhaps a regrettable but probably necessary stage that countries must go through on the path to greater development.

However, a narrow focus on competing factories misrepresents the industry's structure. If the full business value chain is considered, it becomes clear that the cutthroat competition among thousands of small apparel factories in developing countries is fostered by the relatively small number of large brands and retail firms in developed countries that wield oligopsony bargaining power. As we have seen in Part 1, in the global-apparel industry, the big buyers are price-setters and the small factories are price-takers who then attempt to meet the buyers' lower price demands by further squeezing workers who, in most circumstances, have few job alternatives and can rather easily be replaced. The image of free-market competition dispassionately apportioning economic benefits among elements of the apparel sector paints a false portrait.

By committing to pay a 'living wage' and other enhanced labor conditions at the Alta Gracia factory, Knights Apparel adopted a production cost structure that places the brand at a price disadvantage versus other large apparel buyers. As a result, to make up for the increased cost of higher labor standards, Alta Gracia products must be priced at a substantial premium or other offsetting cost reductions must be found. The company decided not to use social labeling to seek a price premium above comparable products, as in the Fairtrade model. As Knights Apparel's Chief Executive Officer (CEO) Joe Bozich summarized the decision: 'Obviously we'll have a higher cost . . . But we're pricing the product such that we're not asking the retailer or the consumer to sacrifice in order to support it' (Greenhouse 2010: B1). In reality, Alta Gracia apparel is priced toward the high end of the collegiate market for T-shirts and sweatshirts, but generally at or somewhat below the price of brand-name competitors of comparable product quality. Knights Apparel seeks to offset higher labor costs through increased productivity and reduced marketing expense.

Productivity gains come from a workforce truly dedicated to producing high-quality apparel because workers know the product must be successful to sustain their well-paid jobs over the long term. Turnover is also extremely low at the factory, less than 5 percent over the first year compared with factory averages up to six times higher. With normal training periods requiring 90 days before new workers are fully productive, worker retention also contributes to better productivity. Social labeling and social-media promotion by student groups on campuses translate into some cost-savings on marketing for Alta Gracia products. This approach must be effective to establish a new brand of apparel in university bookstores, as well as to help offset the factory's higher labor costs.

Finally, Knights Apparel management has indicated their willingness to accept a somewhat lower profit than competitor firms to maintain the higher labor standards. Having established enhanced labor standards in the factory as a 'fixed cost' minimum for the Alta Gracia brand, other components of the business value chain must be treated as more variable. Whatever labor cost elements cannot be offset by greater productivity and lower marketing costs will effectively reduce Knights Apparel's profits from Alta Gracia products. As CEO Bozich recognized, 'Knights will absorb a lower-than-usual profit margin' (Greenhouse 2010: B1). This business-management decision prioritizes worker welfare over profit maximization, altering the dynamics of the industry's oligopsony bargaining model. However, to be sustainable, the factory still must reach some acceptable level of profitability. This goal understandably was not achieved in the first year of operation, but after its second year, Alta Gracia became commercially competitive. Whether or not losses return, and the factory fails, or orders generate enough demand to sustain or expand productive capacity, depends ultimately on universities, the primary retailers of Alta Gracia products through their campus stores, and on the consumer.

5   THE CONSUMER CHOICE CHALLENGE

Social labeling depends on the premise that consumers will hear, understand and care enough about a socially based message to influence their purchase decisions in favor of a socially labeled product. Various studies report an openness and interest among a significant minority of the public, especially youth, to consider such factors and, for some lesser segment, even a willingness to pay somewhat more for products aligned with their social values (Hertel et al. 2007, Millennial Cause Study 2006, Smith 2009). In the collegiate-apparel market, social labeling was not employed in marketing because the minimal 'not a sweatshop' standard for licensing already theoretically excluded products that failed to meet this minimum threshold and rival brands chose not to compete on the basis of comparatively better workplace conditions. Occasionally, monitoring of university codes reveals a brand's failure to enforce code requirements on supplier factories, bringing student protests against the firm and its product sales. However, these actions, to be effective, require substantial energy and their impact is necessarily narrow.[14] The limited resources of activists, and of independent enforcement bodies like the WRC, create a 'whack-a-mole effect,' in which efforts are made to beat down violations of minimal labor standards even as new violations continue to emerge under the relentless price pressure imposed on suppliers (Kline 2010: 8). Little additional time and energy is available for initiatives that could further improve the current baseline standard for minimal workplace conditions.

Alta Gracia breaks this pattern, introducing a higher set of workplace standards with a social-labeling market approach that describes these verifiably better conditions. Thus far, the message has been positive, emphasizing Alta Gracia's enhanced labor standards and its positive impacts on workers and families, without making explicit comparisons with other brands. The Alta Gracia products do not have to surmount the hurdle of asking consumers to pay a premium price, but a substantial number of consumers will have to switch their allegiance from established, better-known brands to purchase Alta Gracia apparel. Social labeling provides a marketing mechanism to accomplish this task, but can it inspire enough consumers to buy Alta Gracia products for the firm to be commercially successful, even at a relatively lower profit level?

As a case in progress, the answer to this question is still unknown but prospects are positive as Alta Gracia enters its third year of operation. Many elements will certainly affect the ultimate outcome, including the crafting of the message and the number and enthusiasm of student supporters. However, the unique circumstances of the case present a challenge, and an opportunity, for consumers to reflect on the meaning of their brand affiliations and the potential impact of conscious, informed choice on market mechanisms. The collegiate-apparel market was shaken by anti-sweatshop protests during the late 1990s, driven by concerns over labor conditions in overseas sweatshops. It took several years and some leadership moves by a few brands to establish the 'not a sweatshop' code standards that have since governed product access to collegiate bookstores. Since all apparel on the floor theoretically meet these minimal standards, other considerations naturally dominate a customer's purchasing decision. Many consumers are likely to be predisposed to a certain brand by a carry-over affinity from other products. Now, confronted with a choice through Alta Gracia's social labeling, how will consumers understand and weigh the meaning of their established brand affiliations?

Within a given price and quality segment of the collegiate-apparel market, product design and presentation in floor displays can influence purchasing decisions. Beyond these factors, brand appeal is likely the most important distinguishing factor. Committed social activists will presumably discern the differential merit in the Alta Gracia brand and readily support its purchase. However, many consumers may need first to examine the basis for their existing brand affiliations before determining whether Alta Gracia's social-labeling story is compelling enough to cause a brand switch.

Often, brand affinities are not adopted or understood consciously or rationally. Extensive and expensive marketing campaigns with catchy slogans, effective imagery and celebrity endorsements can create positive attitudes toward a product that may have little to do with the basic nature of the product itself. Social labeling may also draw on subconscious affinities to some extent, but this marketing approach generally depends more on a rationality-based appeal to the consumer's basic values. In Alta Gracia's case, the impacts of enhanced labor conditions on real workers' lives are being weighed against a subconsciously established preference for—what? The challenge for consumers is to perceive and assess this contrast to inform and guide their own decision-making.

6   SOCIAL LABELING AND ALTA GRACIA'S FUTURE

University retailers and the consumer will ultimately decide the fate of the Alta Gracia factory. Knights Apparel management, the WRC, and especially the workers have committed themselves to a novel initiative that sets down a new marker for higher ethical labor standards in the global-apparel industry. Social labeling provides a mechanism to distinguish Alta Gracia T-shirts and sweatshirts from competing brands in collegiate bookstores, with the WRC verifying the product's substantially better workplace standards. If not enough consumers hear, understand, and care enough about these distinguishing features to choose the Alta Gracia brand over other 'not a sweatshop' apparel, then the effort will fail. The factory will close, and the workers will lose this opportunity to improve the lives of their families and others in the community.

However, if Alta Gracia succeeds commercially, with satisfactory even if not maximal profits for management, then a new challenge can be posed. The justification for accepting minimal ethical workplace standards in the global-apparel industry is that the competitive nature of the sector precludes absorbing any higher labor costs. This claim rests on the assumption that free-market forces, rather than oligopsony power, determine pricing and profit levels as well as the distribution of benefits. If Knights Apparel can start with higher fixed costs from adopting higher workplace standards and yet turn a satisfactory profit, the result will belie the professed dictates of impartial market forces and reveal the latitude of value choices open to large brands and retail buyers.

If enough customers value better labor conditions for apparel workers and express their social concern through purchasing decisions, some brands may even choose to begin a 'race to the top' where they can do good while doing well enough. The entire apparel industry is unlikely to change, but substantial and meaningful progress is possible. It is time to raise the bar, certainly in the collegiate-apparel market, from a minimal and rather ambiguous 'not a sweatshop' standard with uncertain enforcement to the level set by Alta Gracia's embrace of higher ethical workplace standards with strict verification. This case-in-progress presents an exceptional opportunity to meet that challenge.

NOTES

1. See, for example, Wilson 2008, for a discussion of the deflation of retail prices for most categories of apparel since the late 1990s, the point at which corporate codes of conduct and monitoring programs, and promises from brands to improve conditions for workers, became the norm in the industry.
2. See: http://www.workersrights.org/dsp/
3. Factory owners and managers have no greater dedication to worker-rights principles than brands and retailers; they will violate worker rights to the extent that this is economically advantageous and can be done with impunity. In focusing on the destructive impact of brand-pricing decisions, I am not absolving factory owners and managers of responsibility. However, it is vital to understand that the financial constraints imposed on most contract factories by brand and retailer-pricing practices virtually ensures sweatshop conditions, *regardless* of the motives of factory owners. A contract factory owner who genuinely wishes to respect the rights of workers, and acts on this impulse, will have to raise prices—and will be punished, not rewarded, by his customers. Reform of industry-pricing and sourcing practices will make compliance by contract factories feasible; effective accountability mechanisms (unions and genuinely independent monitoring), of course, will still be essential to ensure that higher prices translate into better wages and conditions for workers, rather than being pocketed by factory owners. Absent such reforms, the most effective monitoring programs, and the most effective unions, will not be able to achieve living wages and decent working conditions in most factories.
4. See, for example: 'Our Strategy: Evolving Approach', Nike Fiscal Year 2009 Corporate Responsibility Report (accessed 24 May 2011 at http://www.nike biz.com/crreport/); 'Helping Factories Move Forward,' Gap, Inc. corporate website (accessed 24 May 2011 at http://www2.gapinc.com/GapIncSubSites/ csr/Goals/SupplyChain/SC_Helping_Factories_Move_Forward_Capacity_ Building.shtml); 'Sustainable Compliance: An Evolving Methodology', Fair Labour Association 2010 Annual Report (accessed 27 May 2011 at http:// www.fairlabour.org/fla/Public/pub/Images_XFile/R452/2010_FLA_APR.pdf).
5. 'FLA 3.0,' Fair Labour Association website (accessed 27 May 2011 at http:// fairlabour.org/fla/go.asp?u=/pub/mp&Page=FLA3).
6. 'Briefing: Supply Chains,' Business for Social Responsibility website (accessed 1 June 2011 at http://www.bsr.org/files/Briefing-Supply%20chains_EC.pdf)
7. And one must find this proposition believable, despite the fact that these same brands have had great success compelling these same suppliers to meet their quality and price standards—making very effective use of the powerful economic carrots and sticks at their disposal.
8. The first industry code of conduct was adopted by Levi Straus & Co. in 1991.
9. For more information on these cases, see: http://www.workersrights.org/Fre ports/index.asp#freports.
10. Fireman's income from the sale was reported by Forbes: http://www.forbes. com/lists/2006/10/E552.html (accessed 12 March 2009). The estimate of the cost of doubling workers' wages is based on WRC calculations and assumes

that labor costs at assembly facilities represented 2 percent of Reebok's annual revenue at the time of the sale (US$3.8 billion).

11. Cf. http://www.workersrights.org/verification/index.asp. Last accessed August 2011.
12. For information on WRC's monitoring and verification program, see http://workersrights.org/verification/index.asp (accessed 4 August 2011).
13. For brief pro/con summaries of the debate over sweatshops, see Featherstone and Henwood 2001; Moran 2002, pp. 52–58 and 155–57; Powell and Skarbek 2006; and Varley 1998, pp. 401–27.
14. Examples of such cases can be examined in the WRC's database of factory investigations at http://www.workersrights.org/Freports/index.asp#freports (accessed 4 August 2011).

REFERENCES

Adler-Milstein, S. 2008. 'Resisting the Race to the Bottom.' Brown University, Providence, RI. Unpublished thesis.

Bertoni, S. 2011. 'Paul Fireman on his $250 million Golf Course, Liberty National.' Forbes, June 10. Retrieved July 8, 2011 (http://www.forbes.com/sites/steven bertoni/2011/06/10/paul-fireman-on-his-250-million-golf-course-liberty-national).

Birnbaum, D. 2000. Birnbaum's Global Guide to Winning the Great Garment War. Hong Kong: Third Horizon.

Featherstone, L. and D. Henwood. 2001. 'Clothes Encounters: Activists and Economists Clash over Sweatshops.' Lingua Franca 11(2):26–33.Greenhouse, S. 2010. 'Factory Defies Sweatshop Label, but Can It Thrive?' The New York Times, July 16, p. B1.

Harney, A. 2008. The China Price: The True Cost of Chinese Competitive Advantage. New York: Penguin. Herbert, R. 1998. 'In America; Nike Blinks.' The New York Times, May 21. Retrieved July 16, 2011 (http://www.nytimes.com/1998/05/21/opinion/in-america-nike-blinks.html).

Hertel, S., C. Heidkamp, and L. Scruggs. 2007. 'Ethical Consumption: Who Cares, Who Shops, and Why?' Paper presented at the International Studies Association 48th Annual Convention, February 28, Chicago, IL.

Kline, J. 2010. 'Alta Gracia: Branding Decent Work Conditions.' Research Report, Kalmanovitz Initiative for Labor and the Working Poor, Georgetown University, Washington, D.C.

Kline, J. and E. Soule. 2011. 'Alta Gracia: Work with a Salario Digno.' Research Report, Reflective Engagement Initiative, Georgetown University, Washington, D.C.

Locke, R. and M. Romis. 2007. 'Improving Work Conditions in a Global Supply Chain.' MIT Sloan Management Review 48(2):54–62.

Miller, D. and P. Williams. 2009. 'What Price a Living Wage? Implementation Issues in the Quest for Decent Wages in the Global Apparel Sector.' Global Social Policy 9(1):99–126.

Moran, T. 2002. Beyond Sweatshops. Washington, D.C.: Brookings Institution.

Powell, B. and D. Skarbek. 2006. 'Sweatshops and Third World Living Standards: Are the Jobs Worth the Sweat?' Journal of Labor Research 27(2):263–74.

Ross, R. 2006. 'A Tale of Two Factories: Successful Resistance to Sweatshops and the Limits of Firefighting.' Labor Studies Journal 30(4):65–85.

Ross, R. 2002. 'The New Sweatshops in the United States: How New, How Real, How Many and Why?' Pp. 120–122 in Free Trade and Uneven Development: The North American Apparel Industry After NAFTA, edited by J. Bair, G. Gereffi, and D. Spener. Philadelphia, PA: Temple University Press.

Smith, L. 2009. 'Despite Prolonged Global Recession, an Increasing Number of People Are Spending on Brands That Have a Social Purpose.' New York: Edelman. Retrieved August 4, 2011 (http://www.edelman.com/news/ShowOne.asp?ID=222).

Varley, P. 1998. *The Sweatshop Quandary.* Washington, D.C.: Investor Responsibility Research Center.

Wilson, E. 2008. 'Dress for Less and Less.' *The New York Times,* May 29. Retrieved May 24, 2011 (http://www.nytimes.com/2008/05/29/fashion/29PRICE.html?scp=1&sq="dress+for+less"&st=nyt).

Workers Rights Consortium. 2010. 'Living Wage Analysis for the Dominican Republic.' Washington, D.C.: Workers Rights Consortium. Retrieved August 4, 2011 (http://workersrights.org/linkeddocs/WRC Living Wage Analysis for the Dominican Republic.pdf).

15 Truth in Labeling
Toward a Genuine, Multistakeholder Apparel Social Label

Eric Dirnbach

Advocates of social labeling hold that the poorly regulated, global free market tends to drive production labor standards for some commodities below what many consumers consider socially acceptable, and that these consumers would purchase goods produced under some set of better conditions, even at a higher cost. A system of social labeling can be considered one that makes 'alternative products' to address a market failure, which is the unmet demand of some consumers who would like to purchase the ethical products. In addition to various physical characteristics, these ethically produced goods would also have important social qualities embedded in them that the consumer values. Alternatively, one could view the social-label system as an *alternative market*, whereby goods are produced under different norms than are found in typical markets. In this framework, prices, wages or other factors would be set by mechanisms other than free-market forces, to reach a socially desired outcome the consumer values.

Viewed either way, social labeling has two objectives in addressing the demand for alternative goods and/or the need for an alternative market: to implement progressive social values in the production of commodities, and to build the market for these ethical commodities using 'fair trade,' 'sweat-free,' or other socially desirable labels. A worker-oriented social label strives to improve conditions for workers in the production process. Thus, we can define this kind of social-label system as one where the production of a commodity is regulated by a set of rules designed to produce better outcomes for workers, and where the commodity is presented to socially conscious consumers with an emphasis on the superior labor standards as a key aspect of the product and the marketing message.

Perhaps the most well-known and respected example of a social label is the fair-trade coffee system, managed globally by the Fairtrade Labelling Organizations International (FLO), and locally by national fair-trade affiliates. Following the collapse of the coffee quota-regulation system in the International Coffee Agreement in 1989, and the dramatic fall in global coffee prices, it became clear that coffee producers, primarily in the Global South, were earning too little and often less than the cost of production (Talbot 1997). The fair-trade system evolved a set of alternative market rules designed to empower coffee producers and deliver to them more of the income from coffee retail sales in the Global North. The key principles of the fair trade coffee system are: (1) coffee purchases should be directly from small farmers organized into democratically managed cooperatives; (2) producers receive a guaranteed minimum price per pound of coffee, that is often above the market price, as well as an extra social premium; (3) coffee farmers should receive credit and financial assistance from importers; and (4) there should develop long-term relationships between importers and farmer cooperatives (Levi and Linton 2003). The main innovations in this system involve structural changes in the market that advantage coffee producers (Cycon 2007, Fridell 2007, Nicholls and Opal 2005). A number of studies have shown that many coffee farmers have benefitted from the system, though there are concerns that the system has not helped producers enough (Chambers 2009, Jaffee 2007, Lindsay 2003, Murray et al. 2003, Raynolds et al. 2004, Richardson 2007). Another kind of food-related social label to emerge recently, though one lacking in legitimacy, is the Smart Choices label. Initiated by the food industry in 2009 as a way to label nutritious products, it was widely criticized for claiming that junk food such as Froot Loops is healthy, and it has since been suspended (Neuman 2009). This example shows the danger of corporate public-relations programs masquerading as social labels.

Apparel would appear to be a good candidate for a similar social-label system. There have been well-documented sweatshop abuses in the global-apparel industry for years, there is widespread concern among consumers about these problems, and there is evidence that a significant market exists for apparel that is produced under better conditions (Elliott and Freeman 2003, Kimeldorf et al. 2006, Prasad et al. 2004). Unfortunately, it remains the case that ever since the sweatshop problem appeared on the public agenda in the 1990s, the way the global-apparel industry has been structured, and the manner in which the problem has been framed and reform has been pursued, has resulted in a lack of genuine and widespread improvements in factory working conditions. This chapter will explore these issues further, and discuss in detail the principles and structure of a global-apparel, social-label system that could deliver real benefits for workers.

1 THE UNSOLVED SWEATSHOP PROBLEM

Robert Ross has detailed in Chapter 2 some of the more prominent cases of sweatshop disclosure in the United States in the 1990s. In 2000, the National Labor Committee investigated 16 factories in China, finding extensive wage-and-hour violations at contractors that were working for major companies such as Wal-Mart, Nike, New Balance and Timberland (National Labor Committee 2000). A *Business Week* investigation of another factory in China used by Wal-Mart found similar violations, which were not fixed despite many factory inspections by several independent monitors working for Wal-Mart (Roberts and Bernstein 2000). In 2006, the British group War on Want investigated six factories in Bangladesh producing apparel for major retailers Asda, Tesco and Primark. They found significant wage-and-hour violations, including mandatory 80-hour workweeks, poverty-level wages and underpayment for overtime work, as well as reprisals against workers engaged in trade-union activity (War on Want 2006). These retailers were all members of the Ethical Trading Initiative, which committed them to uphold a code of conduct for decent labor conditions. A visit by War on Want researchers to two of the same factories in 2008 showed that conditions remained the same. The follow-up report stressed that repeated violations represent a systemic problem, stating that 'retailers cannot continue to pay lip service to corporate social responsibility whilst engaging in buying practices that systematically undermine the principles of decent work' (War on Want 2008). A news article about the investigations reported on an interview with a factory owner in Bangladesh that serves different clients who stated that buyers gave him little choice but to keep wages low: 'Buyers who come to Bangladesh tell us, "we are businessmen, we want to make money. If we see cheaper prices in China we will go there"' (McVeigh 2007).

Bangladesh is also notorious for lethal factory fires. Officially, recorded figures detail at least one fire a year since 1990 (Miller 2012). The actual figure is significantly higher. One (unsubstantiated) estimate by the National Garment Workers Federation of Bangladesh estimates that more than 200 fires have caused the death or injury of more than 5,000 workers. In recent years, these include the 2006 fire at the KTS Textile factory, which killed more than 50 workers and injured more than 60, and the 2010 fire at the Garib & Garib Sweater factory, which took the lives of 21 workers and injured another 50. In many of these fires in Bangladesh, the factory exits were locked. There have also been several prominent garment-factory collapses in Bangladesh, including the 2005 collapse at the Spectrum factory and the 2006 collapse at Phoenix, killing or injuring more than 100 workers (Clean Clothes Campaign 2006, Maquila Solidarity Network 2010).

Several years of recent investigations on the soccer ball industry in Pakistan, India, China and Thailand by the International Labor Rights Forum and other groups have found the existence of child labor, sub-minimum wages, large amounts of mandatory overtime work, gender discrimination, and a heavy reliance on long-term, temporary labor in stitching centers and homes. These conditions persist despite over a decade of company and industry labor-rights monitoring initiatives, including the high-profile Atlanta Agreement, which was designed to eliminate child labor in soccer ball production in Pakistan (International Labor Rights Forum 2010).

The Worker Rights Consortium (WRC) has reported that many garment contractors in Bangalore, India, have failed to pay the proper minimum wage to more than 125,000 workers, withholding from workers more than $10 million total in legally owed wages. These wage violations have been happening with the apparent knowledge of major apparel brands such as

Wal-Mart, JC Penney and H&M, which are ostensibly monitoring these contractors. The WRC's report states that 'this situation raises grave questions about the basic integrity of the apparel industry's approach to labor rights' and notes that apparel companies 'have failed to take any action to correct systemic violations of fundamental labor rights in one of the world's major centers of apparel manufacturing, violations that are occurring under the noses of these brands' and retailers' local representatives' (Worker Rights Consortium 2010).

Moreover, recently, the Play Fair Campaign has documented labor-rights violations in a number of factories in China, the Philippines and Sri Lanka that produced apparel for adidas, New Balance, North Face, Columbia Sportswear, Next, Nike, Speedo and Ann Taylor for the 2012 London Olympic Games. Play Fair uncovered short-term contracts, poverty-level wages, forced overtime, denial of freedom of association, and poor working conditions (Play Fair Campaign 2012).

A more comprehensive accounting of historical sweatshop cases is beyond the scope of this article. Without making any claims that these cases are representative of all factories, the appalling working conditions highlighted here, uncovered by investigations from several different groups over the years, reveal problems in factories in many countries producing for numerous apparel brands. Consistent themes have endured over time in this industry. Poverty-level wages often below the legal minimum wage, long hours and mandatory overtime, worker trafficking and forced labor, child labor, unsafe factories and locked doors, violations of workers' freedom of association, pressure on contractors for low prices, and inadequate factory monitoring efforts are normal and persistent conditions in this industry (Armbruster-Sandoval 2005, Bonacich and Appelbaum 2000, Brooks 2007, Collins 2003, Esbenshade 2004, Fung et al. 2001, Rosen 2002, Ross 2004).

2 THE ESTABLISHMENT OF THE CORPORATE SOCIAL RESPONSIBILITY PARADIGM

Moreover, these sweatshop problems continue despite almost 20 years of the corporate social responsibility (CSR) era, during which major apparel-branded retailers and manufacturers (hereafter referred to collectively as the 'brands') have established codes of conduct and factory-monitoring regimes intended to enforce labor-standards compliance on their contractors. These kinds of programs have been widely praised as heralding a new era of corporate responsibility and signifying a new kind of corporation (Conroy 2007, Hopkins 2003, Sethi 2003, Zadek 2001), though more critical reviews have questioned the limitations of this model (Asian Monitor Resource Centre 2004, Barenberg 2007, O'Rourke 2003, Reich 2007, Rodriguez-Garavito 2005, Vogel 2005, Wells 2007). There are generally recognized to be several levels of CSR programs, organized with various levels of complexity (Gereffi et al. 2001). First-Party Certification is the most common, where individual companies such as Nike or Wal-Mart administer their own CSR program. Second-Party Certification involves the administration of a CSR program by an industry association, such as the Worldwide Responsible Accredited Production (WRAP).[1] Third-Party Certification involves the creation of a separate NGO or multistakeholder organization that administers the program. Examples in the apparel industry include the Fair Labor Association (FLA) and Social Accountability International (SAI). Finally, Fourth-Party Certification has the involvement of a governmental entity in setting standards, such as the United Nations Global Compact.

Many of these CSR programs make some of the progressive claims of a social-label system, attempting to market their products as though they were produced ethically. The establishment of these kinds of CSR programs was in response to numerous publicized investigations of sweatshop factories, including some of those mentioned above, and years of protests by activist groups acting as a form of transnational-advocacy network in support of sweatshop workers (Keck and Sikkink 1998). This can be regarded as meaningful progress in so far as the apparel brands have accepted their responsibility, in principle, for contractor working conditions. Moreover, pressure by activists has led to increased disclosure by some brands of previously secret factory locations. A review of labor standards reporting found that four out of 30 brands under evaluation reported some factory locations (Ethical Trading Action Group 2006), and colleges that are members of the WRC require brands that sell their licensed apparel to disclose their factory locations (Worker Rights Consortium 2012). Anti-sweatshop activists have also worked to create Third- and Fourth-Party Certification organizations without corporate oversight such as the Worker Rights Consortium, which deals with university-licensed apparel, and the SweatFree Purchasing Consortium, which involves the procurement of public-sector uniforms (Claeson and Dirnbach 2009, Sweatfree Purchasing Consortium 2012).

However, the brand-dominated CSR efforts are largely inadequate to the task of dealing with sweatshop conditions that are common among the contractors, because they do not address the structural root-causes inherent in the global apparel industry. Major brands outsource to a constantly shifting network of hundreds or thousands of different contractors in multiple countries, and most contractors perform work for multiple brands. The separation of the brands from the direct employment of workers and the use of contractors as intermediaries in production, benefits the brands in a number of ways: by externalizing the risks of employing labor and producing product, lowering the cost of labor, enabling the evasion of legal and moral responsibility for sweatshop conditions, and thwarting worker organization (Bonacich and Appelbaum 2000). Moreover, the relentless price pressure generated by the apparel brands, the intense competition and lack of bargaining power of the contractors, and the desperate need for employment among the largely unorganized workers yield an industry production structure that creates and sustains persistent sweatshop labor conditions as a normal business practice.

There are at least three reasons why current CSR systems fail to improve sweatshop conditions meaningfully. Primarily, there is an inherent conflict of interest at work, because the brands control the code/monitoring regime that is expected to solve the sweatshop problem that they have created through low-price demands, fast-delivery requirements, and the ability to shift production quickly among contractors, creating intense competitive pressures. Second, the current CSR efforts are typically inadequate to the enormous task they confront. There is simply no way to adequately monitor continuously over time the thousands of factories used by the major brands with the relatively skeletal and underfunded monitoring staff that is typically employed. With occasional brief factory visits, it is too easy for contractors to evade detection of violations. For example, investigations have shown that it is common for contractors in China to misrepresent their labor violations, including providing fake records to factory monitors and coaching workers to lie about their wages and hours (Roberts et al. 2006). Third, these schemes fail because workers are not actively involved in their design and enforcement. Workers are the world's experts on their own working conditions, and would be the best 'monitors' of their own workplaces. When workers are meaningfully represented in a CSR system, and empowered to organize and bargain collectively for their interests, sweatshop conditions will improve.

We can see the limitations of the current CSR model when we consider more thoroughly the issue of product prices. One could ask a very basic question regarding prices—are the contractors paid enough to cover their labor compliance costs? True compliance with CSR systems has real expenses, for example, for higher wages, benefits, health-and-safety improvements in the factory, etc., and contractors need to be compensated to cover these higher costs. If contractors are paid enough for their product, then it may be reasonable to expect them to comply with a system that delivers enough funding for that compliance. However, if contractors are not paid enough to cover compliance costs, then we have a different issue, and one that current CSR systems do little to address. In this case, the main problem is that contractors need more resources to comply with the CSR rules. If this is the case, monitoring factories will accomplish little on its own and avoids the principal issue.

We can call the proper wholesale product price (what the brands pay the contractor) that would enable compliance the 'compliance price.' If the bargaining power of the brands allows them to drive the market-product price below the compliance price, then the principal solution to the sweatshop problem is that prices need to rise. If the market price is equal to or greater than the compliance price, then it is possible, in principal, that thorough monitoring of contractors will yield improvements. It is somewhat amazing that after many years of the CSR era, this basic question of adequate pricing receives almost no attention, within either the industry or academia. For example, a 2007 report by Business for Social Responsibility proposed a new framework for supply-chain management that goes beyond monitoring programs and that included some good recommendations such as more closely aligning brands' purchasing practices with their social-responsibility goals and rewarding good suppliers with a more secure business relationship, but the issue of adequate product pricing was never raised (Business for Social Responsibility 2007). Studies to determine contractor-compliance costs and proper product-compliance prices would seem to be at the heart of any genuine attempt to deal with the sweatshop issue. However, most of the research attention has been focused on CSR program structure and outcomes, and pricing is a difficult and controversial issue to investigate, since it deals directly with brand power and trade secrecy. The nontransparency of the industry and a lack of publicly available cost and price data make it difficult to determine if market prices are systematically higher or lower than compliance prices. Addressing this price issue seriously, and the overall terms of trade between brands and contractors, must be a major part of a social-label system. Adequate pricing would be recognized as a necessary but not sufficient condition for proper compliance.

To summarize, the CSR industry, while no doubt correcting some factory problems from time to time, serves largely as a public-relations exercise to reassure consumers and deflect attention from the principal causes that perpetuate sweatshops. Because these programs are not designed to address the pricing pressures that drive poor factory conditions, they have little impact on improving the most common and significant sweatshop abuses regarding poverty level, sub-minimum wages, and extensive, undercompensated overtime work. There is also the difficulty in catching violations among numerous contractors in a complex supply chain using an inadequate enforcement effort. Furthermore, there is no genuine mechanism for other important stakeholders in the production system, especially workers, to influence the program that is intended to benefit them. For all these reasons, corporate CSR programs should be rejected as an ineffective, false solution to the apparel sweatshop problem.

3   PRINCIPLES OF A SOCIAL-LABEL SYSTEM

A social-label system must be designed to address the structural problems that plague the brand's CSR programs. This section will discuss key criteria that a social-label system must adopt, and the next section will discuss in more detail how such a social-label system could be constructed.

For a social-labeling system to be legitimate and meaningful, and result in much better conditions for workers, it should satisfy at least three social-label criteria:

- Good standards: Labor conditions must adhere to core International Labor Organization (ILO) standards, adequate wage and benefit standards, local laws, and other relevant criteria.

- Fair process: All parties in the production system, especially workers, must be empowered to address their needs through genuine collective dialogue and negotiations.
- Full disclosure: There must be transparency in all aspects of the system, including production sites, working conditions, and decision-making processes.

The first criterion—good standards—is the basic requirement for any social-label system that claims to improve factory working conditions. Current CSR systems also have lists of good standards included in codes of conduct, which are often inadequately enforced through their factory-monitoring systems. One crucial standard that deserves special attention, and is usually absent, is an adequate wage level. Prevailing wages in the global apparel industry are far too low for the proper support of workers' families. This chapter proposes that the wage standard for the social-label system be a 'living wage,' defined as an income adequate for workers to support an average size family, taking into account a market-basket of goods, including food, medicine, housing, clothing, transportation, education, and other essential needs (Merk 2009, Worker Rights Consortium 2005a). The issue of living wages is perhaps the most controversial in the sweatshop debate, and most CSR systems mandate only the legal minimum wage, often unenforced. Activists have called for living wages for years, but the industry, along with conventional economic theory, is hostile to the concept of wages that are set by nonmarket mechanisms. This proposal recognizes that since labor costs are a very small percentage of the final retail price, there is enough money in the apparel-production system to increase wages dramatically (Pollin et al. 2002, Worker Rights Consortium 2005b, Miller and Williams 2009).

One example serves to clarify the issue of the unequal division of wealth in this industry. An investigation by the Hartford Courant into a factory in Mexico that produced sweatshirts for the University of Connecticut revealed that of the final $37.99 retail price for each sweatshirt, the retail store made a profit of $4.50; the university earned royalties of $2.28; Champion, the brand manufacturer, made a profit of $1.75; Liga Major, the factory, earned $0.70; the NCAA received a royalty of $0.57; and the workers who made each sweatshirt received a total of $0.18, or about 0.5 percent of the retail price (Kauffman and Chedekel 2004). A serious effort to raise workers' wages could easily find the funds in this supply chain. The main question becomes how to regulate the production system so that wages are raised enough to lift workers out of poverty. In most cases, this will require at least a doubling or tripling of wages over prevailing market rates.

However, as important as the list of social-label standards is, the process by which they are drafted and enforced, and the role that the various stakeholders play in that process, are equally important. This raises the issue of the second criterion for a meaningful social label, fair process. The brand's CSR programs are designed almost completely by company staff and consultants, with advisory input from other groups in some cases. Some multistakeholder initiatives such as the FLA and SAI do a better job of bringing in a wider network of constituency groups. It may be common for CSR systems to survey workers on factory problems, but an occasional survey of a few workers, who may be handpicked by factory management or coached to give approved answers, is inadequate to understand what workers want or what they are experiencing in the factory. It is crucial that workers themselves be central to the setting of standards because they are the experts in what they want and need. For this reason, the lack of worker representation in most CSR systems would be puzzling, if the systems were really in place to improve conditions.

If workers matter in a social-label system, they must have an organized presence to make the case for what they need from the system. And they cannot be 'organized' in ways that are influenced by management and will likely serve management interests, such as advisory committees, quality teams, or company unions. In other words, workers must have genuine, self-controlled, democratic, participatory, worker organizations that are empowered to bargain collectively in their interests. How are we to know what workers want? What wages do they need to take care of their families? What health or retirement benefits would be useful for them? What health-and-safety concerns do they have, whether those concerns involve dangerous machinery, ergonomic problems or harmful chemicals in the production process? What do they think of the shift schedules, and how do they affect their home life? How is the cafeteria food or living quarters at the factory, if any? How are the restrooms, are there enough of them, and do they get enough time to visit them during the workday? An organized presence for workers would answer these questions and ensure that worker needs are incorporated into the social-label system. This is the true meaning of freedom of association and collective-bargaining rights, both core ILO conventions that are often included in CSR standards, but are currently empty of real meaning for nearly all apparel workers.

To create a fairer process in setting standards and enforcement efforts, we must remove some power from the brands in these decisions and empower other actors in the supply chain: the workers, and also the contractors. All of these important aspects of the social-label system, the labor standards, enforcement mechanisms and product-price negotiations, would have fairer outcomes if they resulted from meaningful multiparty negotiations among brands, contractors and workers. In this way, all parties bring their interests to the table for a fairly bargained resolution. For example, the main interest that contractors would be expected to bring to these negotiations is the need to have fair product prices that would cover their costs of compliance with the labor standards. Above, I discussed the concept of the 'compliance price,' and these negotiations, in part, would have the aim of determining these prices.

The third social-label criteria, full disclosure, addresses the lack of transparency in current CSR efforts. The main sources of information on CSR programs are the glossy reports published by the brands that summarize their efforts, and reflect only the information they choose to reveal. While any amount of information on these programs is welcome, they are heavy on positive anecdotes and simply do not provide enough meaningful and comprehensive data on conditions in their contractor factories. Brands have their own standards, monitoring procedures and systems for tracking and reporting data on factory conditions. It is currently impossible, using these reports, for consumers, labor-rights advocates or workers to really know what the overall factory conditions are, or if any changes in conditions over time are real. This hinders the efforts of noncompany stakeholders to engage the brands in a real discussion on the issue, since a genuine conversation is difficult when only one party has all the real information, or if significant data goes uncollected. Activists do investigate factories on their own and report their findings to the public, and this leads to a typical exchange where the brands express concern, emphasize their CSR efforts, and promise to look into the matter, but it is unclear what sustainable changes or improvements are made.

In contrast, a genuine social-label system would use a multistakeholder governance process to structure real discussions and debate on labor standards and enforcement systems, and also to develop a uniform and comprehensive data-collection and reporting system that would be publicly available. This system is more likely to publish meaningful data, and with this more open flow of information, all stakeholders would have an accurate sense of how the system works as a whole and the status of the labor conditions in the factories. This more-transparent process would inspire more confidence in the framework and allow for a vigorous stakeholder dialogue about the system and how it can be changed or improved.

A social-label system based on these criteria of good standards, fair process and full disclosure will be much more likely to improve factory conditions. A more transparent, multistakeholder system such as this could be considered an example of a 'deliberative democracy' framework for governing international labor standards in the apparel industry (Fung 2003). This system is also consistent with the 'commitment-oriented' approach to improving labor standards based on joint brand-contractor problem solving, information exchange, and the diffusion of best practices (Locke et al. 2009). I now turn to a discussion of a possible concrete organizational model for a social-label system that incorporates these principles.

4 CONSTRUCTING A SOCIAL-LABEL SYSTEM

In a previous paper, I outline a possible alternative apparel-production system called the Global SweatFree Apparel Production (GSAP) Agreement (Dirnbach 2008). This agreement is structured as a multinational or global contract between apparel production workers' unions and the contractors and brands within the production system. This framework can form the basis for a progressive social-label system.

The concept for the GSAP agreement is based on the achievements of the International Ladies Garment Workers Union (ILGWU, often referred to as the 'ILG') and the Amalgamated Clothing Workers of America (ACWA, often referred to as the 'Amalgamated'), the two largest apparel-worker unions historically in North America. From their founding in the early 1900s until the middle of the twentieth century, the ILG and the Amalgamated succeeded in organizing the complex, sweatshop apparel industry into union agreements with manufacturers and contractors that raised wages, established health and pension benefits, and improved working conditions in the factories (Fraser 1991, Greenwald 2005, Parmet 2005, Ross 2004, Tyler 1995, Von Drehle 2003). Two key principles that guided these agreements were:

- Integrated production: the unions and the employer associations recognized the close working relationship between all companies in the supply chain and the need for consistent labor standards, regardless of where the workers are employed. Both parties agreed that to maintain high uniform standards throughout the production process, all employers would only deal with other companies that had contractual relationships with the union.
- Joint liability: the unions and the employer associations recognized that it was essential for sufficient payments to be made from the manufacturers to the contractors for the contract workers to enjoy the labor standards to which they were entitled. The manufacturers were held contractually liable to pay the proper amounts to the contractors.

These principles were essential to bring some measure of order to a chaotic and competitive industry, with multiple business relationships and flows of work between manufacturers and contractors. At its high point in the 1950s, these contracts encompassed hundreds of thousands of workers and largely eliminated sweatshop conditions in the majority of the industry. However, during the second half of the twentieth century, the North American garment manufacturing industry slowly moved overseas, and now well over 90 percent of the apparel bought in the United States is imported (American Apparel & Footwear Association 1997).[2] The organizational principles that tamed the North American industry could now be applied on a global scale to handle the global sweatshop problem.

How would the GSAP agreement be structured, and how would it function? A rough sketch will suffice for the purposes of this chapter. The agreement would be a system where the workers and their unions in multiple countries would enter into a global contract, negotiated every few years, with brands and their contractors. The agreement could cover wages, benefits, hours of work, health-and-safety conditions, grievance procedures and other issues; the full range of subjects would be determined in the negotiations themselves. It would also establish the principles of integrated production and joint liability. Integrated production in this case means that all parties acknowledge the need for uniform high standards throughout the global supply chains, with all sourcing by the brands going to organized contractors that are part of the agreement. Joint liability means that the brands agree to pay enough to the contractors to cover the costs of the agreement standards. This contract and these principles impose a measure of worker control over what is normally a chaotic production system with a constantly shifting web of sourcing arrangements, and ensure that enough compensation flows to the workers at the base of the global supply chain.

The GSAP agreement could be negotiated at global, regional and local levels. The global agreement would have some general uniform standards that would cover all factories in the global system. This could include adherence to all local laws, respect for the core ILO conventions, some important minimum health-and-safety standards, a maximum workweek, and a minimum, locally appropriate, living wage and health and pension benefit package (or more likely, an agreed-upon formula for determining these local minima). This global part of the agreement would be negotiated by elected representatives of the workers (unions and/or possibly other representatives of their choosing, for example, in the case of worker cooperatives) and employers (brands and contractors), with possible advisory roles for the ILO, labor rights and consumer advocates, and other stakeholders. There would also be regional or local supplemental agreements where workers' and employer representatives in each country, region or factory would negotiate over local conditions, improving over the global minimum standards. This would include locally appropriate living wage and benefit packages, and any other issues of local concern to the workers and factory management. And, in the interest of transparency, all industry information regarding wages, benefits, working conditions, factory locations and contractor–brand sourcing relationships would be made available to all workers covered by the agreement and to the public.

Returning again to the issue of wages, we can see how the agreement could handle this issue in relation to fair pricing and the interests of contractors and workers. Contractors primarily want to get a fair price for their product that allows them to cover their costs and earn a reasonable profit. Though this system has been principally designed with the aim of improving conditions for workers, this also has the benefit of improving the bargaining power of contractors with respect to brands, as well. Contractors with a more organized presence in the negotiations should be able to use these discussions to press for fair pricing that meets their goals. In principle, a social-label system structured like this agreement could ensure that product prices are equal to or greater than compliance prices in at least two ways. The first is to undertake studies to determine contractor-compliance costs under the agreement, and then establish the wholesale product prices within the system at a high enough level to cover those costs. The analogous situation in the fair-trade coffee system is the minimum floor price for a pound of coffee, currently $1.35/pound for Arabica, plus a $0.20 additional premium (Fairtrade Labelling Organizations International 2012). This minimum price is established to enable coffee producers to cover their production costs and earn extra money as well. However, coffee as a product and coffee production costs may be much more uniform than in the apparel industry, and given the many contractors and myriad different products that will exist in an apparel system, these compliance-price determinations could prove in practice to be a challenging task.

An alternative method is to ensure that price negotiations between contractors and brands are as fair as possible so that fair product prices are determined. The agreement could undertake a combination of the two strategies, where contractor compliance costs are studied and taken into account as negotiations are structured to achieve a fairer price that will cover these costs. Over time, as new prices are negotiated, there will come to be an understanding within the system of what constitutes a set of fair prices for various apparel products. Moreover, whenever there are wage increases, or other higher negotiated costs of any kind, there will also develop an understanding of what product prices would be needed to cover these increased costs. Industry and academic research can assist this process through supply-chain investigations within this framework, examining product pricing, production volumes, scheduling and lead times, factory capacity, and brand/contractor communication. These studies would have the aim of informing the agreement negotiations so that fair pricing is achieved that covers compliance costs. Industrial research can also provide useful information on reforming and restructuring factory-production systems to help meet the overall labor standards.

This proposal is a concrete implementation of the International or Global Framework Agreements that have been negotiated between global union federations and some multinational corporations (Global Unions 2011). In many cases, framework agreements have been structured as fairly general statements of cooperation intended to promote consultation and enforce ILO conventions on freedom of association and other issues for workers employed directly by the corporation and its contractors. However, these kinds of agreements have not generally led to the kind of intensive multistakeholder collective bargaining envisioned here, and the sustainable improvements resulting from these agreements are unclear. A good example is the framework agreement signed in 2007 between the International Textile, Garment and Leather Workers Federation (ITGLWF)[3] and the large Spanish-apparel brand, Inditex. The agreement basically restates the Inditex Code of Conduct, which covers the usual set of issues: forced labor, child labor, discrimination, freedom of association and collective bargaining, harsh or inhumane treatment, safe working conditions, ensuring wages are paid, working hours, environmental awareness and regular employment. It also calls for both parties to monitor developments in the Inditex supply chain, conduct an annual review of the application of the agreement, share information, educate contractors and local union affiliates about the agreement and develop training programs to implement the agreement (International Textile, Garment and Leather Workers' Federation 2007). This kind of cooperation is a positive step and has likely led to some improvements for workers in the Inditex supply chain, but the systemic sweatshop conditions in the industry require a much more comprehensive intervention.

This brief outline gives the essential features of the GSAP agreement. A multistakeholder system such as this would be much more likely to fulfill the three criteria for a legitimate social label discussed earlier and lead to fairer outcomes for workers in the global apparel industry. The first criteria, good standards, will be established and improved over time through rounds of negotiations that bring the interests of all parties into the process. Furthermore, this bargaining between all industry partners—workers, brands and contractors—is designed to fulfill the second criteria, fair process, and will share power, rights, and responsibilities more equitably within the system. Finally, the transparency built into the system and the presence of other stakeholder groups in the process satisfies full disclosure, the third criteria.

This still raises the obvious question of how such a social-label system could be brought into existence, given the likely opposition of most brands and contractors to any new program that reduces their flexibility, raises their costs, and shares power with workers. A full discussion of strategies that could organize such a system is beyond the scope of this chapter, but a few thoughts are in order.

Organizing a social-label system based on the GSAP agreement structure with a significant amount of the global industry involved would be a complex and challenging task. To make this agreement work, it is necessary to convince many brands and their contractors to become part the system. It required decades for the ILG and the Amalgamated to establish their industry contracts covering hundreds of thousands of North American workers, and it could perhaps take even longer to organize a GSAP agreement on a much larger global scale, with many more workers, contractors, and brands involved. The effort would have to start with a small number of companies and their workers and grow from there. For example, there may be some small, mission-driven, socially responsible apparel companies, and their contractors and workers, who will agree to be the first to participate. Once the basic structure of the agreement is established through negotiations between workers and a small number of brands and contractors, it can add new members over time. It is possible to establish a series of increasingly higher labor standards, often called trigger agreements, that would be implemented gradually as various target numbers of companies enter the system. This kind of phase-in of higher standards may make it easier for companies to agree to participate because they will see others do so and will feel that they will not be at too much of a competitive disadvantage.

But, of course, the reality of a hyper-competitive global apparel industry means that few companies will readily agree to a social-label system like this that challenges the familiar sweatshop production model. So, like the ILG and Amalgamated struggles of a century ago, this new global campaign will require some sustained combination of strategic worker organizing at the contractors, and consumer solidarity campaigns aimed at the brands, designed to create disruptive conditions where the contractors and brands want to preserve labor and consumer peace and a stable business environment. For example, the campaign could choose to organize a typical large apparel brand with about US$1 billion in yearly sales, which sources to more than 100 contractors that employ tens of thousands of workers. Workers and activists must determine which contractors are used, and what volume of the brand's product is produced at each site. The end-of-the-year holiday season accounts for a large proportion of the brand's sales and profit, and the production for the holiday season occurs several months before. This is when there should be work stoppages at enough contractors so that a significant amount of the production is halted or delayed. During this time, the activist allies conduct a global coordinated solidarity campaign, launching a boycott that can run through the holiday season, and a series of public protests of the brand. The terms of the settlement are that the brands and contractors must push for some immediate improvements in the wages and working conditions, and they must agree in principle to participate in the social-label system. The campaign would experiment over time with different strategies and tactics at different brands and contractors. A coordinated series of social-label organizing campaigns such as this, identifying and targeting specific contractors and brands, with workers and activist/consumer allies working together internationally, will be needed to bring more brands and their contractors into the system over time. A large-scale campaign would require significant strategic coordination, which could be provided by a traditional entity like IndustriALL, the global union which superceded the ITGLWF in 2012. A governing structure could also come from a new multi-organization global alliance of workers and allies. Examples of similar coalitions include the Asia Floor Wage campaign, which is fighting for higher regional apparel worker wages in Asia (Merk 2009), or Play Fair, a group of union federations and NGOs that is pushing for better labor standards in factories that supply the Olympic Games and World Cup events.

A recent example of this kind of worker-activist coordinated campaign is the successful effort to pressure the Russell Corporation to reopen a union factory that it had closed in Honduras in 2008, throwing 1,200 workers out of work. A WRC investigation found that anti-union animus was a key factor in the decision to close the factory, a significant violation of workers' freedom of association and collective-bargaining rights. A year-long boycott campaign by the United Students Against Sweatshops (USAS) eventually convinced Russell to reach a settlement, where the fired workers would be compensated and rehired into the new plant, and the company would take steps to respect the workers' rights to freedom of association in their other plants in Honduras (United Students Against Sweatshops 2009). A WRC statement on the settlement called it 'one of the most significant advances for fundamental workplace rights in the twenty-year history of apparel industry codes of conduct' (Worker Rights Consortium 2009). Another recent victory is the opening of Alta Gracia, a living wage, union factory in the Dominican Republic, which serves the college-apparel market on 600 campuses (Alta Gracia 2012). As detailed in the preceding chapter, this was the result of years of effort by the WRC and USAS, working with workers who lost their jobs at the former BJ&B factory, and the factory's new owner, Kinghts Apparel. The potent combination of worker organizing and student solidarity activity resulted in these victories.

4 CONCLUSION

A social-label system for apparel should involve genuine three-party multinational negotiations between workers, contractors, and apparel brands that share rights and responsibilities throughout the global supply chain, and be supervised and monitored within a transparent governing system that allows for multiple stakeholder participation. Such a system would establish good labor standards, a fair process to determine these standards, and have much more transparency than current CSR programs. This kind of social-label system would more effectively address the root causes of sweatshop labor conditions and could raise labor standards for apparel workers significantly.

However, it must be asked whether any regulated, market-based, social-label system, however fair and well constructed, is the best solution for the sweatshop problem. An apparel social-label system essentially attempts to construct a partnership of solidarity between poor workers, primarily in the Global South, and wealthier consumers, primarily in the Global North—what we can call a worker-consumer alliance. This is a potentially unstable alliance though, since the interests, experiences and positions of power of both groups are very different, and the key issue of price can divide them. Workers want higher prices to finance higher wages, but if product prices rise too high, even many ethical consumers may abandon the social-label system for cheaper options. This reveals the power asymmetry in this alliance, since it is driven primarily by the purchasing preferences of wealthier consumers—without their demand, the system collapses. Ideally, the rights of workers to fair working conditions should not depend entirely on the whims of distant consumers, however much they are allied politically in a common social-label project (Fridell 2007). Moreover, given the marketing power of the major brands committed to the sweatshop production model, social-label products are likely to remain a small percentage of the total market for the foreseeable future, and they are always susceptible to confusion created in the marketplace by competing products that are falsely labeled as ethical.

An alternative strategy to improve conditions for workers would be through an international and state regulatory model that would strengthen the ILO and the rights to freedom of association, enact a global living wage, and enable stronger labor law enforcement at the national level. These kinds of initiatives have been deprioritized in favor of market-driven models in recent years within the context of a corporate-driven process of globalization. Advocates of social-label, fair-trade or other similar systems should consider whether these market-based approaches are the best solution to deliver social justice for workers, or are merely a better solution within the current corporate-dominated, free-trade framework that needs to change.

NOTES

1. I classify WRAP as second party since it is essentially a creation of the American Apparel and Footwear Association, the main U.S. apparel-industry trade association, but others may classify WRAP as third party, since it is formally an independent entity.
2. Apparel import penetration is the percentage of apparel consumption in the United States that is imported, and has increased over time since the 1960s, reaching above 90 percent in 2006.
3. In 2012 the ITGLWF merged with the International Metalworkers' Federation and the International Federation of Chemical, Energy, Mine and General Workers' Unions to form IndustriALL.

REFERENCES

Alta Gracia. 2012. 'AG Education.' Retrieved August 24, 2012 (http://altagraciaapparel.com/story).

American Apparel and Footwear Association. 2007. *Trends: An Annual Compilation of Statistical Information on the U.S. Apparel and Footwear Industries: Annual 2006 Edition*. Arlington, VA: American Apparel and Footwear Association.

Armbruster-Sandoval, R. 2005. *Globalization and Cross-Border Labor Solidarity in the Americas*. New York: Routledge.

Asia Monitor Resource Centre. 2004. 'A Critical Guide to Corporate Codes of Conduct: Voices from the South.' Hong Kong: Asia Monitor Resource Centre. Retrieved August 24, 2012 (http://www.amrc.org.hk/system/files/critical-guide-to-codeof-conduct.pdf).

Barenberg, M. 2007. 'Corporate Social Responsibility and Labor Rights in U.S.-Based Corporations.' Pp. 223–235 in *Nongovernmental Politics*, edited by M. Feher. Cambridge, MA: Massachusetts Institute of Technology Press.

Bonacich, E., and R. P. Appelbaum. 2000. *Behind the Label: Inequality in the Los Angeles Apparel Industry*. Berkeley, CA: University of California Press.

Brooks, E. C. 2007. *Unraveling the Garment Industry: Transnational Organizing and Women's Work.* Minneapolis, MN: University of Minnesota Press.
Business for Social Responsibility. 2007. 'Beyond Monitoring: A New Vision for Sustainable Supply Chains.' New York: Business for Social Responsibility. Retrieved August 24, 2012 (http://www.bsr.org/reports/BSR_Beyond-Monitoring-Report.pdf).
Chambers, A. 2009. 'Not So Fair Trade.' *The Guardian,* December 12.
Claeson, B. and E. Dirnbach. 2009. 'Making City Hall Sweat: Using Procurement Power for Worker Rights.' *New Labor Forum* 18(1):89–97.
Clean Clothes Campaign. 2006. 'Three Tragedies Hit Bangladesh Factories in One Week, Leaving Scores Dead, Wounded.' Amsterdam, Netherlands: Clean Clothes Campaign. Retrieved August 24, 2012 (http://www.cleanclothes.org/news/three-tragedies-hit-bangladesh-factories-in-one-week-leaving-scores-dead-wounded).
Collins, J. L. 2003. *Threads: Gender Labor and Power in the Global Apparel Industry.* Chicago: University of Chicago Press.
Conroy, M. E. 2007. *Branded! How the Certification Revolution is Transforming Global Corporations.* Gabriola Island, Canada: New Society.
Cycon, D. 2007. *Javatrekker: Dispatches from the World of Fair Trade Coffee.* White River Junction, VT: Chelsea Green.
Dirnbach, E. 2008. 'Weaving a Stronger Fabric: Organizing a Global Sweat-Free Apparel Production Agreement.' *WorkingUSA: The Journal of Labor and Society* 11(2):237–254.
Elliott, K. A. and R. B. Freeman. 2003. *Can Labor Standards Improve under Globalization?* Washington D.C.: Institute for International Economics.
Esbenshade, J. 2004. *Monitoring Sweatshops: Workers, Consumers, and the Global Apparel Industry.* Philadelphia, PA: Temple University Press.
Ethical Trading Action Group. 2006. 'Revealing Clothing: Transparency Report Card 2006.' Toronto, Canada: Ethical Trading Action Group. Retrieved August 24, 2012 (http://en.maquilasolidarity.org/sites/maquilasolidarity.org/files/RevealingClothing_complete.pdf).
Fairtrade Labelling Organizations International. 2012. 'Fairtrade Minimum Price and Fairtrade Premium Table, Current Version: 10.08.2012.' Bonn, Germany: Fairtrade Labelling Organizations International. Retrieved August 24, 2012 (http://www.fairtrade.net/fileadmin/user_upload/content/2009/standards/documents/2012-08-10_EN_Fairtrade_Minimum_Price_and_Premium_table.pdf).
Feldman, P., P. J. McDonnell, and G. White. 1995. 'Thai Worker Sweatshop Probe Grows, Labor: State Subpoenas Department Store Chain and Targets Another. Officials for Both Say They Have Found No Record of Dealings with Garment Firm.' *Los Angeles Times.* August 9.
Fraser, S. 1993. *Labor Will Rule: Sidney Hillman and the Rise of American Labor.* Ithaca, NY: Cornell University Press.
Fridell, G. 2007. *Fair Trade Coffee: The Prospects and Pitfalls of Market-Driven Social Justice.* Toronto, Canada: University of Toronto Press.
Fung, A., D. O'Rourke, and C. Sabel. 2001. *Can We Put an End to Sweatshops?: A New Democracy Forum on Raising Global Labor Standards.* Boston: Beacon.
Fung, A. 2003. 'Deliberative Democracy and International Labor Standards.' *Governance: An International Journal of Policy, Administration, and Institutions* 16(1):51–71.
Gereffi, G., R. Garcia-Johnson and E. Sasser. 2001. 'The NGO-Industrial Complex.' *Foreign Policy* 73 80(4):56–65.
Greenhouse, S. 2010. 'Factory Defies Sweatshop Label, but Can It Thrive?' *The New York Times,* July 18, p. B1.
Greenwald, R. A. 2005. *The Triangle Fire, The Protocols of Peace, and Industrial Democracy in Progressive Era New York.* Philadelphia, PA: Temple University Press.

Hopkins, M. 2003. *The Planetary Bargain: Corporate Social Responsibility Matters.* London, United Kingdom: Earthscan.

International Labor Rights Forum. 2010. 'Missed the Goal for Workers: The Reality of Soccer Ball Stitchers in Pakistan, India, China and Thailand.' Washington, D.C.: International Labor Rights Forum. Retrieved August 24, 2012 (http://www.laborrights.org/sites/default/files/publications-and-resources/Soccer-Report2010.pdf).

International Textile, Garment and Leather Workers' Federation. 2007. 'International Framework Agreement Between Industria de Deseño Textil, S.A. (Inditex, S.A.) and the International Textile, Garment and Leather Workers' Federation (ITGLWF) on the Implementation of International Labour Standards Throughout the Inditex Supply Chain.' Brussels, Belgium: International Textile, Garment and Leather Workers' Federation. Retrieved August 24, 2012 (http://www.itglwf.org/lang/en/documents/ITGLWFPressReleases2007_000.pdf).

Jaffee, D. 2007. *Brewing Justice: Fair Trade Coffee, Sustainability, and Survival.* Berkeley, CA: University of California Press.

Kauffman, M. and L. Chedekel. 2004. 'As Colleges Profit, Sweatshops Worsen.' *Hartford Courant*, December 12.

Keck, M. E. and K. Sikkink. 1998. *Activists Beyond Borders: Advocacy Networks in International Politics.* Ithaca, NY: Cornell University Press.

Kimeldorf, H., R. Meyer, M. Prasad and I. Robinson. 2006. 'Consumers with a Conscience: Will They Pay More?' *Contexts* 5(1):24–29.

Krupat, K. 1997. 'From War Zone to Free Trade Zone: A History of the National Labor Committee.' Pp. 51–77 in *No Sweat: Fashion Free Trade, and the Rights of Garment Workers*, edited by A. Ross. New York: Verso.

Levi, M. and A. Linton. 2003. 'Fair Trade: A Cup at a Time?' *Politics and Society* 31(3):407–432.

Lindsey, B. 2003. 'Should Coffee Drinkers be Activists, Too?' *Consumers' Research Magazine* 86(6):22–26.

Locke, R., M. Amengual, and A. Mangla. 2009. 'Virtue out of Necessity? Compliance, Commitment, and the Improvement of Labor Conditions in Global Supply Chains.' *Politics and Society* 37(3):319–351.

Maquila Solidarity Network. 2010. 'No More Fires, No More Locked Exits, No More Garment Workers Deaths' Campaign Launched.' Toronto, Canada: Maquila Solidarity Network. Retrieved August 24, 2012 (http://en.maquilasolidarity.org/node/939).

McDonnell, P. J. and P. Feldman. 1995. 'Top Retailers May Have Sold Sweatshop Goods.' *Los Angeles Times*, August 15.

McVeigh, K. 2007. 'Asda, Primark and Tesco Accused over Clothing Factories.' *The Guardian*, July 6.

Merk, J. 2009. 'Stitching a Decent Wage across Borders: The Asia Floor Wage Proposal.' Amsterdam, Netherlands: Clean Clothes Campaign. Retrieved August 24, 2012 (http://www.cleanclothes.org/resources/recommended/stitching-a-decent-wage-across-borders-the-asia-floor-wage-proposal).

Miller, D. and P. Williams. 2009. 'What Price a Living Wage? Implementation Issues in the Quest for Decent Wages in the Global Apparel Sector.' *Global Social Policy* 9(1):99–125.

Miller, D. 2012. *Last Nightshift in Savar: The Story of the Spectrum Sweater Factory Collapse.* Alnwick, United Kingdom: McNidder and Grace.

Murray, D., L.T. Raynolds, and P. L. Taylor. 2003. *One Cup at a Time: Poverty Alleviation and Fair Trade Coffee in Latin America.* Fort Collins, CO: Fair Trade Research Group.

National Labor Committee. 2000. *Made in China. The Role of U.S. Companies in Denying Human and Worker Rights.* New York: National Labor Committee.

Neuman, W. 2009 'For Your Health, Froot Loops.' *The New York Times*, September 5.

Nicholls, A. and C. Opal. 2005. *Fair Trade: Market-Driven Ethical Consumption.* London, United Kingdom: Sage.

O'Rourke, D. 2003. 'Outsourcing Regulation: Analyzing Nongovernmental Systems of Labor Standards and Monitoring.' *Policy Studies Journal* 31(1):1–29.

Parmet, R. D. 2005. *The Master of Seventh Avenue: David Dubinsky and the American Labor Movement.* New York: New York University Press.

Play Fair Campaign. 2012. 'Fair Games? Human Rights of Workers in 2012 Olympic Supplier Factories.' Retrieved August 24, 2012 (http://www.tuc.org.uk/tuc files/291/sportswear.pdf).

Pollin, R., J. Burns, and J. Heintz. 2002. 'Global Apparel Production and Sweatshop Labor: Can Raising Retail Prices Finance Living Wages?' Amherst, MA: Political Economy Research Institute.

Prasad, M., H. Kimeldorf, R. Meyer and I. Robinson. 2004. 'Consumers of the World Unite: A Market-Based Response to Sweatshops.' *Labor Studies Journal* 29(3):57–80.

Raynolds, L. T., D. L. Murray, and P. L. Taylor. 2004. 'Fair Trade Coffee: Building Producer Capacity via Global Network.' *Journal of International Development* 16(8):1109–1121.

Reich, R. B. 2007. *Supercapitalism: The Transformation of Business, Democracy, and Everyday Life.* New York: Alfred A. Knopf.

Richardson, J. 2007. 'How Fair Is Fairtrade?' London, United Kingdom: BBC. Retrieved (http://news.bbc.co.uk/2/hi/uk_news/magazine/6426417.stm).

Roberts, D. and A. Bernstein. 2000. 'Inside a Chinese Sweatshop: A Life of Fines and Beating.' *Business Week*, October 2.

Roberts, D., P. Engardio, A. Bernstein, S. Holmes, and X. Ji. 2006. 'Secrets, Lies, and Sweatshops.' *Business Week*, November 27.

Rodriguez-Garavito, C.A. 2005. 'Global Governance and Labor Rights: Codes of Conduct and Anti Sweatshop Struggles in Global Apparel Factories in Mexico and Guatemala.' *Politics and Society* 33(2):203–233.

Rosen, E. I. 2002. *Making Sweatshops: The Globalization of the U.S. Apparel Industry.* Berkeley, CA: University of California Press.

Ross, R. J. S. 2004. *Slaves to Fashion: Poverty and Abuse in the New Sweatshops.* Ann Arbor, MI: University of Michigan Press.

Sethi, S. P. 2003. *Setting Global Standards: Guidelines for Creating Codes of Conduct in Multinational Corporations.* Hoboken, NY: John Wiley and Sons.

Su, J. 1997. 'El Monte Thai Garment Workers: Slave Sweatshops.' Pp. 143–149 in *No Sweat: Fashion Free Trade, and the Rights of Garment Workers*, edited by A. Ross. New York: Verso.

Sweatfree Purchasing Consortium. 2012. 'About.' Bangor, ME: Sweatfree Purchasing Consortium. Retrieved August 24, 2012 (http://buysweatfree.org/about).

Talbot, J. M. 1997. 'Where Does Your Coffee Dollar Go? The Division of Income and Surplus along the Coffee Commodity Chain.' *Studies in Comparative International Development* 32(1):56–92.

Tyler, G. 1995. *Look for the Union Label: A History of the International Ladies' Garment Workers Union.* Armonk, NY: M. E. Sharpe.

United Students Against Sweatshops. 2009. 'USAS Press Release on Jerzees de Honduras Victory.' Washington, D.C.: United Students Against Sweatshops. Retrieved August 24, 2012 (http://usas.org/2009/11/18/usas-press-release-on-jerzees-de-hon duras-victory).

Vogel, D. 2005. *The Market for Virtue: The Potential and Limits of Corporate Social Responsibility.* Washington D.C.: Brookings Institution.

Von Drehle, D. 2003. *Triangle: The Fire That Changed America.* New York: Atlantic Monthly.

War on Want. 2006. 'Fashion Victims: The True Cost of Cheap Clothes at Primark, Asda and Tesco.' London, United Kingdom: War on Want. Retrieved August 24, 2012 (http://www.waronwant.org/attachments/Fashion%20Victims.pdf).

War on Want. 2008. 'Fashion Victims II: How UK Clothing Retailers are Keeping Workers in Poverty.' London, United Kingdom: War on Want. Retrieved August 24, 2012 (http://www.waronwant.org/attachments/Fashion Victims II.pdf).

Wells, D. 2007. 'Too Weak for the Job: Corporate Codes of Conduct, Nongovernmental Organizations and the Regulation of International Labour Standards.' *Global Social Policy* 7(1):51–74.

Worker Rights Consortium. 2005a. 'Sample Living Wage Estimates: Indonesia and El Salvador.' Washington, D.C.: Worker Rights Consortium. Retrieved August 24, 2012 (http://www.workersrights.org/dsp/LivingWageEstimates.pdf).

Worker Rights Consortium. 2005b. 'The Impact of Substantial Labor Cost Increases on Apparel Retail Prices.' Washington, D.C.: Worker Rights Consortium. Retrieved August 24, 2012 (http://www.workersrights.org/dsp/Labor_Cost_Increases_and_Apparel_Retail_Prices.pdf).

Worker Rights Consortium. 2009. 'WRC Statement on the Agreement between Russell Athletic/Fruit of the Loom, the General Workers Confederation of Honduras, and the Sitrajerzeesh Union.' Washington, D.C.: Worker Rights Consortium. Retrieved August 24, 2012 (http://www.workersrights.org/linkeddocs/WRC_Statement_on_Russell-CGT-SitrajerzeeshAgreement.pdf).

Worker Rights Consortium. 2010. 'Preliminary Report on Minimum Wage Violations in Bangalore, India.' Washington, D.C.: Worker Rights Consortium. Retrieved August 24, 2012 (http://www.workersrights.org/linkeddocs/Bangalore%20Minimum%20Wage_Preliminary%20Report.pdf).

Worker Rights Consortium. 2012. 'About the Factory Disclosure Database.' Washington, D.C.: Worker Rights Consortium. Retrieved August 24, 2012 (http://www.workersrights.org/search/about_fdd.asp).

Zadek, S. 2001. *The Civil Corporation: The New Economy of Corporate Citizenship.* London, United Kingdom: Earthscan.

Afterword

At the outset, we posed the question whether a social-labeling approach represents an effective means of improving working conditions and securing labor rights in the global supply chains that comprise today's apparel industry. Based on the research presented in this volume, what tentative conclusions can we draw?

The social-label movement pioneered by American trade unions and consumer organizations at the turn of the twentieth century had two lofty goals: (1) to provide industrial governance by controlling the manufacture of goods in union-organized and collectively bargained workplaces and (2) to mobilize the power of union workers and the wider public in the market as consumers. Despite some important gains, history suggests that neither of these aims was achieved, even before the global migration of apparel production during the final quarter of the last century seriously damaged the viability of a union label for U.S.-made goods.

Both history and current consumer behavior have shown that reliance on a market-oriented social label places the destiny of garment workers at the mercy of a relatively small segment of the apparel-buying public and its fickle purchasing habits. We are open to the possibility that changing social norms and an increased supply of goods manufactured under schemes assuring ethical production could redefine market demand and stimulate business interest in supporting a labeling initiative, as a few of the contributors to this volume suggest. Accordingly, we are intrigued by the possibility that action research, perhaps aimed at collective consumers, could uncover effective strategies for transforming purchasing behavior. It is possible to imagine initiatives that would involve additional groups beyond the university students and government officials in charge of public procurement that current projects target; these might include hotel workers, flight attendants, and other service workers—potentially any large group of employees committed to purchasing workwear produced under fair working conditions.

Of course, government regulation may be needed to ensure that businesses report the information that is necessary for consumers to make informed decisions and to verify that the information reported accurately reflects the conditions of production. We will watch carefully how the world's largest apparel companies respond to the new California Transparency in Supply Chains Act that went into effect on January 1, 2012. The act requires every retailer and manufacturer with annual worldwide revenues over $100 million that does business in California to report on its efforts to eradicate slavery and human trafficking from its direct supply chains. As such, this law may prove an important step in protecting the rights of garment workers in global supply chains.

In the absence of a global approach to the question of labor compliance of the sort proposed by Dirnbach in the final chapter of this volume, national initiatives may represent the most ambitious and comprehensive efforts to promote ethical apparel production. Although we have preliminary data on the degree to which projects such as the *Fibre Citoyenne* label and the *Better Factories Cambodia* program can improve compliance in the apparel sector of developing countries, it is important to note that the jury remains out on the precise relationship between national labeling initiatives and export performance. In our view, this is an area that merits further empirical research, and the extensive data-gathering effort that is being carried out by the International Labour Organization (ILO) alongside the implementation of its Better Work program will provide valuable insights into this critical question.

For those retailers and manufacturers looking to embrace a social label as a mark of the investment they are making in improving working conditions in their supply chains, a number of challenges remain. Given the wide differences across exporting countries in the average size of factories, the type of garments being produced, the profile of foreign buyers sourcing from local suppliers, and the content of national labor laws, it is very difficult to imagine a common standard that could merit an 'on product' social label. Does the solution lie in the direction of 'management system' audits (brand performance checks), which permit standard-setting of management systems, including the whole area of purchasing practices such as pricing, lead times, sourcing criteria, and supply-chain transparency? In short, should we be developing an approach toward labeling that focuses more closely on regulating the production *process* rather than certifying a particular *outcome*? Moreover, if we opt for a process- rather than outcome-based approach, how is the meaning of such a label to be communicated to consumers, without suggesting that such a label will always imply 'perfect performance'?

Finally, allowing the use of a social label entails a responsibility to actively raise awareness about its meaning and its limitations—a responsibility that will have to be assumed by any companies or multistakeholder initiatives opting to use and promote such a label. This effort will need to achieve a delicate balance in terms of pursuing the goal of providing the consumer with clear, usable information while avoiding a 'dumbing down' strategy that provides misleadingly easy answers to what is ultimately a complex political, economic and ethical issue.

While certain markets, such as the public procurement sector discussed by Claeson and the licensed collegiate-apparel segment discussed by Nova and Kline are more auspicious for the development of a meaningful social label, even here, some qualifications are necessary. Workwear for public employees of the sort likely targeted through a public-procurement label is generally a low-margin segment of the apparel market, and manufacturers may have difficulty meeting, for example, a 'living wage' standard, particularly where the buyer is a cash-strapped local authority. In the case of the Designated Supplier Program, only one benevolent manufacturer/licensee, Knights Apparel, has moved toward meeting the terms of the program in respect of living wage and freedom of association.

So, are social labels the answer to improving working conditions and securing labor rights in global apparel supply chains? Although we do not believe that social labels are *the* answer, we believe that they may be part of the solution to improved conditions in global supply chains. Even here, though, we would qualify our endorsement by noting that a host of complicated conditions must be met for a social label to be efficacious and meaningful for workers, businesses and consumers. First, despite the challenges in developing such an instrument, we argue that a single label based upon a global industry standard with clear reporting guidelines and mandated participation would be most beneficial, given the clarity it would provide to workers and consumers, and the 'even playing field' it would create for companies. However, such an initiative would necessarily call for a reconsideration of social labels by the ILO, which is the only organization with the credibility and mandate to oversee such an effort. Second, the label would have to be supported by verification along the global value chain to ensure that what is said on the label reflects actual conditions on the ground. Given the shortcomings of current social-compliance models, this requirement is a serious challenge, and meeting it will require a concerted effort on the part of stakeholders to develop new models of verification. As a first step, we would encourage a systematic and focused approach that builds on the successes and shortcomings of the country, company, and consumer initiatives discussed in this volume. Efforts to develop a successful labeling initiative supported by a wide range of stakeholders might have to begin in a relatively protected, niche market, such as municipal workwear purchased via public procurement or licensed collegiate apparel. While these market segments also pose challenges, some of which we noted above, to designing and implementing an efficacious social label, these are not insurmountable. Furthermore, the successful development of a model social label in one of these areas could bolster the confidence of all participating stakeholders that indeed a thoughtfully developed, carefully monitored social label can play an important role in improving working conditions and labor standards in global apparel supply chains. We would conclude by emphasizing that a meaningful social label may reinforce, but cannot substitute for, the preconditions of decent work in any industry: humane and effective management regimes, mature industrial-relations systems and fully functioning labor administrations.

Jennifer Bair, Marsha A. Dickson, and Doug Miller
November 2012

Contributors

Annelies Goger is a Ph.D. candidate in the department of geography at the University of North Carolina at Chapel Hill.

Drusilla Brown is Associate Professor of Economics and Director of the International Relations Program at Tufts University.

Rajeev Dehejia is Associate Professor of Public Policy at New York University's Robert F. Wagner Graduate School of Public Service.

Raymond Robertson is Professor of Economics at Macalester College.

Arianna Rossi is Technical Officer of the Better Work Program at the International Labour Organization.

Patricia Brien is Senior Lecturer at the Cardiff School of Creative and Cultural Industries, University of South Wales.

Ian Robinson is Lecturer in the Department of Sociology and the Residential College's Interdisciplinary Social Theory and Practice program at the University of Michigan.

Rachel Meyer is Lecturer and Assistant Director of Undergraduate Studies in the Department of Sociology at Harvard University.

Howard Kimeldorf is Professor of Sociology at the University of Michigan.

Llyr Roberts is a Ph.D. candidate at the Centre for Business Relationships, Accountability, Sustainability and Society at the University of Cardiff.

Theodora Valero received her Master of Science degree in Corporate Social Responsibility from the University of Nottingham in 2012.

Heather Franzese is Director of Good World Solutions (formerly World of Good Development Organization) and Senior Category Manager for Apparels and Linens at Fair Trade USA.

Bjorn Claeson is Executive Director of the Sweatfree Purchasing Consortium and Researcher at the International Labor Rights Forum.

Scott Nova is Executive Director of the Workers Rights Consortium.

John M. Kline is a Professor of International Business Diplomacy in the Walsh School of Foreign Service at Georgetown University.

Eric Dirnbach is Researcher at the Green Jobs Campaign at the Laborers Union.

Index

For Product Safety Concerns and Information please contact our
EU representative GPSR@taylorandfrancis.com Taylor & Francis
Verlag GmbH, Kaufingerstraße 24, 80331 München, Germany